The Grotto
Book One

Other Book by Harold Walker

MURDER ON THE FLOODWAYS

The Grotto
Book One

Phu Bai, Vietnam
1969 - 1970

Lt. Col. Harold G. Walker
USMCR (Ret.)

Published by Dragonfly Publishing, Inc.

The Grotto – Copyright-©2018 by Harold G. Walker
http://haroldgwalker.com/

All photographs are from the author's collection unless otherwise indicated in the caption.

Cover design: William Pack
(www.williampack.com)

ISBN: 978-0692160824

Printed in the United States of America.

First Printing, 2018 Dragonfly Publishing, Inc.

"Marines flying the CH-46 helicopter in combat scenarios are among the boldest and most precise pilots and aviation crews in existence."

Tim King

Correspondent

www.Salem-News.com

Operation Hastings

12 – 25 July 1966

Author's Note

In this memoir, I have endeavored to present episodic material in chronological order with real names and issues. The men, the times and the dialogue are based upon current interviews, conversations recalled, reviews of declassified material and reflections of documentable situations. This style is called, literary non-fiction. Very few names have been changed. This is the way it was during the first three months of my twelve-month tour of duty, 10 November 1969 – 13 February, 1970 in the most northern Marine helicopter base in Vietnam. Those three months shaped the scope of my participation as a Marine helicopter pilot in Vietnam. In this book, the word "Grunt" will always be capitalized.

Contents

Prologue

My purpose in writing this book is to provide my thoughts and personal observations regarding my participation in what was the Southeast Asian Conflict, or The Vietnam War, or more commonly referred to among Vietnam veterans as *The Nam*. I was a 23 year old United States Marine Corps (USMC) first lieutenant helicopter pilot when on 10 November 1969, the 194th birthday of the Marine Corps I set foot on Vietnamese soil.

I will provide as complete a picture as possible of my life during that conflict. This work is not an annotated history of my squadron, HMM-262, The Flying Tigers, for I am not a historian, only a person who was fortunate enough to have had a front row seat to a small portion of that cataclysmic event . It is my personal story---what I saw, what I did, and what I felt---with context as to what was happening at that time. Any blame lies with me, no one else. Any accolades lie with the Marines with whom I lived, worked and flew.

My war covered two distinct areas and periods: Phu Bai, Vietnam, 11 November 1969 to 13 February 1970 in the first part of my tour, and 14 February 1970 to November 1970 at Marble Mountain Air Facility (MMAF), Da Nang, in the second part of my stay. This book, *The Grotto, Book One,* covers my time at Phu Bai.

I could not possibly cover every occurrence in our squadron during that year. What I have endeavored to do is provide an overview of day-to-day life in HMM-262, a CH-46D helicopter squadron, during the last gasps of Marine Corps involvement in Vietnam. In order to make this a meaningful experience as seen through my eyes, I must take you back to where I came from and follow my path to Vietnam from a small cotton farm in Southeast Missouri.

I wasn't the kind of person who dreamed of entering the military, nor did I glue model airplanes together. Heck, I didn't even fly kites. I was more interested in an area in Southeast Missouri

called the Floodways, where fishing, hunting, camping and ex-
ploring preoccupied my youth, while keeping an eye out for the
deadly cotton mouth water moccasin, was a rite of passage.

I managed to graduate seventh from a class of 16 at Bragg
City High School, Bragg City, Missouri in June, 1963[1] and went on
to Southeast Missouri State College, now, Southeast Missouri
State University (SEMO), located along the banks of the Mississippi River in Cape Girardeau, Missouri. I went to college because
if I didn't, it would have killed my mother. I was not heavily into
academic achievement and spent much of my free time partying
in a Southern fraternity, Pi Kappa Alpha, and chasing after Kathleen Blanton of Malden, Missouri.

Vietnam as seen through my eyes, at that time, was far removed from the controversial political arena which history has
told us it was, or into which it has evolved. During that bucolic
time of my life, particularly the summer between my freshman
and sophomore college years, the Gulf of Tonkin incident as reported was just another event associated with our involvement
in Vietnam. I had heard the name, but knew nothing about the
event.

I didn't become aware of any reason for the war until I was
in it. To me and those of my era, we were supposed to be stopping the North Vietnamese from taking over South Vietnam, and
the implied danger was that the whole of Southeast Asia could
fall to communism. It was that Domino theory. It was those
North Vietnamese torpedo boats that had the gall to attack the
USS Maddox. Wasn't it? Just what was the USS Maddox and
where was the Gulf of Tonkin?

Late, in the spring of 1966, my junior year in college, Vietnam came into my life. I received a draft notice. The Pemiscot

---

[1] In the 1963 graduating class of Bragg City High school, two of us, Bobby
Mullenix and I went to Vietnam. Bobby, a U.S. Naval aviation jet mechanic, 3rd
class, was a yellow jersey flight deck QC inspector aboard the U.S.S. Franklin
D. Roosevelt aircraft carrier (66-67) and me, Harold G. Walker (author). Other
known Vietnam Vets from Bragg City High School were: Ricky Grantham,
Jerry Marchbanks, Terry Napier, Harry Reed and Austin Wyatt.

County Missouri Selective Service Draft Board No. 82 held court in those days on the second floor of the Post Office building in Caruthersville, Missouri, Pemiscot County, a small river town on the banks of the Mississippi. It was the southeast corner of the state, upriver about ninety miles from Memphis. I appeared before them, asking for and receiving what was called a school boy deferment, so easily obtained I had no idea my time would ever run out.

But run out it did. In April 1967 I received my second draft notice. No problem, I'll just go ask for another deferment. However, this notice was different—they meant it. No more school boy deferments. I told them that I needed to graduate that year, and if they would just postpone my draft until September, I would join up. But I'm almost sure that between the deferments for being married and humanitarian assistance, the school boy deferments or any postponements were gonna take a hit.

"No," was their collective response, "You gotta go." They said, "Ain't you patriotic?" The county of some 50,000 residents was running low on warm bodies, and it was time for we school boys to step up, unless you were married. My attempt to postpone the draft to graduate had come to a screeching halt.

Due to my not having sufficient credits to graduate in June 1967 and having to attend summer school to complete my B.S. in Education degree, with a major in biology and minor in Earth Science, I began efforts to cut a deal with the Marine Corps based upon information I received from Jim Acerback. Acerback was a fraternity brother, who was already in the Marine Corp system, in what he called the PLC program. Jim already had his flight license and was well on his way into the Corps when he told me the Corps was offering "delayed entrances" that would allow me time to graduate.

Jim told me I could swear into the Marine Corps' Aviation Officer Candidate (AOC) program if I passed a written exam and flight physical. Then, I'd be in the Aviation Officer Candidate

(AOC) program rather than be drafted into the Army,[2] providing me with the postponement I needed. Thus, my lifetime association with the Marine Corps came about, due to Vietnam and the draft.

"Prior to 1967 the major university campuses had been in turmoil. The sons of the white middle and upper class had largely been successful avoiding the war through the escape hatch of a college deferment. By 1967 the needs of the Green Machines (Army & Marine Corps) were such that the draft had begun to take significant numbers of them as they graduated..."[3] In retrospect, it was reported that the attack on the USS *Maddox*, under President Lyndon Johnson, was little more than a transparent pretext for expanding the involvement of the United States in Vietnam in a one-two punch. First, media descriptions of the August 2nd attack as an "unprovoked attack" against a U.S. destroyer on "routine patrol" hid the fact that the *Maddox* was providing support for South Vietnamese military operations against the North. Second, the alleged August 4th attack appears to have been fabricated, official accounts attributing the "error" to confusion. Regardless of the cause and without a doubt, the time I spent in the Corps and Vietnam was a very personal period of time that deeply affected my thinking, my opinions...my life.

The group of Marine aviators with whom I was fortunate enough to have served was not all comprised of heroes. Being a hero in the Corps was a high bar. The Corps' history was built of heroes such as Lewis Burwell "Chesty" Puller, the most decorated Marine in American history who sat at the top of the list. I suppose, in retrospect, that I knew some heroes in the Corps, in Vietnam, yet we didn't think of it in that way. There were close calls and death and there was luck, the best of all companions.

---

[2] Another SEMO student, Pat Kenny, was also getting his flight physical at the same time as me. Years later, Pat, in HMM-364, and I would be based at the same location in Vietnam, MMAF, flying the same model helicopter, the CH-46D.

[3] Sheehan,Neil. A Bright and Shining Lie, John Paul Vonn and America in Vietnam. Vantage Books, 1988, 717.

For the most part, I experienced luck. You don't get recognized for having luck. There were those I thought who should have been recognized for surviving close calls and sure death through their flying skills and quick thinking who deserved the label "hero" for their actions, who were never recognized. There were also those who were recognized and decorated that in my opinion didn't deserve the title, most with ranks above captain. But for the most part we first lieutenants were simply young aviators from every corner of America, from every walk of life, with two things very much in common: our decision to join the Corps (no matter what the reason) and our primary Military Occupational Specialty (MOS) designation 7500—helicopter pilot. It was the glue that bound us all together in a common purpose in this, the first and probably last great helicopter war. And no matter what life has since wrought upon us: rags, riches, prosperity or despair; we each and every one take great pride in the fact that we were once in that proud fraternity of men who, on a daily basis "hung it out" for the Corps and our fellow Marines in that valley of death known as Vietnam.

My dreams and aspirations during that time were as simple as my background: to make it home in one piece, get on with my life with Miss Kathy, now Mrs. Kathy, my wife, and take on whatever life might bring. There were many of us, however, that would not have the opportunity to realize that goal. The truth and horror of this "conflict," or any war for that matter, was that many of us would have those dreams dashed by the abrupt rattle of an AK-47, the instantaneous concussion and searing heat of a B-40 rocket propelled grenade (RPG), a high explosive, Anti-Tank weapon, or some booby-trapped landing zone (LZ) on some nameless obscure ridgeline, its significance lost to time...all of this being the product of a shadowy and extremely capable enemy seldom visible from the cockpit of a Boeing CH-46 transport helicopter.

For some, death came not from the enemy but from another facet of our unique and unforgiving environment, now, clinically referred to by the Naval Aviation Safety School in Monterey, California, as a "momentary loss of situational awareness" or by the pilots involved, in less clinical terms, as an "ah shit!" No matter the name, these had the potential of abruptly ending our dreams. For the most part, it seemed to me there were few officially recognized accidents in Vietnam. The other services, Army, Air Force, Coast Guard, could have accidents. But, there are no recognized "accidents" in Naval Aviation, only "mishaps." Any damage that I can recall from a mishap in the Nam was pretty much written off to the overused and time-worn phrase, Direct Enemy Action (DEA).

DEA could be injected into an event if there was any semblance of an enemy presence and did, in my opinion, cover up a lot of pilot error, like vinyl siding on a shack. But, we pilots knew the difference and it haunted us like Christmas Future. Any of us could succumb to that unforgiving mistress who flirted with us each and every day. For, in the sixth or seventh hour of re-supply, troop lifts, medevacs or Recon inserts and extracts, exhaustion could creep up on you like an unseen specter. A micro-second of inattentiveness at a precarious moment when your thoughts turn to home or loved ones could spell your doom and many others along with you.

My year in that violent, controversial and yes, sometimes very humorous world of Vietnam was a normal tour of duty for that era, almost 12 months to the day. I began my travel to the war from the Memphis International Airport on Tuesday, 3 November 1969. On that crisp day, as I walked with my family through the airport, I carried a sea bag along with mixed feelings. I was proud to be going to Vietnam, yet I hated to be leaving Kathy and my family. What could I expect?

I didn't really give much thought to the possibility that I might not make the walk back. That possibility was never talked about, at least not by me or my wife, Kathleen, but that very possibility could easily be read in the faces of my family who had accompanied me to Memphis. Bursting with pride in my dress greens, dark naval aviator sunglasses, Naval Aviator "Wings of

Gold" polished to a brilliant luster with two expert shooting badges earned following a lifetime of shooting on the Floodways of Southeast Missouri, the time had come for me to step up. I was more than ready to go...more than ready to leap into the adventure of a lifetime.

My own personal adventure had actually begun and become real to me about two months prior, when on 15 September I reported to the Marine JAG attorney to sign my will.

1: Thoughts

Vietnam was a lot of things. It was political folly, played out on a grand scale. But on a more personal level, it left hard scars, those you could see and those you couldn't...and death—a high price to pay for folly.

The legend of Vietnam has become what some people hoped was the truth. The characterization of the Vietnam veteran as a rogue bully, raping and pillaging with no rhyme or reason, just out for a body count, or a Rambo-type character with deep psychological scars from his tormented tour of duty, unfortunately, became the public's accepted profile; therefore, the grand generalization about all Vietnam veterans.

Contrary to this characterization, we were not rogue psychotic rapists or killers of defenseless men, women, and babies as Hollywood's movie moguls would have you believe, and as the My Lai massacre anomaly appeared to reinforce in some quarters. Our experience as aviators was normally dull and boring, interspersed with stark moments of pure terror."[4]

Regarding weaponry, to my own personal amazement and chagrin, the CH-46D was armed with only defensive weapons. In time this lack of weaponry became a real concern for 46 pilots. Normally our armament was two .50-caliber M2 machine guns, mounted port and starboard and manned by gunners under verbal control from the helicopter aircraft commander (HAC) or crew chief (CC). On special missions, when a rear defense was deemed necessary, a stinger in the form of a belt-fed 7.62-millimeter M-60 machine gun was mounted on the cargo deck just forward of the rear ramp to dispel any troublesome hitchhikers. There were rumors that North Vietnamese Army (NVA) and Viet Cong (VC) high on hallucinogenic drugs attacked 46s by running up the rear ramp as combat troops were deplaning. Yet there were no defensive weapons such as a forward firing machine gun

---

[4] Author unknown, war reference made during WWI.

turret[5] to protect the cockpit from a frontal assault. Weight and center of gravity issues nixed the idea. We pilots were at the mercy of the gunships assigned to provide accurate fire suppression for us, thus the saying, "sit and take it". We knew that a couple of well-placed rounds into the cockpit from an Ak-47 would put an end to us all. We also knew that a gunship firing from 500 to 1000 feet had little chance of stopping those AK rounds from reaching their mark.

Hero is a high bar in the Marine Corps. I saw very few heroes, but there was a great deal of valor exhibited on a daily basis. My definition of a military hero is someone who does an act for the benefit of others with the knowledge that there is a good chance of being mortally wounded. Jumping onto a live grenade is at the top of the list in Medal of Honor territory. Few helicopter pilots have received that honor. However, one who did was a familiar figure to my group going through flight school in 1968-69, Captain Stephen W. Pless.

In August 1967 Pless demonstrated pure guts and an unnatural talent in flying the UH-1E helicopter gunship while rescuing three U.S. Army soldiers from certain death by the VC. Capt. Pless wasn't part of an organized rescue effort. He and his crew simply departed from a benign mission after hearing a call for help and headed for the trapped soldiers. That part of his decision, allegedly, drove the Marine brass crazy. His fame had reached the level of legend before he met an untimely death on 20 July 69 while trying to jump a motorcycle across the rising sections of the drawbridge (Bob Sikes Bridge) between Pensacola and Pensacola Beach Florida.

A further truth is that he wasn't a fight instructor in VT-1, 2, 3, or HT-8. He was assigned to a non-flying job that required only minimal flight hours to sustain flight pay. He was also well aware

---

[5] In order to accommodate the weight of a forward firing machine gun and retain mission lift capability a myriad of changes would have to be made. The added weight of an internal firing system would decrease mission payload. Therefore, we had to depend on the gunships to keep Charlie from firing into the cockpit.

of his hero status and on occasion pushed his weight around. On one occasion, when then Second Lieutenant Ron McAmis was with his then fiancée at the Mustin Officer's Club, Mainside, NAS Pensacola, Major Pless literally pushed McAmis aside to play his own pick of music, saying to McAmis, "You don't mind do you? I'm Major Pless."

Ron's response was; "No sir, I don't mind sir," but was thinking to himself, may I kiss your ass sir.

The truth of the matter is that CH-46 pilots and aircrews lived and died in the zone.[6] The goal was to remain in place for only six seconds—1001, 1002, 1003, 1004, 1005, 1006—although much longer was normally the case. By definition an LZ needed to be just over 84 feet long and 51 feet wide—the dimensions of the 46 with the rotors spread for flight— but on many occasions, in mountainous zones, the LZ was no larger than a spot in which to place the two rear main mounts of the fixed tricycle landing gear configuration on the 46. In some extreme circumstances only the tip of the rear ramp touched down. On other occasions, a nose-wheel landing was in order to take troops in through the starboard crew door; and of course, there were also the high-risk 120' SPIE (Special Patrol Insert/Extract rig) and ladder extracts that snatched recon teams from the imminent clutches of the enemy.

Contrary to the absurd but popular generalization of most soldiers, including Marines being addicted to mind-numbing substances to help them through their wartime experience, as a Marine aviator I can readily state that I did not personally witness the use of any illegal substances, nor did I recognize the effects of said substances on others. Now before someone reading

---

[6] "When under fire on the ground, Grunts can dive for cover. Helicopter pilots cannot. For a helicopter pilot on the ground in a hot landing zone, there is no place to hide. All you can do is sit there, just sit there and take it. There was not an [enemy] soldier who would not relish a good, clean, close range shot at a Marine Corps helicopter on the ground."Sturkey, Marion F. *Bonnie Sue: A Marine Corps helicopter Squadron in Vietnam* (Heritage Press International,2010), 46.

this says that I was either not there or refused to recognize the use of said substances, think of this for a moment; we were scheduled to fly several times a week and could be required to fly at any moment when we weren't scheduled. To abuse narcotic or hallucinogenic substances would have been stupid and life-threatening. While it's a fact that the drug culture in late 1970 did begin to adversely affect the readiness of some ground units in both the Army and Marine Corps, to my knowledge that abuse did not enter into any of the flight crews.

Another popular generalization of the Vietnam vet was the image of a drugged-out derelict, cringing in the streets of the cities of this country, unable to function due to the memories of his misdeeds in that war. This is undeniably the image perpetrated by those whose agenda was to dehumanize the image of the veteran, thereby advancing the position and stature of those who felt morally justified in refusing to serve by running off to Canada as draft dodgers. This agenda gathered credibility through President Jimmy Carter in 1977 when he granted amnesty to those draft dodgers who fled to Canada.

Furthermore, the actions of individual Vietnam veterans who continue to blame the war for their habitual drug use and the domestic chaos in their lives cause me to question their stability prior to their participation in the conflict. It became a cottage industry in this country to be a dysfunctional Vietnam veteran. How very sad it is that some veterans allowed our detractors to select the tune to which they danced.

The country, no matter how large the bumper stickers trumpeting the tired old phrases of "Support the Troops" and "We Back Our Men in Vietnam," still managed to elect draft dodgers to the highest political offices.

The other 46 pilots that I came to know were also not interested in the political nature of this war. Our mission was simple: support the Grunts that killed the enemy. I never once considered that we would not prevail in that grand endeavor. I instinctively believed in the generals and had the utmost confidence in our unit commanders. However, many years after my tour in Vietnam, I would come to question the war itself, and the competence of both our political and military leaders.

I thought little or not at all of the domestic chaos rattling the United States during that turbulent time. It simply didn't pertain to me. I cared for nothing but the goal at hand—become a squadron helicopter pilot in a combat zone in Vietnam. All the years of relentless training, moving from one level to another in flight school was my total focus. There was no time for anything else. If I had failed, I don't believe I could have endured the humiliation. My sense of duty and honor was honed from an early age by my dad and tempered by the Marine Corps. Anything less than honorable service was unacceptable.

What follows is a collection of events that give some insight into the day-to-day existence of a small group of men who were helicopter pilots. We piloted the workhorse of the Corps, the Boeing CH-46D Sea Knight, affectionately known as the Phrog due to its color and frog-like appearance—a typical bullfrog sitting on its haunches in any ditch in the south. The 46, as we most always referred to it, did have an awkward appearance, but we pilots had great affection for the "aerodynamic beauty" of the beast.

Figure 1 Boeing publicity photo of the CH-46

The 46 came into the Marine Corps in 1964 and was retired in August 2015, but the affection we pilots had for the old war-horse will never fade. Flying the 46 was the best kind of flying. We did everything: combat troop assaults; medevac; resupply; reconnaissance inserts and extracts, which in many instances were emergencies; routine administrative support missions; VIP missions (generals); humanitarian assistance, and any other type of flight imaginable, including flying USO shows to and from fire bases.

Some may find this memoir shocking, absurd, or boring, but it is the truth, or as close to the truth as a human can get. Sometimes, it seems there are many sides to truth. It is well to note that this recitation is not about legends...well, maybe. "When the legend becomes fact, print the legend"[7] is a known theatrical line from a popular movie. I prefer, *when fact becomes legend, then print the legend.*

[7] *The Man Shot Liberty Valance*, starring John Wayne, Jimmy Stewart and Lee Marvin directed by John Ford, 1962.

2: The Beginning

On 2 September 1969, Ho Chi Minh, President of North Vietnam, died of a heart attack. His death gave rise to this barroom ditty sung in military clubs round the world, to the tune of an old toothpaste commercial, "You'll wonder where the yellow went when you brush your teeth with Pepsodent," it went like this:

"Ring a ding a ding ding
Blow it out your ass,
Better days are coming by and by
Bull shit!
You'll wonder where the yellow went,
when the H-Bomb hits the Orient.
Nuke 'em Nuke 'em Nuke 'em
Ho Chi Minh's <u>DEAD</u>!"

A week later I received the following: "By order of the Commandant of the Marine Corps, dated September 10, 1969, you will stand detached from Helicopter Marine Training Squadron (HMMT) 302 on October 11, 1969, and report to the First Marine Air Wing / Western Pacific (Okinawa, Japan) no later than November 7, 1969".[8]

On 15 September 1969, at 23 years old, hard reality had begun to assert itself. In accordance with Marine Corps policy, I reported to the Judge Advocate General (JAG) attorneys at Marine Corp Air Station El Toro in Orange County, California, to have a personal will and power of attorney drawn up. On 29 September 1969 the two-page will giving all of my property "of whatsoever character and wheresoever situated" to my wife, Kathleen B. Walker was signed and notarized.

---

[8] There was a great degree of flexibility built into the order. I did not complete the training syllabus at HMMT-302 until 24 September, at which time Kathy and I were cleared to leave. I was still bound to report to the First Marine Air Wing no later than 7 November, 1969.

Lieutenant Colonel "Panic" Vanek was the commanding officer of HMMT-302, nick-named F Troop. 302 was the advanced training squadron for the CH-46, located at the Marine Corps Air Facility (MCAS), Santa Ana, California off of Red Hill Avenue, where huge dirigible hangars were situated. He prepared the requisite fitness report covering my dates of attendance, 9 July to 3 October 1969, during which my flight log book revealed accumulated flight time of 333.3 hours. In part, the fitness report stated the following:

First Lieutenant Harold G. Walker was, "Amiable and personable and carried himself well, was very enthusiastic and conscientious and accepted assignments cheerfully. He is earnest and a hard worker as reflected by his excellent knowledge of the aircraft and systems. He shows outstanding growth potential."

The above comments were standard fare. Vanek could have stamped each one of our fitness reports with those comments, and probably did. It was an appropriate entry for another new batch of CH-46 helicopter copilots (H2p) completing advanced training and receiving orders to the Western Pacific. Of course, we were all "enthusiastic and conscientious." What were our options? Did we have any choice other than to cheerfully accept our assignments? And how could we have anything other than excellent knowledge of the aircraft systems? That was all we had been doing for the past fifteen months, July 1968 – October 1969, studying and flying with an intensity seldom experienced by any of us at any other time in our lives.

We did have some intrigue other than doing night landings in the Santa Ana Mountains. When returning to base, we descended into thick smog that appeared at two thousand feet above ground level (AGL). We always looked for the fireworks display at Disneyland which signaled the closing of the park at 9:00 P.M. (2100 hrs). Other distractions that summer included my successful testing for a commercial pilot's license. I put the license to use at the Orange County Municipal Airport. Renting a low wing Piper Cherokee 180, Kathy and I toured the beaches from Newport Beach south to San Diego, to Catalina and back to

Santa Ana flying a triangle of beautiful Pacific waters and beaches.

Tragedy also struck. A young neighborhood bicycle rider was hit and killed on Red Hill Avenue, directly in front of where Kathy and I were staying. The Charles Manson Family killings along with recurring warnings that the Zodiac killer may have moved into the Los Angeles area from his Northern California beginnings haunted Los Angeles, and the young wife of one of the flight students committed suicide with a .22 cal. rifle. Another social ill also revealed itself when a flight student revealed himself to be a wife beater.

Our annual physical fitness test during that period was also a victim of our imminent transfer to what was called Westpac (Western Pacific—Vietnam) some of us were getting out of shape, including me. The rituals of Marine Corps fitness borne out of Officer's Candidate School (OCS) had worn off during flight school, thus the separation of the "wing" from the Grunts. The three-mile run had lost its appeal as we managed to run it in just under the maximum time allowed and passed sit-ups and chin-ups by counting two at a time. The feeling was pretty much universal in all but the most dedicated lifers[9] that in the very near future we'd be in Vietnam as CH-46 helicopter pilots and beyond that, the reality that our future was uncertain. Eat, drink and be merry for tomorrow.......was the prevailing philosophy.

With all the things goings on in our training like how to make a high speed low approach to a designated zone or, how to hover on the side of a cliff in a stiff wind, or handle an unannounced engine failure, I didn't even notice Woodstock. It was trumpeted as the largest cultural event in New York's history, maybe the whole country, drawing a half million people, or as some described it, "a half million drugged-out hippies," But, I wasn't focused on anything other than the task before me, and

---

[9] "Lifer" was slang for an officer or enlisted Marine whose goal it was to be a career Marine.

enjoying mine and Kathy's last days together before the big event.

Along with our best friend, Gary Rainey, we had become routine patrons of Disneyland where Kathy and I celebrated our first year anniversary on June 29, 1969 with a candle lit-dinner in the famous Pirates of the Caribbean attraction. We also listened to live concerts by *Kenny Rogers and the First Edition* and heard the melodic sounds of the *Righteous Brothers* and visited Grauman's Chinese Theatre at Hollywood and Vine after a meal at our favorite Mexican restaurant in the Santa Ana area, none of which helped my physical conditioning. It was dreamland for the two of us who had grown up in the Bootheel of Missouri.

Occasionally, over a beer at the O' Club, I'd think of my OCS buddies who were infantry officers and already through their first tour in Vietnam, some of whom had already given their full measure. When learning of each loss sadness swept over me. I knew it was past time for me to step into the breach, and I was ready to go; we all felt the same way.

With the months and years of training completed, the real thing was to come. Having completed all of the training required by the Marine Corps to become a CH-46 helicopter copilot (H2p), Military Occupational Specialty 7562, I headed back to Missouri with Kathy. There I would complete preparations to go to Vietnam, and she would teach school for the coming year in Essex, MO., one of the many small towns that dotted the Bootheel landscape.

What we didn't know at that time was that in August 1969 Henry Kissinger, National Security Advisor to President Nixon, had already begun direct and secret one-on-one meetings with the North Vietnamese politburo which would eventually lead to an agreement with the North Vietnamese and "an honorable end to the war in Vietnam."[10]

---

[10] Richard Nixon campaign promise, 1968.

3: Preparing to Go

During our two-week road trip home to Missouri from California, Kathy and I took a helicopter ride into the Grand Canyon, visited relatives, and ventured into Tombstone to walk the historic streets where the Earps once held sway. It was during this trip, 15 October to be precise, that something called the Vietnam Moratorium Day woke me up to what was happening in the country. I was glad to be getting back to the Bootheel of Missouri where such goings on were unheard of.

In the 24 October 1969 edition of Life Magazine (a little more than a week before I left for Vietnam) Hugh Sidey reported, "It was a display without historical parallel, the largest expression of public dissent ever seen in this country. Across the land the demonstrators gathered, talking, reading names from long lists of war dead, showing the V-sign of peace. As night fell, they moved through the shadows carrying their candles like pilgrims in a cave. ...the crowd chanted, 'Peace—Now! Peace—Now!'"[11]

There were reports of a million participants in what I believed were patently unpatriotic, treasonous, pro-communist demonstrations. In Boston, a hundred thousand people were reported as having participated. At the White House, thirty thousand were reported as having participated. In Chicago, twelve thousand were reported as having participated. No one in my world demonstrated against the war, and I simply dismissed it with prejudice against those demonstrators. But in spite of my dismissal, in quieter moments I wondered why the demonstrations were happening. Did they all just hate us...we folks in the military?

* * *

Kathy and I were unfortunate enough to have experienced anti-war activism first-hand while at HMMT-302. A couple of brightly

---

[11] Hugh Sidey, Life Magazine, 1969.

painted El Toro Marine Corps Air Station buses took our squadron, with wives and girlfriends, to the Los Angeles Memorial Coliseum. We were all enjoying ourselves when we heard the thumping and banging of rocks against the bus. People were throwing rocks at the bus and yelling obscenities at us. Our citizens were doing this to us! The bus driver accelerated. We were calling, "Stop the goddamned bus!" but he didn't and the rock throwers were left behind.

We did eventually leave the bus at a different location and attended the ball game. We recognized a celebrity, Ricardo Montalban, star of the popular TV series *Fantasy Island*. The game closed with the Rams posting a loss. We returned to base, had a few drinks at the club, and called it a night, but it was a night I would never forget.

What I didn't know while I was training: in July of '69, Phase 1 of President Nixon's withdrawal plan from Vietnam had been initiated. 25,000 Marines boarded ships of the seventh Fleet bound for Okinawa, and race riots at Camp Lejune, North Carolina resulted in the death of a Marine; In August '69, HMM-165, a CH-46 squadron known as the White Knights, departed Vietnam for Okinawa; and the last UH-34 squadron in Vietnam, HMM-362, the Ugly Angels, departed Vietnam for Okinawa

In September, my last month in training, Marine Corps Commandant General Leonard F. Chapman, in ALMAR 65, authorized "Afro" haircuts and the use of the upraised fist as a greeting among black Marines,[12] "high and tight" grooming standards for non-blacks remained in place. It has been reported that "black militancy was potentially the most disruptive and, for many white Marines, the most difficult to understand." I knew nothing about this and did not see this type of activity in our squadron or any other helicopter squadron in Marine Air Group 16 (MAG-16). Yet there were very few blacks in the air wing. My first observation of any racial identity action would occur in mid-1970.

[12] Smith,353-365.

* * *

Our trip home was in a two car caravan with Gary Rainey in his '68 Blue Chevy Chevelle Super Sport Convertible with a 396 cu. in. engine and Kathy and me in our '65 Dodge Monaco, a classic "block-long vehicle" with a 383 cu. in. gas guzzling engine. Kathy hated it, but it was a good deal for someone on second lieutenant pay, about $1500. We drove together from Santa Ana to Phoenix, Arizona where we split up. Gary headed for Lake Charles, LA and Kathy and I headed for the Grand Canyon.

Following a great helicopter ride into the canyon in a "Whirly Bird," we headed south to Tucson where we visited with my sister and my extended family. On a side trip to Tombstone, the town too tough to die, it seemed to have done just that, die, as we strolled among the graves at the renowned Bootheel cemetery. The remainder of the trip home took a couple of days.

Upon arriving home in MO. Kathy and I moved our meager belongings into her parents' Missouri home. Her father, a World War II Navy veteran of the New Guinea campaigns, was well accustomed to military service in time of war. Her mother, during her father's absence, had done what Kathy would now do—work and wait.

Figure 2 Kathy, me and my dog Buddy after arriving home in Missouri.

Kathy put on a good face about everything. Any fears she had were internalized until the day before I left. She was moody … thinking… angry… and let it all out when we were walking in the harvested fields of my family's farm. It was cathartic for her, but stunned me. She felt deserted and worried. I felt like crap to be leaving her, but, duty prevailed. We had been preparing for this event since we were married.

* * *

While at home, I received a slight modification of my travel orders:

a) Port of Embarkation (POE): Travis Air Force Base, Fairfield, California.
b) Report to: Marine Liaison, MAC Terminal, building #3.
c) Report by: 1300, 5Nov69.
d) Time of departure: 1700, 5Nov69.
e) Assigned Flight Number: U273/309.
f) Assign Air Movement Designator (AMD): SUU_DNA_2PU_M.

On 3 November 1969 the night before leaving home, President Nixon outlined his Vietnamization[13] policy calling for the unilateral withdrawal of American forces from Vietnam. With the news that President Nixon was calling for us to leave Vietnam, I wondered how his policy would affect my upcoming tour of duty. I had trained for Vietnam. I wanted to go to Vietnam.

Kathy and I checked and rechecked what I had packed in a Marine-issue sea bag and parachute bag including some Primatene Mist, an asthma relief over the counter medication that I always kept in my helmet bag. There was some small talk about President Nixon's policy. I tried to ignore it. Kathy was emotional and angry. Her concerns were simple; we both knew Vietnam was the end result of flight training, but, the enormity of it had not really sunk in for her. I had a restless night with a flare-up of my childhood asthma. My mom and dad were patient, and

[13] In 1960, under President Kennedy, the Americanization of Vietnam was presented as part of the "New Frontier." On 28 March 1969, General Abrams announced we were close to "de-Americanizing" the war. Melvin Laird, Secretary of Defense under President Nixon, suggested what we needed was a new word for de-Americanization: "Vietnamization".

Kathy was quiet, the strain evident in her manner. I was quiet, saying goodbye to my dad, mom, brother, Buddy, and the farm.

The next morning, 4 November, 1969, I patted Buddy, my beautiful Collie dog and my best childhood friend, hugging him in our front yard under the two big cottonwood trees that had comforted me with shade throughout my life. He licked my face, wagged his tail. His eyes seemed sad; he was saying good-bye. I had left him before; when going off to college, when I entered the Marine Corps, when I left for Naval Flight School and when Kathy and I married. But this time was different, much different. This time brought tears to my eyes when nothing and no one else could have. Buddy had been a true and faithful friend, and he would patiently wait for me as he had always done.

Kathy planned to get a teaching job, and live with her parents, so I wasn't going to have any worries on that front. It would have been a lot tougher to go if she were living alone somewhere.

Figure 3 My brother, Johnny, helped me with my baggage on the way to the plane.

The next day, the whole family traveled down I-55, the ninety miles to Memphis International Airport: Kathy and her folks, Sophia and Giz; my mom and dad, Glenda and Fred; my brother Johnny and his wife, Helen, and Laura, their daughter who was three years old. Leaving was more emotional than I thought it would be. Johnny who helped me carry my gear.

Figure 4 Kathy and her mother with tears in their eyes --as Kathy and I parted.

The strain of the event clearly showed on the faces of Kathy and her mother, Sophia. Upon completing good-byes all around, I turned away, tearing myself away from the present, from those I loved, and committing myself to the grand adventure upon which I was about to embark.

The flight to San Francisco was uneventful. In my dress greens, a requirement during that era when traveling on military orders, it was obvious where I was going. The stewardess recognized this and told the pilot, who then asked that I come up to the cockpit. I was really impressed. I'd never seen the working end of one of these 707s. The pilot, it turned out, was a former Air Force pilot who had served his time in Southeast Asia, flying into Vietnam from Thailand. He was happy to talk with me, upgraded me to first class and wished me luck. He, of course, assumed that I was a jet fighter pilot. I corrected his assumption by saying, "I'm a helicopter pilot."

He grinned, and said with true sincerity, "In that case, I really wish you luck."

Upon arriving in San Francisco I met up with friends and fellow 46 pilots Gary Rainey and Joe Smith. We wandered San Francisco's waterfront, going from a restaurant to the night club area and finally arriving at the Playboy Club, where our uniforms gained us admittance. This place was like nothing any of us had ever seen—a real classy joint with a restaurant and bar and Playboy Bunnies. Once settled and realizing we were running low on funds, we vowed dramatically that we would, once putting this Vietnam thing to rest, volunteer as mercenaries for Israel.

There was a motive to our madness. We had taken notice of a table where there seemed to be a celebratory toasting of Israel and the outcome of the June 1967 Six-Day War in which Israel conquered the Sinai Peninsula, Gaza Strip, West Bank, and the Golan Heights. We were all decked out in our dress greens, with one lonely National Defense Service Ribbon and none of the familiar veteran of Vietnam ribbons. It was abundantly clear to everyone who we were, and where we were going.

The table of businessmen toasted us. Upon reflection, I am positive that our benefactors were toasting our uniforms and our destination, not the three first lieutenants who'd had too much to drink on their way to the Nam. Yet what fun it was and what pride we were feeling. We were Marines, pilots, and the great adventure was before us. I'm certain we were just like the fresh young recruits in World War I, anxious to tame the Huns, crowding onto outbound trains as pictured in grainy black-and-white newsreel films and like the 1955 movie, *East of Eden*, starring James Dean, Julie Harris and Raymond Massey, and directed by the acclaimed Director Elia Kazan. After staying the night in a hotel, we would check in to the military air terminal the following day, as ordered.

4: Into the Pacific

Hangovers all around, Gary, Joe and I boarded military charter aircraft, Flight U273. Also boarding that flight was our friend, colleague and former roommate, Roy Prigge, a fellow OCS Aviation Officer Candidate who had been with me since entering Officer's Candidate School. Roy's wife, Faith, his mother and father were there to see him off. Before climbing the stairs to board the aircraft, Roy, who was in line in front of me, knelt down and kissed the tarmac.

I wondered why he did that, and why I didn't care to do that. Was it because I was certain I would be back and Roy wasn't sure? I believe Roy had a better grasp of reality than I did. Our trip to Okinawa would include refueling stops at Honolulu and Wake Island. The aircraft itself was filled to capacity with military personnel—Marines, airmen and sailors. There were new guys—replacements, like us—and there were those who were returning to Vietnam for a second tour or returning from emergency family leave; or returning after having escorted a deceased friend back home.

With us all seated and strapped in, the lumbering jet taxied into position, pointed due west into the Pacific on runway 27. Within moments, the big engines began to rumble like an impending storm. The aircraft shuddered and shook before the climactic release of brakes. The big craft lurched forward into its takeoff roll, slamming us back into our seats. Momentarily I flashed back to the adrenalin rush I felt in the T-28 Trojan when going to full throttle on takeoff with that Radial-1820 engine that cranked out 1425 brake horsepower. That was what I missed upon becoming a helicopter pilot. Faster and faster we sped down the runway. The aeronautical lift created by the shape of those wings became greater than the weight of the aircraft. In a matter of moments, the great wings took all the weight from the landing gear as we crossed over the beach. The aircraft struggled for altitude into the clear skies over deep blue Pacific waters. The squeals of the hydraulic system being pressurized signaled the raising of the massive landing gear into their wheel wells. An audible *thump* signaled the next portion of our odyssey had begun. I settled back into my window seat, closed my eyes and slipped into a much needed slumber.

Our first stop that night was Honolulu, and we were allowed to deplane into a quiet terminal to look for a cold drink, by which I mean a Coke. The flight was full and we slowly became acquainted with other Marines going our way. I had thought that everyone on the flight was going to Vietnam, but soon learned that upon stopping at Okinawa, we would go in different directions to different fates.

All of the military services appeared to be represented on the flight. There were the new guys like Gary, Joe, Roy and me, and the old salts with character lines in their brows—a settled, self-confident appearance with mannerisms that clearly made the statement, "I've been there, don't f**k with me." I recognized that look. I had seen it in my drill instructors at OCS, and my flight instructors at Pensacola. It was the mark of experience.

They all seemed to have the confidence that we lacked, and you just knew their thoughts were off somewhere other than where we were going. The old guys tolerated us new guys as an old, scarred lion tolerates the innocence of cubs, and I instinctively steered clear of those warriors, knowing that I hadn't earned the right to associate with them in a familiar manner. When I earned that right, they would let me know.

In Honolulu my thoughts drifted to Pearl Harbor. My name, Harold, is in honor of my Dad's nephew Harold who survived the attack on Pearl Harbor that plunged the country headlong into World War II. I had not thought of my namesake in years, but memories suddenly flooded into my mind as I recalled his visits to our home, of meeting his wife, Lotte, (of German ancestry), and their daughter Karen. He was a Navy man, and to me he was a hero. He had survived the attack and fought his way through World War II on the sea—only to die of a brain tumor in his later years.

It was all becoming real to me. I was now entering into the arena of a World War II in the Pacific. At an early age, I grew up glued to every episode of *Victory at Sea,* [14] a black-and-white film series narrated by Leonard Graves every Sunday afternoon. Hearing the stirring theme music, I took my place on the couch in front of our Admiral TV console. I played out the battle themes on the floodways in the Bootheel of Missouri, always winning the battle against the Japs or Nazis. Thinking of my namesake and that iconic series, I found myself straining to get a glimpse of Pearl Harbor through the huge windows in the terminal building. If only I could see Pearl Harbor, I could tell my family about it. But I had no idea where Pearl Harbor was in relation to the airport, and anyway, the night was pitch-black. I would, I thought, be back someday to see Pearl Harbor and that exquisite tropical island.

I placed a brief phone call to Kathy to let her know my progress and to reaffirm our commitment to see each other when it was my time for R&R. Finally we reboarded, and the big jet lumbered back into the ink-like night, traveling ever deeper into the Pacific. The muted aisle lights, the sounds of playing cards being shuffled and the wafting of cigarette smoke brought me back to the moment. Next refueling stop—Wake Island! My mind was growing numb but sleep escaped me.

Wake Island, a tiny legendary island, hardly more than a landing strip with only twenty-one miles of shoreline. It was immortalized during World War II by the siege of United States forces by the Imperial Japanese Navy, the day following the attack on Pearl Harbor.

As our big jet sank to runway, the captain immediately reversed thrust on the engines. So quickly was his transition to reverse thrust, I wasn't quite sure we were firmly on the runway before the engagement. The plane shuddered, rumbled, and shook as we slowed to taxi speed. The view of the sand and deep

---

[14] The "Victory at Sea" documentary television series, originally broadcast by NBC, 1952-53.

blue waters of the Pacific mesmerized me. Again, the old *Victory at Sea* series came to mind. In some wondrous way, I visualized the scene and felt the tension as the defenders viewed the armada about to descend upon them. In a way, this was my awakening to what the Pacific represented, and the struggle that surely lay ahead for us in Vietnam.

* * *

The history of that small island during World War II was burned into the psyche of every Marine long before. Of the 500 defenders at Wake, 201 were Marines. On December 8, 1941, only hours after the attack on Pearl Harbor, a Japanese invasion force led by A6M Zero fighter planes bombed and strafed the small island. Marine Captain Henry T. Elrod was one of a few Marine pilots of Marine Fighting Squadron (VMF)-211 who flew against the attacking Japanese fleet. He distinguished himself by shooting down two enemy aircraft and sinking the Japanese destroyer, *Kisaragi,* with the two 100-pound bombs that were strapped to the belly of his Wildcat. The Marines successfully repelled the initial attack, but not the second attack before dawn on December 23, 1941.

During the second attack, the Marines didn't get off the deck. Capt. Elrod then led the Marine's defensive action on the ground, repulsing repeated Japanese marine attacks until he fell, mortally wounded. He was posthumously awarded the Medal of Honor for heroism as both a fighter pilot and leader of the defensive actions of the Marines on Wake. The Marines and sailors not killed while defending the island were taken prisoner and suffered the brutality of the Japanese prisoner of war camps until the war was mercifully ended by the nuclear attacks on Japan.

The history of that small island overshadows its physical size. It is part of our Marine heritage, our Alamo. Our duty as Marines was clearly spelled out in blood at Wake Island. Those 250 courageous defenders, who could have avoided their fate by abandoning the island, definitely fit my challenging definition of hero.

* * *

The sound of the engines winding up after refueling brought me back to the present. The past was clear to me. The future...not so clear. I concluded with a shudder that the NVA was just as determined as the Japanese, a sobering thought which brought me no comfort. Yet I was eager to get on with it. With a now-familiar straining roar, the engines sucked us back into the air on our way to Okinawa.

5: Okinawa

Finally, after what seemed like an eternity in the air, I felt the jet once again begin to settle as the captain reduced power in the final approach to Kadena Air Force Base, Okinawa, Japan, a mountainous island in the North Pacific, known to Marines as the Rock. I, however, learned that Okinawa is much more than an island. It actually consists of 160 primary islands, not just one. It occupies the southern half of the Ryukyu archipelago, with a total land surface of 2,265 square kilometers. Korea and the Japanese mainland are located to the north, China to the west, and Southeast Asia (Vietnam) to the south. Following a horrendous battle that took place on Okinawa in 1945, called the final great battle of World War II, a heavy concentration of U.S. military bases were established on Okinawa, which has remained strategically important to U.S. interests. However, the Japanese hosts are forever trying to get us to leave. Sadly, in my opinion, they have partially achieved their objectives.

* * *

Okinawa was Japanese territory and the last Pacific Island that had to be taken before the planned assault on the Japanese mainland (Operation Olympic), in which a million casualties were predicted. Okinawa was defended by an estimated one hundred thousand of Japan's best troops, who fought until the last man, giving "no quarter"[15] and receiving none in return. There were over fifty thousand American casualties. The battle was regarded by many who were there, and by Victor Davis Hanson, an American military historian and scholar of ancient warfare who studied the battle, as "the most nightmarish American experience of the entire Pacific war."[16]

* * *

[15] The term "no quarter" in military jargon means to take no prisoners and show no mercy.
[16] Hanson, Victor Davis, The Second World Wars: How the First Global Conflict was Fought and Won.

Upon deplaning and locating our gear, the Marines were separated from other service personnel and boarded a bus to Camp Hague, not Camp Butler, the main Marine Corps headquarters of the Pacific and home of the First Marine Air Wing (1st MAW). While passing through Kadena AFB, I noticed a small sign which read "Air America." I took little notice of this small sign other than being vaguely aware of the reputation of Air America being a CIA activity. I would be seeing more of those little signs in the year to come.

Camp Hague was little more than an overflow personnel processing plant to Camp Butler for Marines going to Vietnam, or to bases on mainland Japan. It also served those returning home. The climate was warm and humid, and the camp smelled of canvas, fresh plywood, mud, and sawdust. It was like a tent city boomtown in the 1880s, made of plywood with corrugated tin roofs and Quonset huts. It was raw, to say the least. A sea of Marines with personal effects, seabags, and flight bags moved about in great waves. In one tented area there were mountains of worn, weathered and faded jungle utilities that smelled of sweat and grime tossed aside for re-issue. Jungle utilities (utes) were not issued in the States nor were they allowed to be worn in the States. All the new guys, of which my group was the newest, wanted jungle utes.

We were quartered in temporary officers housing, and told where to get chow and when to muster the following morning. They made it sound like some of us might be going to Japan, not to Vietnam. Now President Nixon's words began to have meaning for me. As I viewed it, the war was indeed winding down. Why else would any Marine be going to the Japanese mainland unless the war was decided?

I wanted to get word as fast as possible to Kathy and the folks back home that I had made it this far without any problems, but there were no telephone booths. However, I was told of a service that we could use which was like a telegram service—a Military Affiliate Radio Service, known by everyone as a MARS station. I sent a message to Kathy through the Ninth Navy MARS District,

Armed Forces Reserve Center, Waukegan, Illinois. My message read as follows: "Dear Kathy, I'm OK, arrived here in Okinawa safe and sound. I love you, will write soon." Kathy received the message on 10 November 1969, the day I arrived in Vietnam.

My group of guys, the helicopter pilots, stuck together. We

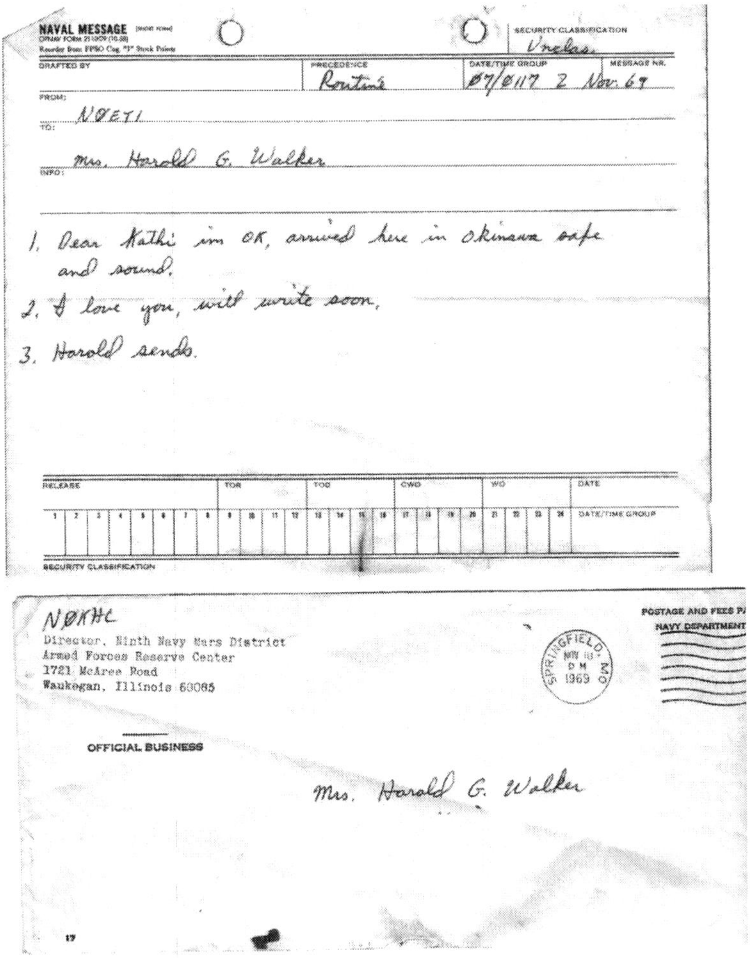

NAVAL MESSAGE

SECURITY CLASSIFICATION: Unclas

DRAFTED BY | PRECEDENCE: Routine | DATE/TIME GROUP: Ø7/Ø117 Z Nov. 69 | MESSAGE NR.

FROM: NØETI

TO: Mrs. Harold G. Walker

INFO:

1. Dear Kathi im OK, arrived here in Okinawa safe and sound.
2. I love you, will write soon.
3. Harold sends.

RELEASE | TOR | TOD | CWO | WO | DATE

SECURITY CLASSIFICATION

NØKHC
Director, Ninth Navy Mars District
Armed Forces Reserve Center
1721 McAree Road
Waukegan, Illinois 60085

POSTAGE AND FEES PA[ID]
NAVY DEPARTMENT

SPRINGFIELD, MO
1969

OFFICIAL BUSINESS

Mrs. Harold G. Walker

Figure 5 MARSGRAM sent to Kathy from Okinawa.

didn't know what to do or where to go or how long we would be at Hague. We initially had enough free time to get off base, have a few beers, and do some shopping, following a briefing to all new arrivals regarding the culture in Okinawa, and encouragement not to do anything that would put us into an Okinawan jail----forever. Also stressed was the VD rate. We were told of the few who didn't go anywhere but to the local hospital after contracting exotic diseases, like black syphilis, causing some to be classified as Killed in Action (KIA), never to go home again. Whether this was true or a scare tactic, only the most reckless would know.

The first order of business was to go to the local town. After hailing a taxi and giving very general directions which were something like, "Take us to a bar," we were off. The cab driver, friendly and English-speaking, knew what he had—another group of thirsty Marines. We were in civilian attire, but there was no disguising who we were. After some time the cab turned down an alley and came to an abrupt halt.

The first thought in my mind was that we were going to be mugged. It was my intention that this not happen, and with no weapons, my feet would do the talking. I knew we could outrun the cab driver, but what if there were other street toughs waiting for us? Gary, Joe, Roy and I were apprehensive, but not overly concerned. We were still Marines, weren't we?

The driver took our money and directed us through the door of a shack. Inside, the scene was surreal; the furnishings, simple tables and straight back chairs, were all covered with what appeared to be white bed sheets. One or two booths were built into the corners of the room. As our eyes became accustomed to the darkness, the forms of others in the room came into focus. There were no other customers, but somber young women were sitting in chairs against the walls. We had no sooner ordered a round of the local beer when the girls came to the table. This was our first experience with the prostitutes of Okinawa. They were all over us and saying, "GI this," and "GI that." Well, the situation was becoming uncomfortable; we just left the beers and walked out with the mama-san pleading that we stay. The cab driver, ever watchful of our group as we wandered about was more than ready to take us elsewhere. We declined and moved on.

It wasn't as though we were naïve or taken aback by the attack of the whores; that seemed to be a routine matter. No, it was that the area was totally unfamiliar to us and seemed really unsafe—there were no other military types, or any other types for that matter, drinking there. We had been taken to this off-street tavern by the cabby. I later learned this action by the cabbie was a common tactic. The owner of a tavern/brothel would pay cabbies to take unsuspecting GIs to their particular place of business. It was all a setup, but we had—at least on this occasion—the good sense to leave.

We later learned that the joint was listed as off-limits to military personnel, which explains why we were the only idiots there. The bar was named Tokyo Bar and was later identified by Naval Intelligence to be a Russian covert operation to obtain intelligence from drunken servicemen.

Not trusting the cab drivers any longer, we walked to what appeared to be the main street and found a reputable bar, if there was such a thing. The bar at least felt safe, and it was full of other military personnel. There we had our fill of grog while meeting other Marines, airmen, and sailors.

We learned Okinawa was also the home of the traditional Japanese steam and massage houses, and we were encouraged by the local military staff personnel that before going to Vietnam, we must experience that cultural tradition. This was another adventure, especially for a guy from a small cotton farm north of Bragg City, Missouri. I really did not trust this, but succumbed to the hype.

The massage parlors were, as I would later learn, legendary throughout Asia. For a few dollars one could endure a steam bath in a wooden cabinet which was painted white. The cabinet was engineered in such a manner that when the clamshell-like doors were opened, a seat was revealed. Upon sitting in the cabinet, the clamshell doors were shut, and your head stuck up out of a porthole. There was a row of these steam cabinets with guys' heads sticking out and steam escaping through the space between their necks and the holes in the cabinets. Some of the more seasoned steamers had placed a towel around their necks to hold in the steam. You were then slow cooked, or so it seemed. The smell from the old steam house was not pleasant; it helped if you had had a couple of drinks first. From the looks of things, a couple of drinks was the least anyone had had.

I became concerned that I could be left in the steam cabinet, because you had to be let out from the outside. This was very uncomfortable. I felt claustrophobic. Once the steam had cooked you, the massage was next. I had never had a massage previous to this, and it was wonderful, so relaxing that I went to sleep only to be awoken abruptly and told to move on as there were more customers waiting. Everyone wanted a tip, but I didn't leave a tip. Instead, I paid the couple of dollars and left, meeting up with Gary, Joe and Roy.

Figure 6 My pin-up, Kathy, modeling the kimono.

Having sobered up from the steam bath and massage, it was time to do some shopping and get back to Camp Hague. I bought Kathy a beautiful kimono and had it wrapped and sent to her. She later sent me a picture of her modeling the kimono, a beautiful picture that I treasured throughout my time in Vietnam. I didn't leave Camp Hague again. I didn't feel that great. I wasn't acclimating to the tropical climate.

For the next couple of days, I was directed to be the officer in charge (OIC) in an area receiving the returnees from Vietnam, overseeing the processing of personal gear before the Marines left for the States. It was utter confusion; Marines coming and going, buses coming and going, clouds of dust kicked up by the heavy traffic and lines of Marines everywhere. There were the new guys, easily identifiable with our crisp new uniforms and confused looks. There were the vets returning in their soiled, faded jungle utes.

"Under the traditions of the Marine Corps, the greatest respect is accorded those who are nearest to danger...they are the infantrymen or, as they call themselves, Grunts. The Grunts have always been called the pride of the Marine Corps because they are the ones who stand on the cusp. They take the most casualties. They have the fewest creature comforts, and they answer in their honor to no one." James Webb, author, *Fields of Fire*. Spoken in the Friday evening, 14 October 1983, "McNeil/Lehrer News hour.[17]"

An unending procession of Marines displayed a deserved pride as they made their way through Camp Hague, being processed to go home. Their personal gear was inspected to ensure prohibited items did not return to the U.S. Among those prohibited items were weapons, pictures of dead bodies, and classified information. This was my first close association with the combat Marines (the Grunts) from Vietnam.

As a wet-behind-the-ears first lieutenant, I was careful not to assume too much authority, allowing the staff of enlisted and noncommissioned officers (NCOs) at Camp Hague to do their job (of which I knew nothing and they knew everything) without my help or interference. This tact on my part seemed to work well.

The men were in different states of mind: some grinning from ear to ear, others appearing in deep thought, quietly going about their business, and yet others who clearly and loudly discussed their trials by fire. Loud mouths! They threw their old jungle utes into a pile. I didn't understand why the Marines were

---

[17] Timberg, Robert, The nightingale's Song. (Touchstone, Simon & Shuster 19950, 331.

not allowed to take the utilities home with them, but that was the rule during that period. A few Ka-Bars, Marine-issued combat knives, were collected, and some gruesome Polaroid photos of enemy dead—their heads on stakes, their pale eyes open, lighted cigarettes stuck into their mouths. Otherwise, there was nothing much of interest. These items were all collected with little or no resistance. Sometimes the Marine simply shrugged and commented, "Who gives a shit?" before tossing the items onto a growing pile.

As I would later learn, any significant war trophies: AK-47s, M-14s, fragmentation grenades, etc., were spirited home by other means well before the individual got into this line. One of the exiting Marines, with whom I struck up a conversation, advised me to find a couple sets of utes in this pile that were a fit and suggested I take them with me into Vietnam because jungle utilities were hard to come by in-country (a phrase indicating service in Vietnam).

I did as he suggested and after finding a pair that fit me and weren't too grungy, I tucked them into my sea bag. Those utilities were the modern day equivalent of the *Red Badge of Courage*.[18]

---

[18] Stephen Crane, The Red Badge of Courage, 1951.

Figure 7 Marine Corps Ka-Bar combat knife given to author in Okinawa before entering Vietnam.

I certainly didn't wear those utilities at Camp Hague, not wanting to appear like an idiot to those who knew me. I would wait until I was in-country. I knew, however, that I would most likely be wearing a baggy Nomex flight suit for the next year. I did have some luck, another Marine who was going to have to turn over his rugged Marine Ka-Bar fighting knife rather than be allowed to take it back to the world handed it to me. The Marine, a Cpl., from whom the knife was to be confiscated, handed it to me. He asked only one thing, for me "to take it back to Vietnam and finish the job."

I began suffering from what was probably a 24-hour viral infection, seemingly brought on by the change in climate. The heat was oppressive, and my body was aching and pumping out sweat at an alarming rate. A fever and dehydration made me weaker. With some trepidation, I made my way to sick call. I was afraid that my schedule to depart to Vietnam would be adversely affected by my fever, but that fear was soon dispelled. The corpsman[19] I saw gave me some aspirin and shared that my condition routinely happened upon arrival from the States. Apparently, I still had not become acclimated.

---

[19] The Corpsman in the Marine Corps is a medic, a naval hospital corpsman attached to the Marine Corps for medical support during operations and battle. No single rating in the Navy is more decorated for valor than the Corpsman.

I decided to try a home cure. I downed a couple of aspirin and a few slugs from a pint of Jim Beam and shared the remainder with Joe and Gary; Roy didn't drink. After several hours of sleep and profuse sweating I was a few pounds lighter and weaker, but ready to go.

* * *

The idea of whiskey being a home remedy had served me well once before. On a junior/senior high school trip from Bragg City, Missouri, High School to Washington D.C. and New York City in 1962 I had begun to suffer from a horrendous sore throat. One evening while in New York City, my friends Don and Wayne and I made a straw purchase of a pint of whiskey. We went to the roof of the hotel and, while looking out over the city, killed off the pint. The next day I was ok—no more sore throat.

* * *

It was nearing our time to undergo in-country processing. The processing was routine, but one thing was ominous. We were provided cardboard boxes upon which we were told to place our name, rank and serial number. After carefully folding our uniforms, we placed them in those plain boxes. I was curious about this and asked the corporal why we were required to leave our greens. His response was prompt and sobering, bringing me back to the stark reality of why we were here and what could happen.

"Sir," he said with a bored look on his face, "when you come back through here a year from now, or sooner, your uniform will be here for you to wear home in accordance with Marine Corps travel policy." That explanation was sufficient, but following a brief pause and a slight smile, he said, "If you are killed in action or are medevaced to Japan or the States, your uniform will be forwarded to your hospital. Either way, dead or alive, you or your next of kin will get your uniform back." Nuff said.

The straightforward, no-nonsense response momentarily caught me off guard. My response was a halting, "Oh … yeah!" as if I had only briefly forgotten why. Now the goal was clear:

come back through Camp Hague alive. As I reflect back, the young corporal probably got a kick out of responding to a new first lieutenant in that manner and seeing my pale response. Whatever the case, no more discussion was necessary.

The next day, Monday, 10 November 1969, it was time for Gary, Joe, Roy and me to enter the fray. After all the training, the anticipation, the news reports—finally it was our time!

6: One Way Ticket

I had never studied a detailed map of I Corps, too busy learning to fly. What will it be like? Will we be fired upon during our approach to Da Nang? These questions would be answered in less than 24 hours.

On 10 November 1969, the 194th birthday of the Marine Corps, my day began in Okinawa with a beautiful tropical sunrise, unlike those seen in the Show-Me State. After boarding a Flying Tigers 707 contract air carrier amid scattered conversations, I took one last glance at Okinawa as the big jet made its lumbering way onto the runway.

This conveyance seemed quite extraordinary to me. I had fully expected to enter Vietnam on a C-130 Hercules or some similar type of military aircraft. Smiling stewardesses, hot coffee, lunch, a snack—this was not what I expected. Not in the Marine Corps. But then, this was a contract carrier that flew people from every service into Nam, every day; therefore, the Corps had to graciously accept the same ride.

The flight southwest across the Pacific Ocean was smooth and uneventful. Light conversation masked my growing sense of excitement. Our status as new helicopter pilots soon became evident to those close to us. We sported the look of new guys with our stateside utilities, bright silver bars, polished wings of gold and spit-shined flight boots instead of combat boots, and we talked exclusively of what flying might be like in Vietnam.

On board was a variety of personnel, Army, Navy, Marine Corps, Air Force and civilian contractors. Some were returning from a week of R&R. Some were returning from emergency leave. Some were brand new Marines and Army infantry types not long out of high school. A few of the Marines were staff NCOs returning for their second tour, and one was on his third tour.

One was an E-7 Gunnery Sergeant (GySgt). Another was a Master Gunnery Sergeant (MGySgt) with those four rockers on the collar insignia of his utes. Two more were Staff Sergeants (SSgts.), one very quiet and seated in front of me, and one very loud in the aisle seat in front of us. He was having fun mouthing off to one of the young privates making his way down the aisle to his seat. He talked about them being "fresh fish," a term I had never heard in that context. He was yapping about some obscure subject having to do with getting killed in Vietnam, telling sea stories as he glanced about to see if anyone else was listening to him.

After some time, while the stewardesses were getting everyone settled, the quiet staff sergeant in front of me shifted around, looked over the top of the seat and spoke to me. "Begging your pardon Sir, but, where y'all headed?"

"Vietnam," I responded. "Where else?"

"Ha," he laughed. "Ain't it the truth." A slight pause, "*F**kin' Nam*," he whispered, mainly to himself..."There ain't no place else."

While I tried to get situated in my seat next to the starboard window he continued, talking to me or himself, apparently recalling his first tour, "Do you have any idea which outfit you'll be flying with?"

"Naw, we're just checking in," I said, thinking that was the end of the conversation. Momentarily, however, he turned around again, his back against the window. He appeared to be thinking about something that was troubling him, something maybe about his past, or his future.

He placed a cigarette in his mouth, but didn't light it as a stewardess grinned and shook her finger. "You'll be able to light up soon as we're in the air."

"Yes maam," he responded with a grin.

"When was your last tour?" I asked.

"'67, '68."

"Wow...you were there through Tet?"

"Yeah," he said. Dropping the Sir. "I spent some time in the dirt there at Khe Sanh, Hill 881 South. It was like the end of the world."

"Excuse me for asking, but isn't it a little quick for you to be going back?"

He looked away, not answering.

Then, in a few moments, he said, "I didn't get along too well back there in The World. Me and the Marine Corps came to an understanding...I fit better there in Nam."

What could I say to that comment? I remained quiet, not wanting to touch his memories of that experience, but it was apparent that he could think of nothing else.

"What are y'all flying?" he asked.

"Helicopters, CH-46s."

"Well, good luck. I was there when some of them things were falling apart in midair."

"Yeah, they had some problems with the tail pylon falling off in the 46A, but those problems have been fixed."

"Y'all wanna play some cards? It'll kill the time."

"Na, I'll pass."

"Any of you other Sirs wanna play cards?" he asked around.

No one was interested. We each needed time to be alone with our own thoughts. Once it became known that we were helicopter pilots, the stories began to fly. There are two types of stories—fairy tales and sea stories. Maybe there are more, but that's what I remember. Fairy tales characteristically begin with "Once upon a time..." and end with "...and they lived happily ever after." Sea stories almost always begin with, "This is no shit..." and can end in any way you want. Sea stories are named particularly for the naval service to which the Marine Corps reluctantly acknowledges a relationship. Tales of the sea lean toward the macabre and can be loosely identified as gallows humor.

The staff sergeant had spoken of Khe Sanh, but he didn't tell it all. Helicopters did litter the earth there.

A loudmouth story teller picked up the beat. He spoke of new pilots mostly being killed within two weeks of entering the war, implying that if we lived past the first couple weeks in a helicopter, we might make it through. True or not, it wasn't anything we hadn't heard before, and it made sense in a funny kind of way. New pilots, not yet adjusted to the carnage and the flights into showers of steel, were susceptible to making a mistake—or were for some reason marked for death, just as pilots who were almost ready to go home, for instance. As Colonel Donald Conroy, the CO of the Marine Aviation Detachment (MAD) at Pensacola, Naval Air Station (NAS) once told me, "Helicopter pilots in Vietnam are dying at such a rate no one should get married before going unless you just want to give your new wife and her boyfriend the $10,000 in life insurance money."

* * *

We had already heard about Operation Hastings and the five CH-46A helicopters that littered the floor of the "Song Ngan Valley," a God forsaken place near the DMZ, now immortalized in Marine Corps lore as "Helicopter Valley." It was a name mentioned in the same sentence as Con Thien, "the Hill of Angels" or as it became known, "The Dead Marine Zone", an abandoned French fort; Khe Sanh, the A Shau Valley, the Battle of Hue and Operation Dewey Canyon. Our helicopter flight instructors at Ellyson Field, Pensacola, FL., Marine Corps Air Facility, Santa Ana and New River, NC. were for the most part, survivors of those hard fought battles from the mouth of the Cua Viet River, west to along the DMZ to Laos and south along the border of Laos. The instructors made sure that upon going in, we new guys knew about it and accepted it as such. We each had to make our own peace with the facts. I did so by doing what I had always heard about military service—never volunteer. Especially don't volunteer for any suicide missions,[20] and never refuse any assigned missions. I would live or die by my decision.

[20] Once I vowed that I wouldn't volunteer for suicide missions, I recognized there was no such thing as a "suicide mission" in Vietnam. The most mundane flight could get you killed at any moment. It was like the air was full of shrapnel and sometimes, someone would just fly into it.

Figure 8 Doomed CH-46 from HMM-265 hit by Antiaircraft Artillery fire during Operation Hastings, July 15, 1966, resulting in the death of 13 Marines. These photographs, taken by Haas Faust, are among the most famous/infamous images of the Vietnam war as reported by Tim King, combat journalist, Salem-News.com.

Operation Hastings was a horrific example of the carnage that occurred in the war. The above pictures were taken by combat photograph Haas Faust on 15 July 1966.[21] The HMM-265 CH-46A shown above was hit by a 12.7MM Soviet heavy machine gun/antiaircraft gun with the North Vietnamese 324B Division in LZ Crow, flown by First Lieutenants Thomas C. McAllister and George Richey. In all, Sixteen Marines died in that one shoot down. Three Marines, who somehow survived, were severely burned.

* * *

[21]http://www.salem-news.com/articles/april232012/helicopter-valley-tk.php via http://wnn,usmcpress/1960svietnam/past21.htm. (350x239pixels) Public domain free of known restrictions under copyright laws – including all related neighboring rights.

The first-tour infantry Marines spoke about having just graduated from high school that past June and then going to either the Marine Recruit Depot at Paris Island, South Carolina, or to the Marine Recruit Training Depot in San Diego. One spoke of having just married his high school girlfriend, bringing out her high school picture. The stewardesses paid particular attention to him, taken with his innocence. The picture got passed around to his buddies, who were laughing and joking around.

"She's nice," said one.

"Let me see," said another.

"Wow," said one. "She's a real looker. You sure she's your wife? She's too pretty to be married to a jarhead like you."

"Yes sir," said another. "Soon as you're killed, I'm gonna escort your raggedy ass home, just to meet her."

The laughter stopped.

"Shut up you dumb son-of-a-bitch," someone said.

The idea of violent death wasn't something the stewardesses or anyone wanted to deal with on this flight. It was too real, too close.

"You Marines better get your gear together, we'll be landing soon," said the stewardess.

Someone uttered, "For you jarheads, that means, get your shit together."

The older second-tour Marines, when not kidding us, were much different, not as buoyant or excited about being in combat again. Some of them were Marines who, upon returning to CONUS (Continental United States) following their first tour, had volunteered to return immediately to Vietnam by waving their Overseas Rotation Date[22] (ORD). They were the ones you didn't carelessly ask about why they were returning to Vietnam, like my question earlier in the flight. I would later learn that many of those who did waive the ORD did it because they couldn't or

---

22 The Overseas Rotation Date at that time was generally a two-year window, meaning that a career Marine could expect to be in the Continental United States for a two year period before returning to overseas duty. The date was arbitrary and could be waived for a variety of reasons.

wouldn't adapt to what they called the bullshit of Marine garrison duty. One Marine, named Mike, flippantly stated his reason for returning to Vietnam was his inability to find the right girl to date in New River, North Carolina.

Soon the stewardesses were serving sandwiches and drinks—no alcohol. Some on board were lulled to sleep by the monotonous moan of the engines. Others turned their attention to an impromptu card game. I finally lapsed into a fitful half-sleep at about the same time the craft began an easy descent, bringing me back to consciousness. How could anyone sleep now?

Over the intercom came the voice of the senior stewardess. "We are now approaching the coast of Vietnam. Please bring your seats back to the full upright position and fasten your seatbelts low and tight across your laps." The stewardesses began their slow walk down the aisle, ensuring all loose gear was stowed, trash was picked up and sleepers gently awakened. "We're landing soon," they'd softly say as they moved down the aisle, stopping here and there.

There was no more small talk, no chatter. Gary and I sat in the same row. Joe and Roy were directly in front of us. I had made it my mission to gain a window seat on the starboard side of the craft. I'd reviewed the route of flight from Okinawa to Vietnam over the South China Sea before boarding that morning. It appeared to me that a seat on the starboard (right) side would give me the best view of Vietnam when approaching the coastline.

It was mid-afternoon, (15 hours ahead of Missouri time) and misty fog had encircled our craft. I strained to get my first glimpse of Vietnam through the porthole windows. Soon a coastline began to materialize out of the mist. I didn't know what to expect, and yet I expected to see something...anything!

Would I see bombs bursting, like Francis Scott Key did when looking at Fort McHenry from his place on the British warship HMS *Tonnant*, or clouds of smoke billowing up from battles enjoined? The faint image of the coastline had a mystical effect on me. I had lived with the image of Vietnam on television since my second year in college, and now here it was right before my eyes, coming closer every moment. The lush greenery of the land was coming into view. It had a surreal quality, truly beautiful yet foreboding. The low-lying coastal plains extended west into the mountains, over which dark ominous clouds hung.

The aircraft made a right turn inward toward the coastline, followed by another right banking turn to the north, lining up on the north-south runway of the Da Nang AFB. As we slowed for approach, the unmistakable sound of hydraulics signaled the lowering and locking in of the landing gear. Once lined up for landing, our position provided me with an unobstructed view of the landscape nearest the coastline.

In many places, the faint geometric imprint of ancient rice paddies seemed to rise from land covered in mossy greenery. Unexpected splotches of white sandy outcroppings (salt flats) were amid the greenery, and they reminded me of the white sand of Pensacola Beach. Randomly scattered about the area were round depressions which I assumed were bomb craters, mute testimony that a war was indeed going on there.

Prior to touchdown, I observed off the starboard side a peculiar cluster of mountainous obelisks rising straight up from the pristine coastline.

I later learned that those large formations were the famous Marble Mountains, a cluster of five marble and limestone hills named for the five elements: Kim "metal," Thuy, "water," Moc "wood," Hoa "fire" and Tho "earth." The dust from those hills is believed to have contributed to the odd outcroppings of white sand found in that area and legend has it that eons ago the mountains rose up from the eggs laid by a dragon. Ancient Buddist and Hindu temples were carved into the mountains and had become places for spiritual retreats and pilgrimages. The faithful believed the cavernous sanctuaries possessed mystical powers.

North of the Marble Mountains I recognized another north-south airstrip, so near the coastline it looked like it was on the beach. I saw helicopters. Could that be where we would end up?

The hydraulics once again began to whine, extending and lowering the flaps. When the flaps engaged, the aircraft lurched forward toward the runway. We passed over a river running east-west. Instinctively, I braced for landing, as the plane slammed onto the runway, the struts seeming to collapse as they absorbed the impact. My immediate thought was that the pilot must have been a carrier pilot. From the manner in which he drove that aircraft into the deck, he must have been hoping for the three-wire. I had experienced that when flying a T-28C Trojan during my carrier qualifications on the USS *Essex*'s 23 January 1969 decommissioning cruise, making me technically eligible to be in the Navy's vaunted Tail-Hook Association.

The lumbering giant of an aircraft groaned and the engines

Figure 9 The Author's 230169 Carrier Qualification in a T-28C on the USS Essex.

screamed as the captain reversed thrust, throwing us forward against our lap belts. Slowing, we turned onto a taxiway. After a brief period of taxiing, the brakes engaged, and we lurched to a stop. We were at the 15th Aerial Port in Da Nang, Republic of South Vietnam. The local time was 1612, 10 November 1970.

An announcement by the captain over the intercom welcomed us to Vietnam. "We are now in South Vietnam. Good luck to all of you and hope to see you upon your return to the world." There was that phrase again, "the world." What I took from that was that South Vietnam just wasn't considered to be a part of the world.

The head stewardess got on the intercom and asked us to remain seated until the door was opened and the stairs leading to the tarmac pushed into place. Gary looked over at me, grinned and said, "Well, I guess it starts today."

"I guess so," I responded, beginning to stretch my arms.

The metallic sound of safety belts clanging and the shuffling of feet signaled passengers were anxious to get going. The big door opened with the sound of a giant suction seal being broken. The first molecules of Vietnamese air rushed into the passenger compartment, heavy humidity and heat I'd not felt in my Missouri home. My first full breath of Vietnamese air filled my lungs.

A military person walked into the aircraft and spoke briefly with the stewardess, who handed the microphone to him. "Welcome to Vietnam," he said. "I'm Sergeant First Class Murray." Murray spoke in military acronyms, on and on about what we were to do upon deplaning. We were tired and ready to get off. "The Marines and Army personnel on their first tour will be transported to Freedom Hill for processing and transportation to your unit. Grab your gear at the baggage area and move to the busses in the parking area next to the terminal building." Everyone stood. With military precision, each row waited until the row before them emptied to get into the aisle. There was no pushing and shoving to get off.

Making my way down the stairs that had been placed against the fuselage, I was looking at the area. It was another plywood city with tin roofs. I wondered who had the contract to supply the plywood and corrugated tin that it had taken to build all of this. We got our gear and made our way to the bus. My path into the country of South Vietnam was at its end. My path into what Vietnam had become was just beginning.

The Staff Marines I had met on the plane, the MGySgt., the GySgt., and the SSgts. were met at the terminal by Marines from the units with whom they were to be attached. The first tour Marines, Pvts., PFCs., LCpls., and Cpls., all boarded a bus to Freedom Hill.

I walked over to the MGySgt and said, "Top, (the respected slang term for Marines at the rank of E-8 and above) I wanted to say good-bye to you and wish you good luck."

With both of us outside and covered (hats on), he looked at me and saluted smartly, taking me by surprise. I awkwardly switched the document package I was holding from my right hand to my left as he maintained his salute, and I returned the salute as best I could, after which we cut the salute. He said, reaching out his hand, "Let me wish you good luck Sir." Then, following a brief pause, and as if he just had an afterthought, he said, "You take good care of yourself Lieutenant. We need you crazy pilots to fly us into and out of trouble. [brief pause] I was here in the Third Marine Division (3d MarDiv) and was waist deep in the siege of Khe Sanh. I've seen what you'll be doing. Those things we spoke of during the flight, the helicopter crashes and the way those gooks shot those 46s down, was all true." With a clear voice, he looked me in the eye, shook my hand once again and said "You be careful out there, yahear?" The perfect salutation to a conversation between two southern born Marines.

"Yes, Sir," I said, realizing too late that I had called him "Sir". I was the officer, still, a new concept for me. I hoped he didn't notice my screw-up. I hadn't been around many senior staff NCOs at that point in my life. Some senior staff NCOs I later learned to take real exception to being called "Sir" by a 1st Lt., usually the offenders of that military protocol. But as I saw it, I was a helicopter pilot more than I was an officer. Anyway, if I offended him, I appreciated him letting it slide—but he didn't.

"No," he said with a grin. "Remember, you're the 'Sir' and I'm the one who works for a living," he chuckled. Then, telling the others with him, "Let's go have fun. We've got a war to fight."

"By the way," I asked, as he walked away, "where're you headed?"

"Seventh Marines, Baldy... Oorah!"

"Good luck!" I yelled. Then, I thought...Baldy... what in the hell is that? I had no idea where or what Baldy was, but it couldn't have been good.

The Jeep, that he was in, pulled into traffic. He was all grins as he returned a thumbs up and yelled back, "Y'all too, Flyboys."

The afternoon was hot and humid; the smell was exotic, almost nauseating. It reminded me of both Okinawa and Nogales, Mexico. The shadows were getting longer, and the day was fast coming to an end as we grabbed our gear and boarded a bus marked Freedom Hill.

7: Freedom Hill

Scrambling onto a rough-looking bus, its open windows covered with chicken wire, we felt somewhat at ease. I asked out loud, "Why the chicken wire over the windows?"

The answer from another person on board was, "To repel hand grenades."

Damn, I thought, this really is Vietnam.

The streets of Da Nang were teeming with small brown people. Every direction up and down the streets strange vehicles of all sizes, small and smaller were everywhere. Those small taxis carrying one or two Vietnamese were three-wheeled bicycle taxis, called cyclos, powered by a driver sitting behind the passengers and pedaling. Vespa scooters and two-cycle engine Honda 50cc motorbikes spewed clouds of blue smoke from their one-cylinder engine that burped, popped and snapped. Two or three Vietnamese or a load of produce and a couple of chickens in small handmade cages were carried in motorized rickshaws, which I doubted would even pull one American. The small stature of the populace led me to question how we could possibly be threatened by this smaller foe. Then I thought of the Japanese in WWII and dismissed my thoughts on the matter.

The women of Vietnam scurrying to and fro wore simple pajama-like clothing, mostly black, with conical hats. The older men and women appeared to have perpetual grins on their faces that revealed smooth ebony colored teeth, the discoloration caused by chewing betel nut, a mild narcotic grown on the Areca tree. To me, someone who grew up on a cotton farm in Southeast Missouri, their appearance was spellbinding—perpetual smiles and questioning eyes. They had seen nothing but war for generations. We were just the most recent occupiers of their land, following the hated French.

The school-age girls, with long raven black hair, were striking in their satiny white costumes called Ao Dai (pronounced ow zeye). The garments had a mandarin collar, tight bodice, and skirt split to the waist, worn over black satiny pajamas. Their flowing apparel made them appear taller and more graceful than those not wearing the costume. Even ladies working, carrying large pots through the district carried themselves with elegance and grace.

Figure 10 A picture of elegance and grace even when carrying buckets." From the HMM-262 1969-70 cruise book. Photo by First Lieutenant Jerry Johnson.

The younger men, for the most part, were dressed in some form of military uniform, most without weapons. I didn't recognize any of the unit insignias, and wondered why there were so many in the street appearing not to be involved in any form of military duty.

The streets themselves were a mixture of red mud and gravel covered by an extra-fine dust of the same color that clung to everything. Heavy military trucks, the 7.5-ton 6X6s (pronounced six-by) rushed about in all directions at speeds well above what appeared to be safe, sweeping pedestrians aside like a tidal wave. The drivers showed little or no outward concern for the crowd. With radios blaring and cigarettes hanging out of the sides of their mouths, they were the lords of the street. Or was it that they were totally aware of the street people, and the very real dangers they represented? Maybe driving the way they did was a survival tactic—to keep moving and not make themselves an easy target.

Military policemen were prominent at many intersections and appeared as unconcerned as the truck drivers. Street vendors sat alongside the roads selling all manner of things out of makeshift crates, including, to my surprise, Coke and Nehi orange drinks. I recalled one of our lectures at OCS, or was it a sea story? Whatever, I was sure I would never drink from a bottle or a water glass with ice from a street vendor. It was reported that military personnel had swallowed ground-up glass that way. The very thought of having shards of glass ripping through my throat and into my stomach almost caused me to give up ice entirely. I resolved to drink only from cans I opened myself, or iced drinks that came directly from the Officers Club.

As we bounced along the streets on the way to Freedom Hill, also known as Hill 327,[23] I took in all the views of the surrounding area. Approaching what appeared to be a theater and a couple of convenience stores, the bus turned into an area surrounded by a

---

[23] A topographic map provides the height of hills and depressions of geologic features in metric measurement. In Vietnam, many locations were commonly known by the height of the hill above sea level, as in Hill 327 or Hill 55.

tall fence topped with concertina wire and under guard by armed military police. An armed guard met the bus, performed a cursory security check, and waved us in. This was the in-country[24] induction center, the entry and exit point for all Marines in I Corps.

Within walking distance of Freedom Hill was the beating heart of the Marine Corps' I Corps war effort. The area included: III Marine Amphibious Force (III MAF) Headquarters, commanded by LtGen. Herman Nickerson, Jr.; the First Marine Division (1st MarDiv) Headquarters, commanded by MajGen. Ormond R. Simpson; and the First Marine Aircraft Wing (1st MAW) Headquarters, commanded by MajGen. William G. Thrash.

LZ 401, the First Battalion Recon headquarters known as Camp Reasoner, overlooked the above commands, including the First Medical Battalion Medical Center (1st Med) where medevacs were taken, and the private quarters of the III MAF general, LtGen. Nickerson at that time.

On 7 November 1969, four days before Gary, Roy, Joe and I arrived at Freedom Hill, the Third Marine Division (3d MarDiv) had left Vietnam for Okinawa in accordance with Operation Keystone, President Nixon's policy of Redeployment and Vietnamization. The departure of the 3d MarDiv denoted the first of many changes in Marine Corps assets in Vietnam.

In the area of Freedom Hill, the signature head gear appeared to be the camouflaged slouch or boonie hat (in Marine-speak, a jungle cover) adorned with hand grenade pins, individual unit insignia pins, and hand written slogans—a collector's dream. The hat was easy to roll up and would fit into the large side pocket on the leg of your utes. It was a favorite among the Grunts and recon Marines, part of the first uniform authorized and issued by the Marine Corps in 1969, designed for jungle

[24] The use of the term "in-country" was introduced to me at Freedom Hill. "in-country" simply meant, "in Vietnam." Freedom Hill was considered by some to be an "in-country" R&R center for those Marines and soldiers who occasionally needed to get away from the mind numbing monotony of that war.

fighting. I had seen the jungle cover at Camp Hague where it was left in large piles by Marines on their way home. The Corps allowed no camouflage uniforms into CONUS.

Again, as a new guy in-country I had no reason to question why so many combat vets were hanging around the Freedom Hill area. I believed all Marines or Army personnel who wore the jungle cover at Freedom Hill were combat veterans. I later learned that many rear echelon service personnel wore them to impress new arrivals and to cover the fact that they had never been in combat. With random combat slogans handwritten on the hats and fresh Marine Corps tattoos on their forearms, visible when their sleeves were rolled to the elbow, their costumes amounted to a modern day version of *The Red Badge of Courage*.[25] They failed to recognize the lack of respect they received from the combat veterans, who referred to them as Remington Raiders, named for the typewriters used in administrative offices of the Army and Marine Corps.

We were soon directed toward the Staff Non-Commissioned Officers/Officers transient barracks by a Marine corporal, who advised that he was on an in-country hold of some sort. He didn't enlighten us as to why, nor do I know why he mentioned it to us in the first place. He was apparently forced into the position of processing incoming personnel and handing out towels. The personnel wandering about the area appeared to be no more than eighteen or nineteen years old and all looked bored—not the uptight we-may-be-overrun-at-any-minute look I had expected. Once the corporal informed us he was on hold he lost interest in small talk, especially with us, so my follow-up attempt at conversation was very lame.

"So, this is Vietnam?" I said, trying to change the subject.

---

[25] *The Red Badge of Courage* is a novel written by Stephen Crane and published in 1895. The story was of how a civil war soldier was propelled to perform valiantly when a wound he had received was believed, in error, by his fellow soldiers to have been received while he was performing heroically. Just as the wound, the red badge, became a metaphor for courage, the jungle cover known as the bush hat became a metaphor for having been a combat veteran, a Grunt.

His answer, "Why...yes sir," was said in a manner which was easily interpreted as yes, asshole, this is Vietnam. Where did you think you were, Cleveland? I felt my complexion change to red, realizing how incredibly dumb I sounded. Gary laughed and said, "You asked for that, Walker," and Roy just grinned as we continued making our way to our quarters for the evening.

The barracks was an overgrown Southeast Asia (SEA) hut with rows of military racks, each with a rolled-up mattress. Bed sheets were provided and chow times were made available to us with the assurance that we would be transported to MAG-16 first thing in the morning.

The daylight turned to twilight and another Marine officer checked in with the four of us. He was a Grunt first lieutenant. His name was William, and he was going home, having served his time. He was friendly—exuberant that his release date had arrived. He had orders back to the World, Jacksonville, North Carolina. His particularly friendly manner caused us to gravitate toward him, but in conversation we kept a respectful distance regarding the war, remembering my encounter with the corporal at Camp Hansen. William had the look of a warrior—slender but not skinny, with deep tanned forearms, face and neck. He had the weather-beaten face of an outdoorsman, making him appear much older than he was. He said he had been a platoon leader, and that was all he offered about himself. The purpose in his manner soon revealed itself. "Marines shouldn't celebrate the birthday alone," he declared, and we were allowed within his world for a brief time.

Yes, it was the Marine Corp's 194th birthday. We'd almost forgotten in our movement from Okinawa. It absolutely was the 10th of November, and he was absolutely correct that this called for a toast among the brotherhood—Grunts and wingers, all brothers to the bone on this day.

William searched through his gear, pulling and shoving aside articles of clothing and coming up with a half-bottle of Jim Beam. Gary and Joe were enthusiastic in their search for some

Styrofoam cups, and the first toast of the evening was raised between the five of us. Even Roy couldn't decline a ceremonial toast, offering up a sincere and sobering wish that one year from this day we would all be able to toast the 195th Marine Corps birthday on our way back to the World. As usual, I was far from that reflective about our situation. The present was what counted and now the trick was to find a real Marine birthday party.

The nights in Vietnam were different. They were mysterious and had an air of unreality. Helicopter sounds were mixed with those of tactical jets taking off and landing at the Da Nang Air Base. There was a row of bright lights, reminiscent of stadium lights, along the crest of a high ridge that formed the extreme western perimeter of Da Nang. Those bright lights against the pitch-black night were buttressed by a series of small outposts, manned by Marines protecting us from whatever lurked outside the perimeter.

The surreal effect was further enhanced by a continuing cascade of huge flares floating down outside the perimeter. They were held in place like lanterns by small parachutes that rocked back and forth, casting eerie shadows on the surrounding areas. This shadowy world I found myself in caused me to reflect upon this place and to sense what Vietnam was all about. During the day the lights were not visible but during the night they brought out the shadows and their presence was clear and startling. The truth of this was overwhelming—the day was ours, but the night was surely theirs.

We eventually found the Officers Club of III MAF with the help of a compassionate duty officer. A Philippine rock and roll band was performing, playing the hits of the 60s. I recognized everything that was being played, and we were treated well, as Marines, not new guys. The celebration was quite civilized in comparison to the two Marine Corps birthday balls I had attended since becoming a Marine. The night ended early, about 2200. After a rousing chorus of the Marine Corps Hymn and a toast, we began the walk back toward Freedom Hill. Having spent a few hours with William, I felt comfortable enough to ask, "What is the war like? What can we expect?"

"I've spent the last year doing one thing—surviving." he said. "The war has calmed down some since '68, no more big frontal assaults like happened in Tet. Mines and bushwhacking is their sport nowadays, and they are coming in from the Ho Chi Minh trail by the hundreds, gettin' ready for something big, someday."

"Where were you?" I asked tentatively, hoping I wasn't prying too much.

Almost whispering, he said, "I was with the 5th Marines, An Hoa, Gonoi Island, Liberty Bridge, Dodge City in Arizona Territory, and what seems like a thousand other places where Charlie lay in wait."

He became quiet for few moments, then, said, "You asked me, what you can expect here." His eyes moved to the lights on the crest of the hill, and he raised his arm as if adding a postscript. Pointing toward the ominous western perimeter he proclaimed with a simple yet chilling directness, "It don't matter where you are out there. All the war you could ever want is on the other side of those lights...so expect anything and everything."

Watching him, it was obvious that he was not prepared to relive his experiences with us that night. He had answered all that was necessary, and it was high time to go home.

My first day in Vietnam was ending. As I shut my eyes that first night, the day in review was like the first time I saw Disneyland—all exhilaration and excitement. The adventure had begun. I was now mentally prepared to learn with which squadron my fate would lie.

8: Checking Into MAG-16

The morning of 11 November 1969 arrived very early, along with a slight hangover. The lieutenant had already begun his journey home. Silently, I wished him good luck and safe travel.

A cold shower, re-heated day-old coffee with grounds floating in the brew that could wake a dead man, along with a dose of excitement and natural adrenaline made my senses razor sharp. All of us, Gary, Roy and I, were up, packed, and in our stateside green utilities with starched and ironed covers, bright shiny gold wings, polished silver bars, and spit-shined boots. With our orders neatly tucked away in a plastic document holder, we were on our way, anxious to begin.

The bus trip from Freedom Hill to MAG-16 headquarters traversed Da Nang from near the western boundary to Marble Mountain Air Facility (MMAF) by the South China Sea, just north of its namesakes, the mystical Marble Mountains. The bus was equipped with what now appeared to be a normal accessory in Vietnam—chicken wire over the open windows. There was a light morning breeze and soft clouds flowed from the western highlands as the first rays of sunshine glistened off cars and motocyclos running to and fro. The streets were the same as the day before, full of people, military vehicles, military uniforms of every description, and each Honda 50 motorbike carrying at least two civilians, a chicken or two, and a basket of produce. Everything seemed to be covered with a layer of that red dust. Riding in the bus was akin to riding a wave of scurrying humanity.

Traveling east, my thoughts and observations were abruptly interrupted as we passed a sandbagged machinegun site with two helmeted Vietnamese military policemen situated under a large yellow flag with three horizontal red stripes, the flag of South Vietnam. They were protecting the approach to the Han River bridge. The Han ran north and south at this point. Two large hospital ships, identified as such by large red-cross insignias were docked alongside the west bank of the river, one north of the bridge and one south of the bridge. Small fishing boats and conical hats seemed to fill the river.

As the wheels of our bus touched the bridge, a thundering section of CH-46s leaped over us, so low I involuntarily ducked my head a little bit. I quickly turned my head to follow the sound. As they settled to the north of the bridge, I caught a glimpse of them. They were headed north and moving fast with a .50-cal Browning barrel hanging out of the side windows. It gave me chill bumps and made my heart beat faster as I strained to see if I could make out any insignia, but no such luck.

I was unsure of our proximity to MMAF at that point, but would later learn that this river was an entry and exit point at MMAF for helicopter traffic from the north, which probably accounted for the complete inattention given those helicopters by the local population. The bus made a tight right turn, heading south, passing by what appeared to be large open storage areas with giant stacks of metal Conex boxes, the kind seen on large ocean going vessels, on both sides of the road and U.S. Army guards on the gates. We continued further south for a short distance, arriving at a gate on the east side of the road, manned by Marines. It was the entrance to MMAF/MAG-16.

The gate guards were picture postcard Marines, which made me realize that the other military posts we had passed were Army posts. We were waved through following a cursory examination by a Marine Cpl. who momentarily boarded the bus.

We continued on the road, heading further into the airbase. Our route took us past the northernmost end of Runway 36 just as a section of UH-1E "Huey" gunships became airborne.

Figure 11 S.E.A hut

The bus now turned south, entering the housing area where rows of SEA huts, or hooches as they were also called, appeared, some of them with squadron markings.

The bus stopped briefly at a small commissary building where some Marines with luggage got off. They spoke of having just returned from R&R. My group and I remained aboard until reaching the MAG-16 administrative area, where we made our way to Personnel Check-In. It was now 1030. Upon arrival, we met up with another arriving Marine, First Lieutenant Ward Holland.

The Marines who were working in the office areas had the distinct appearance of stateside in their starched jungle utilities. Somehow, it didn't seem much different than MCAF Santa Ana, except for the Vietnamese civilians who worked on the base, mainly hooch maids whom we later learned were hired by the occupants of the huts to clean and launder clothes. After checking in with the duty officer we were directed to a familiar face, Lieutenant Colonel Moriarty, the MAG-16 S-1 officer.

LtCol. Moriarty was well known to my group. He had appeared at every juncture of our Marine career to date. He was the officer who had come to speak to us in January 1968 when we were Aviation Officer Candidates in the 48th OCS class at MCB Quantico. He had been there to advise us of the coming naval aviation training change that was coming, the Army Helicopter Training Program.[26] He wanted to know if we would volunteer for such a program. We didn't.

On 1 March 1968 he was the executive officer (XO) of MAD at Pensacola Naval Air Station under the command of Colonel Don "the Great Santini" Conroy, when I checked-in with other 2d Lts. Now, on 11 November 1969 when we stepped into the world of MAG-16, he welcomed us like old friends. We liked him, and his reputation as a straight shooter was well established.

---

[26] The siege of Khe Sanh began on 21 January 1968 and lasted for 77 days. On 28 February 1968 HMM-262 HAC Maj. Edwin G. Neixner and Capt. Robert Lee Sevell, his copilot along with Cpl. Benigni "Benny" Alfredo, their crew chief, were downed by NVA AAA trying to get into Khe Sanh. All aboard (24) were killed. The siege was taking its toll of helicopters and men, bringing the need for more helicopters (CH-46As) to a crisis point. The Army's helicopter training program would become the relief valve.

His presence relaxed me. My mind was spinning, looking for any clue as to where we would be assigned. There were rumors that regardless of the model of helicopter you were initially trained in you could be transitioned to any helicopter squadron. I still held some slim hope that I would get to fly the Huey gunship rather than the Phrog. To be able to shoot back was something that particularly appealed to me following my years while growing up on the farm, hunting and fishing on the Floodways.

The meeting with Moriarty was pleasant enough, but the information he provided caused me some concern. He pointed out general information about MAG-16 headquartered at MMAF, which was hardly discernible from the city of Da Nang. The III MAF, commanded by LtGen Herman Nickerson Jr., was responsible for the defense of the five northernmost provinces that constituted I Corps. The Marine Corps helicopters were located at MMAF and Phu Bai, near Hue and approximately 35 miles north of Da Nang along Highway 1. HML-367 a Huey gunship squadron bearing the greatest call sign of all time, the intimidating call sign, Scarface, was based temporarily at Phu Bai along with two CH-46 Squadrons, HMM-161 and 262 with respective call signs Cattlecall and Chatterbox.

The big picture was that the helicopter squadrons, once located at Quang Tri under Provisional MAG 39, were being relocated to MAG-16, MMAF in keeping with the Vietnamization and Redeployment plan. Those squadrons at Phu Bai would soon be pulled back to MMAF, and the Army's XXIV Corps, directly across Highway 1 from the Marines in Phu Bai, would assume operational responsibility for I Corps. This was a monumental change and clear evidence that the Marine Corps' role in Vietnam was quickly coming to an end.

This was my first direct knowledge of the planned pullout from Vietnam. We, the Marines, had reached our greatest number during 1969–70 when it was estimated that there were 85,000 Marines in Vietnam. My question was, how long can we expect to be here? Col. Moriarty advised that there was "no way to know" as these decisions were based on several factors and made by those much higher in rank than himself.

Moriarty's news concerned me. Had I gone through all of this training only to leave Vietnam before getting the opportunity to fly in combat? And if we had to leave before flying, would we even be recognized for having served in a combat zone? On the other hand, if we did leave Vietnam I thought we might end up in Okinawa or the Philippines, which would also be interesting. The rumors we'd heard at Camp Hague had caused me to fear this might happen.

All of this was speculation and not something I should have been concerned about. As it turned out, Roy, Gary, and I were assigned to HMM-262, and Joe was placed with HMM-161 and Ward was placed into HML-167 a Huey Squadron located at Marble Mountain. It turned out that Ward, who had been in HMMT-302 with us at Santa Ana flying the 46, had also been in the first class of student aviators to fly the UH-1E Huey at Ellison Field while the rest of us were in the last class of H-34s, so, he got to go into the Hueys. Any one of us would have changed places with him. To fly the 46 all year, hauling supplies, didn't rank with being able to drive that Huey with the guns and rocket pods. But, that's how it all worked out. All of us, except Ward would be in the northernmost squadrons, in a holding pattern, before coming to MMAF.

Moriarty further explained that the northern squadrons were, for the time being, supporting the Third Marine Amphibious Force Reconnaissance Company commonly known as Third Force Recon. Their forays into the A Shau Valley, along the border with Laos and in the DMZ, were legendary.

Historically, the northernmost squadrons were heavily involved in Operation Hastings (12 July 1966 – 25 July 1966) in which flights of CH-46s were described as waves of gigantic grasshoppers,[27] and the Song Ngun Valley north of the Rock Pile

---

[27] Vietnam's Helicopter Valley: Graveyard of Marine CH-46s, Salemnews.com/articles/april232012/helicopter-valley-tk.php, and https://www.pinterest.com/ro2650/air-ambulance (November 2015).

was littered with the carcasses of CH-46s, earning it the name, Helicopter Valley.

We were also advised that the living conditions at Phu Bai were much more primitive than those at MMAF, and to borrow a phrase from Force Recon Command[28] a biographical book written by LtCol Alex Lee, USMC (Ret.) who was, as a Maj, the commanding officer of Third Force Recon based at Phu Bai, 1969–1970, there was "no starch, no spit, no polish, and no fakery" associated with Phu Bai. Personally, as a new helicopter pilot, I was not looking for a safe place to go. The lure of being affiliated with the last Marine helicopter base north of the Hai Van Pass was very appealing to all of us.

The feeling I was experiencing was commonly referred to as a golden helmet. Young first-tour pilots could not imagine they might be killed. This fit me to a T. I would eventually learn how wrong I could be.

It was near noon when we received our official assignments, after which we were told to get a meal at the mess hall and then report with our gear to the airfield's control tower to hitch a ride north. The officer's mess at MMAF was outstanding. Good food and ice cream, the first good meal I had had since leaving home. The Officers Club was attached to the mess. It was large and air-conditioned, facing the beach and the South China Sea—a beautiful setting. Maybe, I began to think, MMAF would not be a bad place to stay.

---

[28] Lee, Alex, Lt Col. USMC (Ret.), Force Recon Command (Ballantine Books, a division of Random House, Inc, 1995), 144.

9: Hitchin' A Ride

The method of an individual traveling from point to point within the Marines' tactical areas of operational responsibility (TAOR) as I was about to learn, was mainly by chance. There was no scheduled shuttle service around to the different bases. Told to go to the tower to "hitch a ride" to Phu Bai, we headed out after saying our goodbyes to Ward whose squadron, 167, was there at Marble.

It was a short walk to the Marble Mountain Air Facility (MMAF) Control Tower situated at the center-field off ramp on the east side of the runway, the third "right-off" when landing to the north. It was also the only authorized crosswalk for pedestrians to get to the squadrons located on the west side of the runway with authorization from the tower in the form of a signal. One just had to stand, get the attention of the tower operators by waving, and wait for them to signal you back with a small white flag or hand signal. No one that I am aware of was ever run over by a landing aircraft at MMAF.

Arriving at the control tower we found a small building used for freight and passenger (pax) pickup and drop-off. An officious looking gunnery sergeant (GySgt.) wearing jungle boots, a well-worn Marine green t-shirt tucked neatly into his camouflage trousers over a slight beer belly, along with a starched, shaped and ironed Marine soft utility cover centered on his forehead and sitting just above a pair of aviator sunglasses. A metallic E-7 collar insignia needing some EM-NU (flat black touch-up paint) was pinned to the front panel of his cover where the silk-screened eagle globe and anchor is traditionally affixed. He eyed us suspiciously with a stub of a cigar firmly seated in the corner of his mouth. In the Corps. the GySgt. is a senior non commissioned officer, is most always referred to as "Gunny," one of the most respected ranks in the Corps. A common saying was that Gunnys ran the Corps.

He paced to and fro, in a slow manner, barking out orders at a group of younger Marines, PFCs and Lance Corporals, while eyeing a clipboard full of handwritten notes and invoice-like papers, slowing just long enough to eye us up and down. The Corps. is the world's most experienced logistics machine, and the Vietnam war effort placed tons of supplies in the hands of these experts, who had little time for greeting first lieutenants. A brief salute from the Gunny, more a greeting than a salute, required us to return the salute. He grinned, as we awkwardly freed our right hands from the gear we were carrying to do so. Dropping his gear and returning a proper salute, Gary took charge.

"Gunny, we're on our way to Phu Bai. Anything going our way?"

He shot us a look that said, I got work to do, can't spend time talking to green-behind-the-ear lieutenants. Instead, he said, "I thought you sirs might be headed for a place no one wants to go."

I gulped, put on my best John Wayne scowl and responded without calling him pilgrim, "That's exactly where we want to go."

Gary shook his head at me and turned away. Roy grinned, looked away, and Joe backed me up by saying as clear as a bell, "That's right...Phu Bai."

The gunny chocked back a chuckle and said, "I thought so. I got a 46 coming this way dropping off some paxs (passengers). We'll see where it's headed. Y'all sirs go on over and grab yourself a cold Coke or Pepsi—just 10 cents to the kitty will do."

"Thanks, Gunny. We just got American dollars, will that do?"

"It'll have to," he said. I threw a dollar bill into the jar and we all had our choice, cold Cokes or Pepsis, delicacies enjoyed worldwide.

There being a picnic bench nearby the shack, we piled up our gear and took a load off our feet. The whop-whop sound of helicopter blades was everywhere, beating the air into submission. Some Huey gunships were so full of ammo they could hardly drag themselves to the runway, skids scraping and sparks a-flying. What a show it was, and I got that tug in my stomach that I'd really like to have flown those gunships!

A 46 was being loaded with boxes of gear and a few Marines with M-16s who were waved on board by one of the gunny's LCpls. The Gunny left our presence, removed his cover and trotted over to the 46. He spoke with the pilot through an external telephone located in an access panel on the exterior of the helicopter. The conversation was brief. The pilot with his dark visor in the down position was shaking his head side-to-side as if saying, "no.no.no." Once the helicopter was loaded, the rotor RPM was rolled up to fly, blowing us backwards as we turned our backs.

"He's headed south," yelled the Gunny.

A couple more 46s arrived and departed with no ride north available, and we began to wonder if we were going to get to Phu Bai that day. Then one hard-looking machine came angling into the area sporting a snarling tiger's head on the nose and an ET designation[29] in large letters on the aft pylon. The classic dark Marine green exterior was faded under a soft layer of grit and grime with random riveted patches that stood in stark contrast to the older paint, bearing mute testimony to its combat history. It had the appearance of a war-weary combat veteran.

The chopper was one of 262's Flying Tigers and was on its way home to Phu Bai. Our taxi had finally arrived, and the last leg of our journey was beginning. The copilot, in the left seat, was readily visible through the Plexiglas and to my surprise, was wearing a flowery short sleeved island type of shirt found on every tourist who ever touched the Hawaiian Isles. That was definitely not the regulation green fire retardant Nomex[30] flight suit I expected to see. Yet, I found it both odd and heartening at the same time. As far as I knew, although unconventional, flight suits may have been optional in HMM-262 in Phu Bai. We had heard that Phu Bai was different.

[29] The tail code, ET Echo Tango, identified the aircraft as being assigned to HMM-262.
[30] Nomex is the brand name for a heat and flame resistant material manufactured by DuPont, out of which, our flight suits were made.

As the blades slowed to an idle, the rear ramp of the 46 lowered to the tarmac. The crew chief that I later learned was Sgt. P. R. McIntosh from Pennsylvania, came down the ramp.

Figure 12 Sgt. P.R. McIntosh, HMM-262 crew chief, taken from the HMM-262 1969-70 cruise book.

His helmet had seen some rugged wear. The helmet, normally issued in white, had been painted a dark green apparently so that the white didn't present a target to the enemy. However, the helmet could probably be called speckled due to the random flecks of dark green paint chipped off of it, revealing the original white color underneath. It looked like some speckled bird eggs. He wore aviator sunglasses and sported a raggedy Fu Manchu mustache, not even close to regulation. He was holding a black long cord in his left hand that was plugged into his helmet. In his right hand was a black transmitter with red buttons which he intermittently pressed and released while speaking into the boom mike attached to his helmet and touching his lips. His flight suit was well worn and spotted with sweat, transmission fluid, oil and dust. He had the confident stride of a drill instructor, leaving no doubt as to his position of authority. A black leather western-style cartridge belt with loops full of ammo and a holstered .38 revolver hung around his waist. His flight suit bore a worn regulation black leather name tag with a set of combat aircrew wings pinned to the center of it. It was impossible to read his name.

Figure 13 First Lieutenant Hugo Beck, from HMM-262 1969-70 cruise book.

The blades were still churning at flight idle as the copilot wearing the colorful shirt deplaned through the starboard crew door. He (I later learned was First Lieutenant Hugo Beck) walked around the front of the nose of the 46 in our direction. Besides the colorful shirt, Beck wore jeans, leather loafers and aviator sunglasses. A bag was thrown over his shoulder, and he showed no intention of speaking to us, as he walked through us. But, Joe, being a friendly sort, kinda nodded to him in greeting and said, "hi." The verbal assault caught Beck off guard. He grudgingly acknowledged our presence with a sideward glance and a mumbled guttural sound. The sideward glance, however, gave him away. He was sporting a large black eye under those shades, a real shiner. I later learned what had happened.

That black eye was the result of a "real" Marine Corps birthday celebration at the Phu Bai O'Club the night before. As it turns out, he was on his way to R&R on the day we arrived. Yet, Beck's appearance and demeanor helped to reaffirm the description of Phu Bai offered by Col. Moriarty that Phu Bai was, "more primitive than Marble Mountain." I had a sense that Phu Bai was gonna be very different than Marble Mountain and to me, that was gonna be alright.

The remaining paxs deplaned over the rear ramp. They were combat Marines, Grunts. They held onto their camouflage covered helmets with one hand, their hair blowing in the draft of the big blades. I was face-to-face with the iconic Vietnam combat Marine Grunt for the first time, and I was awe struck. I saw those Marines every night when watching Walter Cronkite. I thought of them as my generation of World War II warriors, but did not think of them as being as young as those Marines appeared to be.

They were like those young Marines onboard our flight from Okinawa the previous morning. They had light beards and barely mustaches and appeared exhausted. They held their M-16s loosely, draped over their shoulders by the olive green slings or gripping the upper receiver hand grips and held closely to their sides. From all appearances they had just come from the field. I was 23 years old and they appeared to be about 18 or 19 years old. My senses being new to everything, seeing those Grunts made me feel even newer. One thing was perfectly clear to me, the fact that I was still on the outside of the Marine brotherhood, looking in.

The crew chief motioned for us to come aboard. Dragging our seabags and flight bags behind us, we stumbled and slipped on engine oil and transmission fluid while making our way up the rear ramp. I couldn't help but compare the CH-46D model we were boarding, with the CH-46F models we had flown back in HMMT-302 at MCAF Santa Ana. Those F models had been clean and fresh; the D model we boarded revealed its advanced age in wrinkled and stressed aluminum skin with numerous splotches of darker green paint the size of a silver dollar. Bullet-holes I later learned, patched up over the years. I liked it. It was a true veteran. I hoped it would take care of us during our stay as I hoped it had done with its previous aircrews—I hoped.

The aircraft had a crew of five and no Plexiglass in the port-hole windows. There were two big, intimidating .50-cal. machineguns positioned on the port and starboard sides near the forward portion of the cabin. It was the port side of the 46 I saw when crossing the Han River Bridge that morning on our way to Marble. The Two .50-cal. gunners stood behind their respective mounted machine gun, staring at us. They wore bib-style bullet bouncers (consisting of heavy ceramic plates inside canvas like material) and the same black leather western style gun belt and holster as did the crew chief.

Figure 14 Interior of CH-46D revealing the two .50-cal machineguns.

The crew door was on the starboard side of the 46 where Beck had exited. It was just like the 46F model we flew back at Santa Ana. It was directly behind the cockpit and hydraulic and power management systems (PMS) closet. A pull-down seat, like the ones used by stewardesses on commercial airliners, was available to the crew chief so he could sit near the crew door, which was in two sections, like a half-door in a stable or barn.

Figure 15 First Lieutenant Larry Ridgeway

We new guys were taking it all in. With Beck gone, who was going to be the copilot? It seemed that one of the crew simply jumped into the copilot's seat. I later learned that the assigned copilot was First Lieutenant Larry Ridgeway.

First Lieutenant Jim Dau was seated in the starboard HAC's seat, speaking to the gunny through the exterior communication system. Turning to his left and looking through the passageway into the cargo area, he waved back at us. The gunny had just told him who we were. His wave meant a great deal to us. Someone acknowledged where we were going.

Figure 16 First Lieutenant Jim Dau

We sat on stained red canvas seats that folded down from the bulkhead on each side of the main cabin/cargo bay area. As the blades were turning at idle RPM, it was only moments before Lt. Dau began rolling the engines up to flight RPM, and I sensed the familiar back-and-forth rocking motion as the aircraft balanced itself. The crew chief was standing outside the aircraft holding that small hand-held fire extinguisher as the familiar high pitch scream of the engines reached flight RPM. Entering the cabin from the rear, he carefully walked up the oily ramp and strode through the length of the cabin ensuring we were safely strapped in as the ramp was raised behind him. Surprisingly, the process was so familiar to me that it made me feel at ease. In moments, the 46 began to move.

If one could learn to taxi a 46, without causing damage to the rotor head, the most difficult part of flying it was accomplished. The 46 has tricycle gear consisting of main mounts under each stub wing, and a nose wheel. Steering is done through the coordinated manipulation of the *cyclic* and *collective*. Many pilots, when safely clear of obstacles, would simply raise the nose gear off the deck, making the 46 easier to maneuver.

In a few minutes we were centered on Runway 36. The cockpit rose higher and higher in relation to the rear portion of the aircraft, like the amphibian whose nick name it bore: the frog. The main mounts reluctantly left the asphalt, and we were airborne, in a hover. The nose section dipped forward as Dau added power and applied forward cyclic. The aft section rose up, throwing us into forward momentum, and the cockpit lowered slightly below the rear of the helicopter. We remained no more than 20-30 feet off the runway, rapidly gaining airspeed.

The flow of air through the cabin offered welcome relief from the heat. The gunners hunched over their weapons, looking out at whatever might offer a target. Or were they just daydreaming? Reaching the end of the runway, the 46 continued to no more than 150 feet AGL. It rolled smoothly to its port side, then leveled out just as smoothly and headed northwest, still at low level.

We were headed toward a river I later learned was the Han River, which ran into Da Nang Bay. The Han River separated Da Nang Air Base from MMAF, and what I later learned was China Beach, the home of a huge Navy exchange, a medical facility and an in-country R&R beach. The Han River was the same river we had earlier crossed in the bus from Freedom Hill that morning.

The helicopter remained at an extremely low altitude, seemingly only a hundred feet or so. It was soon centered in the middle of the Han and gaining airspeed. We hopped over the bridge, flying north. The big hospital ships I had seen that morning on the way to MMAF were a clear indicator to me of our position. I later learned the ships were German. I had never known that Germany was the least bit involved in this war. Their presence was interesting. Maybe we'd take some med-evacuees to those ships?

We eventually entered Da Nang Harbor. The harbor was beautiful, emerald green turning to deep blue as the fresh water merged with the South China Sea. Dau dipped the nose of the aircraft and took up a northeast course, skipping over the waves so low that the nose wheel seemed to be in danger of striking the water. I hoped to feel a spray coming through the open windows. To have felt the mist would have been an unexpected pleasure. I squinted my eyes trying to see where we were.

The sights in the Harbor were exotic. Vietnamese fishermen were in round boats called Bamboo Basket Boats. I had never seen anything like this in the byways and rivers from which my childhood sprang. Flat-bottom boats were the preferred type of boat in the Floodways of Southeast Missouri.

The fishermen of Vietnam were much different. They stood in the fore-section of the boat which could only be determined by the direction it was traveling, due to its bowl-like shape. They worked a long-handled paddle back and forth, like they were whipping up some mashed potatoes. That action, somehow, pulled the boat through the water rather than push the boat through the water.

While the sight of those fishermen was interesting, I also felt somewhat concerned that we were the perfect target from any one of those boats. I repressed this concern, believing that it must be safe if we were doing it. Yet, the thought of what happened to my cousin within close proximity to Da Nang, was a cautioning note for me not to feel too secure anywhere in Vietnam.

* * *

Owen Ray Walker, my first cousin came to mind: On 13 January 1968 just outside of Da Nang, my cousin, Sgt. Owen Ray Walker, a 20 year old squad leader for the 1st Platoon, 1st. Squad, Charlie Company, fourth Battalion, of the U. S. Army's Americal Division, and nine members of his platoon suffered terrible wounds, killing two, 2d Lt. John Scully and the platoon radio man, whose name I do not know) by an NVA/VC command-controlled booby trap. Ray suffered horrible wounds, the loss of one eye and the mangling of his left leg that Ray would not let them amputate. Due only to the speedy reaction of a Marine helicopter pilot who witnessed the explosion, Ray and the others, within moments, were on board the helicopter and being medevaced into Da Nang, saving his life for what became the story of so many, alive, but with debilitating and life changing wounds. Maybe, I thought I could, as a helicopter pilot, do for those men fighting this war like that unnamed Marine pilot had done for my cousin. Time would tell.

* * *

As the 46 neared the northeast point of the harbor, where it meets the South China Sea at a place called the Hai Van Pass, one of the gunners made his way to us, leaned over, and yelled in my ear, "Would you like to fire the fifties?"

I shouted back, "Hell yes!"

The Hai Van Pass at 1640 feet high was a unique geographical reference to us 46 pilots when traveling Highway 1. The highway became a serpentine ribbon crawling up and down the pass into and out of Da Nang during the monsoon season.[31] The French name for the pass is *Col des Nuages* meaning cloudy pass. In ancient times, the pass separated the northern half of Vietnam, called the Province of Hue, from the southern half, called the Kingdom of Champa. Meteorologically, there is supposed to be a distinct weather difference between the southern portion of Vietnam, south of the pass and the northern portion of Vietnam. I hoped to be able to experience the difference while in Vietnam.

---

[31] The monsoon season in the vicinity of Phu Bai prevails loosely from November into the month of April. It is characterized by low-hanging ceilings with visibility on most days below one mile and ceilings as low as 200' with low to no visibility until 0800 or 0900. In one 24 hour period there was 24 inches of rain. During that period of time, restricted visibility was the greatest hazard to flight.

At the top of the pass there are remains of a huge French concrete bunker being used by both the Army and Marines where a large Old Glory waved beautifully in the breeze. I don't believe I have ever seen a more beautiful sight.

With this opportunity to fire the .50-cal, I felt like a kid getting his first opportunity to ride a roller coaster or drive the family car. There was nothing cute or cuddly about those weapons. Their purpose was to hit hard enough to tear through most protective measures and rip the life out of the enemy. However, no matter how lethal these weapons were, on the 46 they were used in a strictly defensive manner. Oddly, we had never experienced the firing power of the .50 cal. during all of our aviation training. We were barely qualified with the .38, the pilot's specified weapon.

The starboard gunner loaded a belt of ammo into the weapon, pulled the cocking lever back, pushed off the safety, stepped back from the weapon, grinned, and pointed at the four of us, then me, waving for me to come to his .50. Not wearing a helmet or hearing protection, I unbuckled and made my way over the rocking and rolling deck, placing my hands on the roof of the cabin to steady myself.

The gunner, grinning at my apparent lack of balance, remained standing steady near me like a seasoned mariner in the wheelhouse of an ancient man-of-war frigate—his sea legs being well tuned. The inherent ambient noise of the two big GE turbine engines coupled with the high speed transmission and synchronization (synch) shaft just above our heads, caused him to have to cup his hand around my ear and yell. He also used his hands to pantomime the proper way to hold the .50 and illustrated that I must shoot downward at a high angle of attack to avoid any possible ricochets skipping off the surface of the water for who knows how far, endangering watercraft or individuals along the shoreline.

I placed my hands on the large hand grips on both sides of the gun and tentatively positioned both thumbs on the pressure

THE GROTTO – BOOK ONE | 79

trigger as Dau, in contact with the gunner, eased into a 10-15 degree right-hand orbit at about 500 feet. The waves were light and
the distance between me and the sea seemed to be just a few feet.
I had seldom been a passenger on the 46 and the differences between what I felt as an unhelmeted passenger and what I felt as
a pilot were extraordinary.

Tightening my grip on the dual handles of the weapon, I
lightly placed both thumbs on the flap that was the trigger on
this weapon. I took a deep breath and slowly pressed my thumbs
down on the flap. Not knowing the sensitivity of the trigger, my
anticipation was such that I caught myself flinching with each
additional amount of added thumb pressure. Suddenly, when
sufficient pressure was applied, the weapon exploded! The report was louder than I expected and without ear protection, my
middle ear took a beating. As I held down the pressure trigger, I
felt that the rate of fire was much slower than I expected. Each
round was individually distinguishable, not like an M-16 assault
weapon on full auto whose rate of fire is so fast individual rounds
are indistinguishable. The smell of cordite/gunpowder quickly
filled the cabin and spent shell casings rained into a metallic fun-
nel feeding into a canvas bag attached to the base of the mount.

I fired a few more intermittent bursts of approximately
three to five rounds each, before Gary, Roy, and Joe took over.
I've never forgotten the sound or the smell of cordite boiling up
in the interior of the 46, nor, for that matter, the ringing caused
by those heavy bursts of fire power into my helmetless ears. It
would not be the last time we would hear or smell the absolute
authority of those .50s when they spoke.

After completing our unofficial familiarization with the .50s,
we settled into a thirty- to forty-minute flight north, staying a
short distance off the shoreline before turning west, crossing
over the beach, and heading inland. Flying at approximately fifteen hundred feet, the land below us appeared to be clumps of
greenery among outcroppings of white sandy land. There were
burnt-out dwellings as well, and no sign of crops. It was evident

that this area was a no-man's-land. The whine of the turbine engines began to lessen as the helo began a slow descent. Phu Bai was dead ahead.

10: Touchdown in Phu Bai

We touched down on the approach end of Runway 27/09, Phu Bai's only runway. I strained to see all I possibly could through the porthole windows as Dau took a right off into the tarmac area. The smooth feel of the runway and taxiway turned to something rough, like turning off of an asphalt road onto a gravel road. The old 46 shuddered and shook and occasionally seemed to slide a little to one side or the other. The surface was much different from anything I was familiar with in the States.

I began to see the tarmac was made of sheets of steel matting with uniform rows of holes in them interlocked together like a giant jigsaw puzzle. I later learned that the matting was known as Marston matting, typically used by Marines to quickly create expeditionary airfields. I would see a lot of Marston matting in my Vietnam tour.

I also had an opportunity to observe what I later learned was 262's maintenance hangar. Its huge doors were opened wide; two or three 46s were undergoing maintenance. After several more minutes of taxiing, we finally came to rest in an area protected by what were called revetments. The revetment was a metal barricade approximately ten feet high that separated individual parking spots.

Figure 17 Helicopter revetments at Phu Bai.

Each revetment was filled with sand. Actually, these things were just big metal sandbag bunkers to limit damage from any direct strikes into the flight line from a mortar or rocket attack, the theory being that any mortar shells finding their mark in the aircraft parking area would land in one revetment with the barrier protecting all other aircraft from damage. This precaution further reinforced the fact that we were in a vulnerable location. I didn't recall seeing any revetments at Marble Mountain.

While looking to the front of the 46 from the main

Figure 18 The console of the 46 cockpit from the cabin area through the tunnel-like opening into the cockpit area.

cabin/cargo compartment where we were sitting, I could see the hands of both Dau and Ridgeway going through the shutdown checklist as the rear ramp was lowered. The extensive checklist is a challenge-and-response between the copilot and HAC with Nomex gloved hands twisting, flipping, and double-checking items being turned off.

Finally, in one last movement, the gloved left hand of the HAC pulled both engine condition levers back to a mechanical stop. The blades slowed to 20%. After a cool-down period the gloved hand reached to the overhead console where he flipped the rotor brake toggle switch on, bringing the blades to a deep grinding stop. After checking the temps, batt-off.

The sounds of the 46's electrical systems and gyros hummed, snapped, and chattered for a few moments till it was all quiet. Shutdown checklist complete! The familiar sounds of seat belts being unhooked and bouncing off the metal seats seemed extra loud, but also reassuring. The flight was over, and we were down safe.

We collected our gear, the sea bags full of personal belongings and flight bags that carried our helmets and flight suits and our orders. The HAC and copilot with their helmet bags were making their way through the small passageway between the cockpit and the cabin. The crew chief was outside, beginning his work on getting the 46 ready for its next flight.

The gunners were gathering up belts of .50-cal. ammo and lifting their respective Browning .50-cal. heavy machine guns from their fixed heavy mounts, each of which weighed near 90 pounds. They cradled their precious cargo in their arms like a father would his child. Dau, the HAC, made his way to us and reached out his right hand, welcoming us with a smile. The co-pilot who had replaced Beck grinned and introduced himself to us as Larry Ridgeway. We were pleased to have a warm welcoming. They seemed genuinely happy to see us.

We made our way to the squadron headquarters next to the tarmac where we found the ready room, the heartbeat of the squadron. A large operations desk sat high upon a plywood dais, similar to a Desk Sergeant's desk at police precincts throughout major metropolitan departments in the States. Furnishings in the room included a refrigerator, called a reefer and arguably the most important item in the room, and a ping-pong table, the second most important item in the room.

Stale cigarette smoke and burnt coffee from an old coffee maker that looked as if it held near a gallon of coffee was the predominant smell. Dark coffee grounds peppered the counter and small spills of coffee saturated a square of cardboard upon which the coffee maker sat, the small red power-on light, dulled by age, still glowed. Plywood and red Naugahyde[32] rounded out the décor. Several rows of metal folding chairs faced the operations desk and chalkboard. The area had a base smell of moldy sandbags first fashioned into bunker-like alcoves when Marines left Red Beach and arrived in Phu Bai in late 1965.

Many missions on the schedule board were marked as outbound and the area was quiet except for the operations duty officer (ODO) in his flight suit, studying his mission board and making changes by using a rag to wipe the board clean, as he carried on a conversation with another pilot who stood near the desk. The sounds in the room were the crackling of the UHF radio set on the squadron common frequency, and the repetitious sound of two additional pilots playing a game of ping-pong at the table in the far end of the room.

A cigarette dangled from the lower lip of a serious-looking pilot studying a map. We were greeted with a casual indifference. Sideward glances and forgettable introductions were made. Joe asked for directions to his unit, HMM-161, and the ODO placed a call to Cattlecall, 161's call sign, explaining that "A few FNGs have arrived and one of them is yours."

"A Jeep is on its way to pick you up," said the ODO with a yawn. "You can catch it outside. Just go through that hallway and out the back door to the road."

"Thanks," said Joe, grabbing up his gear. Gary, Roy, and I said goodbye to our friend as he disappeared into the hallway, headed outside. The ODO's remarks to 161 made the connection. We were now "a few FNGs." the phrase for which the letters stood was, F**king New Guys.

---

[32] Naugahyde is an American brand of artificial leather that is very durable and easily maintained. The only color on hand was red. The paraloft, later, flight equipment shop made everything out of red Naugahyde.

This was not considered a derogatory term but a clear and unmistakable definition of our position in the squadron pecking order. My journey into Vietnam was complete.

Once we were logged into Personnel/Human Resources (S-1), we surrendered our flight log books to the Operations Duty Officer (ODO) who summoned a duty driver to take us to our assigned housing.

As we made our way out the same door through which Joe had just exited. We passed three darkened offices marked Commanding Officer, Executive Officer and Sergeant Major. The Marines working in the S-1 office and Operations wore camouflage trousers with a white T-shirt. Their camouflage blouse hung loosely on the back of their chair, with their soft cover within reach. In another office marked S-2, where secret stuff was kept for those who needed to know, sat a Marine with a high and tight haircut found in Grunt world. He briefly looked up from his desk as we walked by. "Welcome aboard!" he barked, catching us by surprise. I said nothing. I noticed a short-timer's calendar[33] on the wall behind him.

Gary responded, "Thanks, glad to be here."

We exited the offices through that back door, or was it really the front of the offices, into a sandy area buttressed by a large bunker made of sandbags. That large bunker provided a place to duck and hide from whatever might cause you to want to duck and hide, and there were sandbags on the roof, lots of sand bags. I later learned that the roofs would blow off in hurricane-like wind gusts. If there was any doubt as to where we were, the next thing we saw removed it.

An impressive Flying Tigers logo stood right there in front of the entrance into the squadron offices from the airfield road. It was a Bengal tiger baring its fangs against the background of a three-bladed rotor head and the world globe that depicted the unit as a powerful worldwide asset of the Corps. The globe itself

---

[33] The short timer's calendar was normally a made-up calendar for a person who has little time remaining on their tour in Vietnam. Short timer calendars normally began to appear in the last two months of service remaining.

was cradled on a rocker that designated the squadron as HMM-262. It hung on a black pagoda-style support, a tip of the hat to Asia. Wow!

A Jeep, probably an Army retread,[34] was parked in a small parking area near the logo. It bore a red Naugahyde spare tire

Figure 19 Author standing by HMM-262 logo at Phu Bai squadron offices.

cover with the squadron logo produced by the artists in residence in the paraloft. In a few minutes a deuce-and-a-half truck wheeled up to the side of the road. A tall, skinny, pleasant guy from California with a wide grin exited the truck and greeted us. It was Corporal Gaskill. During my stay at Phu Bai, I found that Cpl Gaskill was most always the duty driver, a good man to know. We tossed our gear aboard, scrambled over the rear tailgate into the open bed of the truck and sat on the bench seats along each side.

[34] Jeeps were not commonly seen as much as small military trucks, a deuce and a quarter, or six-by-six normally called a "six-by," and it was not unusual that occasionally one of the Army's jillion Jeeps ended up with a fresh coat of Marine green paint and an unrecognizable serial number. There was bartering and deal making between Marine and Army units throughout the history of the Corps for items in short supply to the Corps. The Corps always turned back some of the monies appropriated by Congress. "More with less" was not just a motto, but a solemn oath in the Corps. Ooh Rahh!

Gaskill was indeed a skilled driver in the muck and deep mud ruts left each day by the monsoon rains. In low gear, the big truck slogged its way toward the officer's quarters, providing ample time for us to view the camp. The moans, groans and smells of the old diesel engine, coupled with the heavy sounds of 46s and Huey gunships, created a cacophony of sounds, diesel smells, and visuals of that place I have not forgotten. One of the crew chiefs from 262, then Cpl. Bill Perrett related that all he could remember about Phu Bai was rain, mud and rats.

Figure 20 A Jeep half buried in the red mud of Phu Bai mud.

My first impression of Phu Bai was that it was just another plywood city like Camp Hague in Okinawa, Freedom Hill, and MMAF. But it wasn't. It had a depth to it that was absent from those other encampments. It was more primitive, more real, more like what I wanted to see and feel. The one standout structure was the maintenance hangar, the heartbeat of any squadron. It was a modern building of steel and corrugated tin, surrounded by murmuring knots of maintenance personnel in work coveralls, milling about while taking a smoke break.

Vietnamese workers and formidable looking warriors stoked my curiosity. Who were they? A few Marines in flight suits and camouflage utilities were walking about, making their way alongside the airfield road. We passed slowly by them, and through a sandbagged community of buildings like the center of a very small town. One of the buildings was lettered *EXCHANGE*.

The Navy exchange was the equivalent of a general store, or what we now call a convenience store. Booze, books, junk food and other miscellaneous supplies could be purchased there if you had military payment certificates[35] (MPC), which we didn't yet have. The building across the road from the exchange was the chow hall. It smelled of baking bread, powdered eggs and strong coffee. I made a mental note of each building.

The camp was just what I had hoped for—a rough-hewn mining camp atmosphere from the 1880s Gold Rush days with a modern military twist. Phu Bai was, indeed, gonna be all right.

---

[35] Military Payment Certificates (MPC) were used in Vietnam rather than dollars and cents. The monopoly money as it was called was, supposed to control the illicit underground market in U.S. currency. Any U.S. currency brought in by the military, like me, was exchanged for MPC.

11: Home Sweet Home

Each Quonset hut was referred to as a hooch[36] and our assigned hooch was the second from the west end of the first row that made up the officer's housing area. A concrete sidewalk ran in between the rows and the showers and restroom facilities were in a separate building, like being at Boy Scout camp.

Figure 21 The concrete walkway through the Phu Bai Officer housing area glistens following a monsoon rain.

In locating our future home, we found all of the hooches, constructed in 1965-66 were protected by a waist-high labyrinth of green sandbags made of a plastic material that oozed dirt, like blood, through the weathered and torn fabric. To the right of the old door leading into our hooch was a much smaller opening offering entry into the bunker. The small doorway required one to crawl in on hands and knees. It was a well-constructed bunker, a grotto of darkness that had protected U.S. Marines from the frequent mortar and rocket attacks on Phu Bai since the Marines first occupied the premises in 1965. I hesitated to crawl into the dark recesses for fear of starving rats jumping onto my back, but in a real attack, rats were better than falling red hot shrapnel.

---

[36] The "hooch" could be any form of sleeping quarters, South East Asia (SEA) huts, Quonset huts, and thatched lean-tos could all be called hooches.

Back at the hooch, Gary pushed against the heavy door. It refused to give way. "Damn," he said. He braced himself, placed his shoulder against the door and shoved. It gave way slowly, dragging heavily across a concrete floor that revealed an arc of deep striations from years of opening and closing. A damp, moldy smell permeated the interior like I imagined the interior of an ancient crypt might smell.

Roy turned his head and placed his hand to his nose with a chuckle and said, "Wow, what a shit-hole."

Trying not to breathe too deeply while choking back a gag reflex, I said, "Looks like home sweet home to me."

Gary ran his hand along the inside wall and found the light switch. Flipping it on, a raw light-bulb in the center of the ceiling produced a yellowish glow. We had stepped into what could only be called a common area, a living room of sorts with a couple of old chairs, a small table, and a refrigerator pushed up against the wall.

Marine graffiti, like stone-age cave art, was scrawled across the walls: "This is a holy war...God hates the gooks too," "Enjoy this war...your congressman went to a lot of trouble to arrange it," and ".30 Cals can't hurt you if your mind's right." A dust-covered window air-conditioning unit rested in a crude hole cut into the outer wall. Due to the cool temperatures this day, it was off. Its very existence, however, was evidence of the heat to come following the monsoons. We turned the dial to on and the vintage machine rattled and began blowing dust and rat droppings into the air. "Turn it off before it poisons us," yelled Roy.

Holding my nose, I tugged on the handle of the old refrigerator. The seal broke and I opened the door slowly. A dull glow and cool air spilled out. It worked, kinda! A half-package of mystery meat, green at its edges, was accompanied by a couple of rusty cans of Black Label beer. Maybe... just maybe, there was life here in this old hooch after all. The reefer itself was a testament to the many years our country had been fighting in that land, fighting over the same ground day after day and year after year, as was done by the French in the Indo China War. According to what I knew, unlike the French, we had won all our battles. Yet in spite of that fact, we found ourselves entering into what can only be described as a full-blown military retreat and artfully labeled Vietnamization and Redeployment, or peace with honor? The initial phase of the redeployment had already begun. It was code named, Operation Keystone Eagle.[37]

A second light switch beside a curtained doorway provided electricity to five bare light bulbs, equally spaced down the center of the ceiling inside the bunk area. Three of the bulbs were not working, leaving much of the bunk area in dark shadows. Stepping into the windowless, poorly lit area, our senses were again assaulted by the dark, damp interior. I was glad I had listened to my flight instructor in HMMT-302 when he told me to be sure and take an electric blanket, not to keep warm, but to keep the bunk dry—a very smart thing to do. The interior of the bunk room was half filled with stacks of old bunk frames and crude furnishings like desks, small tables, book shelves and bar-like structures constructed from old ammo boxes, plywood and red Naugahyde.

Another dim glow at the far end of the room, near what appeared to be the rear door of the hooch, caught our attention. The slight glow was produced by a small desk lamp, evidence that someone else, maybe a hobbit, resided in this dark, damp realm. An unmade bunk and a makeshift desk upon which the small lamp was set were the personal belongings of one 1stLt. Tom McCormack. The papers lying on his desk identified him as a communications officer who worked in the message center.

[37] Smith,U.S. Marines In Vietnam, High Mobility and Stand down, pp. 132-133; "On 8 June,[1969]President Nixon and South Vietnamese President Thieu met on Midway island... both Nixon and Thieu [made] the decision to begin unilateral redeployment[with]the initial redeployment of the 3d Marine Division code name Keystone Eagle...by mid-June [1969]."

Figure 22 First Lieutenant Tom McCormack, from HMM-262 69-70 cruise book.

We'd meet Tom later. Our first order of business was to put together a place to live and call home. Gary, always the drill instructor, tossed his sea bag into the center of the room and took charge. "Okay Marines, let's get to work."

Roy and I dropped our gear alongside Gary's and did just that, putting together three more bunks. With us three and McCormack, the hooch that normally held six to eight men was near half full. When we finished setting up our bunks it was late in the afternoon. We decided to check out the mess hall and visit the exchange. Walking back through the housing area we met pilots and aircrews, many with combat aircrew wings, coming and going. I wondered which ones were with HMM-262. They just eyed us with that "who are you?" look. I was hoping we'd run into Joe and see how it was going with him in 161.

We made it to the mess hall, which had just opened for the evening meal. It was also a plywood palace, with a heavy double-door entry. The doors opened inward. I noted that there was a long piece of heavy timber, maybe 4x12, leaning against the wall inside the entry. It was like an old fort. Those doors could shut out the hordes by placing that heavy yoke across them. As Gary, Roy, and I made our way in we saw Joe, who we began to call. "Smitty!" When he saw us he was talking to a group of pilots with a big grin on his face. It was apparent that he was busy getting acquainted with them. He waved. Joe was a big likeable fella who made friends easily; it appeared he was doing well.

We, on the other hand, ate by ourselves, not knowing who was or was not in 262. There were three squadrons at Phu Bai, HMM-161, 262 and HMLA 367, each with near fifty pilots. I recognized Jim Dau and assumed those within proximity to him were 262 pilots. It was like walking into the Crystal Palace Saloon in Tombstone, Arizona, during the 1800s. The air crews had a rugged appearance and confident air about them.

Figure 23 Phu Bai pilot caricature, drawn by First Lieutenant Jerry Johnson.

Some wore various styles of mustaches that reminded me of black-and-white Civil War images captured by Matthew Brady.[38]

I later learned that the commanding officers at Phu Bai were lenient when it came to personal appearance, but demanded proper haircuts and facial hair in conformity with Marine Corps standards when going on the week-long R&R trip out of country

---

[38] Matthew Brady was a famous 19th-century Civil War photographer.

or on Marine business, like Night Vision School in Thailand or Jungle Environment and Survival Training (JEST) School in the Philippines. As I was advised by one combat vet, "The CO wants us to avoid the look of misfits and desperadoes when possible."

They were all dressed in the standard Nomex flight suits, originally green but turning a brownish hue in the tropical heat and the syrupy humidity of Vietnam. Their boots and ours were covered with the red mud that was everywhere. Well-worn black leather name tags or custom embroidered name tags from Okinawa or the Philippines in Marine Corps colors (gold and red) with gold wings, rank, and call signs or just nicknames were visible on their flight suits. Their unique camouflaged covers were custom-made from a material design called tigerstripe[39] favored by the Special Forces. The sweatbands of their covers bore various identifying details including tour of duty dates (i.e. 69-70), and places of duty. When the pilots, who were at Quang tri, ordered their covers after arriving at Phu Bai, both duty posts (Quang Tri and Phu Bai) were on the sweat band. The golden wings of a naval aviator were embroidered on the front panel of the cover where the eagle, globe, and anchor would normally appear on Marine Corps issue covers. Those covers were highly prized by their owners. In years to come they would be worn at reunions and displayed in man-caves, taverns or wherever we veterans sat, remembering when.

There was no prohibition against wearing a sidearm in the camp. Most of the crews were armed with the Marine Corps issue weapon, a Smith & Wesson .38 cal. revolver with a four-inch barrel. Yet, many favored other personal firearms, most often the Browning 9mm. First Lieutenant Marion Wood had a beautiful 9mm Browning automatic. Some preferred the Marine issue .45 semi-automatic and many were seen carrying personal combat knives. The famous Marine Ka-Bar was the perfect knife, carried

---

[39] Tigerstripe camouflage was originally worn by the ARVN Marine Corps and U.S. Army Special Forces. It was never issued by the U.S Marine Corps or the Army. However, the Marines were able to get the Tiger Stripe material made into the shape of the Marine issue cover, worn by many pilots.

either on the same cartridge belt that held a firearm or, in some instances, strapped to the lower leg[40] or affixed to the survival vest with the knife scabbard down, making it easier to retrieve the knife with a downward sweep of the hand. A few wore the Mark I Gerber fighting knife or a Bowie knife. Some wore a cartridge belt across their chest or a shoulder holster.

In the final analysis, the pilots and aircrews from Phu Bai all appeared formidable in or out of the cockpit. I had been told there was nothing at Phu Bai except rain and boredom, but I sensed something more, the opportunity for a grand adventure.

After our meal we politely excused ourselves, trying not to be noticed, and returned to the hooch. There we met Tom McCormack. He was a big burly fellow with a full mustache and mellow attitude. He appeared to be at ease with us and welcomed our rude behavior. He advised us of many things. The hooch maid that did his laundry was Missy Noa. He was absolutely positive that she would be overjoyed to learn that she was going to have a hooch full of Marines to care for, as well as the income that would come with the job.

That night there would be more house-cleaning in the hooch, but there was one more place we wanted to visit on this, our first day in Phu Bai—the Officers Club. It was unique. Right here in Phu Bai, South Vietnam, was a building similar to a ski lodge. Situated about a hundred yards from the hooches, the O'Club was a meeting place where one could chill out after a hard day of flying. It was located near the eastern perimeter of the base, directly under the watchful eye of a guard tower manned by XXIV Corps Army personnel at night.

---

[40] The wearing of a knife on the lower leg made the knife accessible. The wearing of the knife on the outside of the survival vest, handle up also made the knife accessible.

During the evenings, the place was normally always full of pilots. It was the place where I learned the most about flying in Vietnam, not tactics, but the politics of 262, which played an important role in how I dealt with my coming year. The other thing

Figure 25 Phu Bai guard tower with officer's club visible in rear.

that crossed my mind was if the enemy had any idea how full the clubs were at night with pilots and crews, they would have ended the war much sooner than anyone could have imagined.

Figure 24 O'Club courtesy of John & Linda Kosinski.

The club décor consisted of a large bar made of natural stone and plywood, trimmed in the ever-present red Naugahyde. There was a small stage area used by transient USO shows and a lodge-like stone fireplace big enough to place large logs. This would be our gathering place.

Heavy drinking was commonplace, even among some of those who never drank in the States. A strong mixed drink cost the equivalent of 10 to 35 cents in monopoly money. While in Vietnam, you could draw an amount of money for the month and leave the bulk of your money in your account. I doubt I ever drew more than fifty dollars a month in MPC and when leaving on R&R, you could request your money in U.S. Currency, but upon your return if you had any money remaining, it was changed back into MPC.

Movies were a nightly event. Our arrival day being Armistice Day, the feature for the evening was *Victory at Sea*—footage of World War II narrated by Walter Cronkite. In later days we learned that sometimes the second reel of the movie was mislabeled as the first reel by some clown who passed it along to our squadron. We all became quite comfortable with seeing the second reel first. All in all, it was a very comfortable setting.

12: Gettin' the Scent

November 1969.[41]

The period of 1-30 November 1969 marked a transition from support of the 3d MARDIV to the 1st MARDIV. This event had an immediate effect on the squadron, sending helicopters south rather than north to conduct missions in the Da Nang area. Eight officers and thirteen enlisted transferred to HMM-262. Four officers transferred from HMM-262. The average number of aviators was 42. Heavy monsoon rains and low ceilings continued to hamper flight operations and resulted in reduced flight hours.

HMM-262 COMMAND CHRONOLOGY

Our first night in Phu Bai was behind us. It was time to get the scent[42] of the place. When Gary, Roy and I arrived, the squadron hierarchy consisted of two majors. The CO was Major Donald J. Meskan (normally a billet held by a LtCol) and the XO was Major Howard M. Whitfield. Both were chosen from the HMM-262 squadron in which they were serving, not a violation of any particular Marine Corps doctrine, but, an oddity at this time in this war.

It was whispered that the deficit of field grade officers, especially lieutenant colonels, endemic in Quang Tri Province, was because no lieutenant colonel wanted to be placed into the Quang Tri squadrons due to the horrific battles and deaths of helicopter personnel experienced there. There seemed always to be a lack of helicopter pilots, which helped me understand why the Marine Corps was so ready to offer the kind of deal I got when trying to graduate from college. The Corps began sending

---

[41] Texas Tech University, The Vietnam center and archive, https//vva.vietnam.ttu.edu/ repositories/2/digital (Aug 31/2017)

[42] Getting the scent is the manner in which a good hunting dog gets his bearings, knows where he is, knows where he's going, and who or what he's after. Getting the scent means not bringing attention to yourself. Be quiet, listen, and determine how things are going in a new and different place.

new second lieutenants straight from Quantico to Pensacola, by-passing The Officer's Basic School (TBS) normally 6 months in duration. Eventually, following the 46th OCS class that concluded on 2 February, 1968, many newly commissioned second lieutenants, going to pilot training, were sent directly to Mineral Wells Texas to begin training as helicopter pilots in the U.S. Army training process, with a contractual opportunity to fly jets when their tour in Vietnam was completed,[43] slicing months from the Naval Aviation training process in which me and my group were involved. There were only two flying Captains in the squadron: Captains Simon F. Stover, the Operations Officer (OpsO) and David L. White, the Aviation Maintenance Officer (AMO).

There were three non-flying officers, W.W. "Capt'n Jack" Gustin, the OIC of S-1, Capt'n Gross (an officer I never saw in the squadron) in maintenance and "Buzz" Verbanik, the maintenance Quality Assurance (QA) officer. Two pilots from my group's era were already there: First Lieutenants Terry Driskill and Robert "Bob" Lloyd had arrived in late September at Quang Tri just before the squadron moved to Phu Bai on 30 September '69. Terry was a Californian, born and bred and a semi-celebrity. He came from a generation of garage bands that hailed from the Golden State. He was pictured as one of the band members on the album cover of *Sailor*, the second album of the Steve Miller Band. Lloyd was a quiet intellectual whose presence and demeanor had a calming effect on rowdiness. Those two were the tip of the spear of the new guys coming to 262, and we couldn't have had better representatives of us.

Other than that, I knew nothing about the squadron, especially the depth of its earned honors on the battle fields of Vietnam.[44] I'd heard of HMM-364, the Purple Foxes, due to First

---

[43] By not going through the Navy's aviation training syllabus where the student Naval aviators have an opportunity to get the aircraft of their choice, be it Jets, helicopters, C-130s, etc. they were provided that opportunity following their tour in Vietnam.

[44] Crumley, Beth, Walking With Giants-The Tigers of HMM-262, www.mca-marines.org/mcaf-blog/2011/07.

Lieutenant Joseph P. Donovan who, during a 77-day period in early 1969 had been awarded two Navy Crosses, Two Distinguished Flying Crosses (DFCs), and a Purple Heart, making him a legend. But what about 262, where were they?

December 1967 through mid-1969, CH-46D squadrons under MAG-36 included HMM-262 in support of the 3d MarDiv. Marines were in constant battles with hardcore NVA Army units. The names of those battles are written in blood. The stories scream at you from hundreds of pages of AA reports and individual unit chronologies. Mid-air collisions in congested airspace, B-40 RPGs, heavy 82mm mortars, AAA, automatic weapons, and the NVA tossing hand grenades into the zone, were as common as monsoon rains and fog.

Unverified rumors not found in AA reports emphasized the kind of enemy they faced, and we new guys would face. There were rumors of arrows—as in crossbows—and crazed charges by uniformed NVA believed to be high on narcotics of some kind. Some told of the enemy attempting to run up the ramp of the 46 when Marines were disembarking. Some told of enemy prisoners, who, while tied and placed on helicopters attempted to chew through electrical cables that are like lattice work inside the fuselage and cargo decks of H-34s and CH-46s. The image in Life Magazine showing the dead Marine at the feet of the Marine gunner on the H-34 could also not be forgotten. Sea stories or myths, it all set an image in our minds of a maniacal enemy and heroic stands by Grunts against the communist horde.

During the TET offensive of '68, several of us FNGs were in the 48th Officer Candidate School at The Marine Base, Quantico, VA. The entire class consisting of two companies of officer candidates, A & B Companies, volunteered to give blood at the Bethesda Naval Hospital. Riding in "cattle cars,"[45] we were specifically told that the blood was for the Marines in Vietnam who were engaged in the TET offensive battles. Having volunteered

[45] Cattle cars were troop carrying vehicles with a few windows too high to look out. I felt like we were riding in a horse trailer.

our pint of blood, I felt at that moment we all, at least, had "blood in the game." I always wanted to know more about those battles and the Marines who faced the human waves.

Studying the activity of CH-46s in the Vietnam War, I began to read of the horrific ground war in that period, border wars, beginning with Operation Hastings in July, 1966. The head on fight with the 324-B North Vietnamese Army Division, 10,500 men strong and the 90th NVA Regiment, with 1500 men, entrenched and waiting in the rugged Song Ngan Valley with the 803rd and 812th NVA Divisions together with the 341st NVA Division poised for attack in the DMZ. Every helicopter pilot, copilot, crew chief, .50 cal gunner and corpsman of every squadron that flew into that hell on any occasion did so knowing they would be bloodied.

Figure 26 Lance Corporal Ernesto Gomez, HMM-262 crew chief, receiving the Navy Cross. Courtesy of Beth Crumley's "Walking with Giants."

From the Marine outpost at the mouth of the Cua Viet river west to Dong Ha to Con Tien (the "Hill of Angels" that became known to Marines as the "Hill of Dead Marines") to the Rock Pile along highway 9 to Khe Sanh and hills 881 N and S, and 861, a labyrinth of high ground, unnamed ridges and deep jungled ravines had to be cleared of NVA regulars by Grunts, taken to, taken from, supplied and medevaced by Marine H-34s and CH-46As from early 1967 through TET[46] and Operation Dewey Canyon. Legendary HMM-262 crew chiefs like Lance Corporal Ernesto Gomez, who was awarded the Navy Cross for his actions on 25 January 1968, Hill 881S and Corporals "Jake" Jacobs, Robert

---

[46] Corporal Kreig "Hip" Loftin, Crew Chief, advised that HMM-262 did not participate in the battle of HUE because of all the battles going on in the most northern portion of Quang Tri Province.

"Lead Ass" Harrison and Kreig "Hip" Loftin who spoke of stacking the dead like cordwood, were outstanding examples of all the crew chiefs who came through that hell.

Figure 27 Major Dave Althoff. Courtesy of Beth Crumley

The legendary Major David L. Althoff commanded the HMM-262 detachment known as the "Poor Devils" to supply emergency lift capabilities to the Special landing Force coming off the USS Tripoli from Okinawa. Later, Major Althoff's Poor Devils joined with the main body of 262 in Okinawa and moved into Quang Tri. During Major Althoff's tour of duty, he was awarded 3 Silver Stars, 3 DFCs and more than 50 air medals exemplifying the pilots of HMM-262. He was the first Marine helicopter pilot to receive the Alfred A. Cunningham Award, recognizing him as the Marine Aviator of the year. It was noted that each pilot and crew chief during that era averaged more than 100 hours of flight time each week, thus, supporting the overall need for more pilots and CH-46s.

I believe upon reading and studying what the war was like along the DMZ and Laotian border, I had a slight grasp of the deep historic legacy of HMM-262 in Vietnam, but there was more to come.

Officially, Operation Dewey Canyon was the last big sweep of the 9th Marines through the Song Da Krong Valley, on the border, between Vietnam and Laos, some 35 miles west of Phu Bai and Hue. The operation, which ran from 22 January – 18 March 1969, was aimed at destroying the staging and assembly areas of the NVA, which had been poised to attack the population centers of

Dong Ha and Quang Tri. During that operation the border of Laos did not protect the NVA from the onslaught of the Marines. For

Figure 28 HMM-262 Helicopter revealing patches covering several hundred bullet holes, typical of helicopters operating in the vicinity of the DMZ and Laotian Border. Courtesy of Beth Crumley's "Walking with Giants."

the Marines involved, it yielded four Medals of Honor (three posthumously), three Navy Crosses and six Silver Stars. Silver Stars and DFCs were abundant among the helicopter and fixed wing communities during those hard days.

Although the Dewey Canyon[47] operation was officially considered complete, the battles never ended as several regimental sized enemy units of the 6th and 9th NVA Infantry Regiments remained. Third Force Reconnaissance (Maj. Alex Lee) under the mandate of Lieutenant General Herman Nickerson, Jr., Commanding General (CG), III Marine Amphibious Force (as of 26 March 1969) was extremely active in response to intelligence requests on the enemy units that remained actively moving men and material into the Northern A Shau Valley and eastward into the provinces of Quang Tri and Thua Thien,[48] and battles with no names ensued through April, May and June.

The following event involved two First Lieutenants who were still in the unit when I arrived—First Lieutenants Steve Bravard and John Parnham. A Third Force Reconnaissance Team, code-named Carpet, located just inside the Laotian border near LZ Vandergrift became the setting for another dramatic and awe-inspiring event in the months preceding my arrival.

---

[47] Crumley, Beth, Green Hell – Operation Dewey Canyon, www.mca-marinew.org/mcaf-blog/2011/07.

[48] Smith, C.R. U.S. Marines in Vietnam: High Mobility and Standdown. 1969. Washington, D.C.: History and Museums Division, Headquarters, U.S. Marine Corps, Washington, D.C., 1988. 67-68.

The following is a brief description of an important part of the 262 legacy into which we new guys found ourselves.

April 1969

At 1800H [24April69] Chatterbox [event 93-9], ET 14, [piloted by Maj. L. J. Ihli with First Lieutenant Steve Bravard, his copilot] and Chatterbox [event 93-10], [the chase 46 piloted by First Lieutenant T.M. Ewing and his copilot First Lieutenant John Parnham] attempted an emergency extract of [3d Battalion] recon team [code named] "carpet" at YD 023 194. Chatterbox 93-9 was shot down, crashed and burned, causing injuries to crew and passengers. Chatterbox 93-10 was also shot down attempting to extract the crew and passengers. Chatterbox 93-11 and 12 arrived on station shortly after and inserted a reactionary force simultaneously extracting the injured crew members

HMM-262, PROVISIONAL MAG-39

First Lieutenant John T. Parnham, April 1969–April 1970, currently a retired circuit judge in Pensacola, Florida, recalled the following:

"On April 24, 1969, we were flying resupply west of Khe Sanh, near Vandergrift. It was near dark and there was a call for an emergency extract. I was flying copilot with Lt Terry Ewing in the chase bird [ET-15]. Maj Ihli was the HAC in the lead 46 [ET-14], and Team Carpet was pinned down in a zone located just across the line from South Vietnam in Laos. I was a brand new copilot.

"Upon arriving at the extract location, it was determined that a landing was impossible, requiring the team to be hoisted out of the zone by Ihli and Bravard. This required the 46 to remain in a steady hover for several minutes, in the most vulnerable position imaginable, while presenting an appealing target and absorbing intense enemy fire from an enemy who had successfully surrounded the team on the ground. This was a situation that no helicopter pilot wanted to withstand, requiring nerves of steel, and luck. Luck, however, was not in abundance that day. The situation appeared hopeless as the recon team fought off a company-size force of NVA regulars. Ihli and Bravard's 46 went down. Steve suffered the worst injuries, having been thrown from the helicopter while still strapped in his armored seat.

"Ewing and I were next into the fray to pick up whomever we could. We made attempt after attempt while enduring intense enemy fire which ultimately brought us down. All of us were now in the zone with the recon team.

A reversal of roles had occurred. The recon team had now become the rescuers of the downed pilots. The condition of the crew on Maj Ihli's 46 was unknown to us. No one could get to Ihli and Bravard's 46, ET-15, while Ewing and I remained with the recon team far into the night as the fight raged.

"An A-4 Skyraider dropped a bomb containing flechette[49] rounds in very close proximity of the LZ to prevent the NVA from over running our last stand. I (Parnham) was lying between two recon Marines when one of the flechette bombs exploded in close proximity to our position, killing one of the recon Marines lying next to me and injuring another lying on the other side of 'em,"

Figure 29 First Lieutenant John Parnham

Parnham recalled.

[49] A flechette is a one inch arrow or dart with guiding fins. A bomb or artillery shell contains approximately 8,000 flechettes. A cloud of flechettes can impale the enemy into the trees, usually fired at massed enemy troops.

John Parnham, whose nickname when my group arrived in country was "Stumpy," allegedly, because he had landed on some stumps, at one time, impaling his 46. He sported a drooping mustache and was one of the most respected old guys in the squadron due to his gentile manner and impeccable combat experience. He was eventually awarded three DFCs for actions taken while flying with 262.

Regarding Lieutenant Bravard, Sgt. Dale Riley, the crew chief of Major Ehli and Lieutenant Bravard's helicopter, while injured, made his way to the cockpit of their 46 where he found Ihli unconscious, hanging upside down in his straps. Riley cut the shoulder and lap straps, Ihli began regaining some consciousness, and Riley helped him out of the wreckage. While getting Ihli out, Riley realized that Bravard and his armored seat were gone. His thoughts were, "Where the hell is the lieutenant?" Riley said he looked around and saw Bravard's armored seat, which had detached on impact and was flung from the 46, sliding down the hill into tall elephant grass. Bravard appeared dead, still strapped in his armored seat.

Lt. Bravard estimated he was unconscious for approximately 10 to15 minutes. Upon regaining consciousness, he found himself still strapped in his armored seat and in tall elephant grass, approximately one hundred meters down the hill from the downed 46. Sounds of battle filled the air. With a broken jaw and leg, deep lacerations in his face and covered in blood, he managed to release the straps and fall from the seat. Seeing the helicopter he had so recently copiloted broken and lying several meters away, his instinct was to crawl toward it. Fighting against passing out and not knowing where his crew was, he eventually made it to the helicopter. Lt Bravard was discovered by members of the recon team and carried into the recon group where he endured the pain and a great deal of blood loss, floating in and out of consciousness.

Figure 30 Facial injuries received by Steve Bravard on April 24, 1969, Courtesy of Steve Bravard.

Bravard's initial condition in the armored seat had given the NVA every indication that he was dead. His flight suit showed signs of having been searched by the NVA—his survival radio, maps, and personal belongings were gone. It was his good luck that they didn't confirm their kill by applying a coup de grace. Though he suffered serious injuries, Bravard never left country for treatment, finding himself back in the cockpit in May 1969.

First Lieutenant Robin Tomlin, HMM-262, was scheduled on standby to fly a Bald Eagle mission, 1600-2400, a standby mission at Quang Tri for any type of emergency extract to rescue Marines. The call came in to Quang Tri that a rescue was required for Team Carpet and the two helicopter crews shot down in the zone. The Bald Eagle mission was launched. Included in this mission were two Huey gunships, an OV-10 from VMO-6, and a stack[50] of fixed wing.

Tomlin and his crew braved heavy enemy fire as they made multiple attempts to get into the zone. Maj. Ihli, on the ground in the middle of the battle, all but ordered Tomlin to leave them for fear they too would be shot down. Tomlin refused.

Lt. Tomlin and his crew displayed nerves of steel, following a strobe light held by one of the recon Marines into the pitch black zone. Against all odds, he did it. With the sounds of battle all about him, he brought out two air crews and one recon team,

---

[50] A "stack" of jets (A-4 Skyhawks or F-4 Phantoms) is slang for more than one jet in holding. The jets would go into a holding pattern in proximity of the action, like "in holding" by commercial aircraft to land at a particular airport. Each aircraft would have its own altitude in order to avoid a mid-air. That group of jets represents the "stack."

a total of 23 Marines. They arrived safely back at Quang Tri at 2325 hrs.

Later that evening Lt. Parnham asked Tomlin, "Why didn't you leave us when Maj. Ihli suggested you do so?"

Tomlin replied, "I knew if I didn't get you guys out right then, I'd be coming back in the morning to pick up your bodies." He wouldn't leave them, upholding the highest tradition of the Corps, to leave no man behind, a place of rare air, where only real heroes dwell. Uncommon valor was clearly apparent that day in that zone by Lt. Tomlin. Tomlin was considered for the Navy Cross, but that recommendation was reduced to a Silver Star, then it was further reduced to a Distinguished Flying Cross. No one could understand how it was that some received a Navy Cross or Silver Star while others received the DFC, and some a Single Mission Air Medal still, many received nothing for what were clear acts of heroism.

Later, as the Marine Corps' participation in Vietnam was nearing its end, a commanding officer voiced that if there were no bullet holes in metal or flesh it was a single mission Air Medal, whereas if holes were in both metal and flesh it was a toss-up between DFC and Silver Star. Some voiced that no First Lieutenant would be receiving a DFC and made section and division leaders only of Majors and senior Captains. It did not go unnoticed.

Figure 31 Relieving Stress: A celebratory gathering by Provisional MAG-39 pilots in "The Zoo" at Quang Tri, like many such get-to-gathers following long days of flying. L to R: Lieuten-ants John Parnham, John "Wags" Wagner III, Flight Surgeon (unidentified) Paul David, Steve Bravard and Ken Boyack.

13: Our Reception

At near this same time back home (on 12 November, 1969) 35 newspapers across the United States broke the news of the My Lai massacre. I knew very little about My Lai while in Vietnam, but it was headline news in the Sea Tiger newspaper.

* * *

By the time Gary, Roy, Joe and I arrived in Phu Bai, the war as those men had known it was pretty much coming to an end. The 3d Marine Division was well into the process of redeployment. PMAG-39, which included among others, HMM-161, 262 and 367 was deactivated in-country at Quang Tri on 31 September and moved to Phu Bai.

How could we believe anything other than we might not be in Vietnam long enough to fly any missions. All of the chaos and redeployment gave rise to raging rumors every day, not lost on us new guys.

Upon our arrival into Phu Bai, we newly arrived pilots going into HMM-262 in Phu Bai were welcomed by most of the old guys[51] on check-in. Therefore we were not as yet combat veterans, and strangely that fact appeared to be a source of difficulty for one of those veterans, who projected a deep hostility toward our little group of misfits.

Following our official check-in with the personnel department, S-1, I was assigned to First Lieutenant John A. "Wags"

---

[51] "Old Guys" was a metaphor. It had nothing to do with age. It was for pilots who were there before us. The truth is that many of those Marine helicopter pilots who were in 262 before we arrived could easily have had dates of rank junior to ours. The reason harkens back to the decision by the Marine Corps in early 1968 to have Marine helicopter pilots trained by the Army. Army helicopter flight training concentrated entirely on flying helicopters which allowed the Army trained pilots to be designated as helicopter pilots in much less time than if they were trained by the Navy. Naval flight training, by signed contract, included both fixed wing and helicopter training that dramatically increased the time it took to become a designated helicopter pilot. Therefore, if two people entered Army flight school and naval flight school at the same time, the Army trainee would be designated much earlier and be able to get into the fray sooner as was the case.

Wagner III as the Assistant Paraloft Officer. He was a likeable guy and the word was that he never received his HAC designation due to some alleged problem between him and the XO.[52]

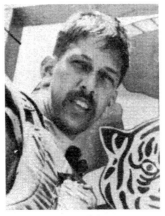

Figure 32 First Lieutenant John A. "Wags" Wagner III, from HMM-262, 1969-70 cruise book.

Far from seeing that as a deficiency, the FNGs viewed it as an indication Wags bowed to no man. He had a very good reputation as a pilot. His conundrum was one I never figured out. Yet, he was not the only pilot who felt they were dealt a bad hand by Meskan and/or Whitfield. The animus toward the current leadership by the old guys was palpable.

Wags was in the area when I was getting my assignment and welcomed me by saying, "Welcome to Phu Bai. I'll show you the way to our kingdom. You sound like you're from the south, where you from?"

I accompanied him to the paraloft on the second deck of the maintenance hangar, where I was introduced to the troops who really ran the shop: A humongously fat SSgt. who disappeared shortly after I arrived and Sgt. Grit Patton from North Carolina. The others in the shop were Cpl. C. F. Summers from Nevada and

---

[52] First Lieutenant John A. "Wags" Wagner in later years said that he had refused to fly what he considered to be a mission solely for the benefit of overall squadron flight hours in one month, to attain 1000 hours in a contest with HMM-161. That refusal, he said, kept him from receiving a HAC check.

LCpl. D. F. Delp from Ohio. I could see that Wags was clearly at ease with the way things were run, and as his assistant, so was I.

My primary duty would boil down to picking up mail, writing fitness reports and staying out of the way of the Marines who

Figure 33 Paraloft/flight Equipment crew from HMM-262's 1969-70 Cruise Book) Left to right: LCpl. D.P. Delp, Cpl. Summers, unidentified, and Sgt. Grit Patton

ran the shop. Wags introduced me to Capt. Verbanik who was our OIC. However, I was never in a meeting with Capt. Verbanik and Wags didn't seem to meet with him either. The Marines in the paraloft were artists in their craft of making almost anything—helmet bags, map bags, coverings of every conceivable shape and size, even reupholstered furniture—from the ever-popular and readily available red Naugahyde, of which there was an inexhaustible supply.

My first impression of 262, as a whole, was that they had a cautious optimism and anticipation that just maybe, at any day, the squadron could be ordered out of country. Maybe the whole squadron would be going home soon, back to Hawaii, home base for 262. As for me, I correctly perceived my primary role was to maintain a low profile, keep my head down and get out alive. As a matter of fact, the main thing happening on the hangar deck was the making of embark boxes for the impending move south to Marble Mountain.

Figure 34 Lt. McClure, USN "Doc" from HMM-262 cruise book.

The next step of checking into the squadron was the medical check-in. Navy Lt. M. McClure was our flight surgeon. We were told to just call him "Doc". He was a great guy and lived in a hooch with pilots. Not until seeing the movie *Mash* upon my return from Vietnam could I identify his character. He was Hawkeye Pierce. There were no female nurses around Phu Bai, so his likeness to Hawkeye stemmed from professional similarities. The storyline on McClure was that he took advantage of every symposium in the Pacific, not held in Vietnam. He was well liked and had definitely seen his share of trauma medicine. The big vaccination, when entering into country was the gamma globulin shot to give one's immune system a boost upon acclimating to the tropical climate. The shot was rumored to be extremely painful and to bring on flu-like symptoms, causing some to be taken off the flight schedule. When I checked into medical, Doc asked me, after explaining what might happen, "Do you still want the shot?"

I responded by saying, "Hell no, I don't want the shot. Do I have a choice?"

He said, "Yeah."

"Then, no." and that was that. No argument, no problem, and I never became sick in Vietnam, except for hangovers.

It was rumored that on one occasion, when an older Marine dropped dead of an apparent heart attack, Doc was awakened early one morning by an excited young corporal asking him to hurry to the aid of the man. Doc allegedly woke up, rolled over, rubbed his eyes, looked at the clock, and said, "Is he dead?"

The young Marine answered frantically, "I think so."

Doc replied, "Well, go back and find out. And if he's dead, just throw a blanket over him. I'll get to him in the morning." That was the image I had of Doc, and the telling of the story, true or false always got a laugh.

Another interesting thing about Phu Bai was the Montagnards. They were the real deal.

Figure 36 Montagnards patrol being led by a Special Forces Green Beret Advisor

Figure 35 Montagnards in battle gear pictures from Special Forces online publication, photographer/s unknown.

I first saw them when Gary, Roy and I were being driven to our Quonset hut quarters. The CIDGs[53] were housed in two-story barracks and they worked for the Military Assistance Command, Vietnam (MACV) Studies and Observation Group (SOG) under the direct control of the Special Forces. They were primarily

---

[53] CIDGs (Civilian Irregular Defense Group), South Vietnamese paramilitary force, composed largely of Montagnards, the nomadic tribesmen who populate the South Vietnamese highlands, and "advised" by the U.S. Army Special Forces.

transported by the Vietnamese Air Force's 219 (H-34) Helicopter Squadron whose call-sign was King Bee, and they received support from the Huey gunship squadron based at Phu Bai.

When I was walking past their area, they appeared to be a happy group, always laughing and tossing knives in some sort of game. Their happy disposition contradicted their deadly reputation. I tried to stroll by with one eye on them, hoping they wouldn't notice me in my new jungle utilities and combat boots. I didn't yet have enough courage to wear the combat-worn utilities I'd picked up at Camp Hague. However, the Montagnards always spoke at me, not to me, in Vietnamese phrases I certainly couldn't and didn't want to understand.

Figure 37 Military Assistance Command Vietnam (MACV) Studies and Observation Group (SOG) patch; sounds like a benign research unit in the Pentagon, but it's anything but benign.

I always returned their comments with a wave and nervous smile, to which they would say something, then look at each other and laugh hysterically…at me. My feeling of inadequacy was heightened as they intuitively recognized I was an FNG and sensed my uneasiness as I walked past. They were real guerilla warriors, more than equal to the NVA or VC.

Another group of real warriors was the Third Force Reconnaissance Marines also located on the north side of the runway in the Marine encampment at the easternmost edge. Their compound was closed to all visitors unless they had received access permission from the CO or his direct representative, the XO. Their encampment was fenced and surrounded with concertina wire, and the fence was covered with a canvas like material that totally shrouded the place. They were an elite Corps of Marines,

every bit equal to the Montagnards in guerrilla warfare expertise. Their deadly reputation was amplified by their skull and
crossbones logo and their motto, "Swift, Silent, Deadly." The
whole thing had an aura of mystery that intrigued me. Where
did they go and what did they do? Their existence was critical to
understanding the nature of the conflict going on in the deep
jungles where the sun's rays never touched the ground and the
world was not watching. There was no right and no wrong in
those jungles—only survival. I was never tempted to visit inside
that compound.

The officers of 3d Force Recon were: CO, Maj. Alex Lee; XO,
Capt. Norman Hisler, and Operations Officer, Lt. Buck Coffman.

Maj. Lee, a tough, cigar-chompin' Marine's Marine, and his
XO would occasionally come to the O' Club to play poker with
Majors Meskan and Whitfield. In 3d Force Recon's cloistered
compound, the 3d Force Recon's club was a wooden plank bar
with a chest of cold beer. They never used any kind of soap or
deodorant, nor did they wash their field clothes in anything
other than cold water. Any scent other than the jungle itself
could mean their life. They were pure warriors from a different
age. The Montagnards and Recon warriors' were found in dense
jungle paths along the borders of Laos, Cambodia and Vietnam.
They were intimately familiar with the Ho Chi Minh trail, and
their reputation was legendary within the Corps.

Third Force flew with both 262 and elements of the 101st Airborne's XXIV Corps, specifically the 2d Squadron of the 17th Air
Cavalry. In reality, Maj. Lee preferred flying with the Army rather than the Marine Corps. Lee,[54] in his book *Force Recon Command*, stated, "If the Marine air wing could not or would not support us fully, we could seek help from the ready and willing Army
aviation assets of the 101st Airborne Division." And "despite [his]
congenial relationship with the Marine pilots, the difficulties
and obstacles [he] encountered with the First Marine Air Wing

---

[54] Lee, Alex, Force Recon Command, Ballantine Books, 1995. Pages 69-70,
145-146.

brass in Da Nang made the Army [Lee's] primary transportation choice." Lee further advised in his book that his ace in the hole remained to be the Marine Corps in that he, "knew that any combat difficulties they might encounter with the enemy [even if the Army had taken them into the bush] would bring all the might Marine air could muster."

Additional insight into Maj. Lee's reluctance to use Marine air was revealed by Maj. Sellers, who replaced Capt. Stover as the Operations Officer upon Stover's departure at the end of his tour. Major Sellers was a second tour pilot with a long and distinguished career in the 46. On one occasion, according to Maj. Sellers, he had some heated words with Major Lee regarding Lee's favoritism of Army Air over the use of Marine Air.

Figure 38 The death card appeared much like the 3rd Reconnaissance Logo.

Our war in the 46 was more distant than the Recon teams; theirs was up close and personal. They ambushed the ambushers and left their calling card—a 3d Force Recon playing card with a death head inside a triangle and the words Swift, Silent, Deadly on each plane of the triangle.

The enemy so feared them that a bounty was placed upon the head of each 3d Force Recon Marine and Major Lee's head in particular. My war, meanwhile, would be viewed through a thick Plexiglas windscreen while enveloped in an armored seat and bullet bouncer[55] in which I felt I could hardly move, like a small child whose mother shoved him into a thick snowsuit.

I truly wanted to meet those warriors whose legends were being formed, but intuitively, I refrained from approaching them for fear of being considered too familiar without having yet earned that privilege. In time, I would feel more comfortable in their presence, but for now I would keep my distance.

---

[55] The pilot's bullet bouncer differed from the crew chief and gunner's bullet bouncers in that the pilot's vest consisted of only one ceramic chest plate. The pilot's armored seat protected his back.

My main emphasis was upon not killing myself or my crew while ensuring the safe delivery of my cargo, be it men or supplies. Recon's war was to locate, identify, report upon, and when necessary, kill the enemy by whatever means available. Our jobs were symbiotic. We needed each other. We respected each other and depended upon that truth, of which we both were only too aware.

Third Force thrived on combat, the kind of combat I could only imagine. They routinely ventured into the A Shau, the Valley of Death, and beyond in small teams, six or seven men at the most. Returning after a week or longer, they would pick out an LZ and call us or the Army in to pick them up. A saying about Recon was they were the only unit that could "stir up shit and get out before it hit the fan." Yet that was not always the case. Sometimes—no, many times—they didn't get out before it hit the fan. I feel very fortunate to have been a copilot on a couple of 3d Force inserts and extracts. I salute them.

The essence of Phu Bai unexpectedly enveloped me. It was visceral. The primitive nature of the base and its proximity to the Vietnamese countryside made me feel that I was indeed at the tip of the spear, beyond the bridge, the most forward element of MAG-16 during that period of time. I couldn't have been in PMAG-39 or any of the other squadrons that participated in the hard fought border wars of the DMZ and Laos. Being in 262 in Phu Bai was as close as I could get, and I was where I wanted to be; no starched covers and little noticeable military protocol other than traditional courtesies. Red mud, red dust and monsoons, on one occasion, twenty four hours brought 24 inches of rain, accompanied in the background by the muted popping sounds of helicopter blades moving at the speed of sound, slapping the air into submission. I wanted to truly experience that place before we moved to MMAF, before this world was forever lost to me. I wanted to experience what it was that separated us FNGs from the old guys. It was something I could not define, quantify, or otherwise explain.

It was in their walk, a kind of swagger. It was in their eyes. It was a feeling. It was the smells of mud, plywood and moldy sandbags, combined with the beauty of this tortured land. And it was the terror and ugliness of it. What was at Phu Bai, for our group of FNGs, was the essence of the Vietnam experience. They, the men who had flown into that war had "seen the elephant,"[56] and I longed to have the same experience.

One could not look at us FNGs and in any manner believe we were experienced and battle hardened. We tried to look the part, to fit in; but one had to be careful about trying this lest one be caught up in a situation as I both experienced and witnessed.

During a bout of drinking, one of the best storytellers, John Parnham, had our rapt attention as he described what seemed to be an impossible situation. Parnham began by saying that on one occasion, he and his crew had flown into the A Shau Valley to collect the last of a 3d Force Recon team that had been ambushed. While in the zone, the NVA was attacking with everything they had, including RPGs and small arms fire, destroying their helicopter and killing or wounding most of the remainder of the team. He and First Lieutenant Terry Ewing, the HAC, were among the last to be pulled out of the mangled helicopter when a surprisingly large force of NVA overran the zone. We FNGs had eyes wide open and mouths agape; we tried not to show how in awe we were of his current presence among the living. He stopped telling the story and just looked out into nothingness with a forced stare, allowing the silence to do its work. I waited until I bit, "Then what happened?" I said.

Parnham looked at me, took another swig of some odd smelling liquid, let the tension build a little more, and said, "They killed me." Then came the big gotcha-laugh. I had been had. I heard the laughter as I had bit hard on the story. Then I also laughed and sat back, relieved that it had been a joke. There were

---

[56] "To see the elephant" is a phrase taken from several sources dating back to 326bc when Alexander the Great fought against elephants. The phrase was used by Civil War Soldiers of both the North and South armies to mean, having experienced combat and been wounded.

many variations of this type of story told to FNGs. However, as I was to learn, most Vietnam War stories had some element of truth to them. Maybe, just maybe, Parnham had wondered why he wasn't killed in the zone on that April day in Laos. The truism was that 46 drivers did die in the zone even when the war was almost over for Marines.

14: Paraloft

The next order of business was to get our flight gear. With so many deaf helicopter pilots walking around, a new helmet was making its appearance into the helicopter community. Sonic ear cups were introduced to guard against that big high-speed transmission that sat just above our heads, producing frequencies above 800 hertz—causing a mind numbing amount of damage to the hearing apparatus in our brain housing group, similar to that suffered by artillerymen. Our old training command helmets also had to be dulled down. No more flashy reflecting tape like we plastered on our helmets to reflect our own identity. My old helmet had the outline of Missouri with the state motto "Show Me" highlighted. I thought it appropriate for the training command. Yet, the paraloft crew stripped the helmet clean and used Ultra-flat non-reflective Marine-green paint to repaint the helmet and replaced the microphone package from the training command with the one in use in MAG-16.

We were issued survival vests complete with a first aid kit, emergency rations, survival knife, a big survival map, etc. We were also issued a bib-like bullet bouncer with a chest plate composed of heavy ceramic layers with of all things, "do not drop" embossed on the piece. It was to be worn over the survival vest. A small emergency radio was fitted into a pocket sewn onto the front of the vest. It reportedly would fly out of the pocket in which it was fitted and smack you in the mouth if you had a hard landing. But, it was invaluable to you if you needed it.

For the most part, we pilots, when fully dressed for flight in Vietnam and strapped into that iron-maiden-like seat had protection generally equivalent to that worn by EOD (Explosive Ordnance Disposal) personnel. Yet, unlike EOD personnel, our arms, head, shoulders and our legs from mid-thigh to the bottom of our feet remained vulnerable. Another real danger was fire. It was believed by pilots that the 46, although there are no official findings because there were no known survivors, would burn up before hitting the ground at altitudes of more than 2000'. Getting out of the cockpit quickly if on the deck had to be done through the emergency exits located on both sides of the cockpit. The danger there was if the helicopter was lying on its side, the pilot on the side lying against the ground might crawl over the top of you, planting one of those steel toed flight boots in your face.

The ceramic bullet bouncer was reportedly capable of stopping a .30 cal. round (AK-47) fired at point blank range up to 1500'. At an altitude of 3500', the helicopter was considered safe from a .50 or .51 cal. I was unaware of anyone who had actually been hit in the chest with a .50 cal. round while in the cockpit and survived, but, the thought that it might just slow up a .50 or .51 cal. round made us all feel a little safer. The true effects of either the .30 or .50 or .51 Cal would soon be realized.

We drew our standard issue firearm, a Smith & Wesson .38 caliber revolver and standard flare-tipped survival rounds of ammo for making our position known if downed. Although we were required to carry the .38, many pilots and aircrew ignored the rule and carried personally owned weaponry. I checked out a .45 automatic along with a web belt and holster to wear when not flying and an M-16 to keep in the hooch, just in case.

Figure 39 First Lieutenant Steve Bravard pictured the proper positioning of the holstered firearm when in flight.

We were told by the old guys that the best way to carry the .38 was to get a western-style gun belt and holster made by the Vietnamese. The holsters were purchased from a Vietnamese mama san shop, a ragtag little store that sat on the side of Highway 1 just outside the main gate of our base. I also learned that wearing your sidearm in a low-slung manner, like the western gun fighter, was one thing; however, wearing a sidearm in the 46 was quite a different matter. Fully dressed, the arms of the armored seat were above your lap and a snug fit for me at my height of six foot three inches and normal weight of 210-215 pounds. The dimensions of the armored seat made retrieval of the weapon impossible if worn on the side. The answer was to utilize the .38 Smith and Wesson as added personal protection, like an athletic cup, by rotating the gun belt so that it lay directly between your legs, directly behind the cyclic as demonstrated by Steve Bravard in the picture. In this location, the firearm was easily accessible if needed and also provided armor for your most private parts.

We also received a USAF flight crew check list booklet full of classified radio frequencies and call signs as well as coded routes of flight. The first thing we put on was the flight suit and flight boots, followed by the survival vest and firearm, followed by the bullet bouncer, then the helmet and Nomex groves with the sleeves of the flight suit pulled over the Nomex gloves and tightened around your wrist, making sure there was no skin showing in case of fire. All of this in relentless heat and humidity causes you to sweat gallons of fluid. Then and only then are you ready to fly.

For a while, I also carried a large Bowie knife that I had purchased at the El Toro Marine Corps Air Station Exchange, based upon a recommendation by one of our HMMT-302 instructors, Lt. Tom Sullivan, who commented that the small, and always dull, survival knife made available in our survival vest was insufficient when on the ground in Vietnam. He urged us to get the Bowie knife. I did, but eventually discarded the cumbersome Bowie in favor of a Gerber Mark III combat knife worn in the lower leg pocket of my flight suit. Many of the old guys favored a variety of personal side arms, of which the 9mm Browning seemed a favorite. Some, however, placed their trust in the .45 cal. M3A1 submachine gun, commonly called a grease gun, developed at the end of WWII for tank crews. One of our crew chiefs always carried an M1918 Browning Automatic Rifle (BAR) in a hunting case. It was rumored that he had once been shot down and had to walk out of the jungle, along with the recon team he was supposed to have been rescuing. Next time, he said, he'd be better armed.

The crew chief that brought the Browning along with him, mentioned above, may have been with Captain Dave White and First Lieutenant Larry Fenton in their 7-10 June 1969 trek through the jungle, a for-real war story. Although Capt. White was a quiet, intense man who would never have spoken of his "adventure," the story has come out through then Lt. Larry Fenton.

Marine recon teams were being inserted into the DMZ to confirm size and scope of a known enemy battalion presence. Two of those teams going into the DMZ in that period of time were *Fighting Mad* and *American Beauty*.

The "Fighting Mad" recon team consisted of eight Marines. They were inserted deep inside the DMZ in mid-afternoon that day and moved rapidly away from the insert zone deeper into enemy infested territory. The team was immediately detected by the enemy, through a fluke occurrence by an enemy soldier, and a fire fight ensued. The recon team killed two NVA soldiers. Two recon team members however were badly wounded and the team was being surrounded. The team leader, a Lt. Gross, with two of his eight man team down called for an emergency extract.

The decision, at Recon headquarters in Da Nang by the powers that be, was to input more Marines into the area to assist Fighting Mad in fending off the enemy and moving to a location accessible to the 46s that were coming for them. In accordance with that decision, a section of HMM-161 46s, call sign Cattlecall, were dispatched to pick up 20 Marine reinforcements at Quang Tri and to insert them within close proximity of Fighting Mad.

During that same period of time, Capt. Dave White and Lt. Larry Fenton of HMM-262, call sign Chatterbox, with Lt. Jim Dau and John Parnham as their chase 46[57] were also sent out to extract the team. Captain White's section remained high, at 3500', reportedly, a safe distance from the .50 cal. the enemy most always had at their disposal. As they watched HMM-161 from their

[57] The "chase" bird as it was sometimes called was the second aircraft in a section of two helicopters.

high perch above the action, they saw Marine enforcements successfully deplane from the lead 46.

Lt. Fenton watched as the HMM-161 chase 46 landed in the zone and successfully inserted the remaining Marine reinforcements. Lt. Fenton advised that he also observed heavy muzzle blasts in the zone directed at the 46 trying to takeoff. The pilot of the 46 announced that he was hit, had lost an engine and one of his gunners was down. All hell was breaking loose.

The damaged 46 was able to get out of the zone, but wobbled just above the trees for about three kilometers from the zone where they had inserted the Marine reinforcements. The pilot did an outstanding job of landing the 46 in an area without crashing. The lead 46 from 161 was with the battle damaged aircraft and immediately landed near the downed helicopter, picked up the entire crew, and headed back to the hospital at Quang Tri.

Marine fighter bombers, A-4s and F-4s were directed to bomb the downed 46, keeping the .50 cals. out of the hands of the NVA. On each pass, the fast movers, who bombed the hell out of the 46, were coming under heavy Anti Aircraft Artillery (AAA) fire with each pass. A reassessment was underway...what to do next?

The original recon team, *Fighting Mad*, was still on the ground with seriously wounded men. Now, with no successful extract, an additional 20 Marines were with the team, making 28 Marines on the ground, some seriously wounded.

Capt. White and Lt. Fenton who had been in a position to observe the happenings were getting low on fuel. Capt. White led his section to Fire Support Base (FSB) Vandergrift to refuel and await further orders. At about 1800 hrs, nearing dark, the decision to attempt an extract of the near 20 Marines on the ground was left up to Capt. White, the section lead. The Forward Air Controller in charge of coordinating the rescue attempt stated that it was beginning to get dark, and if they wanted to undertake the rescue, they should act quickly as the mountains in the west were beginning to turn purple. Capt. White advised that his section was going in.

The Marine Grunts on the ground waiting for the 46s to come and pick them up were in radio contact. They formed up in two lines, called sticks,[58] one for each helo and waited. For some reason, the fighting had oddly died down. There was virtually no firing from the NVA.

Capt. White asked his chase, Lt. Dau, to remain high as he went down in a high speed pass to see what it was like and, to draw out the enemy. There was no response from the enemy. Maybe the NVA had had enough for the day and had gone home, deciding against tangling with the bombers that would inevitably be there in moments if needed. Whatever the reason, Capt. White did not receive any fire from the NVA.

On the next pass, as Capt. White briefed his crew chief and gunners that they were going in, he and Lt. Fenton checked their inertial-reel locks locked. Fenton again scanned the instruments, ensuring he could easily get to the hydraulics switch for isolation if needed. With Dau and Parnham above, the approach was begun. There were no problems...and no enemy as they reached their objective and about to touch down. Fenton recalled that while they were still airborne, he saw the Marines standing in their sticks turn toward the jungle and begin firing. Some, he said, were "firing from their hip... John Wayne style[59]." Others "went to the ground, firing under their 46 into the area where he and White had intended to land.

"Aw shit!" was all he could utter.

Streams of tracers were then arcing toward their helicopter. Their port .50 cal gunner opened up filling the cabin with cordite. For a brief time, Lt. Fenton said, "I saw two trails of red tracers the size of beer cans arching toward each other from the .50 cal gunner on board his helicopter and the enemy .50 or .51 cal. gunner on the ground. It was a duel, two .50s firing point blank at each other, a fascinating view, almost dreamlike."

---

[58] A "stick" is a slang term for a predetermined number of Marines selected and lined up to board a helicopter upon its landing.

[59] This is when the proper noun "John Wayne," became a verb. To John Wayne meant to be an aggressive warrior.

A .50 cal round slammed into Lt. Fenton's seat, the impact stunned him but did not hit him. The aircraft was going down as Capt. White controlled as much as was possible. "The earth seemed to be coming up at us, rather than us going down...an odd visualization of what was happening." When they hit the ground, the helicopter began flipping over and over before coming to a stop.

Miraculously, Capt. White, Lt. Fenton and their crew of three made it out of the inferno that only moments before was their 46. The fireball that erupted caused the FAC to transmit to Lt. Dau, "There's no need to try and rescue the crew, and no one could have lived through that crash." Lt. Fenton, upon hearing the conversation over his survival radio, interrupted their conversation by announcing "Hey! The Phantom's here and everyone got out!!" They were all alive and Lt. Fenton identified himself as the Phantom, a nickname that Lt. Dau and Parnham would recognize. The shoot-down of White and Fenton brought the full might of the Marine Corps and Air force into play.

During the next four days (7-11 June) their group of approximately 30 Marines were shadowed by an NVA force that was kept away from them by the use of all available artillery and air power including, the Air Force's Puff the Magic Dragon.[60] On 11 June, they were rescued by Maj. Meskan. Fenton said, "The man (Maj. Don Meskan) had his detractors, but he never shied away from a tough mission and he was good at his job."[61].

The story of their trek has all the earmarks of a feature film. Two of the Recon Marines were badly wounded. One was shot in the chest and one had a shattered thigh bone. They were both on stretchers. The Marine shot in the chest died the day after

---

[60] "Puff the Magic Dragon" was an Air Force Douglas AC-47D side firing aerial gunship that could put down 18,000 rounds per minute with three General Electric 7.62mm Gatling Mini-guns. The plane could blanket every foot of a football field in 60 seconds. Its reputation was one of horrendous power, like the devil pissing fire.

[61] Thanks to Larry Fenton, former Lieutenant, now, LtCol Retired, who kindly allowed me to read his personal memoir of that trek through the jungles of the DMZ. It's a remarkable story that only he can totally relate.

their trek began. The Marine with the shattered thigh bone survived through pure agony as the corpsman did what he could. They were in constant radio contact with a forward air controller (FAC) and were headed toward LZ Beaver, a place not far away that would be a good pickup zone.

They were determined not to leave anyone behind. So, they brought the body of the dead Marine with them on a stretcher as they struggled up and down steep ravines, chopping their way through the jungle undergrowth. The heat and humidity caused the body to rapidly decompose; the stench too ghastly for the stretcher bearers to endure for periods longer than a few minutes before switching off with each other.

At one point, Lt. Fenton and a recon Marine were both shot. Lt. Fenton was shot in the left knee and the recon Marine was shot in the shoulder, by either the NVA or our own close air support; they couldn't be sure which. During the night, a Marine platoon joined up with them providing more security. It was a miracle they were found by the Marines as the NVA followed their every move, like they were bait, just looking for a chance to shoot down more helicopters. On one occasion, Capt. White, a former artillery officer before becoming an aviator, working in concert with Lt. Gross, made the decision to call in artillery on top of their small group because they were closely surrounded and in fear of being overrun. Capt. White made the call and explained to Lt. Fenton that in reality, most artillery missions seldom land on the exact coordinates they are supposed to hit, but they come very close and that was exactly what they needed at that time.

They dug their holes and the artillery came in all around them within close proximity, doing the job that Capt. White wanted; to keep the enemy at bay and to let them know that Marine air and artillery could get to them at any point on the map. It was a long grueling trek but, they all got out when Maj. Meskan led a group of HMM-262 46s to pick them up. This episode gives real meaning to the advice I once received. I was told by a senior pilot "When on the ground, the Grunts are your god. Listen to them and keep your head down. When in the air, you are their god. They look to you to get them to their job and safely home. Don't attempt to do their job, and they won't attempt to do yours."

Lt. Fenton was taken to the field hospital at Quang Tri where he underwent immediate surgery by an overtired and stressed out doctor. Upon being placed in a bed following his surgery, and at about the same time as he regained consciousness, he heard rockets slamming into Quang Tri. Unable to move by himself, he watched as anyone who was able to be evacuated from the Quonset hut hospital into a sand bagged bunker, was evacuated.

Finally, a hospital worker took pity on him and helped him out of bed, but deposited him under the bed. Once he was under the bed, the worker ran from the building to the relative security of the bunker. Having survived the trek and then the rocket attack, he was moved to Da Nang then to Yokosuka Naval Hospital Japan, never again to return to Vietnam.

During the same time Lt. Fenton and Capt. White were making their way out of the DMZ to safety, First Lieutenant Ron McLean, Jimmy Stewart's step-son, a recon Marine who was in the 48th OCS class with me, A.C., Eric and Roy, was killed. His body was removed from the DMZ during the same period of time the trek was happening.

The incident described above was but one small portion of that war in which the 3d MarDiv, MAG-36 at Phu Bai and MAG-39 at Quang Tri CH-46s were involved. The era of Vietnamization and Redeployment began in late 1969 when 3d MarDiv redeployed to Okinawa.

Lt. Fenton was promoted to Captain and continued his Marine Corps career, transitioning to jets and retiring at the rank of LtCol. During that same time period, He also became an Airline pilot and retired in 2014 from Delta as a Captain of the B-767-400 after 28 years. He had a remarkable career.

15: Getting Scheduled

I was told the time between arriving at Phu Bai and getting on the flight schedule was anywhere from a week to two weeks, give or take. But it was the monsoon season, and it rained and rained and rained. We three FNGs, Roy, Gary and I had little more to do than get acquainted with Phu Bai until being placed on the flight schedule for some benign administrative mission. Yet depending on circumstances, we could be placed in the cockpit on a for-real combat mission. Only time would tell.

Figure 40 First Lieutenant Jack Page, the weather watcher, "A hundred foot overcast, one-half mile visibility, hmm, we can make it. Launch 'em!"

With the unremitting torrential monsoons came the ever-present low ceilings and minimal visibility which produced white-knuckled flying and the tongue-in-cheek phrase First

Lieutenant Jack Page perfectly demonstrated when he appeared in HMM-262's 1969-70 cruise book.

Assignments from MAG-16 for missions the following day in the Da Nang area were called frags. *Frags* arrived in Phu Bai by midnight or later, keeping the operations folks working 17-hour days or longer. That meant the assigned aircrews had to have their helicopter preflighted and the mission briefed as per the schedule. Then, with the monsoons like they were, the flight crew would begin the ready room wait for any amount of ceiling that would permit takeoff.

During those days, the ready room would be full of pilots playing ping-pong, sleeping, writing letters, reading, reviewing maps, or just dreaming about R&R or what to do following Vietnam.

For us FNGs the poor weather gave us additional time to mark up our own area maps with compass headings and unit locations within the Da Nang TAOR: Hai Vanh Pass, Hill 55, Hill 64, Hill 34, Hill 25, Liberty Bridge, An Hoa, Twin Bridges, Hoi An, Thuong Duc, Go Noi Island, Alligator Lake, LZ Baldy, Ross, etc., etc. There were no such markings necessary for Northern I Corps, but there were plenty of old maps for I Corps should the mission arise. Some did, for Third Force Recon.

I managed to write a brief letter home to Kathy each day. The letters required no postage as long as you wrote the name of the squadron, HMM-262, and Fleet Post Office (FPO), San Francisco 96602 into the return address and the word FREE where the stamp would normally be placed.

For the most part, the letters were a rambling discourse on the living conditions and day-to-day events rather than military matters followed by "Luv Ya." Kathy's letters to me were similar. She wrote about her first-grade teaching job. Her letters were filled with how her days were spent. Because her parents both understood war and the military, they were very supportive.

Like many, I had no worries on the home front and could fully concentrate on surviving the coming year.

Figure 41 Free mail from Vietnam with FREE written where stamp goes.

We had been warned not to divulge any strategic information, and not to discuss mission-specific information. The S-2 (Intelligence) warned us that the letters we received from home should be destroyed. The warning was due to the knowledge that in some instances the Vietnamese hooch maids had been caught stealing the letters from home and then taking the material to NVA sources, which in turn used addresses and information that loved ones may have inadvertently repeated, like squadron strengths, mission descriptions, etc.

Each hooch had a Vietnamese hooch maid who was paid approximately five dollars a month by each occupant. The earnings, which averaged $36.00 per month, were a great deal of money for Vietnam, as much as or more than an ARVN captain. The women washed all clothes and cleaned the hooch. They had received a security clearance through Vietnamese and military intelligence to work at the base and were for the most part very trustworthy. They were allowed to purchase items from the exchange in limited amounts and spoke minimal English. They even helped us learn some Vietnamese, but the majority of pilots didn't bother to learn more than a few simple phrases, like *dinky-*

dau which means crazy or *didi* which means to hurry up or to run.

The majority of Vietnamese with whom we came into contact spoke English much better than we could ever learn to speak Vietnamese. It wasn't an ugly American thing; it simply wasn't necessary for us to speak Vietnamese.

Our hooch maid, Missy Noa, was an efficient housekeeper and always pleasant. On the rare occasions when she wasn't pleasant, we gave her plenty of room. All of the Vietnamese women were referred to as Missy, Missy this, or Missy that. She was small in stature as were all the Vietnamese. Her teeth were a shiny smooth ebony color, stained from chewing betel nut leaves. She routinely wore shiny black pajamas, though many wore white or lighter-colored clothing and always the traditional conical hat. I never felt quite comfortable in her presence.

Her age was difficult to determine. The Vietnamese women led a hard life and aged early due to agricultural work and the extreme primitive living conditions. Her eyes were always alert. She walked with a shuffle, her wooden sandals clop, clop, clopped against the concrete sidewalk that ran the length of the officers' hooches. She appeared to enjoy her day, cleaning flight suits, polishing boots, visiting and having lunch with the other hooch maids.

Figure 42 Parade of hooch maids

They ate fish, rice, and heavy helpings of Nuoc Mam, a nauseating concoction that was totally Vietnamese. It was a fish sauce, produced by compressing fish and salt into earthenware jars and allowing it to set nine months to a year in direct sunlight. The horrific smell of the sauce permeated the air during the noon lunch hour as the hooch maids met for lunch. But I came to accept this smell as being thoroughly Vietnamese and soon it became almost unnoticeable—meaning you can get used to anything.

The Vietnamese civilians who worked on the base were allowed through the front gate in the morning at 0800 following a close inspection of what they were bringing in, at about 1600 hours they would leave. The clippity-clop of their wooden sandals heralded their retreat back into their village where they would spend another night, surviving. It was like a parade; we called it the parade of the hooch maids.

The daily flight schedule was delivered in a peculiar but necessary manner. Frags requested by MAG-16 at MMAF for the following day were received at the communications bunker where Lt. McCormack worked. Once the squadron Operations Department (that included Gary Rainey) received it, they fit the mission with the pilots and published it. Schedules were delivered to the O' Club and to each hooch by an operations runner.

The runner would enter the hooch, and if like on so many occasions it was either very late or very early in the morning, the hooch was asleep. The scheduled pilot's bunk would be located, and he would be awakened by being simultaneously shaken and having a flashlight shined into his face. The question came fast. "Are you so-and-so?" While partially blinded by the strong light and trying to block that light from your eyes with your hand, the faint outline of a hooded figure with no face was looking down upon you. It was the monsoon season and all it did was rain. The runner would always have on hooded rain gear. We never knew his identity and the hooded silhouette struck me as akin to that of the grim reaper.

At zero dark thirty[62] in our hooch, the worn and sagging door squeaked and scraped in its time worn arc in the concrete floor as it was pushed opened. Ominous footsteps would begin and stop as the hooded runner worked his way down the length of the center aisle, stopping at each poz.[63] Holding the flashlight so he could read the schedule and also see the face of the pilot,

---

[62] "Zero dark thirty" generally means very early morning. Officially, it is 30 minutes after midnight.

[63] POZ is slang for position or location, as in what is your poz? Where your bunk was located could be called your poz. It was a common use term.

he would ask, "You Lieutenant Walker?" "You Lieutenant Prigge?" "You Lieutenant Rainey?" The response was "Yes," or "No," or shaking one's head from side to side or nodding in the affirmative. If the response was "Yes," the flashlight would be redirected from your eyes to the flight schedule and the raspy voice from under the hood would read the mission number and type: resupply, medevac, admin, etc., along with the brief time. All the while you were trying to adjust your eyes to the unexpected light. All I could really get out of that was that I had a flight and to get to the ready room ASAP! Once the grim reaper made his rounds in the hooch, if you were not selected, relief set in and hopefully you were off to sleep once again. As it was oft said, "If you sleep half the time, it cuts your tour of duty in half."

My personal philosophy about flying was taken from some of my flight instructors in HMMT-302, Santa Ana, known as F-Troop. They were combat veterans, and they preached that we must always fly in accordance with the Naval Air Training and Operating Procedures Standardization Program (NATOPS). Some of the instructors just winked at the idea of flying NATOPS in a combat environment, yet, it was NATOPS that guided our every waking moment in pilot training. I was told by one seasoned veteran, "Don't worry about dying, 'cause if it happens, it happens. But don't go hot doggin' and doin' high speed buttonhooks[64] into the zone. Those maneuvers place high stresses on the airframe.

---

[64] The classic buttonhook was entered at cruise speed, (120 kts) and no higher than a hundred feet. Upon approaching the LZ, a high drag turn (the buttonhook) would result in a rapidly decreasing air speed into a landing. It went something like this, approaching the LZ from a direction that allowed you to quickly lower the collective, while raising the nose to maintain altitude (like a low level quick stop)then roll the aircraft into a right bank not exceeding forty-five degrees while applying left rudder to keep the aircraft in balanced flight and roll out on the desired heading substantially increasing the collective. If done correctly the aircraft will be in a position to land, hover or need a CH-53 to take its carcass home. I never tried to do a buttonhook. The risk was not worth it. And, I always believed the maneuver was too much stress on the airframe. Lt. Fred McCorkle however was one of the exceptions who routinely and successfully flew this maneuver.

Remember Station 410?[65] They beefed it up, but who knows for sure it won't happen again. And you're flying a helicopter as big as a billboard and damned near as slow. No amount of twisting and turning can keep a half-decent rifleman from hitting the CH-46 at any point during the approach and takeoff. Remember, you're low and slow, and your belly is exposed when you flare that green monster. Best you worry about flying NATOPS and make the enemy kill you. Don't kill yourself!"

The early morning flights from Phu Bai to MMAF meant a 0300 wake-up, suiting up with the aid of a flashlight to keep from bothering the others lucky enough to be able to sleep. Getting our Nomex flight suits on, putting on heavy socks, slipping into our steel-toed leather flight boots and rain gear (if it was raining), and strapping on our personal sidearm and knife before heading off into the dark rain-soaked night was, in itself, a daunting task. Next was heading to the chow hall or, in my case more often than not, directly to the ready room to ensure the flight was still on and to learn the side number of the aircraft assigned. I wasn't much of a breakfast eater. The ready room coffee, strong enough to walk on, was normally sufficient.

The flight crews and crew chiefs were well ahead of the co-pilot. By the time the copilot got to the maintenance office, checked through the yellow maintenance sheets listing everything done to the bird and began his walk to the helo, the crew chief would have already conducted his very own preflight, readying the aircraft for the Copilot's preflight which would be the second done on the craft before daybreak. Upon completion of the copilot's preflight, it was time for a mission brief from the HAC.

The briefing could be long and intricate, addressing all aspects of the mission, or just "let's build a fire (meaning to start

---

[65] In 1967, CH-46A models were crashing, killing the entire crew, when the aft pylon that contains the engines, main transmission, and aft rotors broke off in flight. The fix was to strengthen a point called station 410. The 46A model, following the necessary modifications that also included more powerful engines, was renamed the CH-46D.

the engine) and get at it." After the crew chief and copilot assured him that the bird was ready to go, the HAC normally made his way to the maintenance office and signed for the aircraft. He then conducted his own walk-around preflight, the third set of eyes on the aircraft. Only then could a launch take place.

The launches during monsoon season were flown under Visual Flight Rules (VFR) into weather so bad I couldn't imagine why we were doing it. When flying due east to the sea, we flew at extremely low altitudes, while being blasted with monsoon rains and fog so thick we depended upon anti-collision lights to maintain separation. We flew so low I believed we could have been hit by the bad guys with a slingshot. Upon reaching the coastline, we turned south keeping the shoreline off our starboard side. It was a treacherous route. The vegetation along the shoreline, being darker than the surrounding fog, rain and seascape, was the only thing resembling a horizon. The radar altimeter in concert with the whitecaps, visible through the all-encompassing gray, kept us out of the water as we cautiously moved south to the Hai Van Pass and into Da Nang Bay.

In contrast, when flying south by way of Highway 1, we stayed on the right side of the highway just like driving a car in the States. The UH-1Hs of the Army's 101st Screaming Eagles and the 82d Airborne made this work for them, and we simply complied. It all worked, no-mid-airs along that route. Many of the Army helicopter pilots were not Instrument Flight Rules (IFR) qualified, or were flying helicopters that weren't equipped with the necessary navigation aids. They flew through everything, occasionally tucking in close to one of our 46s to get through IFR conditions. They were a gutsy lot of 18-, 19- and 20-year-old Warrant Officers (WO1) who were totally fearless.

The reason we didn't go south using IFR was due in part to the Da Nang area being full of military jets and commercial airlines: World Airways, Flying Tigers Charters, and Continental Airlines. In order to get radar contact for a ground-controlled approach into Da Nang, we 46 drivers, speeding along at 120 knots, had to climb into a particular high threat environment saturated by those fast movers—not a good idea.

We had to go through all of this to get to MMAF and on many occasions only to be placed on weather hold for conditions less restrictive than what we had just flown through. That "can-do attitude" exhibited by the HMM-161, 262, and HMLA-367 squadrons at Phu Bai was one of the reasons why the veterans of Quang Tri, Dong Ha, and the associated battles of Tet '68 had an attitude when it came to MMAF. Without saying it, the veteran pilots at Phu Bai considered the squadrons at MMAF as pampered and more stateside-like.

16: First Scheduled Flight

Following a brief period of acclimation, we FNGs were beginning to fly. Skills get rusty. When I learned that I might be on the 14 November flight schedule, it had been six weeks since my last flight in HMMT-302—an eternity. I hardly slept at all the night before. The booming of what was called harassment and inter-diction[66] (H&I) artillery fire by the Army's 105 Howitzers seemed to go on all night. Sometimes the thundering barrages seemed all too close. Was it incoming or outgoing? I didn't know.

I remained in the hooch the night of 13 November, not going to the club. I wrote a letter home telling Kathy that all was well, cleaned my firearms (which now consisted of an M-16 and .45 Auto in addition to my .38 S&W service revolver with the tracer rounds) and played a game of Acey-Ducey[67] with Roy while we waited to greet the operations schedule runner.

Near midnight the schedule runner pushed the door open, allowing the fog and dampness to roll into the hooch like an old Dracula film. Mumbling a few words ending with "sir," he pushed a handful of schedules into my hand. Scouring the document, I quickly learned that I was indeed scheduled. It was a 0500 takeoff with Maj. Whitfield, the XO, which meant that I had to get to the ready room at least an hour or more beforehand. Setting my college-worn travel clock for a 0300 wake up...three hours to sleep...I dozed some, unable to go entirely to sleep.

After a half hour of tossing and turning I gave up on sleep, turned off the alarm, gathered up my flight gear and stumbled into the common area, careful not to let the light from that room

---

[66] Harassment and Interdiction firing was artillery strikes (normally by 105 Howitzers around the Phu Bai military complex). The purpose was to deny the enemy freedom of movement and to destroy enemy morale.

[67] Acey-Ducey is a board game played by two opponents on a playing board with fifteen checkers and a pair of dice. There was hardly a hooch, bar or ready room in the Marine Corps that didn't have an Acey-Ducey game board lying around. During the long hours of monsoon season, the board was in perpetual use.

streak into the bunk area where Roy and Gary were competing for who could snore the loudest.

I donned my flight suit and boots, strapped on my firearm, pulled on my rain gear, placed the rain hood over my head, grabbed my flashlight, then headed out into the thick fog and drizzling rain. With my head slightly bowed, watching each step, I tried unsuccessfully to avoid the soupy red mud holes that were everywhere in the camp. The H&I firing by the Army's 105 Howitzer crews was still going on. It created what I thought of as a symphony composed of dozens of bass kettledrums mimicking rolling thunder.

I suppose the Army's XXIV Corps was extra concerned on such nights, when you couldn't see more than a few feet in front of you. Mr. Charles[68] could have been walking along the same road and neither of us would have known the other was there. As I walked, I wondered what my first day in the Vietnamese air would bring. If the fog didn't clear, I presumed we'd be doing a special instrument takeoff.[69]

The scent of the area at that early hour was distinct. There was the strong musty smell of old sandbags and mildew, not as noticeable in daylight hours. The smells of powdered eggs, cardboard bacon and strong coffee flowed from the chow hall, along with the distant cacophony of artillery sounds that carry further in the night air. It was surreal to actually be in Vietnam.

I didn't know the chow hall would be open that early. It may have been the last of the midnight rations called *mid-rats*[70] provided to those mechanics who work all night long, never see the sun, and without whom we'd never meet the needs of the flight

[68] The Viet Cong was referred to in the phonetic alphabet as "Victor" "Charlie" (VC). The North Vietnamese Army regular was referred to as NVA and called "Mr. Charles" by those from the 3d Marine Division who fought the NVA in those epic battles before redeployment and Vietnamization.

[69] A special instrument takeoff is a takeoff without sanction from a clearing authority, i.e. an FAA or similar authority. The takeoff could be performed by the aircraft commander if the weather was below minimums for a normal takeoff and the aircraft commander held a Special Instrument Rating.

[70] Mid-rats or "midnight rations" are meals for Marines on a midnight shift, mainly maintenance and medevac crews and security guard details.

schedule. They were the unsung heroes of the endless days in Vietnam.

Nervous and anxious, I was ready to get into the air. An old saying goes, "The more you fly, the more you want to fly." Oddly enough, the reverse was also true, "The less you fly, the less you want to fly." It would seem that saying was perpetuated by someone who had chronic air sickness, but it was true to an extent. Getting back on your horse or bicycle quickly following a fall goes right along with not staying out of the cockpit too long. We new guys all needed to get back into the sky.

My pace quickened the closer I came to the squadron offices, making my way to the ready room. I needed to see the big schedule board on the wall that was always being worked on by Operations. I needed to see if there were any changes. There were no changes for me. As I was scheduled with the XO, I knew I had to do this right...by the book, which was really the only way I knew how to do it.

I made my way to the squadron pilot's cubby-holes along the wall in the ready room where pilots kept their flight gear. I located the one with my rank and name embossed onto a strip of red label-maker tape. I checked to see if everything was still there: my new red Naugahyde helmet bag inside of which was my helmet, knee board, a small clipboard with note-size paper configured to fit on the leg just above the knee (your work station where you kept the raw data that would go into your AA report), my Nomex flight gloves that I normally kept in the zippered pocket on the lower leg of my flight suit when not flying, making them easy to get to or put away; and the frequency booklet that contained the most important items in any flight, especially for a copilot. It was full of classified frequencies, call signs, routes of flight, weights associated with known resupply items and technical data on the CH-46D that you might never use, but was available if necessary.

My survival vest and radio and the all-important bullet bouncer were also stuffed inside the cubicle. We could actually get all of this stuff in those cubicles 1'sq., 14" deep. I grabbed my new red Naugahyde helmet bag and made the short walk to the maintenance hangar. It was time to review the yellow sheets that contained the maintenance history of the aircraft we were assigned, ET 153956.

The maintenance records, legal documents, that tell the history of each aircraft were maintained in the area we called the maintenance shack, even though, it was simply a small room off the main hangar. Off to one side was Capt. David White, a man of few words who was all business and whose background in this war ran deep.

As I reviewed those yellow sheets, I was seeing the war's activity in the life of our assigned 46. The metal benders[71] had patched dozens of bullet holes throughout its past and replaced the blades, damaged by gunfire at different times. The avionics (electronics) department had also made it their hobby. But on that specific day, at that specific time, most of the gripes[72] had been dressed and signed off as ready to fly, except for some that were addressed with the ominous words *"could not duplicate and/or next pilot check* or even worse, *ground checks good.*[73]*"*

I walked down the center of the taxiway that ran between the revetments. As I approached the aircraft in the still drizzly night and fog, I walked up on the crew chief completing his morning preflight ritual. He assured me that everything was in order as we addressed the open items carrying the title of *next pilot check* and *cannot duplicate.*

---

[71] Metal bender is slang for a Structural Mechanic who knows patching techniques for damages, including bullet holes in the aircraft.

[72] Gripe is a slang term used when addressing concerns a pilot has regarding any kind of issue associated with the aircraft. The gripe is written on a form that traditionally was yellow, thus a yellow sheet, and is presented to the appropriate maintenance department for review and correction. A "downing gripe" is a serious matter that must be resolved before the aircraft could be scheduled to fly.

[73] "Ground Checks Good" or "could not duplicate," or "next pilot check" were responses to gripes that raised concerns for pilots. Sometimes, there's an unusual vibration in the flight controls or a brief RPM surge, or a bad feeling, whatever. It was something unknown and something unknown could kill you.

The preflight ritual is an eyes-on process, two sets of eyes go over everything, the crew chief and the copilot and on occasion the HAC, too.

The process begins by doing a walk-around looking for any obvious problems, like your first look at a used car. Then, enter the helicopter by the rear ramp, normally covered with a slippery layer of engine oil, which is normal for the 46. Moving from the rear of the cabin/cargo bay toward the cockpit, I placed my survival vest and bullet bouncer on the red nylon pull-down bench seats that were along each side of the aircraft and moved toward the cockpit. Crouching or almost kneeling in the small walkway tunnel opening into the cockpit between the electronic and hydraulic closet areas, I conducted a visual inspection of the cockpit area, primarily to ensure all the circuit breakers were in their correct position. A couple of circuit breakers were pulled and wired so they couldn't be pushed into the console. After ensuring all the circuit-breakers were in their proper position, I took the copilot seat, plugged the pigtail on the helmet into the helo's intercom system (ICS) placed my helmet on my head and flipped the battery switch to on. The radios had to be thoroughly checked. A bad primary radio problem (avionics) would be an immediate downing gripe to be addressed before the craft would be given an "UP" for flight status. I made sure all the radios were in working order by conducting a radio check with the Phu Bai tower, UHF 241.0, "Phu Bai tower, Chatterbox radio check."

"Loud and clear Chatterbox" came a heavily accented Vietnamese voice.

"Roger that, thanks."

Then, check the navigation instruments (navaids). Dial channel 69 into the TACAN navigation aid at Phu Bai. Check the direction measuring equipment (DME) that gives both the bearing and nautical miles to the station, a short distance away. It all checked good. But, with the fog and drizzle not letting up, it was becoming apparent that an early morning launch, as scheduled, was questionable at best. Even though we were all instrument-rated pilots, flying in instrument conditions in the U.S. was one thing. Flying on instruments in Vietnam was quite another. I learned most of the veteran 46 pilots didn't trust the navaids in Vietnam, except when there was no other way to get home. I was told most of the instrument flight time logged by the pilots was simulated, like Ground Controlled Approaches into Marble Mountain on a clear day. To be in actual instrument conditions would be easy enough, just punch into the clouds at 500 feet and flail about, but that didn't often happen, because there were jets in those clouds too.

Stories exist of CH-46s flying in the mountainous western regions of Vietnam near the Laotian border, running into what we called inadvertent (unexpected) IFR conditions. In those instances, the pilots try to climb to altitudes that let them clear the highest peaks in the area and head east toward the sea in order to descend below the cloud coverage. In some instances, 46 drivers were known to pop into a cloud layer when taking fire from AAA, moving out of the area as quick as possible. In those instances, both HAC and copilot work as a team, one flying, the other communicating with known clearance agencies and artillery (Arty) control stations. On occasion, an Army Huey would hug in tight with a 46, like a pilot fish next to a shark, to be led through the IFR conditions.[74] Or, as I was told, when coming out of the A Shau Valley, enemy tracer rounds light the way for you. Either way, I found all of the radios worked as advertised, there and then, in the revetments at the base. Who knew what would work when you needed it.

The exterior preflight was a different matter. Climbing to the top of the helicopter to check the fore and aft rotor heads,

[74] All naval aviators are instrument qualified which extends the training period before being designation as a naval aviator. The Army, during the Vietnam Conflict needed hundreds more helicopter pilots than the Marine Corps. and they pumped them out in the fastest way possible. They were not trained in instrument flying before going to Vietnam. There were designated Instrument pilots in the Army who led groups of helos through IFR conditions into and out of combat, but on occasion that system didn't work. On occasion they would hug in tight to a CH-46 as they both made their way through the goo. Flying in the lowlands, in the Da Nang area, there was much less chance to be caught in inadvertent IFR.

sync shaft and blades, required a walk on top of the 46. Doing that walk during a dark and rainy night was probably the most dangerous thing you could do outside of being shot at by Charlie, which was probably equal in probability of death.

The fore and aft rotor heads, the synchronization (sync) shaft, and hanger bearings had to be inspected for discolorations and loose fittings. As I carefully made my trip back and forth along the wet and slippery centerline of the aircraft, I found nothing to make me think the aircraft was not in good working order. I felt we could, based upon the current weather, file a tower to tower flight plan and go on instruments. I was excited to think we might do that. I kinda wanted to experience an instrument approach into Da Nang. It'd be a red letter day for my flying career. I was ready and upon completing the outside inspection, I reentered the cockpit to get my knee board for the anticipated preflight brief, leaving my survival vest and bullet bouncer in the red canvas seats with my helmet hanging above the copilot's seat on a hook provided for that purpose. With my knee board in hand, I walked back through the rain to the ready room feeling that I had accomplished a thorough preflight.

I found a seat in the ready room, pulled out the instrument approach for Da Nang, and waited. The time passed slowly as the squadron struggled to come to life: 0400, then 0430, then 0500. Finally, the XO strolled into the ready room wearing rain gear with a hood over a vintage beige-colored navy flight suit, a large bowie knife on his side. The flight suit was not the green Nomex as was now required by the Marine Corps. I didn't think anything of it, except to briefly wonder where he got the beige flight suit. That suit might have been from when he first became a naval aviator. Word was that the XO was a graduate from the Air Force Academy and chose the Corps over the Air Force. Old flight suits were cool, and it was considered a myth that Nomex would protect you from fire. I didn't recall any Nomex flight suit protecting anyone from fire. But, I also recognized that altering flight gear was acceptable, regarding unit patches, etc.

* * *

When I first arrived in Pensacola in March 1968, the old orange flight suits had been recently replaced with the green Nomex flame retardant flight suit. We student naval aviators who had admired the Marine Corps' naval aviation recruiting posters in which the pilot was standing next to an F-8 Crusader, known as "The Last Gunfighter." We purchased the old orange flight suits from a local Army-Navy store in P'Cola. We couldn't wear the suits, but it was neat to have them.

* * *

I met the XO, by introducing myself. "Good morning, Sir. I'm Lieutenant Walker," I said with as much enthusiasm as I could muster. I was certain he had no idea who I was.

"How's the helicopter?" was his response.

"It's good, Sir. I've completed my preflight."

With no additional brief, I walked with the XO to the maintenance office where he briefly spoke to Capt. White while asking for the maintenance book on the helo. He flipped through the yellow sheets, occasionally pausing to read certain entries, before returning to the ready room. I followed.

Up to this moment there was no discussion by the XO as to the mission—nothing. No "Let's go brief," "Let's check weather," no nothing. I was nervous but tried to appear calm when another pilot appeared in the ready room. I didn't recognize him, but he appeared to be a senior officer. He had that easy self-confident stroll I'd come to recognize as that of a seasoned combat veteran. His helmet bag was tossed over his shoulder like he was flying that morning. I thought nothing of it.

First Lieutenant Gene Tolls, a tough-as-nails veteran combat pilot and one of the top flyers in the squadron, ambled over to greet the man. "Mornin' Colonel..."

So, the stranger was a colonel. Could that have been full Colonel, or Lieutenant Colonel? I didn't have a clue.

Tolls added with an air of familiarity, "How ya doing this fine morning?"

"So far, so good," responded the "colonel" with a smile as he shook a cigarette out of its pack and lit it with a flick of his Zippo.

"Love the nice weather you got up here," said the Colonel as cigarette smoke flowed from his nose and mouth, "reminds me of '65." Both men laughed. The colonel coughed.

Up here? It was apparent this colonel wasn't from Phu Bai. He had to be from Marble Mountain or 1st MAW headquartered in Da Nang, or III MAF. I heard they had colonels running over each other up there. Then I looked at the big schedule board and saw my name was being replaced with the name Mann. I had been scheduled just to preflight the XO's bird. The realization swept over me that this was not going to be my first flight in Vietnam.

The XO barely looked at me, said, "Thanks," then turned his back and continued talking with the colonel. I wondered which one of them was to be the copilot. My first scheduled mission in Vietnam was over for the day. I went back to the helicopter, gathered my gear and returned it all to my cubby-hole.

Disappointment was all I felt, and a little anger at being used as their servant. Rank has its privileges, I suppose, and I was just an FNG. That day, I decided, I would spend time with the guys in the paraloft, get to know them better . As I walked in, Sgt. Patton was working on a helmet. I grabbed some coffee and made myself at home. It was time to check things out in the hangar.

On November 15, the following day, HMM-161 CO Maj. R.W. Carr was relieved of command by LtCol Benny Mann (First Helicopter Pilot Navy Cross recipient). The Marine Col. who took my place the day before. Mystery solved.

* * *

Note: I had arrived in Phu Bai on 11Nov69 to begin my year of living dangerously. However, as an FNG, I was not viscerally connected to the squadron. I knew no one but those who came with me and the results of that were that we didn't know anything about what was going on. I'll simply recite some of the November 1969 Squadron chronology available through Texas Tech.

THE GROTTO – BOOK ONE | 147

The period of 1-30 November 1969 marked a transition from support of the 3d MarDiv to the 1st MarDiv. Increased enemy activity in the new area of operations [Da Nang] resulted in a substantial increase in fire incidents, and battle damage to six HMM-262 aircraft. Heavy rains and low ceilings continued to hamper flight operations, and resulted in reduced flight hours once again."

And:

On 17Nov69, "Chatterbox 7 [First Lieutenant Don Esmond, HAC and First Lieutenant Tom Reid, copilot] was called out on an emergency medevac in the ROK Marine area (BT219494). The aircraft sustained approximately 24 hits resulting in one crewman, the crew chief, Cpl. Thomas Franklin Rogers, age 24 from Spencer, Tennessee instantly killed when one .30 cal round entered his chest near his heart.

Rogers was well liked in the squadron and was one of the men who barbered, J.J. Hall being the other barber in the squadron.

Lt. Esmond was wounded, treated and released. Sgt. McReynolds a .50 cal. gunner received life threatening wounds and was hospitalized for the better part of a year with wounds from a .30 cal rounds that hit his jaw, tore into his stomach and ripped into his leg. LCpl L. Strickland, a .50 cal gunner was wounded, treated and released and credited with killing six attacking NVA/VC. The copilot, First Lieutenant Tom Reid, was the only one to come through it unscathed.

The crew of Chatterbox 7 was rescued by First Lieutenant William "Babs" Babcock and his copilot First Lieutenant Robert Lloyd. The helicopter was recovered, repaired and back in the air within days.

I had been in the squadron six days when the first Marine from our squadron, in my tour, was killed. My eyes became less wide. It was going to be a long year.

Figure 43 Corporal Thomas F. Rogers

17: First Real Flight

(November, 1969 flight hours: 19.8)

On 18 November 1969, following the bloody day before, I once again found my name on the flight schedule for a 0800 takeoff. My innermost thoughts were of what happened the day before. How did they get shot to pieces? I learned that they were on the deck when it happened and that the .50 cal. gunners were keeping the enemy at bay. I wanted to know more about what happened, but, it was time for me to prepare for my first *real* flight; or would it be just another preflight. My concerns about the squadron being shut down and sent out of country remained constant. The rumors remained rampant, but with this coming flight, at least, I would have one red ink[75] Vietnam mission in my log book.

First Lieutenant Ken Boyack, the HAC with whom I was scheduled, was a quiet guy and a Silver Star recipient. However, I was feeling rustier and less sure of myself due in part to my last for-real flight being in HMMT-302 now 46 days ago. I recognized that my job was to learn my job—to be a copilot—and that phase of my existence would last until I could become a HAC.

To be a HAC you must have a total of 500 hours and pass a check-ride with a senior aircraft commander, like the CO, XO or NATOPS officer. Like most helicopter pilots that went through the west coast training squadron, I had only the minimum hours required to become an H2p (certified copilot). In my case, I had a total of 333.3 total flight hours when I arrived in Vietnam, 167.7 hours to go.

Some copilots came to Vietnam with more than 400 hours. They, for the most part, were from the 2dMAW at New River,

---

[75] Red ink was used in our flight log books to denote combat missions. Later in life, a log book full of red ink was something special and remains so.

North Carolina and had been on a six month cruise[76] before getting orders to Vietnam. Many of those copilots were light years ahead of us west coast types due to their experience aboard ships.

Our designation as an H2p was sufficient to conduct an in-depth preflight, take off and land in good weather and light winds. Becoming a real combat-qualified copilot in a squadron like HMM-262 was more like being a prospect in an outlaw motorcycle gang. You had to take care of the edges of flying: preflighting; keeping notes on all of the activities of the day, learning the distinctive communications in that wartime environment and all the while, "skillfully monitoring the instruments."

I considered my previous preflighting for the XO, however disgusting it was to me, to be a part of that world in which I wanted to belong. If you performed well, a benevolent HAC might let you get some stick time. If you attained 500 total hours in the 46, and if the HACs had total confidence in your ability to handle situations thrown your way, then and only then, would you get the opportunity to have a HAC check conducted by one of the senior officers. If you did well, you would be invited into their brotherhood and allowed to wear the colors.

The early wakeup on the morning of 18 November 1969 went okay, or as we were learning to say, "as per usual." I got up, dressed, and once again walked out into the heavy, almost suffocating humidity of the Vietnamese night. Being a fan of the old horror movies and mysteries, the eerie lighting effect on condensed water droplets made me think of the gaslights of old London and the stories of Jack the Ripper, The Wolfman, and Dracula. The rounds of the hooded schedule runner in this atmosphere enhanced the effect.

[76] Helicopter Aircraft Carriers were identified by the letters, LPH (Landing Platform Helicopter). Examples of that type of ship were the USS Tripoli (west coast),and the Iwo Jima, Okinawa, Guadalcanal and Guam (East Coast). They carried a full Battalion Landing Team that included helicopters and a detachment of Marines. The LPHs were constantly on cruise throughout the world, waiting for the next hot spot.

The ground was quivering from what felt like low grade earthquakes caused by the Army's H&I artillery. During my years of growing up on the farm in Southeast Missouri, I had become accustomed to feeling the low grade earthquakes emanating from the New Madrid fault line, which in the early 1811/12 era had generated the great earthquake that caused the Mississippi River to run upstream for more than a day. I was still too new to this environment to know for sure what was and what wasn't incoming mortar rounds or rocketry. I figured I'd wait to see if anyone else ran to a shelter, and if they did, maybe it was the real thing.

A memory that came to me gave me some relief from my indecision about the thundering barrage. While I was at Santa Ana, I recalled a conversation between the flight instructors who were just back from Vietnam. One of them, talking about a particularly difficult time at Dong Ha or Quang Tri when those locations were under attack by mortars and/or rockets, said, "If you had to think about whether it was incoming or not, it wasn't." But...I still wasn't so sure.

But on that one occasion, when I was about ready to head to one of the bunkers whether anyone else was doing it or not, the booming stopped. Whew...I thought, I just about made a fool of myself; as some would say, better dead than to do that.

Arriving at the mess hall, I found a group standing outside the closed doors, waiting for breakfast. I stood to one side and waited, taking up time with small talk among the pilots. It was interesting conversation; the talk was about the rumors of when units were returning to the states, reemphasizing to me what LtCol. Moriarty told my group when we checked into MAG-16 at MMAF, "Don't unpack!" was the unwritten message. I was more than ready to get into the air. With even one mission in-country, I would have red ink in my flight log book.[77]

---

[77] An actual mission, not an administrative flight, was always logged into our flight log books in red ink. To have a book full of red ink was a prize to be acknowledged.

I scooped up some powdered eggs and cardboard bacon and washed down the morsels with hot black coffee (no sugar or cream, too much trouble) and darted back through the door into the night that was turning to dawn.

Making my way past the Montagnards' barracks, even though it was early morning, I watched for any threat from the knife throwers. I was lucky. They were nowhere to be seen. Approaching the squadron offices, I stopped off first at the paraloft shop. Someone from the crew was always there.

Lucky again. Sgt. Patton was there and had coffee percolating. Patton was a country boy like me. He was from North Carolina. The smell of coffee and fresh-cut Naugahyde was a new smell for me. It filled the air. After checking to see if I had any mail, (I had none. I hadn't been there long enough to get mail) I headed for the ready room, greeting Wags, who was coming up the stairs to the paraloft. We passed each other on the staircase as I was descending to the main floor of the hangar.

"Wags," I said. "anything I should know?"

Wags nodded a greeting and said, "Nothing much happening. Oh yes, we're missing a Staff Sergeant, but meet me in the club tonight and I'll go over a few items."

"What Staff Sergeant?"

"Never mind, I'll tell you tonight."

"I have my first flight today."

"With who?" he asked, with seemingly genuine interest.

"Boyack?" I blurted out.

"Good," he said and turned to continue up the staircase. He then paused, turned back towards me and said, "He's a good guy, not an asshole like some."

"That's good to know," I responded.

Then, Wags added, "He was shot down a while ago by AAA, bad shit, and crashed into a river."

"No kidding?"

"No kidding," Wags responded. "Get this...he had to keep from drowning...get out of the helicopter and keep the Major with whom he was flying, who couldn't swim, from drowning.. Ha...Have a good flight."

I really wanted to learn more about Boyack's shoot-down, and I hoped I would be able to talk at length with Wags that night, maybe even talk with Boyack, too, depending on how the flight went.

The squadron area was still quiet, but coming to life. The ODO (Operations Duty Officer) was First Lieutenant Chuck Fleischer.

Figure 44 First Lieutenant Ken Boyack

Like all ODOs, he was in his t-shirt, standing by the big schedule board with a marker pen in one hand, a phone in the other, and a lead pencil tucked behind his ear, dealing with last-minute matters and making minute adjustments to the flight schedule as necessary.

I double-checked the scheduling board and verified my flight. I asked Fleischer, who had just put down the phone and was busy with another issue, "Is this a real flight or am I just doing the preflight?"

Fleischer looked up from his paperwork and with some irritation and his patented smirk, said "Whataya mean, flying or preflighting...what the f**k else would you be doing...?" then turned back to his work before I could answer.

Figure 45 First Lieutenant Chuck Fleischer, taken from the HMM-262 1969-70 cruise book.

Not comfortable with Fleischer's flippant response, I more accurately stated my concern. "I just want to know for sure. My last first flight I had, I was the duty preflighter for the XO, and no flying."

"Really...?" he smiled, like he enjoyed that...then, his patented smirk. "Well, not today, you're flying."

The flight had a flight purpose code of 1R4 (Administrative/SAR/VIP). We'd be flying for the Republic of Korea (ROK) Marine Corps the famous Camp of the Blue Dragon, south of MMAF who came to I Corps in the fall of 1966. It was indeed going to be a real first flight.

Feeling much better, I retrieved my flight gear and made my way from the ready room back to the bright lights of the maintenance hangar, which had come alive. The smells of hydraulic fluid and engine oil, mixed with the soulful lyrics of Jimi Hendrix' "Purple Haze" emanating from a portable radio or tape player near where some metal benders were working on a piece of fuselage, patching bullet holes—imagery I would not soon forget.

It began raining again.

Crew chiefs, gunners, and last-minute maintenance issues were being attended to before the yellow sheets could be signed off. Capt. White was going over a pile of documents with Capt. "Buzz" Verbanik,[78] who was in charge of quality control and our paraloft. He was a tough-looking Marine who could have cut his teeth with Chesty at the Chosin.[79] He was holding a handful of

---

[78] Capt Buzz Verbanik was a mustang (prior-enlisted)Captain who was well respected. He loved to play handball and during the next few days following my first flight, he was medevaced out of the country due to being hit in the eye with a speeding racket ball. He was the only person to whom I reported. The paraloft following Verbanik was functioning as an independent entity.
[79] The Battle of Chosin Reservoir was fought during the Korean War (1950-53). The fighting around Chosin Reservoir was 26 November to 11 December 1950. Col. "Chesty" Puller played a key role. When surrounded at the Chosin Reservoir, Chesty said, "All right. They're in front of us, they're behind us...they can't get away this time."

documents. Verbanik and White always gave me confidence that everything was as it should be.

I conducted the standard reviews, making mental notes of the last few gripes and paying particular attention to the "cannot duplicates" before conducting my preflight of the bird. After the standard preflight, during which I found no problems, Boyack appeared to conduct his own preflight, and as I watched he gave it a good going over too—I was beginning to see that the combat vets who had survived to near their full tour always conducted their own preflight—or, since I was so new that trust had not been built as yet. I returned to the ready room with Boyack, who was friendly and easy to talk to.

After his briefing we were on our way to MMAF. At 0800, after a short weather hold, we were finally off. I was leaving Phu Bai as a bona fide, certified, exemplified copilot for the first time. I couldn't have been more proud of myself.

The process of learning how to fly in Vietnam had begun in earnest. I learned about obtaining clearances from artillery missions along routes we would be flying. There were two routes we could have used going south. One way was to go "feet wet" over the sea, retracing the route Lt. Dau had taken when I arrived eight days before.

The optional route, the one we would end up taking south that day, was straight down Highway 1 at about 100 feet AGL or less, offset to the right, like driving a truck. Flying at that level was always dangerous. There was the very real possibility that some trigger-happy Victor Charlie would take a shot at you, and he would have to be a relatively bad shot to miss something as big as an eighteen wheeler at tree top level (only a slight exaggeration).

An array of military vehicles clogged Highway 1. Armored cavalry assault vehicles, each one with a .50 cal. machine gun, augmented by two M60s protected by massive shields both led and followed six-by cargo trucks filled with supplies. Intermixed in the bodies of the convoys were gun trucks, six-by cargo trucks outfitted with sandbagged gun emplacements. The convoys contained up to two hundred vehicles, occupying miles of highway. Armored personnel carriers could also be observed, along with the M48 Patton Tanks in use by both the Marine Corps and the Army. Vietnamese farmers and their water buffalo walked the shoulder of the highway with carts full of produce going to a market; I supposed. Yet, I never saw a farmer's market, only simple roadside stands with a mamasan clearly in charge.

Arriving at the Hai Van Pass, we followed the snake-like route up, over and down into Da Nang Harbor. We crossed Da Nang Bay north to south at approximately six feet AGL with the radar altimeter bouncing on zero and wove ourselves into the mouth of the Song Han River, avoiding the fast movers (jet traffic) leaving and entering the Da Nang Air Base. Boyack called MMAF tower on UHF 281.2. We were cleared to enter a left downwind for Runway 35, a route I would fly hundreds of times in the coming year. He called out the 180 and was cleared to land. Requesting a left-off[80] at center field, we parked at the fuel pits to top off the fuel.

I was nervous as a T-28 flight student on a check-ride. I couldn't help but consider each flight a check-ride since I had been grilled and judged on procedures during each flight since my first training flight in a Beechcraft T-34B Mentor at Saufley Field on 5 July 1968. It was a difficult mental transition to feeling like a fully qualified copilot. Even knowing I was now a member of the team, I still suffered from the post-student syndrome. I was trying so hard not to screw up that I must have been robot-like. This was my first opportunity to fly as a squadron copilot, and I didn't want Boyack to sense any weakness in me.

Watching Boyack flying the craft, revealed the ease and confidence he had while flying. I envied his poise. He made the clearance calls, allowing me to learn, and to my surprise, treated me as an equal, actually allowing me stick time. It was a safe admin

---

[80] "left off" or "right off" at a particular taxiway was a request to the tower that you wanted to leave the runway and to which side you wanted to go.

flight. However, my attention was drawn to the countryside, getting a sense of the different areas in which I would be flying. The area south of Da Nang along the coast was primarily the responsibility of the ROK Marines. The Que Son Mountains were within the responsibility of the 7th Marines who were headquartered at Baldy.

Liberty Bridge, Go Noi Island, Arizona Territory, and the Thuong Duc corridor were in the backyard of the 5th Marines headquartered at An Hoa, an old French military base. The views were hypnotic. The land was exotic, beautiful, and frightening, all at the same time. It was magically alluring, as if I was watching a TV back home in Missouri and not actually here.

I steadily learned that the most important aspect of flying as a copilot in Vietnam was to know your role, shut your mouth, and be a good recorder of events. How many sorties[81], from where to where, what were the grid coordinates, how many passengers were carried, how much cargo was carried? Listen to instructions from the clearing agencies, be prepared to dial in the proper frequencies, obtain azimuths[82] of artillery missions passing through the different TAORs. Quick plot the artillery coordinates from where to where and stay under the arc of the trajectory, or find an alternative route around the artillery mission. Know exactly where you are at all times. Learn the names of the different clearing agencies. Always obtain clearance and be familiar with direct air support control (DASC) agencies: Da Nang DASC when entering the Da Nang TAOR; Gia Le Arty, to be called upon when entering the Phu Bai/Hue TAOR, and Red Devil Arty that controlled the Quang Tri/Dong Ha area.

---

[81] A sortie was a movement of the aircraft from point A to B. Helicopters flew hundreds of sorties. For example, a resupply mission could require several sorties to resupply a position. Each sortie was recorded on an AA report. Twenty sorties equaled one air medal.

[82] An azimuth is a direction. When identifying artillery missions to a pilot, he wants to know from where to where (the azimuth) and at what altitude the artillery shell will take.

There were a vast number of frequencies available to the flight crew, and when briefing a new pilot it was the responsibility of the HAC to ensure the copilot had a general idea of what frequencies to expect. At the end of the day, we returned to Phu Bai/Hue, north along Highway 1. I was allowed to fly the entire re-entry into Phu Bai; the first stick time I'd had since leaving the training command. I was careful to stay approximately 1,000 meters to the right of the road and approximately 1500 AGL—much higher than the altitude we'd flown when leaving Phu Bai. At approximately five miles south of Phu Bai/Hue, off of TACAN Channel 69, Boyack dialed in 241.0—the Phu Bai Tower— and requested clearance to land.

Boyack pointed out that the Army's XXIV Corps and the 101st Airborne were situated west of the highway and urged me to take extra precautions when coming into the Phu Bai/Hue traffic area. The 101st seemed to have an overwhelming number of Hueys and small observation helicopters, but they did not land or take off at the Phu Bai/Hue airstrip. They were taking off and landing in their own area. It was always rush hour along Highway 1. Helicopter traffic in the air—Army, Marine, and Vietnamese. Everyone's head had to be on a swivel. The crew chief, knowing I was new, took particular notice of the airspace on my side of the helicopter, calling out the position of other aircraft, "Three o'clock, our level, closing fast." Information was coming in to me in rapid Marine speak. The key to survival in that traffic jam in the sky was immediate reaction to information received.

We received clearance to land on Runway 27. Closer to the airstrip, we heard the tower clear a section of HMM-161 46s to enter a right downwind for 27. We were directed to follow the pair in a modified left base off Highway 1. I announced to Lt. Boyack it was time to perform the landing checklist, really not much to do on a fixed gear helicopter.

"Cargo ramp, check,"

"Shoulder harness, locked."

"Crew, checked."

"Landing check complete."

18: King Bee

With Phu Bai dead ahead, I had begun reducing power about one mile out in order to enter a smooth 500 foot-per-minute flight-school descent. At the quarter-mile point, and at about six hundred feet, I felt the approach thus far was flawless. The section of HMM-161 46s that preceded us had landed and were clearing the duty with a right-off onto the second taxiway, announcing, "Tower, Cattlecall, going ground." I was set up for a turning base acknowledgement to the tower when from out of nowhere the excited voice of a tower operator with a thick Vietnamese accent, ordered us to do an IMMEDIATE 360.

Seeing the 46s taxiing to their line, Boyack, the crew chief and I were looking for the traffic called by the tower. I did as instructed and without delay entered into a banking left turn as the crew chief called out, clear left. I completed the turn away from the runway, still unaware of the exact position of our unidentified traffic.

"Traffic at our eight," the crew chief called out. "Hell Sir, it's King Bee."

"What the hell is King Bee?" I blurted out.

"Remember this moment," said Boyack. "Their call sign is "King Bee" and it's the damnedest thing you'll ever see. That's the South Vietnamese Air Force, and they wait for no one."

Completing the 360 degree circle and rolling back onto our original course, I saw the flight of three Sikorsky H-34s at various points in the landing profile.

I later learned that King Bee pilots were real showboats and probably the best H-34 pilots in the world. They paid little attention to directions from the tower and would come and go as they pleased. Rather than King Bee responding to the tower operators, the tower operators were forced to keep up with King Bee's movements and warn other aircraft to get out of their way. Their armament was an M-60 machine gun, locked and loaded at all times, even on the deck, and the pilots would bail out of their 34s before the blades stopped turning—a cardinal sin in the helicopter world. But probably their rotor brakes burned out years before.

They worked with Military Action Command Vietnam (MACV) – Studies and Observation Group (SOG), taking the Montagnards to and from Laos, Cambodia, etc. in the dangerous business of harassing the NVA traffic up and down the Ho Chi Minh trail.

* * *

I had learned early in my flight training at VT-2 Whiting Field, Millington, Florida (August 1968 – December 1968), to keep an eye open for the Vietnamese pilots. There was a large contingent of Vietnamese pilots going through the syllabus. One of my first instructions was to watch for the Vietnamese and Laotian flight students. They were small people, and we Americans were giants among them. In the T-28, during engine run up, prior to take off, when the power of the R-1820 Cyclone 9-cylinder radial engine 1425 brake horsepower was checked, there was such a thing as "creep." The power run-up primarily consists of setting the parking brake, advancing the fuel mixtures to enrich them, and advancing the throttle to 1500 RPM. At my body weight of about 205 pounds I felt it took all my strength, standing on the brakes with my upper back and shoulders jammed against the seat just to hold the beast as it shook and shivered for the brief time required to check the prop, magnetos, and nacelles (openings in the engine cover).

The small physique of the Vietnamese pilots during these moments of the run up could be overwhelmed, which would allow the T-28 to creep forward into the taxiway on which other aircraft were taxiing to the duty runway for takeoff. You had to be ready to stop taxiing and let them wander around until they pulled the throttle back to idle.

* * *

I had to take my eyes off King Bee and concentrate on the few remaining moments of the flight. I touched down on the runway, transitioned into a slow taxi, and requested a right off onto the Marston matting near 262's maintenance line. The matting was slick as usual during the monsoon season. The old 46 swung back and forth as it swaggered slowly to the revetment indicated by the ground crew.

The flight was over, and I drew a sigh of relief. Reading off the shutdown checklist, expecting a formal response to the challenge and reply items, I only heard myself. Boyack's hands went through the checklist as if he were shutting down the family sedan. He didn't miss an item all the way down to, "batt…off."

I removed my helmet and sweat dripped down my forehead into my eyes, burning them. The unmistakable sound of the electronics closet and the gyros winding down seemed much louder than I recalled from HMMT-302. The engines were shutdown but still snapping and crackling as the super-heated metal cooled.

The crew chief was busy unbuttoning the engine doors and using a rag to mop up the hot oil that dripped onto the flooring. The metallic sounds of the big .50s being pulled from their mounts and long links of .50 cal. rounds being shoved back into their ammo boxes heralded the end of the flight. The sounds of shutdown were reassuring, and I had a great feeling of relief.

Seated in the left seat, I noted the shutdown time on my knee board and waited until Boyack cleared the cockpit. He moved cautiously through the tunnel-like passageway into the cabin section where he stopped to talk with the crew chief. I soon followed, crawling through the tunnel, bypassing the crew door in order to walk the 24.5 ft. length of the 46's cabin, committing sight and smells to memory. The engines were still making that popping sound and the sight of red hydraulic fluid, the life blood of the 46, mixed with the grit and grime of engine oil that covered the surface of the ramp provided further evidence the day was done.

Having been raised with horses, I couldn't help but recognize similarities between the 46 being placed in its revetment, and the crew tending to its needs as I had done with my horse,

Rebel, before turning him out to pasture following a good workout. I knew the history of that aircraft from the yellow sheets that read like a patient in intensive care. I knew it had scars from hard battles and had seen death and destruction. I also knew it carried its crew back to base after each fight and would be ready to do the same thing tomorrow when it came time to fly.

I had, for the first time that day, seen some of Vietnam from a front row seat and when the day was done, I slid awkwardly down the ramp and when both my feet touched the deck I knew I had no further aspirations in life. I was finally doing just what I wanted to do — be a squadron helicopter pilot in Vietnam.

The flight time that day came to 5.5 hours. I was satisfied that I had not screwed up and was comfortable with what I considered a successful first hop. In the post-flight debrief, which was very brief, Boyack raised no areas of concern. With a grin on his face, he pointed out that it was the responsibility of the copilot to complete the paperwork—recording the events of the day in an AA report for his review and signature. I was more than happy to take it on. I had begun to feel comfortable, a little bit.

The mission system code for the flight with Boyack was a 1R4. That literally translates as follows: First, a number; 1 means day, 2 means day/instrument, 3 means night/visual, and 4 means night/instrument. Second, a letter; for the CH-46 that's an R for transport, like an eighteen-wheeler. The third figure is a numerical code; 4 means administrative transport.

There were many mission codes: 1R4 was administrative transport-VIP; 1R5 was combat troop lifts, troop inserts and extracts into and out of enemy fire, which was common to mission 80 (quick reaction) and SOG missions to Laos; 1R6 was medevac; 1R7 was recon inserts and extracts; 1R9 was resupply, from which the vast number of air medals originated; 3R6 was night medevac; 3L2 was night test.

* * *

Air Medals:

The system for air medals was in place for fixed wing aircraft long before helicopters were in use, and it had not been amended during the period of 1969-70. The original intent was that a "mission" was one takeoff into harm's way, and a return landing. Within that system, helicopters in Vietnam conducted many takeoffs and landings into harm's way, i.e., an unsecured area in support of the war effort. Each landing was counted as a mission credit.

If a pilot received hostile fire, that was a strike credit. Therefore, landing in a hostile area and also taking fire equaled two mission credits. Twenty mission credits equaled one air medal. The air medal was earned by first accumulating twenty mission credits. Each additional twenty mission credits was represented as a numeral on the air medal. Yes, it's somewhat confusing.

Therefore, an A-4 or F-4 pilot might fly 200 missions in a year's tour, which represented 10 air medals. A helicopter pilot serving a year's tour in Vietnam may have had more than a 1000 mission credits which translated into 50 air medals. This distinction between the fixed wing and helicopter communities resulted in many happy hour "discussions" between the two communities.

I've heard them go at each other in the following manner:

The fixed wing community would scorn and laugh at the ungodly number of air medals a helo pilot may have. The helo pilot responds with, "You had an equal opportunity to fly down low, get shot at every day and swelter in the heat, rather than fly at 30,000 feet in air-conditioning and be finished for the day after an hour-and-a-half, rather than 8-10 hours." Albeit much more colorful language was used between the two communities than represented here; the two communities actually hold each other in high esteem. Ha! The last gasp is the fixed wing pilot saying to the helo pilot, "I'd rather have my sister in a whore house than have helo time in my log book." Then, it really gets to be fun when the helo pilot responds, "I'd rather screw myself across the sky than blow myself across the sky."

* * *

On that same day, 18 November, during my first real flight with Boyack, six more FNGs arrived in Phu Bai; First Lieutenant's A.C. Allen, Marty Benson, William W. "Bird" King, Fred McCorkle and Donnie McGlothlin. Benson went to HMM-161, where Joe Smith landed. Allen and McGlothlin were assigned to our hooch, bringing the total number of pilots to six and the total occupancy to seven counting Tom McCormack.

The remainder of November 1969 would bring more FNGs to Phu Bai: First Lieutenants Mike Glynn, Pete Hanner and Ron McAmis and five more flights for me. The days were taken up with making our living quarters more habitable and preparing maps, marking points we could use for navigation purposes. When the sun was out, which wasn't often in the monsoon season, it really cooked. I found it odd, that the pilots who were not flying had an opportunity to get a tan. The best place for tanning was on top of the sandbagged bunkers between the Quonset huts. They'd drag an old lounge chair up on the top of the bunker, put on their shades, grab a beer and think they were on R&R. Take it when you can get it was the motto. I would learn to do the same.

The hooch was becoming home. Acey Ducey was the game of choice and cold beer was the drink, there or at the O'Club. The beer we found to be most available was Carling's Black Label. Some of those cans had been around so long, they showed signs of rust. The good beer, Budweiser, when available, went fast. When a fresh load of brew came to the small exchange, you had to be there first to get Budweiser. A.C. Allen purchased a refrigerator from the exchange, one of those small ones, about the height of a small lamp table. It sat directly to the side of his rack. It seemed that A.C. always knew when a new supply of beer came in. I can still see him coming into the hooch with a case of beer on his shoulder and a grin on his face.

During periods when flights were cancelled or there was ample downtime, impromptu Volleyball games would break out.

Bad weather, coupled with boredom and beer brought forth this phenomena in a muddy area near the hooch area. A volleyball net stretched between two posts and as many men that were available played. The rules were simple there were no rules which was referred to as "jungle rules." More pilots were hurt playing this game than anything else. Twisted ankles, busted noses and loosened teeth were not uncommon. Slamming the ball over the net into the opposing team was normally accompanied by a kick under the net with steel toed boots. It was great fun and relieved tension. The toughest of the tough were: Lieutenants W. R. "Wild Bill" Davis, W. R. "Hud" Hudson, Gene Tolls, Eric "Bones" McGrew, Dean "Gorilla Monsoon" Davis, and Ed Mowry. But of course, anyone who showed up for the game had to be ready to take the bruises in good fun.

The days were also filled with one rumor after another about when we would either leave the country entirely or move on to MMAF. It was a sure bet that we would be leaving Phu Bai sometime in January, as HMM-161 was hearing the same rumor. Whatever the case, I now had one flight in red ink in my log book.

Meeting "Hoss":

Enroute to an early morning flight in late November 1969, Pete Hanner and I were headed for the chow hall. Upon arriving, the doors had not yet been opened. Hanging out with the few pilots who were all getting ready to put in a full day, probably a max crew day of resupply, we waited. Momentarily, a formidable looking major from the gunship squadron called Scarface strode up to the door in full flight gear and no cover (hat). The other pilots, all lieutenants, gave way. His eyes were fixed upon the closed door. He had a ruddy, red-faced complexion and reddish colored thinning hair and was built like an NFL guard. He arrived like a loud clap of thunder out of a sudden summer storm. They called him "Hoss."

I had heard the name once since arriving at Phu Bai. The name itself brought to mind *Dan Blocker*, who played *Hoss Cartwright* one of the stars of the classic TV western, *Bonanza*. It was more than apparent to Pete and me that Hoss was a tough, no-nonsense character. I later learned that he was originally an A-4 Skyhawk pilot who was among many jet pilots who were arbitrarily reassigned to fly helicopters. The need for helicopter pilots among both the Army and Marine Corps because of Vietnam had become a pressing issue. Our own CO and XO, LtCol Bancroft and Major Sellers had both originally been jet pilots. I was still unfamiliar with how that kind of transition from jets to helicopters affected the pilot.

However, it was apparent to me that Hoss was flying the right machine. Being one of the biggest bulls in the pen, he was in no mood to wait. Cursing a blue streak while pounding his massive fist against the mess hall door, he demanded attention. The door was flung open wide by a cook who, immediately upon seeing and probably recognizing Hoss, shrank back into the recesses of the chow hall as if he had just seen *Beowulf's Grendel*.

I didn't know if Hoss' presence caused them to open the mess, or if it was time to open, nor did I ask. Both Pete and I steered way clear of Hoss. Yet, I was curious about that larger-than-life gunship pilot but that could wait. Both Pete and I had to get to the squadron office. Years later, we would know much more about Malcolm T. "Hoss" Hornsby.

19: First Medevac

On 28 November 1969, my 24th birthday, I was scheduled to fly my first medevac mission. I would be copilot to Babs who had rescued Lieutenant Esmond down south at Hoi An. Babs' background was that he had once been written up for the Distinguished Flying Cross up in Quang Tri. The write-up was approved at both the group and wing level only to be denied, with no given reason, at Headquarters, USMC. No amount of inquiry into the issue was responded to by Headquarters Marine Corps leading to his belief the declination was due to direct animus from the CO/XO level of HMM- 262.

Figure 46 First Lieutenant William "Babs" Babcock

Babs was a tall blonde-haired lanky fellow with the cadaverous look of an ultra-marathoner, not the least bit caught up in the "I'm the HAC and you're the copilot so act accordingly" bullshit or the "sit down strap in shut up and don't touch anything" attitude held by at least one of the veteran combat pilots toward us new guys. Babs and I were scheduled to fly chase to First Lieutenant Nelson and his copilot, First Lieutenant Winston "Hud" Hudson, also an "old guy."

The dedicated Marine Corps medevac package, based at Marble Mountain's medevac hot pad consisted of a section of CH-46s and a section of gunships from HML 167 or HML 367. I was more than ready to begin flying "real" missions instead of administrative flights. A medevac flight was the answer to my dreams. My preparation to fly the medevac went without incident, checking and re-checking the yellow sheets in the maintenance shack, and preflighting the aircraft with crew chief Cpl. Billy Garvin of Houston, Texas, before Babs showed up.

Moments later, Babs made his way into the maintenance shack as I was returning from the preflight.

"How's it look?" he asked.

"Looks good," I responded, before mentioning a couple of minor gripes marked "unable to duplicate."

Figure 47 A section of medevac CH-46s.

Babs turned to Capt. White to chat about something, pausing long enough to tell me to go on over to the ready room and see what the weather looked like for flying south. There was no need to check with weather; it looked like crap, it was always crap. I almost needed a guide to get through the fog and drizzle to the ready room.

In the ready room, I met First Lieutenants Bill "Fuels" Nelson and Winston "Hud" Hudson, who were scheduled to fly the lead medevac in the section lead. Both gave the appearance of supreme confidence. The place was full of pilots briefing missions that probably wouldn't get off the deck.

Nelson was a quiet guy who had that "can do" look of confidence, and thus gave me confidence in what we were about to do. Having heard so much about the action that comes with a medevac mission, I was both curious and confident with the level of pilots I saw there.

Hud, a tough looking hombre, with a scar near his right eye, sipped on a cup of black coffee while seated, at ease with himself

and reading what appeared to be a letter from home. When Babs arrived we gathered in a corner of the crowded room for a mission brief from Nelson that went something like this. "It's crap weather, and we have to be at MMAF to assume the medevac package at 0600." Crap weather meant another day of monsoon season in Vietnam. But those vet-

Figure 48 First Lieutenant W. "Bill" Nelson

eran combat pilots had flown several hundred hours in some of the worst weather in the world, in the mountainous regions of Vietnam and knew exactly what to do. I was the only one in that flight that didn't know what to expect.

Nothing stops a medevac package. The air crews: pilots, crew chiefs, gunners and corpsmen all knew the risks that had to be taken to help those Grunts whose lives hung in the balance. Yet, there were no guarantees. Many medevac flights ended with catastrophic results. The name "Ugly Angels," was an appropriate call sign for the first Marine helicopter squadron (HMM-362, an H-34 Sikorsky squadron) in Vietnam that was the first Marine helicopters to fly medevacs in Vietnam in all-weather conditions.

Nelson continued, "We'll be going feet wet," which meant we'd be flying due east to the South China Sea, then turning south while remaining offshore a brief distance. Upon reaching the Hai Van, we would turn right into Da Nang Bay, between the high pass on our right and Monkey Mountain on our left, into Da Nang Bay—standard operational procedure (SOP). "I'll call frequency changes. Any questions?" There were never any questions.

My personal yet unasked question was, why don't we go down Highway 1. I did not have the gravitas to speak out. But, I learned about Highway 1 with Boyack, during my first real flight. If we went down for any reason on our way to the coast, I thought, who knew what hell we'd be in. There was nothing between Phu Bai and the coast but burned out villages, VC, and salt flats. It looked every bit like a no-man's-land. If we went down while flying Highway 1 south, the route I'd flown with Boyack, we could probably step out of the helicopter, put out our thumb and catch a ride with one of the dozens of Army Hueys and Chinooks going our way.

Many pilots liked going feet wet. They wanted to be out over the water, following the coastline down to Da Nang Bay, staying away from potential small arms fire and the heavy helicopter traffic along Highway 1.

The accepted range of small arms, which included the AK-47, was reportedly 1500feet AGL. Now, I was certain that a .30 cal. could pump a round further than any 1500 feet, so I never wanted to test the accuracy of that measurement and neither did Babs. He had a reputation for flying at or near 10,000 feet if he could possibly get there, and, if the fighter/bomber F-4s and contract air charters into Da Nang didn't complain about a 120 kt. big ass helicopter being in their way, he'd never come down from that altitude.

But on this day, 1500 feet was impossible. We would be flying at approximately 150 to 300 feet in gray soup—seeing only the ground over which we were flying while straining to get a glimpse of the pulsing anti-collision light on the lead bird's aft pylon. I hoped that any curious VC or NVA would be so shocked at seeing us at such a low altitude we would be able to pass over them and be gone before they could use us for target practice.

No excuses! We launched! Nelson called the tower for departure to Da Nang with a right out[83] to the coast. Departing on Runway 27 into prevailing winds of ten to fifteen knots, we made a 180 degree turn to 090, on course toward the sea. Passing over Phuong (pronounced Fu Long), the Chieu Hoi village just north of the runway, we were almost on top of the hooches. Clearances were handled through Gia Le Arty 36.4 FM, and we switched to UHF Button 1, squadron common, to maintain communication with Nelson.

As a copilot, it was necessary to read the earth and to know where you are on the map at all times. The land mass between Phu Bai and the sea was flat, a few feet above sea level, with no real geographical features other than a small river we passed over, that according to the map, linked up with a much larger bay area south of us, which I didn't recall having ever seen due to the ever present monsoons.

As close as we were to the Phu Bai TACAN station, the signal should have been strong. But it was iffy. We could be solid on the tail of the needle, 090 degrees one moment and the next moment the needle would twirl around like an errant wind-mill. So, the magnetic heading was the most useful. We were flying something like partial-panel instrument flight (needle ball and airspeed) all the time.

* * *

The unwritten rule, I learned, was to not trust your life to instrument flight when some stations were intermittent or inaccurate. Furthermore, flying into Da Nang or Chu Lai, you shared the air space with F-4s, A-4s, ARVN Air Force, and whatever commercial carrier might be landing or taking off at that time, a nightmare scenario when you are traveling at 120 knots or less; it was much safer to remain in our very own low flight environment. Tactical

---

[83] When launching out of an airfield with a control tower, Phu Bai, MMAF, An Hoa, it was necessary to tell the tower which way you intended to go, right, left or straight ahead. The Tower would then have information to relay to anyone flying through the area or entering the pattern to land. "Tower, Chatterbox 28, right out feet wet." "Roger, 28," etc. etc.

entry patterns under instrument conditions were published and used in some instances in order to check the weather in the TAOR. Fly at 1500 feet into the TAOR and when the weather sucks you in, grab a Ground Controlled Approach (GCA).

* * *

Giving up on knowing our exact position, I simply resorted to keeping an eye on the engine gauges to ensure everything was within the green or normal range—another key flight responsibility for the copilot. Reaching the coastline, we continued a hundred yards or so out to sea before turning south. The visibility was even worse over the water because there was no semblance of a horizon. Over land you could differentiate between the dark ground and the fog. This was not so over water, which was the same color as the clouds. Babs maintained a semi-loose cruise[84] position off Nelson's port side. I would have felt much better had we simply filed IFR into Marble Mountain. What I learned in Vietnam, however, was that we hardly, if ever, flew IFR except when absolutely necessary to stay current or for instrument flight in an extreme emergency.

Traveling at 110 knots, ten knots less than the recommended operational cruise speed,[85] we soon arrived at the now-familiar Hai Van Pass, where we transitioned to the Bravo Tango (BT) tactical map and dialed in Channel 77, the Da Nang TACAN channel, since Marble Mountain did not have a TACAN channel of its own. We entered the area through the normal entry pattern over Da Nang Bay and upstream over the Han River, passing by the German hospital ship and hopping over the bridge, landing at MMAF. After hot refueling at the pumps on the western edge of the runway, we taxied to the medevac bunker and assumed the

---

[84] "Loose cruise" was two to three rotor lengths back from the lead aircraft on either side of the lead, with a high-enough step-up to avoid being kicked around by the rotor wash of the lead aircraft.

[85] The NATOPS operational cruise speed of a CH-46 was 120 kts., the airspeed by which the helicopter could best maneuver at cruise, although 150 kts. was routinely reached when taking an emergency med-evacuee to a medical facility.

day's responsibilities at 0600. The night shift, handled by a sister squadron, was in contact with Marble ground control, leaving the medevac revetments and making room for us, two fresh 46 crews of six each, with a corpsman. We officially assumed the daytime medevac responsibilities.

The medevac shack itself was on the west side of the runway, north of the midway point and the fuel pits, officially known as POL (petroleum, oil, and lubricants). Two revetments near the medevac shack were for the 46s on duty. The location of the revetments allowed immediate access onto the parallel taxiway for takeoff. Some crews had been known to lift directly out of the revetments on takeoff.

For the most part, pilots remained in the shack and received missions over the land-line phone. A large map of the Quang Nam Province was affixed to the wall for rapid location of mission coordinates. The inside of the shack smelled awful. At night, the mess hall would send mid-rats near midnight. That food usually consisted of baloney on stale bread and warm milk in those small cartons like we used to get in school. Hardly anyone ever risked eating the stuff for fear of ptomaine poisoning and themselves being medevaced.

Aircrews were required to clean up after themselves, but there appeared to be no one responsible for emptying garbage cans. Inside and outside the shack, garbage cans overflowed with reeking leftover food from previous crews.

There were six racks set up with mattresses and pillows encased in plastic. Blankets and sheets were present but no one would touch them for fear of catching something penicillin couldn't cure. Activities between calls consisted of catching up on letter writing, playing cards, Acey-Ducey or just dozing off. One of the problems however, mentioned in speaking about the shack was that the dice for the Acey-Ducey board was always missing[86]. The crew chief normally remained with his helicopter,

---

[86] Regarding the missing dice. Most pilots carried their own pair of dice for that purpose. My dice have remained in my flight suit for the past 49 years.

lounging on one of the bench seats on the cargo deck. The corps-man was also always near the helicopter and the gunners were within proximity to their big .50s, ready to go. I learned from them that the best place to be was outside, rather than inside, depending on the mosquito infestation.

Babs took time to brief me on SOP in the shack. When a call for a medevac was received Babs wanted me, the crew chief, Billy Garvin, the gunners and the corpsman to "immediately get to the helicopter" while he remained in the shack with Nelson cop-ying coordinates and receiving a quick brief by Nelson. By the time Babs got to the aircraft, he wanted the start checklist com-pleted and the blades turning, or as close to that as I could get. It was protocol for a CH-46 medevac helo to be in the air within two minutes after the HAC strapped into his seat. Therefore, the 50 + items in the pre-start and start checklists had to be boiled down to battery on, rotor brake off and engine condition levers to fly in less than one minute.

Intent on doing things right, I went back to the 46, sat in the copilot's left seat and completed the Pre-Start checklist item by item down to "Aux Power Plant-On," for an expedited start-up. The rest of the morning was monotonous. I started a letter to Kathy to be mailed later. I always wrote about things I was in-volved in, but not in detail enough to be useful to anyone who shouldn't be reading it. Nothing we did was worthy of a Top Se-cret designation, but we were warned anyway about detailing squadron locations or future actions.

Totally bored, I walked to the front of the 46 the nose of which was only a few yards west of the runway and watched the weather slowly melt away. Toward mid-day the ceiling was lift-ing and a few flights were beginning to take off. I hoped we would get at least one medevac in, just to see how it all worked. That would happen sooner rather than later.

The medevac phone (also called the bat phone) rang loudly. Nelson picked it up, listened intently for a moment, and with the phone still held to his ear, looked at Babs and Hud, twirled his right index finger in the air, mouthing the word, "Routine," before grabbing a pen and jotting something down on his knee board. Hud looked over at me and said, "Let's go." Babs dropped the magazine he was reading, grabbed his knee board, and walked toward the map.

When a medevac call was received in the shack it would consist of the following information:

1. Precedence. Emergency was the only category when an attempt would be made regardless of weather, time of day, or military circumstance. The medevacs that were not attempted at night were classified as Priority, Routine, or Permanent Routine. Permanent Routine meant that the individual was dead.
2. Number of killed in action (KIA) and wounded in action (WIA) along with branch of service or nationality.
3. Nature of wounds.
4. Coordinates.
5. LZ secure or not secure. An unsecured LZ always made for some tension.
6. Marking of LZ, usually smoke.
7. Best approach direction (dependent on wind direction/enemy situation).
8. Medical assistance required.
9. Requesting unit call sign and frequency.

Seeing Hud and me leaving the shack, the crew chiefs became animated without us saying a word. A choreographed movement had already begun. My heart began pounding and I struggled to contain my excitement. Just be cool, was the thought in my head as I made my way out of the shack to our helicopter in the second revetment not running, but at a brisk walk.

Stepping onto the rear ramp, I almost slipped in the fresh oil that was always there. I grabbed my survival vest from the bench seat where I had left my gear, threw on the heavy bullet bouncer, adjusted my cartridge belt, squeezed through the small access opening into the cockpit, and slipped into the copilot's seat. I pulled the harness over both shoulders to my lap belt and buckled them into the 3-point safety buckle, grabbed my helmet from the hook over my seat and placed it on my head with both visors, clear and tinted, in the up position. Leaning forward, I ensured the inertial reel lock wasn't locked so that I could move my upper body with no restraint. Again I adjusted my service revolver so that it was aligned between my legs and within reach of either hand, as we had been taught. All of this was completed in a matter of moments. Then I flipped the battery switch to on, awakening the helo's nervous system. The whirring sound of the gyros and radios coming online was reassuring.

The gunners, corpsman, and crew chief moved throughout the cargo deck. Their professional behavior was quite impressive. There were no lost movements or irrelevant words. I felt very new at this point; not wanting to screw up, I remained quiet and began doing my job, which was to get the blades moving.

"Billy, how do you read?" I said, checking the intercom system.

"Loud and clear." came his immediate response.

Then the words that no CH-46 pilot will ever forget, "Ready APP (APP is pronounced Ape)."

Garvin responded, "Ready."

"Ready one," (Engine 1). "Ready two," (Engine 2). Both engines were soon online as I continued with the checklist while Babs was strapping himself in.

"I have the aircraft," he advised, and I took my hand from the engine condition levers (ECL). He now had total control of the aircraft.

"Rotor brake off," he said.

"Rotor brake off," was my response.

"Walking 'em up," he said, easing the ECLs forward.

"Aye aye, sir," Garvin responded, standing outside the aircraft with the fire extinguisher in-hand.

Babs flew through the checklist by rote memory. I read from it. He was way ahead of me and so was Hud. The blades of Nelson's helicopter were already a blur. I was indeed the FNG.

Our blades began to turn causing the craft to begin that rock-ing/swaying movement that occurs when both sets of rotor blades are waking up and going through the initial stages build-ing to supersonic. As they passed into the 98% flight RPM, Garvin gave the okay to Babs that there was no fire and climbed into the helicopter over the rear ramp, closing and securing the engine doors behind him. Babs beeped the RPM up to 100%. There was no confusion. All crew members were aboard. Crew chief, gun-ners and corpsman were all at their stations and waiting.

From the other helicopter our flight leader Nelson took con-trol, initiating frequency changes through challenge and re-sponse. The communication went something like this:

Nelson: "Chase, go ground, 290.3." (Switch to the frequency 290.3.)

Babs: "Switching."

Nelson: "One's up." (This means that the flight leader is on the desired frequency and is asking if the chase bird is also on that frequency.)

Babs: "Two's up." (The flight leader is now referred to as One and the chase as Two.)

Nelson: "Ground, medevac package requesting taxi to the parallel for takeoff."

Ground control: "Medevac is cleared to taxi as requested, contact Marble tower, 281.2."

Nelson to Babs: "Go tower."

Babs to Nelson: A double click on the communications trig-ger. (Confirming—same as "Roger".)

On Marble's tower frequency, we overheard the Comprise gunships[87] being cleared for takeoff. Our position in the revet-ments provided me with a clear view of the two gunships. The Hueys were taking the runway at the mid-point of the runway where the tower was located. Heavy during takeoff, with a max-

---

[87] The gunships were sometimes just called "guns" when in the heat of an extract or insert you were referring to them. As in "The guns targeted a tree line from which we were receiving fire."

imum load of ammo, they had to move forward, attaining transitional lift to get into the air. They were literally only a few inches off the deck, skipping and scraping along with sparks bouncing off the airframe each time the skids scraped the concrete. They appeared to literally drag themselves off of the runway. Off first, their job, I learned, was to lead the flight, obtaining artillery clearances to the medevac pickup coordinates and making initial contact with the unit where the med-evacuee was waiting. Once they were in the air, it was our turn.

Nelson: "Ground, medevac, flight of two taxi to the parallel."

"Roger medevac, cleared to the parallel, contact tower." The call for taxi to the parallel allowed us to forego the long taxi route from the medevac shack to the normal entry point onto the runway taking several minutes off of our time of takeoff. Any minute we could save meant the evacuee would have a better chance to live.

Nelson: "Tower, medevac, flight of two, for takeoff with a left-out."

From the tower, weather and altimeter: "The weather is overcast with a 1,000 foot ceiling, rain and fog with quarter-mile visibility." We could see that. "Winds are light and variable from east to northeast, altimeter 2-9-9-5, cleared for takeoff." Besides being cleared for takeoff, the clearance read back to us provided a current altimeter reading, the second most important part of the clearance.

Positioned behind Nelson on the parallel taxiway in a slow forward taxi, I observed the lead 46's tail section rise in that awkward way the Phrog takes flight—the aft rotor head high in the air with the forward rotor head much lower. Our section was off and on our way.

20: Follow The Leader

Babcock's eyes were fixed on the lead 46. He gently pulled up on the collective, adding small amounts of power, easing us ever so gently to the right-rear of the lead, in anticipation of the next turn. I couldn't take it all in fast enough. The movement was smooth. Reaching the end of the runway at an altitude of 100 feet AGL, Nelson repeated his intentions to the tower, "Left-out to the river."

"Roger medevac. Cleared as requested. Have a good day."

"Roger..."

A few moments later, Nelson rolled left toward the Han. Babs slid right, through rough air buffeting caused by Nelson's rotor draft, settling into a loose cruise position to the right rear of Nelson—textbook. Our route was west over the Han River, which soon branched off and became the Cam Le River. Helo flights in and out of MMAF through that area were restricted to a maximum altitude of 150 feet. The restriction kept helos out of the approach portion of Runways 35, left and right, at the Da Nang Air Base—a good reason to be low.

Nelson called clear of Marble's control tower. "Chase, go squadron common" which was button 1 on the UHF dial. As copilot, I made the switch. When the switch was made, Babs made a brief, "twos up" response to Nelson who followed with a double click of the UHF. All was well.

During this short portion of the flight, the small side windows available to the pilots were slightly open and the air that blew through the cockpit was refreshing. Our crew chief, Corporal Billy Garvin, from his starboard drop-down seat, was keeping an eye out for other aircraft on the river that neither the pilot nor copilot could see—his left arm on the half door, his right hand holding the ever present mike cord available to him for immediate contact with the pilots and gunners who hovered over the barrel of their 50s, looking into the distance, looking for trouble. The Navy corpsman, seated on the port side of the cabin on the red canvas bench seat calmly checked and rechecked his medical supplies. A huge airliner on short final into Da Nang crossed over the river just in front of us, so close I could easily see the pilot fixated on runway 35 where he was about to land. I wondered who was checking into the war that day, counting myself lucky for already being there.

I couldn't help but think of how exciting this was, racing over small round fishing boats manned by local fishermen like their ancient ancestors had probably done in that same type of boat for hundreds, maybe thousands of years. It was surreal. Our low altitude allowed the musty smell of the river water into the cockpit, taking me back to the days when I fished in the floodways of Southeast Missouri with my best friend, Raymond. The river bank alongside the river was covered with lush green undergrowth. It seemed to me to be perfectly suited for an ambush, but no one else appeared to think so, so I kept my mouth shut. Still to my surprise, the fishermen, like those in Da Nang Bay didn't bother to look up or in any way appear the least bit curious about us. In this helicopter war, the sight of low flying helicopters of all sizes and configurations over the waterways near Da Nang had become commonplace. I always thought, maybe too commonplace.

Our speed began to increase, the nose wheel still only a few feet above the river as we approached a steel bridge, the Cado Bridge. It was Highway 1, the great north-south thoroughfare from Saigon to the DMZ and beyond. Nelson called for a frequency change to Da Nang DASC 313.9 and Babs responded with a double click of his mike. The request was for clearance down Highway 1. DASC responded with azimuths and altitudes of ongoing fire missions, primarily 105 Howitzers. Being clear of the missions, we were cleared on course.

The bridge was within a few hundred feet as Nelson's aircraft began to gain altitude. With a slight roll to the left when traveling at near 120 kts, he entered into what was known as a cyclic climb. A slight amount of back pressure when applied to the cyclic while maintaining the same power setting (not raising or lowering the collective) allowed the craft to climb while the air-speed slowly decayed. Once the desired altitude was reached, the airspeed is allowed to build to the desired airspeed, normally 120 kts. Babs followed suit, rolling further left and also entering a cyclic climb that pegged the vertical speed indicator (VSI) in an ascent of nearly 1,000 feet per minute, forcing me back and down into my seat.

The entry from the Han up and over the Cado Bridge wheeling south over Highway 1 was exhilarating and the first of many hundreds of times I would do the same in the coming year. The altimeter jumped to a 1000 feet AGL. A few moments later we were back in loose cruise on Nelson's starboard side, just below the scud layer of clouds. Babs maneuvered from the right rear of Nelson to the left rear position, placing him in a better position to keep an eye on the lead as his seating position as aircraft commander is on the right side of the cockpit.

The section of 167 Comprise gunships was in front of us at a much lower altitude, skimming the treetops like they always did, like hunters, and soon coming up on the pre-briefed fox mike (FM) frequency. We were cruising at 120 knots. The gunships cruised between 80 and 100 knots with a full bag of fuel, a full load of rockets, and 4,000 rounds of ammo. We overtook the gunships and within minutes we were approaching the medevac coordinates—north-northwest of the Blue Dragons. Nelson called for an FM frequency change, and finally we were all on the same frequency, the Grunts, the gunships and us. The ROK Marines in the zone were giving us a zone brief. Nelson would be picking up wounded ROK Marines.

The LZ brief required the following information or equivalent:

1. The LZ is (rice paddy, hilltop, etc.).
2. Obstacles to flight are (wires, trees, etc.).
3. Recommend approach from (N, E, S, W).
4. Wind from (N, E, S, W).
5. LZ is marked with (panels, smoke, strobe, etc.).
6. Friendlies extend from LZ (N, E, S, W meters).

7. Enemy positions from LZ (N, E, S, W meters). Last fire received from (N, S, E, W), consisting of (.30-.50 cal., automatic weapons, rocket-propelled grenade, mortars) at (date and time).
8. Cleared/not cleared to fire (N, E, S, W meters).
9. Type and number of medevacs (emergency, priority, or routine).
10. Departure route (N, E, S, W).

As the chase 46, Babs kept us well clear of the LZ, setting up an orbit just below the cloud layer at around 1100 feet AGL. The clouds were ragged; as the day became warmer, visibility varied moment to moment, from less than a mile to two miles and more. The Gunships' responsibility was to take the brief, clear the area, and clear the lead 46 into the zone while providing fire suppression. Today the zone was considered secure. No enemy fire had been reported within the past 24 hours; a piece of cake!

Nelson was cleared into the zone on our UHF common frequency. He advised us to remain high as he began his approach. We moved west approximately one click (a 1,000 meters), below the clouds, which kept us well within small arms range.

Nelson took over the fox mike communication with the radioman in the LZ. As the chase bird, we monitored both the FM and UHF common frequencies for the flight. The medevac was going smoothly because of the skill and coordination developed by the Marines through practice and application. I had the best seat in the house.

As Nelson approached, he called for the Marines on the ground to "pop-a-smoke." The smoke is a canister of charged smoke powder, available in varying colors and tossed into an area to mark it for landing. It revealed the direction of the wind and, without doubt, the exact spot to land.

The radio operator in the LZ responded, "Roger. Smoke's out," as the canister began to spew the colored smoke identifying the LZ.

Nelson: "I've got your scarlet."

LZ: "Roger, scarlet."

The LZ radio operator confirmed the color only after the color was identified by the medevac. I learned later that this sequence of acknowledgements happened for a reason. Apparently, during 1966, '67, and '68 in the border battles of Laos and the DMZ, when an LZ popped smoke they may have identified the color of the smoke for the pilot. Enemy monitoring the frequency had on occasion popped smoke in the same color, luring the helicopter to land off target with catastrophic results. It became SOP for the pilot to identify the color of the smoke to the Marines on the ground, leaving them to acknowledge the color. It made good sense to conduct the smoke dispersal in that manner and not risk an ambush. It was also reported that on one occasion, the 46 pilot requested the Marines start a fire so they could be identified from the different smokes that were popping up. Then, additional fires began to pop up. True or not, it illustrated the situations that could occur.

Figure 49 A CH-46 in its iconic flare following a corkscrew approach just before touchdown with its belly dangerously exposed and the rotor wash approaching hurricane strength.

Nelson nosed into the wind, and when directly over the zone at an altitude of approximately 1200 feet, announced over Fox Mike (FM radio) "Down right." What followed was a dazzling display of aeronautical artistry—the nose-down corkscrew approach perfected by the 46 community and called the death spiral by some. Nelson, with the nose of the 46 never leaving the center of the LZ, swirled down, rolling out on final with the 46 rearing up like a wild stallion before its main gear touched down, and its nose wheel settled gently into the dirt. The flare at the conclusion of the approach is the iconic image of the 46 in Vietnam. It can be found in many photos snapped by combat Marines in the zone, and in combat art from that era. Throughout the corkscrew approach, the gunships played leapfrog, ensuring total coverage of the 46.

The wind whipped up by those six big blades blew poncho liners, C-rations, cardboard, and miscellaneous items high into the air as the helicopter touched down. Many of the ROKs threw themselves across their gear, turning their heads away as the rotor wash blew fine red dirt into them like tiny stinging pellets. Off to one side was a corpsman and the ROK Marine to be picked up, standing, bracing themselves against the storm of dust and dirt particles that stung like bees, when slamming into uncovered flesh.

Nelson announced he was in the zone and all was well. I began counting to myself, 1001, 1002 … for a full six seconds. Comprise, the HML-167 Huey gunships had set up a wagon-wheel pattern at a 1,000 feet AGL, covering the ground all around the LZ. All remained quiet …I was spellbound, and becoming more and more aware of the skills and senses required to become an aircraft commander. How did he do that? I wondered.

The image of that nose down spiral remained fixed in my mind for future reference. At a later time, in trying to explain the maneuver Babs told me, "Just lower the collective, go hard right with the cyclic and nose down while keeping the aircraft in balanced flight through the use of the rudders and make it into the zone in one 360 degree spiral. "That's all there is to it." He said. "But remember; don't pass over the same ground twice." The fully articulating head of the 46 rotor system was what allowed for this maneuver.

As I 'skillfully monitored the instruments,'[88] Babcock maintained an easy orbit. I strained to take in all that was going on down on the ground as the radios crackled with cryptic comments between the gunships, Nelson, and the Grunts. Also, a wide cinematic view of the Da Nang lowlands was beginning to

[88] The phrase "skillfully monitored the instruments" is invariably found in any write up for the copilot no matter the extent of his personal performance and has become a satirical phrase used by copilots to describe their performance.

come into view as the day wore on. From my port-side copilot seat, I could see the twin bridges over the Thu Bon River near Hoi An, the Que Son Mountains to the south-southwest and several puffs of white smoke in the areas of Alligator Lake, Go Noi Island and An Hoa where the 5th Marines were taking care of business.

21: Taking Fire

I later learned that the white puffy smoke I admired was both

Figure 50 White Phosphorus aka Willy Pete or Whiskey Poppa.

beautiful and deadly. It was White Phosphorous (Willy Pete) an incendiary weapon that can melt the skin right off your bones and is also used as an effective smoke-screen for infantry move-ments or to screen medevac and Recon helicopters from enemy forces during contested inserts and extracts. The firing could have been coming from 155 Howitzers from hills 55, 65, 37 or An Hoa, or from mortars by Marines close to the enemy. Apparently, all hell was breaking loose in that low-land canopy of green on that overcast day.

The pickup coordinates for the medevac that day was north-east of an old battered and broken French fort, a relic of the past where graves of unknown foreign intruders lie. There was al-ways action in that area. But the overall appearance of farmers dressed in traditional garb, black peasant pajamas and conical hats woven from bamboo straw tending their rice paddies be-hind huge Water Buffalo, could lull you into a false sense of se-renity. The black attire was an official trademark of the Viet Cong, because it was worn by the peasants working the fields. Yet, the additional presence of small children and women walk-ing to and from the paddies flicking the great beasts with small branches both reassured and blurred reality.

I could only imagine how many of the "peasants" that day were VC and how many were not VC; and of those who were not, how could they withstand all this craziness going on around them. The gentle farm scenes side by side with the puffs of Willy Pete were difficult to comprehend.

Billy Garvin, our crew chief, a tough veteran who reminded me of Raymond Busby my boyhood friend in Missouri, called up front to the cockpit. "Sir," he said, like he was talking about where we would be having lunch, "we're taking fire." Then, with a little more emphasis, "We're taking hits." My mind raced. What? Taking fire? From where?

My head was on a swivel as those thoughts whizzed through my mind. Babcock coolly notified Nelson, the lead medevac, then in the zone picking up the sick or wounded Marine and the gunships overhead, that we were taking fire, and they should turn northwest upon leaving the zone.

As Nelson was departing the zone after picking up the medevacuee, he notified us and the gunships that he too was being fired upon and taking hits. The tranquil scene had turned into a shooting gallery, and we were the clay pigeons. Yet, I couldn't see the enemy or hear the hits. Babcock raised the collective, applying more power. The two big GE engines immediately responded. We began climbing into the lower edge of the now ragged overcast while moving north-northwest to put more distance between us and the area where we took fire. The clouds were dissipating rapidly. The ceiling was much higher than it had been a few minutes before, and the visibility was becoming unlimited below those clouds.

The .50-cal. gunners reported no sighting of muzzle flashes on the ground. The Comprise gunships, however, reported they were taking up the fight around the pick-up zone at the request of the Marines on the ground. They had no defined target, but were working out on the tree line from which the Marines on the ground believed the fire was coming. We overheard them say they were dropping a few rockets into the trees to dissuade any wannabe bad guys. The sniping had apparently promptly ended as quickly as it began. Babs, maneuvered so as to keep us on our course, headed north as Nelson climbed to our altitude.

The gunships after shredding the tree line from which the fire was believed to have originated, announced they were breaking off their attack and remaining with Nelson. Babcock directed me to note the coordinates of the firing and asked Billy, our crew chief, if anybody was hit. No one was hit. But, during all of the excitement, I had forgotten to carefully monitor the instruments, so I quickly checked the gauges, especially the No. 1 and 2 hydraulics. I was prepared to flick the hydraulic toggle switch to "isolate" if needed (a total loss of hydraulics can kill you quicker than a heart attack). But there was no indication of a loss of hydraulic pressure, no movement from normal on any gauges. Where were the hits?

Garvin reported that the blades must be hit because he happened to see the tracers going through the forward rotor arc at what looked like a few feet from the cockpit. But, I didn't see anything, nor did I feel anything like a tremor or shaking. But Babcock, with his hands on the cyclic and collective, acknowledged that he felt some slight vibrations. He reduced our speed to ease any undue stress on the blades and reported to Nelson that we had suffered battle damage and were heading to MMAF with possible blade damage. Nelson immediately acknowledged and approved.

After a minute or so, Nelson responded saying he had also taken some hits, but was otherwise okay, and was heading for NSA hospital nearest Marble with the medevacuee. The flight had split up. Not the best thing to do. But, sometimes it was necessary. This was one of those times.

The gunships advised they would remain with Nelson until he reached the hospital, but then they were going back and hunting down the VC. They knew, however, that the enemy had blended back into the countryside as quickly as he had attacked, probably placing his AK-47 back in its hiding place, then continuing with his farming. I was told that we were most certainly just a target of opportunity for a lone VC farmer, "a common occurrence" they said.

The peculiar thing about the event was that there had been no report of enemy activity in the immediate area of the medevac and the zone had been considered a secure zone. Also, the Camp of the Blue Dragon was approximately fifteen miles southsoutheast of Da Nang, near where we were, and they had pretty much pacified the area, making it an unfriendly and risky venture for an organized group of VC to target us in the middle of the afternoon.

But one gutsy bastard had taken two 46s out of commission and would cause our squadron to have to reconstitute the medevac package. Another lesson learned. There were no cakewalks in Vietnam. You had to accept the fact that the most benign mission, even a routine medevac in what appeared to be a benign pastoral scene, could take an unexpected bad turn. I had to, begrudgingly, give Charlie his due.

My attention during this incident was on doing anything asked of me by Babcock and hoping for the best, but oddly, I felt no particular fear, just excitement...adrenaline I suppose. We were finally able to get to 1500 feet with near unlimited visibility. Babs handled it in a professional manner, picking up a direct heading to Marble while at the same time informing DaNang Air Support Control (DASC) of our circumstances. Fortunately, no ongoing artillery missions complicated our route home.

Changing frequencies to Marble Mountain tower, we re-

Figure 51 This image was what we saw when on short final onto runway 36 into the Marble Mountain Air Facility. The medevac pad was to the left (east) of the far end of the runway, hardly visible from this point.

ceived priority clearance to land, and for anyone also attempting to land at Marble, to remain clear. As we approached Marble, I quickly ran through the landing checklist. The crew was quiet. Babcock remained steady on the flight controls and the 46 flew smoothly to the runway.

It's odd, but during those few moments before we touched down, I noticed large white letters P O W painted on the tin roof of a building in a compound just outside the southern boundary fence of Marble Mountain Air Facility. On 10 November 1969, when I flew into Da Nang on World Airways, beginning my year in Vietnam, I briefly noticed the helicopters at Marble Mountain Air Facility, wondering if we would be based in that venue. But, I didn't notice the big bold white letters P O W on that occasion.

On this occasion, the letters seemed to be as large as the Hollywood sign on Mount Lee overlooking Los Angeles. The men in the compound whom I presumed to be prisoners, were milling about in the exercise yard. Some appeared to be kicking a ball around. Others milled about in small groups...wow. Thoughts came to mind of the difference between our treatment of the POWs in accordance with the Geneva Convention and the treatment our guys were receiving in the Hanoi Hilton. I hoped we could free those men. I was still new to our Vietnam policy.

The voice of the Marble Mountain tower operator renewed my concentration on flying. He asked if we needed immediate attention upon landing. Babcock responded "No ambulance needed, and we want to land in an area near the approach end of the runway.

"Roger that" was the tower's response.

I could see the crash crews in their silver flame retardant suits, placing the hoods of their suits over their heads and climbing onto their trucks. The silver suits were on top of the trucks manning the big foam cannons in case of fire. An ambulance, its red lights flashing, was waiting for us. Red flashing lights were everywhere it seemed, the crews were ready to walk through fire to get to us. The sight of those fellas gave me an overall sense of well-being. I have the utmost respect for people who, without hesitation, would hurl themselves into an inferno if necessary to save our lives. Their world was a high bar.

Babs avoided a hover landing for a smooth airplane-like roll on landing, keeping the overall weight of the CH-46D (11,585 lbs.) off the blades until the nose and main gear were on the deck. When our main mounts touched down, Babcock steadied the 46 into a slow taxi as he spoke to ground control. "Right off," he requested; It was the first available turn off the runway.

With the immediate danger of crashing over with, the danger of losing a blade and causing the 46 to go into ground resonance[89] and beating itself and maybe us to death, remained a distinct possibility. The MMAF crash crews followed us off the runway, and we were taxied to a temporary holding area as directed by ground control.

We hurriedly went through the shutdown checklist. The engine condition levers (ECLs) were brought back to the detent and the one minute cool down was accomplished. After completing the cool down period, the levers were moved back to off. Babcock didn't activate the rotor brake as would have been done in a normal shutdown, instead, he allowed the blades to coast down to a stop. An immediate braking action could have caused the blades to crumple if damaged in the way we expected.

Garvin remained attached to the long cord, reporting during the shutdown that he didn't see any sign of structural failure, but as the blades slowed he did see damage. The gunners and corpsman deplaned, well clear of any potential problem as the blades and aircraft coasted to a stop. Babcock and I completed the shutdown, grabbed our gear, and cleared the cockpit. My first medevac mission had ended early, but, I had learned lessons that would see me through the coming year.

The damage assessment revealed no hits in the body of the aircraft. However, as Billy had earlier noted, a couple of blades in the forward rotor head were pretty well chewed up. Two jagged holes, believed to have been caused by a .30 caliber AK-47;

---

[89] Ground resonance is an imbalance in the rotation of a helicopter rotor. The loss of a section of a blade could throw the helicopter into ground resonance. It has been described as a demon, It has demolished helicopters and killed pilots, passengers and bystanders.

holes were large enough to fit your fist through. The holes were through the spar of two blades, that portion of the blade providing overall structural support to the blade itself. Normal stresses on the affected blades could have caused catastrophic failure and certain death for us. We lucked out...pure luck. It was my birthday; I was now 24 years old and still alive.

It turned out that the Nelson and Hudson in the lead helicopter had also been damaged too much to fly...so, that benign routine medevac, with probably one VC and an AK-47 took out two CH-46s for the remainder of the day. The good news was that the med-evacuee was taken out of the field and no one was hurt. We would spend the night at Marble and wait throughout the following day for the blades to be replaced.

22: Happy Birthday

On that day, 28 November, I felt at liberty to celebrate both my 24th birthday and my first encounter with the enemy, even though it could only be considered by combat vets as a trivial occurrence. I hoped that Kathy and my family would have baked a cake on my behalf. We took our flight gear to the transient hooch, only a few yards from the Marble Mountain O' Club. This occasion would be my first opportunity to take in the Officer's Mess for dinner and then settle in for a movie that evening, just like I was back home.

Figure 52 Marble Mountain Beach with concertina wire and Monkey Mountain in background

The facility, all in the same building, was situated near the beach and was very nice, probably because MMAF was the headquarters of MAG-16 and by all accounts over run with brass (majors and above). It would soon be the home of every Marine helicopter in Vietnam as the Marines collected around DaNang.

On the east side of the building facing the sea, an asphalt perimeter road, a chain-link fence and rolls of concertina and razor wire was what separated the club from one of the most picturesque beaches in the world. The white sand, composed of material from the marble and limestone hills that made up what we called the Marble Mountains, caused every naval aviator to recall the beauty of Pensacola Beach, Florida.

The interior of the club was large enough to hold several squadrons. It had a long bar behind which was a row of windows that provided a panoramic eastern view of the beach and the deep blue waters of the South China Sea. If not raining or storming, a large concrete patio provided seating for first run movies projected from the club over the perimeter road and onto a large outdoor screen built on the beach, like a miniature drive-in movie from back home.

Upon entering the facility through the main entrance, a door that opened onto the west side of the building leading from the street that ran the length of the base, there was a short hallway perpendicular to the entrance. Two interior doors, one to the left leading into the Officer's Mess and the one to the right opened into the O'Club. A sign on the door to the club prohibited the wearing of side arms. I found this distinctly different from Phu Bai where there was no such prohibition, probably because in Phu Bai it was known that the next guy in the door might very well be Charlie; as in VC.

The food was terrific with pie or ice cream or both for dessert, not a bad deal. The squadron pilots were more stateside-looking than those at Phu Bai. I had begun to feel like I was from Phu Bai, and I enjoyed the difference. Though I had been in-country only 18 days, I had received my first enemy fire (though I didn't recognize that we were under fire until being told we were by the crew chief) and the battle damage had put our helicopter out of commission. The feeling of being an FNG was beginning to fade, just a bit slower than I had hoped for. I enjoyed that night at the MMAF O'club, renewing old friendships with Ward Holland and other old training command buddies while drinking about two dollars worth of Budweiser and watching whatever movie was playing. Later, I used my bullet bouncer as a pillow and slept like a log.

The next morning, 29 November '69, I asked one of the Marines working on our helicopter to snap a picture of Billy and me. I hammed it up a bit with Billy's M-16, at the nose of the helicopter. Much later, after getting the film developed, I sent the picture to Kathy. I wrote in the letter that when we meet on R&R I would tell her about that day. I couldn't tell her any of the details for fear of providing prohibited information. (I was always super careful about not providing any information that could be considered vital information, and I always burned letters from home, to my chagrin, to keep them away from the hooch maids.)

Back at Phu Bai, Following an uneventful flight back, when

Figure 53 Cpl. Billy Garvin and the author with the helicopter we were in when the blades were hit.

filling out my first after-action report for Babs, I took my time; ensuring I did it correctly. After that, I had nothing scheduled. I spent the remainder of the day writing letters and tidying up my living area in the FNG hooch. I checked in on the paraloft, shot the breeze with Wags, learning more about him and stopped by the exchange on my way back to the hooch.

My grand adventure was beginning to take shape. The Squadron's Command Chronology for the month of November 1969 addressed our medevac in this manner:

"Chatterbox medevac and chase received intense .30 caliber fire flying under low ceilings. Both aircraft received two hits and were forced to shut down at Marble Mountain after completing the assigned medevac."

Nelson had written in the remarks section of his AA report, "Routine Medevac." For Nelson, Hud and Babs, it was just that, a walk in the park. For me, it was the first time someone tried to kill me!

I was told by one of the pilots that being shot at and hit at altitude was unusual, but it happens. He said, "You'll always be shot at and most of the time you won't even know it unless those rounds get into the cockpit, and then, you're in trouble."

We were lucky. The .30 caliber rounds that hit our blades opened them up like they were made out of paper. Although no one was harmed, two helicopters and their crews were taken out of the flying business for more than a day, at a cost of thousands of dollars in man hours and material, and they could do that to us all day long. I saw it as a bad omen for the overall war effort, especially since the world knew we were already pulling out of Vietnam. The knowledge that we were leaving was not in the interest of the poor Vietnamese farmer. He was now forced to get on the good side of the VC and not be killed by us as a collaborator with the VC. He was between the devil and the deep blue sea, a hell of a line to walk.

23: First Recon Insert with Gorilla Monsoon

December 1969
Total Dec. Flight hours: 35.3

Significant Happenings:

- President Nixon announced that the third round of American troop withdrawals from Vietnam was to be completed by 15 April 1970.
- Marine strength in December 1969 stood at 54,559. The peak Marine strength in Vietnam was reached in 1968 when more than 85,000 Marines were in Vietnam.
- Chicago: December 4, 1969. Illinois Black Panther leader Fred Hampton, age 21, and a Black Panther party leader from Peoria Illinois, Mark Clark, were killed in an early morning police raid at 2337 W. Monroe St. a stronghold of the Illinois Black Panther Party. In the past two years, the Black Panthers engaged in eight gun battles nation-wide with police. Racial unrest and Anti-War demonstrations were rampant throughout the country. But, in Vietnam, we were blissfully unaware of the everyday chaos in the states. At least, in Vietnam, it was controlled chaos.

Figure 54 North American T-28 Trojan at VT-2, Whiting Field

Being in Phu Bai was exciting, and it was the first time that I could remember when there were no outside pressures on me. During the training command, each flight had been a drill on procedures, both normal and emergency, with the only respite being solo flights in the T-28. Those few times flying solo in the T-28 Trojan at Whiting Field, Millington FL. are treasured memories. There were times in the training command that I thought I might never enjoy the simple thrill of flying, like I did when I was at Santa Ana, CA and flying the beaches in a Cessna 180 out of Orange County Municipal Airport with Kathy. But, helicopter flying in Vietnam was very close to that, almost mystical.

In Vietnam, I felt it was such luxury to just do your job, learning each day how to twist and turn that Phrog into tight zones; zones that were sometimes surrounded by skyscraper trees, where you had to descend straight down for 50 feet, then gingerly touch the correct pedal so lightly that it seemed that your very thoughts could steady the craft, just to get below an awkward tree limb. All this with the reassuring words of the crew chief, the one person in the world you allowed into your head, at that moment in time.

"Steady...steady...steady...good...down...steady...hold...steady...down. Hold! ...Stumps!"

"Damn!"

How could I not love it? All you had to do was fly...kinda like Jonathan Livingston Seagull.[90]

Figure 55 First Lieutenant Lt. Dean Davis, HAC, on left. Author, copilot, on right.

---

[90] The story of a seagull who broke away from his clan and reveled in the sheer love of flying higher, faster and with more precision than any other

On 02 December, I was scheduled with First Lieutenant Dean "Gorilla Monsoon"[91] Davis, an easygoing giant of a man and a standout collegiate football player. The brief hour-long mission was a rare opportunity to work with Third Force Reconnaissance because Third Force nearly always used Army assets. The insert was between the Hai Van Pass and Phu Bai, near the coastline in an odd outcropping like a small Marble Mountain.

The flight was uneventful when juxtaposed against future contested inserts and extracts into the Que Sons and Thuong Duc corridor, but, Davis' piloting skills were nothing less than re-markable to me.

The mission was to insert a small team of recon Marines onto an outcropping near the coastline, southeast of Phu Bai and north of the Hai Van pass. We were accompanied by our escort, a couple of Scarface gunships led by Maj. "Hoss" Hornsby. Once we reached the coordinates, Davis deemed the LZ too small to land the 46. The decision: a main mount landing, something discussed, demonstrated and performed in HMMT-302 during the last stages of flight training. The goal was to back into the zone with a slight five to ten knot wind out of the west- northwest and place the two main mounts, one under each stub wing, on a sliver of land with the front portion of the helicopter hanging over the abyss. I was about to experience a *for-real* main mount landing, with elite combat troops.

Scarface was flying about with eyes on target, relaying information to us.

"No sign of enemy activity."

"Roger that."

"Isolate my radios," Davis commanded.

seagull ever dared to try. The story was a runaway best seller by Author Rich-ard Bach.

[91] There were two "Gorilla Monsoons" First Lieutenant Jack Williams of HMM-161 at 6'5" tall and 250 Lbs was another. He was known to sometimes wear a full Gorilla mask fitted with a mike when flying, scaring the heck out of the Vietnamese.

I switched off his UHF and VHF radios so the chatter would not interfere with his total concentration. I continued to monitor the radios, responding if necessary. It was Dean and the crew chief, joined as one brain, without any outside interference. I had now become the voice of the flight, in direct contact with Scarface. My job was to monitor the instruments and keep my mouth shut.

The maneuver Davis and the crew chief were coordinating was no different from backing an eighteen wheeler up a ramp to a second floor loading dock with only inches to spare on each side and no safety railings. It had to be done with great precision. I struggled not to show any discomfort, only wide-eyed amazement. Hovering at 500 feet, level with the outcropping, Dean evaluated the area. It was no wider than about ten feet, with a depth of only a few feet. A pedal turn caused the 46 to groan, lurch and wobble in the breeze that inexplicably had turned into a more powerful quartering wind from the northwest. Davis' concentration was fixed on controls, power, altitude. Back, back we went, with only feet between the blades and the embankment and 500 feet straight down through the Plexiglas under our feet. The contour of the LZ narrowed enough above the lip to allow the aft blades unobstructed movement, but little more.

The crew chief, hanging out of the right-side of the crew half door, guided Davis back. "Back ... steady ... steady ... hold ... down ... steady ... down!"

Witnessing the professional intimacy between pilot and crew chief that can never be broken, it became clear to me that this was how to survive Vietnam.

The main mounts settled on the lip of the outcropping. A breath could be taken, but only a slight breath. This was the stepping-off point. I stole a glance back through the small door into the cabin area. The Recon Marines were up and ready to go, looking every bit like the warriors they were. Two voices rang in my headset.

"Ramp," came the crew chief's voice.

A millisecond later, Davis commanded, "Ramp." With my finger poised on the switch, I "skillfully" lowered the ramp until it touched solid ground.

The team was off the aircraft in seconds, disappearing like ghosts into the bush. The crew chief reported them clear.

"Ramp up."

"Ramp up," I responded, activating the toggle switch.

Davis added power as the ramp rose, lifting the 46 slightly and disengaging the main mounts from their precarious perch. The crew chief called us clear and Davis moved the cyclic gently forward, sending us into a dive toward the deck.

"Thank you, Chatterbox," came the gruff voice of the Recon radioman.

"Good work," came Hoss' gruff voice from the Scarface gunships. "You need us any longer?"

"No, thanks for your work today," responded Davis.

"We're going hunting now. Have a better day." Off went the Scarface gunships.

And with that, the mission was over for us. My first Recon insert was done. We quickly picked up airspeed, hurtling toward the valley below as we headed west for Highway 1. Scarface had begun their inexhaustible hunt for Charlie. By Vietnam standards, the insert was considered uneventful, routine. It was routine to Davis, the crew chief, and the Recon Marines, but it was new to me, and I wanted to experience it all before we had to leave Vietnam. Moriarty's cautionary note when we arrived in Vietnam, that we could be leaving Vietnam any day, haunted me. Dean gave the controls to me. "Take us home," he said.

With my feet on the rudders, my left hand wrapped around the collective and my right hand on the cyclic, I felt strangely at peace. That was my first Third Force insert. I had now worked, albeit in a very peripheral position, with the legendary Third Force Recon, commanded by Maj. Alex Lee. This mission greatly influenced my understanding of the Recon missions, and made me feel a little more comfortable.

Back at Phu Bai, I resumed my collateral duty in the paraloft. It was a non-job that gave me the luxury of throwing myself into flying. Yet how did you do that when there were almost 50 first lieutenants who wanted to fly, and only a few HACs to fly with? It was winter and the weather was bad. Ready room time at either Phu Bai or Marble Mountain was the norm.

24: Marble and LZ Baldy Medevac

On 4 December 1969 I found myself scheduled to fly as copilot on the lead medevac bird. Finally, I thought. I'd get to go into the f**king zone. The squadron XO, Maj. Howard Whitfield, was scheduled to be the HAC.

Also on that same day, the Marines of Phu Bai were to have a couple of distinguished visitors. Gen. Lew Walt, the first Assistant Commandant of the Marine Corps to become a four star general, was being escorted to Phu Bai on an informal visit by MajGen. (three stars) William G. Thrash, the 1st MAW Com-manding General. I would have liked to have seen Gen Walt. He was more popular with the troops than the commandant, and, like WWII

Figure 56 General Lewis Walt, Assistant Commandant of the Marine Corps.

5-star General Omar N. Bradley, the "G.I.'s general," He, (Gen. Walt) was the only general I would have recognized. He visited the troops on the front lines, and they loved him for it. And, like General Bradley, General Walt always placed the welfare of his men and country ahead of his own.

Yet, I was also very excited about being in the lead medevac bird and to be flying as copilot with the squadron XO, Maj. Howard Whitfield, even though I'd been disappointed that I was scheduled only to preflight his helicopter for him on my first scheduled flight. I didn't know anything about Maj. Whitfield except that he, like most every combat veteran of the hard war along the border with Laos and the DMZ, had at least one DFC and a handful of air medals. My only experience on a medevac mission thus far had been as copilot on the chase 46 with Babcock and we barely completed the first medevac before being hit and having to reconstitute the medevac package.

The crew of the helicopter ET 29 assigned to Maj. Whitfield was: crew chief, Sgt. D.W. LaPlante; G.E. Moore; and Cpl. D. Martinez were the .50 cal. gunners. The Corpsman, picked up at MMAF, was HN W.C. Moore

The flight schedule identified First Lieutenant John R. Whitworth, another DFC recipient, and his copilot H. R. "Bob" Weber, a recipient of two Purple Hearts and a DFC in the chase bird in ET 21[92]. The medevac Flight Purpose Code (FPC) was 1R6. The Mission number was 11.

Medevac missions were all categorized as "mission necessary." Bad weather and low visibility (monsoons) was still the daily diet of weather. The XO and Whitworth decided on going feet wet to Marble Mountain, a route with which I was becoming familiar.

All of the pilots on this mission had flown these routes several times. Even me in my first flight with Ken Boyack on 18 November and with Babcock on 28-29 November. Arriving in the Da Nang Harbor, we passed by Monkey Mountain and China Beach and entered the Han River, cruising upstream by the hospital ships. Approaching Marble Mountain, the XO made the call.

"Chase...go tower."

"Switching," responded Weber, who was on the controls of the chase bird at the time.

I tuned in Marble Mountain tower, UHF 281.2 written on my knee board. The XO asked for and received permission for a left downwind to Runway 35. He called a flight of two at the 180 and our chase bird swung to an outside starboard cruise position. As we turned on final, he slid further back to our 6 o'clock position, with a step-up to avoid our rotor wash as we lined up on 35. The XO performed a smooth roll-on landing just short of the center field taxiways and called for a left-off to the fuel pits and medevac shack. Whitworth touched down a few seconds behind us.

Once we had both topped-off (refueled) the XO called Marble Ground Control (290.3). He requested taxi clearance to the medevac pad and prior to shutdown, he called Da Nang DASC 313.9, notifying them the Chatterbox medevac package was onboard and assuming the daytime medevac responsibility.

---

[92] At the time of the mission, November 28, 1969, there were no individual numbers assigned to the Aircraft Commanders, i.e. Chatterbox numbers. Those would come soon.

The XO deplaned and got set up in the medevac shack, as did Whitworth. Weber and I remained with the helicopters, setting them up for a quick start by completing the start checklist down to Battery On and Ready APP (pronounced Ape).

Inside the medevac shack, the XO was on the landline talking with DASC, and Whitworth was getting comfortable. The Corpsman from either the 1_{st} Marine Division Hospital (1_{st}. Med) or the Naval Support Activity Hospital (NSA) was already in place. Soon, all were accounted for and the crew chief, corpsman and gunners went on about their business of preparing for anything.

The XO conducted a quick SOP briefing. Then the monotonous waiting began, which meant: letter-writing, playing Acey–Ducey, a game of ping-pong, napping or working on some collateral duty like typhoon control officer. We were like firemen, spring-loaded to react to a fire alarm from a dead sleep. Crew chiefs were always caring for their helicopter. It was their home and their child. The gunners were busy ensuring the belts of .50 cal. ammo were stacked so that no jams would result when firing got hot and heavy. As the sun rose higher and higher, the fog and rain dissipated and the sound of helicopters increased as they began taking the duty runway to fill the air.

I meandered out to where our 46s were parked and stood by the parallel taxiway, next to which sat our helicopters, separated from each other by a high metal revetment. Standing by the nose of my 46, just a few yards short of the parallel taxiway, I had a clear view of the 46s taking off on Runway 36.

The awkward-looking but iconic image of helicopters launching into the air, nose down and tail up was exaggerated in the 46. The aft pylon rotors, the same size as the forward pylon, gave them that super-sized look that caused the uninitiated observer to think it was going to do a header into the runway.

Most were turning hard left after takeoff, south into the Da Nang lowlands where the fire bases were located, or west toward Freedom Hill, III MAF Headquarters, or maybe Camp Reasoner LZ 401, where First Battalion Recon was located. Some made a modified right, heading back the way we had come, north over the

Han River, past the German hospital ships on the west bank, into the bay and over the Hai Van pass to the northern provinces.

I wondered what the day would bring for them...and me. I eventually made my way back into the shack. I considered writing a letter to Kathy, but the phone rang and everyone went on alert, like a blooded Pointer that sensed a flock of pheasants.

25: Choreography

Following the nod from Maj. Whitfield, everyone became animated. Weber, resting in an old easy chair that had seen its last days some years before, got up, stretched and began walking to the door. I followed suit. As we both exited through the door, the crews seeing us began to move in a choreographed manner to their respective helicopters. The XO and Whitworth remained by the phone and map. Each person had a job to do and did it. Hardly a word was spoken.

Weber, a seasoned pilot and veteran of the border wars, had just recently returned from a hospital stay after being wounded earlier in the year. He was glad to be back, and to resume flying.

As I walked briskly toward my 46, the familiar metallic sounds that came from movement on the helicopter by the crews announced that the preparation for flight was underway. The gunners were donning their bullet bouncers with heavy front and back plates of honey-combed ceramic plates and placing belts of ammo into the breach of the machinegun. The crew chief, with his long-cord and fire extinguisher in hand, was positioning himself just a few feet from the port engine.

I entered over the rear ramp, slipping and almost falling down in the perpetual layer of oil and transmission fluid. It has been said, if a 46 isn't leaking engine oil, don't fly it. Recovering, I ducked and twisted to avoid the engine doors that hung from the roof in the aft cargo compartment. The crew chief would secure those doors once there was a successful start.

The corpsman, who had been napping on the battered and oil-stained red nylon bench seats, sat up and began arranging his gear. He was obviously a veteran of this process. The gunners nodded to me as I passed and ducked to squeeze into the cockpit through the cramped entrance between electronic and hydraulic compartments. I hoped I didn't look like a new guy to those veterans, but I'm sure I did.

I strapped into the left seat, ensured that both shoulder harness straps were locked into the lap belt, placed my helmet on my head and pulled the chinstrap tight, buckled my kneeboard above my left knee and flipped on the battery. The 46 came alive with electronic sounds and the whine of gyros. Grabbing the cyclic and squeezing the red trigger to access the ICS, I spoke into the boom mike, "Anyone up?"

"Yes sir," responded the crew chief.

"Let's go round once. Gunners, port?"

"Yes sir, loud and clear."

"Starboard?"

"Loud and clear, sir."

"Corpsman?"

"Yes sir."

"Okay then, let's do this."

I then spoke those immortal words we 46 drivers will never ever forget, "Ready APP."

"Ready APP," came the crew chief's voice in response. "Switch on." The APP wound up in an ever increasing high pitch scream till it produced the power necessary to start the engines.

In a few moments I said, "Ready one."

"Roger," responded the crew chief, "Ready one."

Bringing the Number 1 ECL up to and around the detent that starts the engine; I moved my hand to the Number 2 ECL and did the same, thus both engines were on-line[93]. Reaching up to the console above my head, I flipped the rotor brake toggle switch to "brake-off." Sluggishly, the big blades began to move, their weight gently rocking the 46 side to side. With my right hand now positioned onto both ECLs, I announced to the crew-chief, "Walkin 'em up?"

"Roger sir, walk 'em up."

Moving each ECL forward, at approximately the same time, required a side-to-side movement of the hand, like a slithering snake movement. Each back and forth movement of the hand moved one ECL forward, then the other in small increments thus

[93] "on-line" was common language when an engine started properly. In the above comment, both engines started properly and were, "on-line."

the descriptive term *walking ém up*. The blades moved faster and faster as the ECLs were moved forward until both ECLs reached 98% or *fly*, at what I called the *blur stage* then beeped the engines up to 100% RPM. NATOPS guidance is not to go from 20% to fly in less than 60 seconds. I did it in less than 60 seconds, yet I had still lagged behind Weber whose blades had become a blur as I advanced my ECLs through 60%; so much for following NATOPS procedures if you had to get started quickly. Weber beat me fair and square and had shown me that I was indeed the new guy. Damn, I thought, I gotta find out how he did that.

The old war bird groaned, like an exhausted fullback, who could barely get up after twenty or so punishing carries, but was too proud to accept help. I admired this old Phrog, this warhorse, that had flown through every level of hell and which on any given day held my life and others in its weathered grasp.

I heard the XO making his way through that small tunnel opening into the cockpit. Like all tall people, he had to almost bend double to ease himself into the commander's seat. On his kneeboard were the coordinates of the medevac pick-up. He moved quickly once seated, adjusting his shoulder harness and lap belt as I completed the remaining items on the takeoff check-list. After locking the inertial reel lock of his safety harness, he took control by saying, "I've got the aircraft."

As I felt the controls being taken, I released my grip and re-sponded in accordance with SOP, "You've got the aircraft." Pos-itive transfer of control is a big deal. It sounds kinda corny, but it's necessary.

"It's a routine," explained the XO, and provided me the co-ordinates.

The HML-167 Comprise gun package—two Hueys, both with a full load of 2.75-inch rockets and a door-mounted M-60 ma-chine gun—were always at max gross on the first mission of the day. When cleared for takeoff, with full power applied, their skids appeared to be no more than a few inches off the deck. The takeoff run was more like a wallowing than a run in search of translational lift, recognized by a shaking and shuddering of the airframe. Dozens of heavy drag marks across the runway was testament to their presence and proof that helicopter pilots can learn to fly anything. Once in the air, still near max power, they wobbled slowly and awkwardly until achieving an altitude of less than 150-feet, in keeping with the ceiling restrictions for helicopters around the Da Nang Air Force Base. They could then begin increasing their airspeed, call clear of MMAF air space, and breathe a little easier.

With our UHF on the working frequency, the XO keyed the mic and said to Whitworth, "Go ground."

Whitworth double-clicked his affirmative rather than taking up precious time with a verbal response, the sign of someone who wasn't an FNG. However, after switching frequencies, Whitworth came back with a solid, "Two's up," an affirmative response to having switched frequencies—positive switches.

XO: "Medevac package requesting taxi onto the parallel for takeoff."

Ground Control: "Roger, Chatterbox, cleared to taxi as requested. Contact tower, 281.2."

XO: "Chase, go tower."

Whitworth double keyed the mike.

XO: "Tower, medevac package requesting takeoff from present position."

Tower advised us of weather, winds, traffic and altimeter setting, and cleared us for takeoff. We were on our way.

We followed the Hueys, remaining low. The fishermen in their round boats took no notice of us. The ceiling, though much better than on our trip down from Phu Bai, was still less than a 1000 feet, with two to three miles of visibility. Approaching the Cau Do bridge at 120 knots, the XO eased back on the cyclic, sending the 46 into a smooth climb to just below the cloud level while turning left to a due south heading along the left side of Highway 1.

The gun package had already obtained the necessary clearances, informing us over medevac common frequency that we were cleared direct to the LZ coordinates. I traced a straight line from our current position to the designated coordinates, folding the map to a manageable size. At altitude, near one thousand feet AGL, due to the ceiling, I could clearly see the Comprise gunships down low in front of us, flying a loose spread. It was the classic Marine Corps medevac package. I could only imagine how good our arrival must look to those needing us. It always made me proud to simply be a small part of it all.

As we approached the LZ, we remained on the UHF common frequency and dialed in the FM frequency for the unit. This zone was considered to be secure, and the Marine was suffering from a high fever, not war wounds. When he was satisfied that we had received all the necessary information from the Grunts in the zone, the XO took over direct communication with their radioman. In an easy, calm, reassuring manner, he asked for smoke.

"Roger smoke," responded the radioman.

At this point, Whitworth communicated that he would be taking up a position a couple of clicks to the west of the zone. The XO rogered Whitworth's transmission and, so far as I could tell, everything was going according to SOP—normal.

Although I had flown a previous medevac mission in the chase bird with Lt. Babcock on 28 November, that entire mission had been an anomaly. Both helicopters had been disabled by enemy fire, and the mission had needed to be reconstituted with new crews and aircraft while we waited for our aircraft to be repaired. I was, therefore, still too new to know what was considered normal operating procedures when performing a medevac.

Smoke made its way through the trees, creating a splash of crimson against the backdrop of deep green foliage, lazily drifting southeast. It looked like an impressionist painting, something Monet might have thrown onto a canvas. All the colors looked rich and deep, like some of the forests in the Bootheel of Missouri. I had grown up playing in the jungles of the Floodways. I felt comfortable here in Vietnam.

The XO set up his approach into the wind, what there was of it, and with one last check with the crew, he began the descent. The Comprise gunships were entering their covering pattern. In one of those 360 degree nose down spiral approaches, we were suddenly on final, flaring to touchdown. We were in the zone. "If you ain't in the zone, you ain't in the war," was the mantra CH-46 pilots chanted when poking fun at Dimmer, the CH-53 squadron, because they were prevented from landing in hot zones, due to a fear of losing them. Those rigs were very expensive. The 46s were expendable.

The most vulnerable times for a helicopter are on approach to landing, sitting in the zone, and during takeoff. At one of these points, you will be fired on if an aggressive enemy force is present. I was acutely aware that both of us, the chase 46, Whitworth, and our 46 could both be hit by ground fire at any moment. I expected to take fire, even though there was nothing to suggest we would, just like before. The earlier mission was similar to this one. We had Comprise yet they didn't get hit. We did. I wondered why two gunships hadn't at least intimidated the enemy on that earlier mission. These thoughts flashed through my head in a millisecond.

Upon approaching the zone, 300 feet... 200 feet... 100 feet... 50 feet... touchdown, I pushed myself back into the armored seat. Positioning my right hand near the ramp switch on the center console, I waited to feel the main mounts settle on the ground. The XO brought the bird down directly to the deck in a smooth no-hover landing. The crew chief asked for the ramp; down it went. The Marines in the zone were covering themselves from the hurricane-force winds of the rotor blades. Loose gear, sand, and debris were blown away due to the power applied for landing. The radioman was crouched down with a flak jacket and no helmet, his back to the helicopter, his hair blowing in the windstorm we created. As we settled into the zone, the XO reduced the collective, reducing the lift characteristics of the blades while keeping the power at 100%. This eased the winds some. The radioman then turned toward the helicopter, communicating as necessary to the XO. The sick Marine was helped into the aircraft, and upon receiving a report from the crew chief that we were set to go, the XO advised the radioman that we were lifting and advised him to be vigilant on future medevacs to secure the loose articles in the zone before the helicopter arrives. The radioman screamed over the sound of the blades, "Roger that, sir."

The next few moments, coming out of the zone, were always dangerous as we clawed for altitude. We were super-vulnerable during this procedure because we were big, low, and slow. The XO called out over working UHF, "Out right." A Comprise bird responded, "Roger, right," then moved into their covering mode for egress. I could hear their communications, "I've got his six," meaning that one of the gunships was rolling in to cover the area behind us. However, during this time, I became unaware of where the gunships were located because I was primarily fixed on monitoring the instruments. It was the responsibility of the gunships to stay out of our way. Pulling max power, we departed in a nose high right spiral to altitude. Luckily, the weather had now lifted to almost unrestricted visibility at or above 1500 feet. The XO leveled out at approximately 1200 feet AGL, asked Whitworth to contact Single Parent (code name for the unit responsible for coordinating the medevac birds to a receiving hospital).

There were two hospitals in Da Nang: First Med, located on the western edge of Da Nang near Third Marine Amphibious Force (III MAF) Headquarters and the Naval Support Activity (NSA) Hospital, due west of the MMAF. We could also be diverted to one of the hospital ships, the *Repose* or the *Sanctuary*.

Whitworth announced that we were being directed to First Med. The Gun package advised they were returning to base (RTB). Whitworth accompanied the XO and me to the medical facility. After depositing the medevaced Marine, we also returned to MMAF, refueled, and assumed the ready position for the next call. I had now officially completed my first medevac. My experience was growing, and so was my confidence.

Whitworth, during our down time, reminded me that the goal was to remain in the zone, ramp down, for no more than six seconds. I would never forget this, even though on most occasions, remaining in the zone for only six seconds wasn't possible.

26: Hand to Hand

As soon as we returned to the medevac hooch, we were directed to relocate the entire package to LZ Baldy, also known as Hill 63 (Coordinates BT 136455), the home of the 7th Marines. The relocation seemed like a strange request, but according to the XO there were going to be changes enacted on a daily basis. LZ Baldy was a garrison located south of the Twin Bridges and west of Highway 1 on Route 535, the southeastern approach to the Que Son Mountains. This area was in what was commonly referred to as Indian Country, a term reminiscent of a John Wayne movie used to depict any place where the VC/NVA lived and fought. All of I Corps was Indian Country as far as I could tell. The real challenge would have been trying to find a place that wasn't Indian Country.

On that day, 041269, there was action on Barrier Island, some 34 miles south of Hoi An within the TAOR of the 2d Brigade, Camp of the Blue Dragon, ROK Marines. The island, a strip of sand that vaguely meets the minimum geological requirements to be designated an island, is separated from the mainland by a skinny north-south river called Troung Giang that angles southeasterly into the sea. The north end of the island is defined by the Cua Dai Song, a river that runs from the mountains west into the sea. By being based at Baldy, our medevac team was within 20 minutes of any medevac that might be needed in that treacherous area. The "Baldy" medevac was destined to be a regular daily medevac location. It was always hot at Baldy!

The ROK's were well known for their disciplined behavior and relentless pursuit of the enemy; and they wore distinctive and very cool-looking tiger-striped jungle utes. They were known not to take some prisoners, and those who were taken were normally brought to the ROK Marine headquarters where they were vigorously interrogated. The ROKs never gave nor asked for any quarter from their enemy, and we U.S. Marines admired and respected them above all other military units.

Historically, LZ Baldy had been held by both Army and Marine units. It was always hot at Baldy. The base had a short runway with a control tower and heavily sandbagged buildings and bunkers. The outer perimeter was enclosed in double concertina wire with cleared fields of fire backed up with Claymore mines— the ones marked "THIS SIDE TOWARD ENEMY" in bold writing[94]. The base looked every bit like the set of John Wayne's movie *The Green Berets*, except LZ Baldy also had a touch of Mel Gibson's *Mad Max*. Marines walked around the base in flak jackets and weapons at the ready. This was the real deal. There was definitely an atmosphere of heightened awareness that Charlie could be lobbing in mortars at any moment.

Further west from Baldy, along the rugged and mine-swept road that continues west into the rich greenery of the western approaches to the Que Sons was the remote outpost of Fire Support Base (FSB) Ross. Ross was overlooked by FSB Ryder; a small observation and support base appropriately named for being located on a geological saddle; quite literally a backbone, connecting separate portions of the Que Son Mountains. A small boulder near the helo pad with the name, Ryder, scrawled in red paint reminded me of blood. Ryder also overlooked An Hoa home of the big 175MM self-propelled guns and was near Antennae Valley.

[94] 1.5 lbs. of C-4, a plastic explosive, is in each Claymore mine. When ingested in small quantities, seizures and vomiting occur. However, there are no long term impediments caused as a result. It was known that some medevaced individuals purposefully ingested the C-4 in order to get out of the field. This was happening more often as the drawdown grew closer and many did not want to be the last person to die in Vietnam.

Figure 57 One of the "Big Mamma" 175 mm self-propelled guns at An Hoa.

Upon our arrival at the Baldy medevac pad, First Lt. C.K. Doi and his copilot "Butch" King arrived in ET 11. For whatever reason, we were swapped aircraft. Doi took ET-29 back to Phu Bai along with the crew chief, Sgt. La Plante. ET 11 and its crew chief Cpl. J. Poulos remained with the XO and me. The gunners and corpsman all remained with us.

At about 1400 a call came in for an emergency medevac. The XO and Whitworth took the information as the rest of us ran to the aircraft. The start sequence was the same as always—hurry up.

I learned from Weber that the rotor brake should be released before starting Engine 1, the port engine. The procedure was not in compliance with NATOPS. But, contrary to what I originally believed coming out of the training command, the practice was never addressed as being wrong. The number two engine would be brought to 20% in the same manner. This allowed the blades to begin moving at the beginning of the start sequence, saving maybe twenty seconds in bringing the rotor speed to flight RPM before the aircraft commander was strapped into his seat.

I started the turn-up as Weber had described. When I reached 98%, I glanced at his blades. I couldn't tell if he had beat me or not, but I felt that I had learned one of those little secrets that makes you a better copilot—a better Vietnam helicopter pilot. I then beeped the engines to 100%. I began to feel that I had washed a little of the FNG off myself. Moments later the XO and Whitworth were headed for the birds. The Baldy tower frequency on UHF 327.0 granted us clearance to lift and depart to the east.

The Comprise gunships were with us and began making their way to the pickup point. The coordinates for the pickup were on Barrier Island. It was owned by the ROKs. The zone was only a few minutes from Baldy and the preliminary brief, as stated to me by the XO, was that the zone was hot, and there had been hand-to-hand fighting there as recently as 15 minutes prior to the call. The words excited me. This was it! The XO had not defined the mission as an emergency, but then it must have been, or why would we be flying into a hot zone with active combat ongoing.

Finding the zone wasn't difficult. The gunships had already found it, which was obvious by the time we reached a few hundred feet AGL coming out of Baldy. We continued to climb to 1500 feet while the gunships circled the scene like chicken hawks. Their presence was comforting. The Comprise lead directed us to the FM frequency where we could hear the zone brief being given by the radioman in the zone. "There is no enemy action at this time."

With Whitworth in a loose cruise on the outside of our orbit, everything seemed okay. Yet, this was the kind of situation the instructors at Santa Ana spoke of—times when it seemed there was no action, when only moments before, action was hot and heavy, and vice versa. Which would it be was the question in my head.

The sea stories, probably exaggerated, about situations like this were all over the place. But the core of those stories was probably true. When going into a hot zone, where hand-to-hand combat was reportedly going on, be prepared to get in and get out as fast as possible and have the door gunners ready to fire.

Well, that seemed like good advice on any landing in Vietnam. I was full of anticipation, and not afraid. I was excited. My internal dosing of adrenalin was high. I now wondered if that wasn't how everyone felt—not afraid, just excited—and that made you better, maybe.

The XO was the picture of cool and calm and showed no outward signs of anything but professional behavior. He took over direct communication with the radioman in the zone from Comprise. The radioman in the zone identified himself as a Marine liaison officer assigned to the ROKs. He re-emphasized the situation in the zone; several casualties with various types of wounds including bayonet wounds from close combat no more than 15 minutes prior to our arrival. It seemed that everyone was using '15 minutes' as the catch-all time frame for when the last incoming fire was received. The XO rogered the brief and asked for smoke. Whitworth keyed the mike and advised that he was going to set up a couple of clicks away; the XO double keyed his affirmative to Whitworth.

The crew was briefed on the situation. The .50-cal. gunners charged their weapons by pulling the bolt back and releasing it, ensuring the round is properly seated for firing. The XO advised that there were no known friendlies outside the wire of the zone and to return fire when fired upon. This was rogered by the crew chief and both gunners.

The XO set up the entry into the spiral as yellow smoke briefly rose from the zone to a height of 12 to 15 feet before it was swept toward the sea by a gentle yet steady 10-15 knot westerly breeze. Dropping the collective, the XO put us into the standard CH-46 tight 180 degree nose-down spiral. At the same time, the Comprise package went to 1,000 feet AGL, setting up a covering pattern. It was another one of those dizzying rides where it seemed that the nose of the aircraft remained stationary, pointing directly into the zone, and the tail seemed to rotate around as we rolled in on final and flared for touchdown. I did what copilots do—took notes and carefully monitored the instruments. As I pushed as far back in the armored seat as possible, I visually went through the landing checklist. My right hand was poised for activating the hydraulic isolation system just in case a lucky shot hit our hydraulics—the heart of the system.

The flare of this 11,585 pound flying machine will always create a windstorm. Ponchos, shelter halves and anything not tied down flew into the air. Luckily, we blew everything away from us and nothing was sucked up into the rotor arc or into the engines. The ROKs, who had just had their hands full with either VC or NVA or both, had not secured their gear prior to our arrival—understandable in this situation. As the main mounts settled into the sand, I lowered the ramp. The corpsman ran down the ramp to prepare the evacuees for transport. I began my silent count: 1001 ...1002 ...1003 ...1004 ...1005 ...1006—and we were still in the zone. There were no signs of the evacuees.

I began to feel like a sitting duck and forgot about counting, keeping my hand near the ramp switch and waiting for the crew chief's okay, all the while mindful of keeping myself well inside the wings of the armored seat. At regular intervals, I could see the shadow of Comprise through the blur of the blades. The gunships were not in the zone with us, they were at 1,000 feet, or more. Thankfully, there was no shooting. As a matter of fact, there was nothing going on. How could a place be reported as being in hand-to-hand combat with battle casualties minutes prior to our arrival and then upon our arrival be so utterly calm?

Barrier Island was just sand with sparse vegetation. The name Barrier Island should have been replaced by the name Barren Island. The word was that the ROKs had bulldozed the whole island. There was no place for Charlie to hide there. So where was he? Were they all killed and put in a pot to be cooked to perfection? Maybe given the circumstances, it was not an idea to be summarily dismissed. The ROKs were all milling about, disheveled and pissed off at us, while trying to keep their gear from being blown all over hell's half-acre.

These guys were not like the ROKs at the Camp of the Blue Dragon, all spit and polish. These guys looked like ancient warriors, like the Hwarang Warrior Knights of ancient Korea—tough, real tough. I half expected to see a VC staked to the ground with ants chewing on him.

One story told back in the squadron came to mind. A VC sapper[95] who had the misfortune of being captured trying to throw a satchel charge into a ROK-protected village, was hanged between two long poles that crisscrossed over the entryway to the village. The body hung there throughout that particular day as a warning to any future saboteurs. They knew how to get their point across. We Marines loved the ROKs.

Still sitting with full power, I was getting anxious. It'd been five minutes in the zone, a very long time. What happened to the six seconds stuff? Maybe the six seconds crap was thrown out to me as a joke. The XO was completely quiet. He hardly ever spoke. I began to wonder if he was with me in the cockpit or somewhere else, like Hawaii or somewhere. Some chatter over the UHF frequency between the Gun birds broke the silence. "Everything okay down there?" I wanted to say something like, "Yeah...there ain't shit down here. Did we come to the right zone?" But I didn't. Hell, I was just along for the ride.

The crew chief announced, "They're coming" then he briefly paused before saying, "I think?"

The XO called on the liaison officer, "What's up?"

After a bit, the answer came. "They're coming; the corpsman, a makeshift stretcher fashioned from a shelter-half and a couple of walking wounded." I cautiously leaned forward in my seat to see how far the med-evacuees might be from reaching us. With my back partially turned toward the XO, I felt a hand on my shoulder pulling me back into the armored seat.

[95] Sapper: a special elite combat element trained to penetrate installations to carry out assassinations or sabotage. The NVA Sappers were a much-feared force. They normally wove themselves through outer defenses of fire bases, etc. in complete silence.

"I'd rather not have a dead copilot, yet!" he said. "Don't make it easy for Charlie to kill you. We have no cover that amounts to much, so don't give Charlie a clear shot." I immediately fell back into the FNG mode just when I was beginning to have some confidence.

Finally, the evacuees were onboard. The crew chief cleared the ramp to be raised. The XO squeezed the trigger on the cyclic and made the call "out-right" to the gunships and Whitworth. The gunships responded by setting up their wagon-wheel coverage as the XO, with a "good to go" from the crew chief, pulled up on the collective. The ROKs turned their backs, bracing them-

Figure 58 LZ Baldy medevac pad with control tower in right rear.

selves as some were pushed along by the storm. We came out right with full power and in one 360 degree turn we were back at altitude headed toward Baldy, only a few minutes away. We dropped the med evacuees off at Baldy's hospital then repositioned to the fuel pits before returning to the medevac pad. I made notes regarding the medevac for use on the AA report and thought about my lessons learned. Never, never give Charlie a clean shot at you; remain far back in the armored seat while on the deck and keep the rotors at 100% when in the zone, for you may have to leave in a hurry and if you were at idle, you'd probably be dead before you could get the ECLs to flight RPM.

I later learned that although Barrier Island had been bull-dozed clean; the island was a veritable ant hill rumored that the ROKs had discovered near a 1,000 "spider" holes within each 1,000-meter grid square. The VC could launch lightening raids and disappear before your very eyes, like a circus magician stealing away in a false compartment. They were there! It was a sobering thought.

I recalled the Comprise gunships circling us at a 1,000 feet. My thoughts, at that time, were if they had attempted to lay down protective fire from their orbiting altitude with 7.62 rockets or a door mounted M-60, the whole 46 would have been sprayed. No one was that good a shot from one of those airframes, unless it was that insulting VC farmer that hit Babcock and me when we were at altitude. But he wasn't firing from a flying platform. Furthermore, even though we were armed with pistols, what good was it? I had the distinct feeling that the only reason we had a sidearm was to fire flare rounds if we survived a crash or assault and were lucky enough to still have a sidearm. Hell, all they had to do was attack the 46 from the front, where there was no firepower and that would put a stop to it all. I don't recall any helicopter crews being taken prisoner by Charlie and none being released by the peace-loving Army of the People's Republic years later, following our ouster.

"Everything okay down there?" had been the extent of the communication from the gunship to the XO. A double key of the mike had been his response. We had no forward firing capability, only our firearms that were terribly insufficient. The fantasy of a 46 shooting its way out of a zone was just that, a John Wayne fantasy. On the ground in that zone, the XO and I had been sitting ducks, totally dependent upon covering fire by gunships or ground forces. For the most part, the action was at the rear of the helicopter, around the ramp, with the pilots looking out into nothingness. "Don't worry about it. We're covering you," was not very reassuring. Something had been different this time. Comprise didn't get down into the zone with us like they had during my first medevac on 28 November.

27: Medevac Common

My thoughts about the ROK Marines and Comprise gunships were interrupted by yet another Baldy medevac request that day—a routine medevac. The pickup coordinates were northwest of Baldy, in the foothills of the Que Sons. The time was approaching for us to head back to Phu Bai, and this medevac would probably be the last of the day for us. So far, so good, and I had learned something else by watching Whitworth and Weber. Don't run to the helicopter for a routine medevac. I was actually beginning to feel a little relaxed.

After a normal start-up and takeoff, we departed Baldy to the northwest. The Comprise guns were out in front and below us, probably about 500 feet AGL. I was on the map and had the zone fixed. The XO knew where he was going and didn't need the map. My thoughts were to visualize the area and orient myself as to where we were from Baldy, in case I had to walk back. We continued on a direct heading, coming under the gaze of the majestic and sinister-looking Que Son Mountain. The bucolic jade green rice paddies were turning to rolling terrain with dense jungle-like foliage, but it was not a jungle, just very rough country.

In a few minutes, the gunships made contact via FM with the zone; we were all listening in as the zone brief was made. It was a by-the-book-brief, a no-sweat. There was sufficient room for a three point landing in the zone, no main mount landing with the nose hanging over a 500 foot drop, or jungle so thick you couldn't see outside of a few meters when landed. Yet, there was a geological peculiarity. The hill seemed out of place with the surrounding low ground. It was obviously a frequently used spot because it looked like an old camp ground area. The Marines were set up around the zone. It appeared the Marines were conducting a normal sweep of the area for spots where Charlie could congregate and be an immediate threat to Baldy. A sweep was always underway around Baldy, one of the most active enemy targets in the war. The evacuee had probably twisted his ankle.

The gunships set up their wagon-wheel formation and Whitworth took his place approximately one click (a thousand meters) to the east of the zone. The radioman advised there was no immediate enemy activity. The winds were light and moderate; we could have landed in any direction without worries about the winds; however, we were in Indian Country and anything could happen.

I was preoccupied with copilot duties, my finger on the map, like we were taught in HMMT-302 when navigating our way through the Surprise Canyon Wilderness into Death Valley and keeping track of coordinates and sorties for the day's activities. The approach was routine—to the northwest, where purple smoke spewed from the zone. The XO began what I would now call a modified spiral, not the usual tight nose-down death spiral as the approach into Barrier Island had been. This one was more like a casual cruise. There was no indication of enemy contact in that zone, therefore, no tactical combat approach was necessary. Our airspeed gradually reduced to 70 knots as we turned on final. It was a smooth NATOPS descent toward the bare knoll that sat just above the glare shield of the 46 — textbook!

A quick glance told me the gauges were all within the normal range as I ran through the landing checklist concluding with a shrug of my shoulders to ensure "Inertia reel lock—locked." We passed through 150 feet with an airspeed of 30 to 40 knots, down to 75-100 feet where the airspeed ceased bleeding off as the altitude continued down to approximately 25 feet. Our intended point of landing was just above the glare-shield (like the dashboard of a car) and beginning to disappear under the aircraft as it was supposed to do.

Then I began to have an uncomfortable feeling, that sixth sense of foreboding; the one experienced by all helicopter pilots when at some point, for some reason, at the bottom of an approach, things just don't seem to be going right. Not too bad, but we were too high and too fast for the point we were at in the approach; the airspeed wasn't bleeding off. The drill is, announce a wave-off and go around. Just go around. Do it again.

There's no reported enemy activity. Don't try to salvage a bad approach. That's the drill, that's good headwork, and it's pounded into every flight student, by every flight instructor, day in and day out. Sink rate should be 500 feet per minute in the approach, reducing to zero with airspeed reducing to zero at the point of landing. We could have done a no-hover landing that would have lessened the storm of dust on the ground, but none of that happened.

We were too high and too fast, it seemed surreal. I was confident that this was just one of those approaches that didn't happen in the way it was intended—it happens. Yet instead of waving off the approach, the correction applied by the XO was to perform a quick stop, the nose well above the horizon, while simultaneously lowering the collective to arrest any forward progress. The nose of the 46 then dropped through the horizon. The vertical speed indicator (VSI) bounced around briefly, then plummeted. The XO's immediate response was to raise the collective into the armpit, applying sufficient power to slow the descent into the zone. The hair on my neck and arms rose up. I instinctively braced for impact, pushing back hard in the armored seat while simultaneously ensuring the inertia reel lock on my shoulder harness was indeed locked. My mind raced as to where we would finally land, or better yet, where the crash would end as we fell off the knoll and possibly caught fire. The maneuver worked. The big T-58 engines spooled up[96] and stopped us right at the moment of probable impact. He pulled it out. But what had happened? What the hell was that all about?

The rule of thumb is not to use more power to land than is required to take off. Granted, on some occasions, especially in Vietnam, it can be necessary to apply a large amount of power as speedily as possible, surpassing the amount of power required

---

[96] Spooling up refers to stabilizing the jet engine before applying power. In layman terms, it means that when the collective is raised in a quick movement, trying to avoid a hard landing, it takes a few moments for the T-58 engines to react. During that brief time required for the engines to come up to speed, you may not avoid a very hard landing.

in a normal take off. But on this particular occasion I failed to see the exigent circumstances that required anything more than a normal approach.

The following saying was written on the walls of our hooch by some unknown former resident. "Lose not thy turns lest the earth rise up and smite thee." A truer saying there never was. We were lucky this time; no lost RPM, and the power was available, primarily because we were light, not heavily loaded. My mind returned to the remainder of the medevac in which the evacuee was ambulatory, walking alone to the aircraft.

Throughout the process, there was nothing but silence from the XO. I said nothing. The silence made me uneasy. I made a sideward glance at the XO, waiting for him to say something, to explain, or to just say, "Ah shit!" Something! He said nothing, staring forward as if transfixed. Wow, what had I just witnessed? Had I, as a student at HMMT-302, done something like that, my flight instructors would likely have had me doing spot landings until I retired, or more likely, just shipped me directly to Paris Island to serve out my hitch as point man on some lost platoon in the Thuong Duc Corridor.

Upon leaving the LZ, Whitworth fell into a cruise position as we began picking our way back to Da Nang with the evacuee. It was at this point that the second situation of the day happened. Whitworth told us that Comprise gunships wanted us to call Single Parent, the organization that told us where to take the evacuee. Single Parent wanted more information about the patient. I figured the wounded soldier might just have been bored because he didn't appear to be sick or hurt. Whitworth directed us to come up on "Button Red." I said nothing. The XO, Whitfield, directed me to input "button red."

"What's that frequency?" I asked.

"Don't you know?"

I had no idea what Button Red's frequency was, and without responding immediately I went to work trying to thumb through the frequency cards on which there were hundreds of frequencies listed, none of which were labeled "red" that was associated in any manner to medevac. I was finally forced to respond that I didn't know the button red frequency and couldn't find it.

I cringed, waiting for his response. He was quiet for a few more moments, then he keyed the mike and responded to Whitworth, Comprise gunships and, I suppose, anyone else listening in on that UHF frequency. "My copilot doesn't know the frequency for button red. Please pass it to me."

Hell, he's the XO, and he doesn't know what button red is either. No wonder it wasn't briefed. Whitworth without hesitation passed the frequency over the air, "35.5," an irregularity, if not some kind of violation due to me not knowing that damn frequency. I immediately dialed in the frequency and waited for the XO to make the call, but there was nothing but silence for many moments. Finally, he directed me to make the call to Da Nang medevac, which was actually called, Single Parent, to find out where we were to take the evacuee. Humiliated and sick to my stomach, I did as directed. I will never forget 35.5.

I felt small enough to crawl up under my armored seat cushion. Louis Puller Jr.,[97] in his Nobel Prize winning biography *Fortunate Son* described a "visceral humiliation" at having straggled

---

[97] Louis B. Puller, Jr. killed himself on 11 May,1994. He had lost both his legs just below his waistline and parts of both hands when he stepped on a land mine in Vietnam on 11 October 1968. Son of the Legendary Lewis (Chesty) Puller, the most highly decorated Marine in history. "Lou," was in the same OCS class as A.C., Eric, Roy and me. We were in different platoons, but I recall how the Drill Instructors (DIs) seemed to target him for every little almost inconceivable infraction. I recall him doing pushups in the middle of the hallway with two or three DI's standing over him, yelling at him, telling him he wasn't anything like his old man, Chesty. I remember his name that was placed on the back of his utility blouse, like all of us, when he could not place one foot in front of the other on those early, grueling forced marches, crawling when he couldn't walk, suffering that "visceral humiliation" that I could have never known unless Chesty had been my father. I made my way around him as the struggle not to straggle pushed men to their limits and beyond. I believed then as I do today that he was targeted so that no one could say he slid through OCS on his father's reputation. I remember the DIs when we were commissioned as Second Lieutenants in the Little Theater on the Marine Base, Quantico, Virginia. They swarmed around Chesty hoping for a glance from him, to touch his sleeve, to acknowledge his every motion as the news media smothered both Chesty and his son, Louis. He was medevaced by

on conditioning hikes over the hill trail in OCS Class No. 48 in 1967-68. On the day of that medevac, I understood what he meant.

The gunships passing the frequency over the air, in the open, was a violation of something; it had to be, I thought. But they had no choice. A medevac bird that didn't know the frequency of Single Parent must never have happened before and the XO had put the whole thing on me, the FNG. Why not?

Once the evacuee was deposited at First Med, we made our way back to Phu Bai in absolute silence—the longest trip I had experienced to date. What now? On this, my ninth flight in-country, I felt it was all over. I was certain that I would be sent to the Communications Bunker with Ridgeway or much worse, forward air controller (FAC) duty for the remainder of my tour, because I wasn't FAC trained.

Finally we landed back at Phu Bai. Following shutdown, and as I gathered up my gear, I bumped into the crew chief. He looked at me and just rolled his eyes. I was certain he was disgusted with my performance, and if there is anyone from whom a 46 pilot wants respect, it's the crew chief, above all.

262 HAC, Jim Dau from that hell in Vietnam to his hell on earth. Rest in Peace Louis Puller Jr., you are missed, Semper Fi.

28: The Debrief

My goal was to complete my post flight duties as fast as possible. Flight crews were returning from all sorts of flights: troop lifts, recon inserts and extracts, resupply, administration, and maybe record-setting altitude attempts by Meskan and a sandbag. After writing up the flight information, sorties, number of evacuees, any enemy fire taken, etc., I gave the paperwork to the XO, who never mentioned the incident, and I never asked how he felt about the flight. Feeling like crap, I just wanted to get the hell out of there.

I thought it was a good time to go to the paraloft to check on any mail that I might have and to just get away from the crowd in the ready room. While putting my flight gear away in the cubby hole assigned to me, I heard someone say, "Welcome aboard."

It was Mike Delong. Like many in the Corps, he was a Marine legacy. His father was Colonel Phillip C. Delong, the Marine Corps' thirteenth-highest scoring ace. He flew nearly 200 combat missions in Corsairs in WWII and Korea. Mike was in Operations under Captain "Smokey" Stover, and he pretty much knew what was going on at any level in the squadron at any time. Because of the time he spent in the ready room around the operations desk, he had become one of the best ping-pong players in the squadron, maybe in the whole wing. He was affable with a sly smile that could rapidly twist into a wicked grin. In a quiet response to him, I simply shrugged my shoulders and said, "Yeah, thanks. I think I need a drink."

Mike somehow must have known of my faux pas and said, "See you at the club."

"Yeah."

I made my way through the maintenance hangar and up the stairs to the paraloft to check for any mail. Sgt. Patton was working on something and said without looking up, "No mail today, Sir." I always felt self-conscious about men near my own age call-

ing me sir. But that's the Corps and tradition rules. I hadn't begun receiving any mail yet, and I didn't want to read any letters
anyway.

With Sgt. Patton busy, I shot the breeze with Lance Corporal
Delp, a farm boy from Ohio. He and I had that in common, and
we often spoke of hunting and working on the farm. He told me
he was a qualified .50 cal. gunner and received extra pay for flying and shooting—the best of both worlds. I told him how I grew
up shooting snakes on the floodways of Southeast Missouri, and
told the story of the killing of Harry "Fats" Shell by Donald "Hokey" Busby on our farm when I was twelve years old, something
I could never quite forget.[98]

Delp laughed and said, "I know what you're talk'n about
when it comes to shotguns, hunt'n, crazy drunks, and women."

"Ain't it the truth," Sgt. Patten said.

I thought I had interfered with them enough and was about
to take my leave but thought of one more thing. "Y'all ain't heard
anything about our missing Staff Sergeant have ya?"

"Hell no, we ain't heard nothing" responded Sgt. Patton.

"How about Wags? Seen him today?"

"Yes sir, this morning."

"He okay?"

"He seemed to be."

"Okay, guess I'll go. I had one hell of a bad day today."

"It'll get better tomorrow," one of the crew said as I turned
to leave. That was a perpetual thought that some didn't exactly
believe. In Vietnam, there was always something that could be
worse tomorrow.

I finally made my way to the hooch after stopping by the
small exchange, looking around, and leaving with a five cent can
opener. I thought we might need another one in the common
area. Although pop-top cans were nothing new, occasionally an
old can of beer from some unknown source would show up with

---

[98] I later wrote a book named *Murder on the Floodways* about my life and
experiences on the Floodways of the Bootheel of Missouri, detailing the killing of Harry Leslie "Fats" Shell, by Donald Ray "Hokey" Busby.

signs of rust on it and without a pop-top pull tab. In that case, we needed an old fashioned church key.

The hooch was beginning to take on all the comforts of home, including an old easy chair (the kind you see on the front porch of fraternity houses or cotton patch shacks) which looked like rats might have made it their home. I grabbed a cold beer, trudged to my rack, kicked off my boots and tossed my pistol belt and cover on the back of a chair. I laid down on the electric blanket that kept the bed warm and dry, reached over on my ammocrate bookshelf and flipped on a cassette tape of The Mamas & The Papas. "Monday ... Monday, can't trust that day." And, without taking another sip of that beer...dozed off into total darkness. As I always contended, each hour of sleep was an hour out of country, and if you slept half the time, it cut your tour of duty in half.

Damn ... what's that? The screeching and dragging of the hooch door across the concrete floor brought me back from that delicious unconscious state of deep sleep. The reefer door opened and closed followed moments later by the distinct crunching sound of a pop-top beer being opened and the recognizable click of a Zippo lighter, followed by the smell of a freshly lit cigarette. It was Gary.

"Well ... well, you're here," he said. "How'd it go today?"

"Fine, just great, couldn't have gone better." Then I told him of the events.

"Wow, better you than me," he said with a smile. "Have a beer and forget it." That was the best advice you could get or give in Vietnam for most anything that happened—just have a beer and forget it. Another saying was, "Nothin' means nothin'."[99] I proceeded to act accordingly.

Following the beer, we went to the chow hall, then on to the club—a haven from the nasty weather that was always coming in from the west-northwest. Gary and I sat, talked, and listened

---

[99] "Nothing means nothing" was a common phrase in Nam. It literally meant there is no value that can be given to anything in Vietnam: words, deeds, material things...nothing...means anything (nothing).

to the music flooding the bar from that common accessory, the 4010 TEAC reel-to-reel, sipping a cold beer. Then, in came some more desperate-looking pilot types: John Parnham, Tom Reid, Bill Nelson and Gene Tolls. They sat together in their group, laughing and talking about whatever happened that day. Alone at the bar was Capt. "Smokey" Stover shooting-the-breeze with a pilot I didn't know while a couple of Vietnamese waitresses tended bar and took orders at tables. Mike Delong, Mike Glynn, Pete Hanner and Ron McAmis soon arrived, along with Joe Smith and some 161 pilots included in which were First Lieutenants Jerry Berry, Brian Duniec, Joe Smith and others. Soon, the movie would begin, maybe.

After some time elapsed, I went to the bar to buy another round of drinks and an impromptu conversation ensued between me and Stover. Stover's demeanor made him easy to talk to. You'd think he was your best friend and in that conversation I told him of my concerns regarding the flight with the XO, the approach, and my FM 35.5 debacle. He dismissed my not knowing the frequency as simply being an FNG occurrence, but didn't address the XO not knowing the frequency. However, the approach I described did get his attention. I was surprised that he proceeded to tell me that the XO had recently (10 May 1969) crashed, killing five Marines in a similar manner to what I described—going in high and fast, having to perform a quick stop out of ground effect, pulling power, losing turns, and crashing into the zone.

Unaware of this previous incident, I wondered why there wasn't some way to address these happenings.

Stover warned me, "Be careful talking about this incident any further."

I thought, maybe it's just me, but didn't that incident and what just happened to me look like a trend? My immediate thought, in response to Stover's comment, was that I didn't really care what might happen to me. It seemed there was a real problem with the XO, and that the old guys knew of the problem.

The problem may have been as simple as a depth perception issue. Why wasn't it addressed-especially after the May 1969 crash.

Even at my early age in flying, I knew that a poor approach can happen to anyone. The XO's alleged response to a bad approach was to try to salvage that approach rather than to wave off or go around. Trying to salvage a bad approach rather than to wave off or go around was not good headwork, yet in a combat environment, a go-around or wave-off might be worse. Like the umpire at home plate, the final decision could only be made by the aircraft commander. Also, the old axiom of not flying over the same ground twice is indeed a factor in that decision making. God help the person who makes the wrong call.

I was beginning to understand what kind of war the old guys had checked into when they came to Vietnam, the legacy they inherited, the legacy we inherited: flying into a large enemy presence every day, eyeball-to-eyeball with small arms, automatic weapons, hand- and rocket-propelled grenades, mortars, and maybe the mythological anti-aircraft weapon, the quad-fifty. Occasionally, it was finding a fragmentation grenade in the cargo area with the pin partially pulled and midair collisions as occurred in Operation Hastings and in the siege of Khe Sanh. Most of these men had received Silver Stars and DFCs with clusters and a bucketful of air medals. Many had been wounded, patched up, and sent back in, like First Lieutenants Steve Bravard and Robert "Bob" Weber, Capt. White, and many more. That kind of day-to-day survival had to leave some scars.

At the root of it all was to try not to present one's self to the enemy as a big, slow target, in a machine that could only be big and slow when landing or taking off. I knew that the XO had been flying in that environment for months, maybe years, before I had arrived. I now knew that those months had been bad, really bad, and who was I to say anything.

After a while, Mike Delong made his way over to me at the bar. He chuckled a bit and said, "How did you like your first medevac with the XO?" He'd overheard me talking about the flight.

234 | Harold G. Walker

I turned toward Mike and said, "No, my second medevac. The first one was cut short." I added, "Guess I'll never forget what Button Red is." Everyone in hearing distance burst out laughing, relieving the tension and relaxing me. Mike sat down on a stool by me, grabbed a cold beer, and downed a big gulp.

"Don't worry about it," he said. Mike then took time to educate me about what had happened out there. "The brief should have included you. The working frequencies for a medevac are known, and probably the XO didn't deem it necessary to recite it in the brief, especially the medevac common frequency 35.5."

"Yeah," I said, "but why didn't the XO know the frequency if it was deemed to be so well known that it was unnecessary to brief?"

"I don't know," he responded, taking another drink. "It was an odd thing that happened, yet it was obvious he had not briefed it because of his over-the-air comment holding you responsible for not knowing the frequency when he, the XO, didn't know."

"Yeah, what the hell was that?"

"The XO's over-the-air comment was not an indictment of you, the new copilot, but of him, the HAC … As for the approach made by the XO, sounds like you may have had a near crash on your hands." Mike paused, then after a few moments, lowered his voice and continued, "You know the XO has already crashed once [in May '69] killing several Marines. It was officially listed as the result of direct enemy action, but changed to unknown. There was talk that the real cause was pilot error. The copilot turned in his wings—quit, the poor son of a bitch."

I began to feel very fortunate to have survived these past couple of weeks, what with my flight with Babcock and this flight with the XO. What can I expect next, a court martial? Well, maybe. Listening to the old guys, it was becoming apparent there was an abundance of dislike for the CO and XO. Meskan was generally described as a medal monger—an eccentric who would do anything to get a medal. He already had a handful of DFCs. The XO was described as a recluse and an oddity, a graduate of the

Air Force Academy. Very few seemed to have any respect for his flying ability; however, they were the veterans, and I was an FNG. Could I, should I, go to someone else, or just forget it?

29: An Awakening

On the morning of 6 December, Gary, Donnie and I went to breakfast together, enjoying a big helping of powdered eggs, canned bacon, toast, and coffee strong enough to hold up the roof. Afterwards we went our separate ways. Gary headed to operations and me to the paraloft to shoot the breeze with Sgt. Patton, and then made my way to the ready room. Upon walking into the ready room, Capt. Stover sidled over to me and in a quiet voice said, "The CO wants to talk to you."

"Oh shit, what now?" I quietly asked.

"I don't know, but I can guess," said Smoke[100] with faux concern spread across his face like milk on a Cheshire cat. "Honest, he just told me to get ya for him. I didn't ask any questions."

Damn. It was my intent from the beginning of this sojourn to maintain a low profile in the squadron. I wanted nothing to do with the CO or XO. After flying, the day before with the XO, a low profile wasn't going to happen what with my loud mouth at the O'Club. That wasn't going to happen again either, I vowed. I knew the CO's sudden interest in me was about that flight. Hell, he didn't know I existed. I was sure that Smoke had been in with the CO, probably the first thing that morning. Maybe, I thought, the CO wants to hear in person about what happened. Maybe he had some unresolved concerns about the XO based on what I was being told about that crash in May: an unexplained power loss, no enemy fire[101] and the copilot turning in his wings afterward? WTF![102]

---

[100] Capt. Stover's nick name, "Smokey" was sometimes shortened to just, "Smoke."

[101] Then Capt. Dave White, one of the officers conducting an investigation into the 10 May 1969 crash, found no evidence of enemy fire, identifying the bullet holes as points where the post crash fire caused ammo to cook-off, exiting through the skin of the helo.

[102] William "Babs" Babcock, in the years following his tour in Vietnam, conducted an in-depth, unpublished and copyrighted investigation into the May, 1969 incident, and noted a similar incident when he was flying with the XO on 8 September 1969.

Years later, the copilot on that flight spoke to Bill Babcock about having been questioned by then HMM-262 Operations Officer, a bald headed major. When the copilot tried to tell how he and the crew chief had tried to override the major's grip on the collective to avoid the crash, he said he was told that nobody wanted to hear stories about pilot error on the part of Maj. Whitfield.

"Walker," said Smoke, "just be cool and agree with him."

I nodded at Smoke, not wanting to get into any kind of a back-and forth discord with him, got up out of my seat, and grabbed another cup of coffee.

"What was that all about?" asked Gary, who was in the area and had seen Smoke talking to me. I filled him in on the sordid details.

"Okay," advised Gary, "when you go in there, remember, just the facts."

"Just like Jack Webb, huh?"

"Yeah, just like Jack Webb." responded Gary.

I appreciated Gary's advice, but, it was becoming abundantly clear to me as to who had snitched me out, other than my own stupid comments. I was getting my first lesson in squadron politics.

I presented myself in the door of the CO's office just as I had been taught in OCS—at attention, standing tall, heels together, hands at my side but I didn't slap the frame of the doorway like required in OCS. "Lt. Walker reporting as ordered, Sir." He looked up, as if he had expected me at that precise moment and said, "Come in."

His reputation as a loner and hard drinker came to mind. He was seated behind his desk with command flags draped, according to tradition, from their staffs behind him. He was in his flight suit, with his well-worn camouflaged cover carefully placed on the desk to his right. It bore the gold leaf of a major dead center in the front panel, where the eagle, globe and anchor decal is normally set.

Maj. Meskan was one of only two majors commanding combat helicopter squadrons at that time. The other was Maj. Carr, the CO of HMM-161, who would soon be turning his command over to LtCol. Bennie H. Mann. It was rumored that Maj. Meskan and Maj. Carr had been promoted to the positions of CO in their respective squadrons because no Lieutenant Colonels wanted to take command of those squadrons that were in the thickest and deadliest fighting of the war.

Quang Tri Air Facility, where HMM-161, 163 and 262 and VMO-6 were based under PMAG-39, sat alongside Highway 1 near Dong Ha, both of which were within "spittin' distance" of the DMZ. The NVA assaults would eventually come south in human waves. The battles along the DMZ were vicious and hard-fought. Loss of aircraft and crews threatened the availability of CH-46s. Operation Hastings in July 1966 had been the beginning of a level of battle that would characterize all the fights along the DMZ and the Laotian border. A whole valley would become known as Helicopter Valley because of the carcasses of CH-46s that littered its floor. Maybe this place was where his kind, the complete warrior, was made.

I stopped in front of his desk and stood at rest, my left arm behind the small of my back. Meskan gave the appearance of reviewing some paperwork, but it was apparent that he was waiting for my appearance, letting me sweat. I remained at rest for several moments wondering what my fate would be. He let me stand, my eyes focused on a point on the wall above his head. I could see that he was looking directly into my eyes. Eventually, he gave the order, "At ease." I continued to stand erect, but looked dead into his eyes.

"Lieutenant Walker," he spat out.

"Yes, Sir," I said in my most officious OCS manner.

"It has come to my attention that you dislike flying with my XO."

This was about as direct and to the point as he could be, and no less than I expected. His demeanor had not disappointed me. His words froze my soul. There was a heaviness in my stomach.

I instinctively knew that every detail of the medevac had been replayed to Meskan by Maj. Whitfield, no doubt with Smokey's added perceptions from the club conversation. My intent was to slow my heart rate and show no emotion either way. My course was clear, I told him everything, from the screwed up approach right down to the part where the XO blamed me, over the air, for not knowing the button red frequency. I had read him correctly; he wasn't surprised by anything I told him, nor did he attempt to correct or challenge me.

Meskan responded, "Lieutenant Walker, let me tell you a few things about living here." His speech was slow, deliberate, easily understood, but surprisingly, not as arrogant or as hard as I had expected. "First of all, all pilots do not fly alike. Secondly, as a new guy in Vietnam, don't bad-mouth your commanding officer or executive officer. You've already screwed up, and you owe the XO an apology. Do it. And by the way, before you leave...I've got a staff meeting tomorrow at Marble, and you will be my copilot."

That was it. I couldn't read the CO's response. On the one hand he was soft-spoken, which I did not expect but which was of little reassurance. I couldn't call this an ass chewing. I didn't get the impression that any more was in store for me. But here I was, an FNG, new in-country, wet behind the ears, and already hip-deep in shit with both the CO and XO. It was a helluva situation for a guy who wanted to maintain a low profile.

"You're dismissed. Go find the XO."

Going to see the XO to apologize was something I wasn't looking forward to doing. Smokey snuck up to my side and said, "What did he say?"

"Apologize to the XO."

Once again, he gave me the same advice, "Just be cool and agree with him."

Apologizing to the XO was a hard pill to swallow, even when ordered to do so. I really didn't want to do this. What would happen if I didn't? I figured my Vietnam tour might already be over. I had no choice.

This was it. Do as ordered…or not. Finally, repeating to myself, "F**k it! Here I go. Whatever happens, happens," I walked directly to the XO's office…and found that he was unavailable. I left the ready room and looked for the XO at his quarters. No luck. An immense feeling of relief came over me. I'd have to see him the next day.

The rumors didn't stop about the XO, probably the work of Stover. It was as if a floodgate had been opened to pent-up past frustrations and problems, and I was the one who opened the raw wound, a hell of a situation. It seemed that everyone was aware of my impending doom. Glances in my direction were redirected upon meeting my gaze. Everyone was wondering where I would land—probably in Special Services at wing headquarters in Da Nang, handing out basketballs.

30: Take a Deep Breath

The hooch was now full of FNGs: A. C. Allen, Kentucky; Pete Hanner, Illinois; Ron McAmis, Kansas; Donnie McGlothlin, Arizona; Roy Prigge, Minnesota; Gary Rainey, Wyoming by way of Louisiana (dual citizenship) and me, Harold Walker, Southeast Missouri, the Bootheel, orphaned from Arkansas and a stepchild to Missouri, a state within a state.

Everyone there, although looking into an uncertain future, seemed to be happy to be in Vietnam, in HMM-262, and in Phu Bai in particular. All of us were from different areas of the country, all of us ready to do our duty. I felt as comfortable with the men in that hooch as I was with my own family. It was true that we were forming into a band of brothers. There were other hooches there with new guys but not one comprised totally of new guys. And soon enough it happened; we were vandalized by a masked man who scrawled "F**king New Guys" across the front of the outside door door leading into our inner sanctum.

On 6 December 1969, I flew a 1.2 night maintenance test with Bill "Fuels" Nelson.[103] Early 7 December,[104] I found myself scheduled as the CO's copilot on a 1R7[105] mission code, an administrative flight to Da Nang. It was the same day HML 367 officially moved to Marble Mountain. Here it comes, I thought, we'll all be leaving soon. However, I was wary about what might happen this day with the CO.

---

[103] Bill Nelson was one of the good guys, amiable and easy going. His nickname was "Fuels," due to an incident in Quang Tri. He allegedly pulled away from the fuel pits with the fuel hose still connected to the 46. Nothing more than a loss of fuel and gaining a nickname occurred. However, it reflects just how nicknames were won.

[104] Pearl Harbor Day, 1969. I had to think of my namesake even as I was preparing for my flight with Major Meskan. Harold Bunch, my cousin, was on liberty from a battleship anchored on Battleship Row in Pearl Harbor when the Japanese attack occurred. The exact ship he was on was lost in time. But I seem to recall that he was serving on the Oklahoma at that time and the man who relieved him from his duty that weekend was killed in the raid.

[105] The scheduled mission code 1R7 was wrong. The correct mission code would have been 1R4.

My flight with Major Meskan was scheduled for a leisurely 1100 takeoff time, after the morning combat launches. I began the morning as usual; stopping by the chow hall then on to the ready room to verify the flight with Meskan was still on or if I was just supposed to pre-flight. It was a real flight.

Grabbing my flight gear, I headed to the maintenance desk where I reviewed the yellow sheets, seeing that the names of the crew were affixed. Cpl. J.J. Hall, a highly experienced crew chief was assigned and there were no gunners on this flight. However, a Jeep with a weight of 2,265 pounds was listed as cargo and was being loaded and secured onto the cargo deck. Hall knew just what to do. He lured two or three of his buddies to go along on the trip on the off chance they'd get to go to the China Beach Exchange, the largest Exchange in Southeast Asia, if they agreed to help load and unload the Jeep at Da Nang.

With J.J.'s assurance that the Jeep was safely tied down and wouldn't roll out the back of the 46 on takeoff, I made my way back to the ready room to await the required preflight brief by Maj. Meskan. I was fixated on this brief as I nervously awaiting the CO's arrival.

After about a half-hour Maj. Meskan came out of his office. He had been there the entire time. I wondered if he had been busy, or if he was just letting me sweat. He conducted a simple brief, telling me that our flight this morning was to Da Nang—little or no further explanation other than we were to land at the Naval Support Activity Hospital LZ, immediately west of MAG 16's MMAF, while he attended a meeting somewhere in Da Nang. I assumed the meeting may have been about the coming change of command, when he would be replaced. Maybe he was headed for III MAF, but if that were so, we could have landed much closer. Also, if the meeting was at MAG-16, we could have easily landed at Marble, parked the 46 in the transient area, and avoided being in the way at the hospital complex.

Well, no matter what he was going to do, the Jeep was for his use, and I would remain with the helicopter until his return sometime that afternoon. My response to Meskan was a very cautious, by the book, "Aye aye, sir." Yes, sir...whatever, sir! After signing for the aircraft, Meskan told me that I would be flying the helicopter to Da Nang. I would have to change my gear from the copilot's seat to the aircraft commander's seat.

Hearing that, I quietly took a deep breath. My senses went to full alert, and I resolved at that moment to fly strictly NATOPS, reverting to the training command out of a sense of self-preservation. Having to prove yourself on each flight was how you got through the training command. Having to do it again, for Meskan, was routine.

Everything I had heard about Meskan was that he was a medal monger, a hotdog, a risk taker in the mold of Pappy Boyington.[106] He had already earned a handful of DFCs, maybe more, and had attempted to and possibly did set an unofficial altitude record in the 46 while flying daily combat missions. I had, during my time as a student pilot, flown with his kind before, in VT-2 at Whiting Field, Millington, FL. and HMMT-302 at the Marine Corps Air Facility, Santa Ana, CA. I knew how to do this.

My path was clear. I would bore him to death with NATOPS, and sir him to death. It was only in this manner that I felt I could hope to offset any criticism of my flying ability that may have been presented by the XO, while defending his own poor piloting skills—giving rise to this whole situation. It might be boring, but it would be safe, and it would offer Maj. Meskan no opportunity to question my flying ability. To get rid of me they would have to show that I was not a responsible pilot. They would have to take me out, without my help!

The early morning combat missions had been launched, allowing me an unobstructed taxi followed by an equally unremarkable takeoff into a standard NATOPS five hundred-foot-

---

[106] Pappy Boyington was an ace in support of the WWII Pacific campaign. He was a prisoner of war and earned the Medal of Honor. His fame was worldwide and the subject of books, movies and a successful television series. Furthermore, Boyington and Steve Pless, the Marine Helicopter MOH earner, were much alike. Hard drinkers, partiers and just what was needed in a war. They were in a way, role models whom we cherished. I believe I can say we did quite well by following in their paths.

per-minute climb to an altitude of 1500 feet. Maj. Meskan switched radio frequencies requested by me, true to his briefing that I would be doing all of the flying. He directed that I follow Highway 1 south. It was a beautiful morning. Traffic on the old rugged highway, as usual, was heavy with military vehicles, farmers, and the occasional water buffalo pulling a cart laden with produce, and an ancient farmer or small child walking alongside with a switch, urging the beast forward.

We kept to fifteen hundred feet AGL, offset to the right of the thoroughfare, making our way down to the Hai Van Pass, up and over the peak and down the south side, passing near an orphanage courtyard filled with little kids playing in an organized manner. I took us across the Da Nang Harbor at about 30 feet, purposely staying much higher than what I was used to seeing and well within the restriction of 50 feet. We passed Monkey Mountain and China Beach off to our left, entering the Han River on the south side of the bay. We passed by the German hospital ships nestled against the west bank of the Han. I eased back on the cyclic into a smooth cruise climb, hurdling the east-west bridges over the waterway teeming with the usual human traffic moving to and fro in waves. I always wondered why they were always in a hurry. Guess if I lived in their world, I'd be hurrying too. The simple act of hurrying would seem to be an escape.

My thoughts were broken as I automatically called for a switch to Marble's tower frequency, advising them of our intent to land at the NSA hospital pad. They cleared us with landing instructions. To do this correctly, I called for a landing checklist, which to my knowledge was not normally done here in 262. Maj. Meskan, however complied in the manner of a skilled pilot, reading the challenges as I responded. I made the normal downwind portion of the landing. At the 90-degree position, adjacent to the landing spot, I gently rolled the helo into a 180-degree turn north, setting up for a NATOPS no-hover landing to a spot near the upper-right corner of the large landing pad, in accordance with Meskan's instructions. The no-hover landing minimized the rotor wash into the triage area. The remaining shutdown was accomplished in the same manner as the flight—challenge and reply.

Maj. Meskan advised that we were preauthorized to remain in this position for the remainder of the day. The familiar sounds of shutdown brought an immense relief to me. Whatever his thoughts, I had done my best. Half the flight was complete. The flight had been as I had hoped; uneventful, unremarkable, boring. Maj. Meskan's comment following shutdown was, "That was a good landing (pause) for the training command."

Yes! Just what I wanted to hear.

"However, as you fly more, you'll have to get faster in the landing."

My strategy had apparently worked. My by-the-book flying had bored him to death. He recognized the NATOPS approach but had also, by suggesting that I would have to get faster, provided some relief from my main concern that this might be my last flight in Vietnam. I would be flying more, maybe not in 262, but at least more. I felt much better.

Also, at no point during the flight or afterward did Meskan raise any issues or question me as to systems, etc., therefore not totally treating me as a flight student. I had expected something much different.

J.J. and the Marines on board unloaded the Jeep. Meskan informed me that he would return at approximately 1300 hours and wanted the helicopter readied for immediate takeoff—jumped into the jeep and in moments disappeared into a cloud of dust. With Meskan's departure, J.J. told me that he and the other Marines were going to the China Beach Exchange and asked if I wanted to accompany them.

I knew they had shopping to do, and I didn't want to impose on their personal time. I decided to remain close to the helicopter, maybe get some lunch at Marble Mountain and take in the local sights. Plus, I needed some time alone with my thoughts, time just to breathe. Just maybe, I could make a MARS call to Kathy. I wanted to share this experience with her, and I needed to hear her voice.

There I was at the NSA hospital, one of the main receiving points for combat casualties and my first up-close view of such a unit. Due to prevailing winds at MMAF/Da Nang, most landings and takeoffs at NSA were on a northerly heading. The landing pad was large enough to accommodate maybe three CH-46s, but little more. Because of this limitation I felt uncomfortable taking up room in this hallowed place. Why didn't we just land at MMAF and park in a transient parking area. He could have easily driven the Jeep to wherever he was going. I just didn't understand Meskan's reasoning for taking up medevac pad space, nor did I ask.

The facility consisted of the familiar plywood architecture and Quonset huts, but with nurses, doctors, and orderlies going to and fro, passing by me as if I wasn't there. Near the landing pad, which was composed of Marston matting, was the receiving area. Rows and rows of what appeared to be sawhorses (the kind used by carpenters) were set up. I soon learned this area was known as the "tree farm." Why the tree farm? Because, when the injured and dying were brought off the arriving helos by the corpsmen, and assisting aircrews, they placed the stretchers on the sawhorses. Alongside the sawhorses were the free-standing bright aluminum poles, common in hospitals, from which the doctors and nurses hung plastic bags filled with life-saving blood and plasma while they were performing triage. The appearance of those bright aluminum poles gave rise to the term, tree farm.

The place was mesmerizing, and sobering. I noticed the availability of several garden hoses, the need for which was not to water flowers, but to wash away the blood, to disinfect. It was the gruesome truth of this place. This place, continually cleaned and disinfected, smelled of death and those who had recently struggled for life. Nearby an unmarked refrigerated Quonset hut evoked a chill in me, causing me to give it my undivided attention. "What is that place?" I asked a busy orderly. Without pause, he responded over his shoulder as he drew the last few puffs on a cigarette, flipping the butt into a bucket of sand. "That place?" he asked. "That's the morgue."

Although the hospitals were known for having good chow I lost my appetite. I walked away from the facility, north along the dirt and gravel roadbed that led past the gate into Marble. I felt an incredible emptiness. My mortality was never more fragile than at that moment. I needed to touch someone outside this place. I needed to be reassured. I needed to talk to Kathy.

Leaving the hospital, I walked to the gate into Marble Mountain and upon identifying myself was waved through by a Sergeant, who wondered why I was wandering around in a flight suit. After a brief explanation, that my helicopter was at the hospital and that I wanted to make a MARS call, I was waved through the gate. Making my way on foot to the MARS station I saw many young Marines only a few years younger than myself waiting in line; even to me, they seemed young. They were laughing and carrying on like kids. Hell, I guess we were all kids, even me at 24—a truth I was hesitant to acknowledge.

I pondered their circumstances. Those "kids" were Marine Grunts, killing machines, the kind that Confederate General J.E.B. Stuart wanted in his cavalry, youthful, unmarried and as dangerous as the horsemen of Genghis Kahn. I didn't know why they were at Marble Mountain. Most Grunts on an in-country R&R were at Freedom Hill enjoying a movie or on China Beach. Yet, they had no way of knowing when they would have another opportunity to call someone at home, if ever. Knowing that I would have many more opportunities than they to make such a call home, I stepped out of line and headed back to the hospital.

31: A Flying Lesson

At approximately 1300 hrs. just when I was beginning to get antsy about whether they would be back before the CO returned; J.J. and his crew showed up carrying shopping bags. Our down time was a good perk for both me and them. It had provided me time to acquaint myself with the hospital complex and to give some thought regarding what I was experiencing.

With no hesitation, J.J. began his preflight, after which I performed a walk-around and preflight. The weather being pretty good for a monsoon day, J.J. and the Marines who accompanied us sat at one of the picnic-type tables close to the helo pad, making light conversation about their trip to the exchange. The men described their purchases from "the largest Navy exchange in the Pacific."

"Hell, sir," said one, "China Beach is an in-country R&R site. You don't have to go to Hawaii for this one. There's a real beach and everything but girls there." (It had been lost on me how little these men got to see of Vietnam. They were mechanics and electronics technicians who were always in the hangar, working all hours, never leaving the base. Their dedication was what made everything work.) He continued with glee, "There's a hospital there, too, with a bunch of round-eyed American nurses.

"But, you gotta be dying to see one of them," one laughed.

"You can actually buy a car or a Harley there for a lot less than you can buy 'em for in the States, and pick 'em up when you get home...everyone does that, they said...I'm gonna do that, too." Then he abruptly stopped, seemingly just noticing the medevac surroundings—the tree farm, the morgue—and in a more somber tone, he said, "...that is, if we go home."

J.J., always one to think of the quirkiest thing to say, thought for a moment and said, "Don't worry, you'll go home...one way or the other," then chuckled.

"Damn you, J.J." said the Marine.

As they continued their sparring with each other, I thought, going home hadn't crossed my mind. I still had a huge hurdle to get over with the CO, and I hoped they'd all be buying that new car; a red convertible, I thought... maybe a Corvette, a dream of mine since seeing those sparkling blue Corvettes driven by the Blue Angels in Pensacola. Hmm...I thought. Maybe a Corvette is still a possibility in my life: now *that* would be worth a tour in Vietnam!

The CO arrived in his Jeep at about 1330 hrs. Without further ado, J.J. and the crew loaded the Jeep while the CO did a walk-around and inspected the strapping down of the vehicle in the cargo bay. There was no small talk. Hell, I couldn't tell if he even noticed I was there. His mind was obviously elsewhere as he went about his routine. There was something about him that was hard to figure out or put my finger on. I'd never been around anyone so complex.

Our brief was Meskan's lone comment to me: "Let's go!"

Soon we were both strapped in and J.J. was giving us a thumbs-up. As the CO got comfortable, I began with the NATOPS check list. He didn't verbally respond to my challenge, yet his hands bounced from switch to switch in a quiet, introspective manner, with precision derived from years of flying experience; not rudely ignoring me but preoccupied. He didn't have to think of the checklist, but he let me go on as if it mattered.

I was seeing a trend. The combat vets had no time for challenge and response. They knew the procedures. Once someone began reading from the checklist, it nailed them as a new guy. I was learning.

He started the engines and called Marble tower for clearance out of NSA with a northbound departure back along the Han to the harbor. I wasn't asked to touch the controls, and I was satisfied with that. I had just about convinced myself that all was well with the world.

We were initially going home feet wet, circumnavigating the Hai Van Pass to the east; the same route Jim Dau had taken on my first ride in-country. We were about a football field distance from the Hai Van and about eye level with the highest point of the pass. The weather turned out to be okay, a high ceiling of clouds with plenty of visibility. I was actually beginning to relax somewhat, believing that whatever it was that I feared about this flight was not going to occur. My solitude was broken by the distinctive keying of the ICS button.

"Walker, I'm gonna show you some of the area." I had barely responded when he abruptly lowered the collective while moving the cyclic forward in a smooth coordinated manner. The 46 nosed down as we entered a dive to the sea, pulling out at the last moment from dipping our nose into the salt water. We were headed due west, 270 on the nose. I was about to find out firsthand how good a pilot Meskan really was.

We skimmed over the waves as we headed toward the beach. Our nose gear seemed only inches above the water as some spray beaded on the Plexiglass just below my feet. We approached the beach north of the Hai Van Pass at 130-140 knots. Upon reaching the sandy beach, we jumped the sand dune that abutted the beach along the shoreline, and made a dizzying sharp right turn. To my amazement during the aggressive moves, the balance ball remained centered. He zigzagged for a quarter mile or so, then, with an abrupt cyclic climb he entered a steep 90 degree left turn. The attitude indicator swung from horizon to horizon seemingly touching the 60-degree mark on each maneuver. All of this felt as comfortable as sitting in an easy chair, the ball remained centered as if it were glued. During the turn the big blades were popping and snapping as they slapped the compressed molecules of air. The engines screamed. Damn ... it was becoming an exhilarating ride and the skill of the pilot was obvious.

In what seemed like a few moments I realized we were approaching Highway 1 from the east over a large grassy area, not a rice paddy, more like a scenic pasture one could find in my home state of Missouri. Meskan finally broke his silence by saying, "Look for a tree standing alone."

To our starboard side, approximately three hundred meters away, was a lone tree, an oddity. He slowed the 46 and air taxied to the tree at about a 10 to 15 foot hover. Now I was really wondering what was going on. My former belief, that the test was complete, was a wrong impression.

The tree was 40 or 50 feet high with branches reaching out to about 12 feet at the very top. As Maj. Meskan eased the 46 forward, the arc of the blades came within 20 feet of the tree. He told me to take control of the aircraft.

"I have the aircraft," I said.

"You have the aircraft," was his response. His eyes fixed upon the horizon, not watching me.

The next direction from the CO was the first and last time I have ever heard such a command. "See that top branch?" he asked. There was one branch that appeared out of place, longer than the others by a couple feet. I acknowledged that I did see it as my knuckles turned white, and I squeezed the black color out of the cyclic. He said, probably without cracking a smile, "Take off about ten inches from the tip of that limb."

He was dead serious. However, intentionally placing the blades of my helicopter within close proximity to a tree was completely foreign to me, therefore, rejected by all of my instincts. It was similar to when I was in the first or second grade, and a classmate brought a garter snake to school in a bucket. We were encouraged by the teacher to touch the reptile, to learn the skin was not slimy but dry and coarse, and, furthermore, to learn that not all snakes were poisonous. My experiences with snakes taught me at an early age not to waste valuable time trying to determine whether or not a snake was venomous before killing it. In the Bootheel of Missouri the vast majority of snakes were extremely aggressive and deadly. The worst of those was the semi-aquatic Cotton Mouth Water moccasin. A big "Moc" will come at you full speed, slithering back and forth with its large triangular head held high for the slightest irritation it might feel you caused him. At that time in school, under those circumstances, I forced myself to touch the snake, momentarily overcoming all of my better instincts.

This was the same as that snake. I would do as the CO requested because had I not, the CO may have in some manner justified actions against me, the worst of which could possibly be my leaving the squadron. What recourse did I have? However, in doing as ordered I would again have to touch the snake and force myself to overcome natural inhibitions.

The direction of the CO was clear: take off about 10 inches. He didn't say touch the limb with your blades. He said take off the limb. With this concept firmly set in my mind, sweat popped out on my forehead, and my grip, if possible, tightened on the cyclic and collective. I felt stiff and awkward—not believing I could accomplish this test to his satisfaction, yet knowing that I was now committed. Come hell or high water my blades were going to go into that tree. As I made the conscious decision to accept the challenge, the responsibility for this decision clearly shifted to the aircraft commander regardless of rank. How could he explain to the satisfaction of any mishap board why we were in the middle of a field, with neither military objective nor purpose, with our blades entangled in the only tree in that ample clearing? This realization had a cathartic effect on me as my tension subsided and my focus intensified.

As the 46 inched forward into the tree limb, the winds began to blow stronger, rocking the limb to and fro. I pulled back sharply as the blades came within inches of the trunk of the tree. My concern wasn't a scratched blade but a damaged blade requiring a report. Debris was being blown from the tree and swirling through the air, reminiscent of an oncoming summer storm and its effect on the fragile limbs at the top of the Cyprus trees on our family farm. The CO appeared relaxed and unconcerned. I noticed that he was not hovering over the controls as was the position of instructors in the training command when a student was performing a hazardous maneuver. My thoughts were twofold: he had either total confidence that he could overcome any disastrous circumstance I might get us into, or total confidence that I wouldn't get us into such a circumstance. But if the latter was true, why the test? Or, maybe he was simply a madman.

Once again, I eased the cyclic forward until the blurred arc of the blades, traveling at the speed of sound, struck the limb. The debris field in the air momentarily thickened, and my reflexes instinctively reversed motion, pulling the blurred arc back from the tree into its original safe path. The rapid movement set the 46 to rocking fore and aft. What's next, I thought, different limbs or a different tree until he was satisfied that I could remain a member of his merry crew?

On the next try I floundered into the tree, not making the surgical strike he envisioned. Finally, with the words, "I've got it," my test was over. Maj. Meskan took charge of the big craft and with no further comment conducted his own trimming session of the tree. He trimmed the tree at will, here and there, without a word. I watched, knowing that I was witnessing something very special. I didn't have the feeling that he was trying to impress me, but that he might just do this for the fun of it, like his attempts to set the high altitude record. As abruptly as it had begun, it was over. He turned toward Highway 1, and we were off to Phu Bai. I had either passed or flunked the test; I had no idea which.

The approach and landing at Phu Bai was uneventful. After engine shutdown the CO unstrapped, gathered his flight gear, and left for the ready room. Following the post flight paperwork the CO directed me to follow him to his office.

Maj. Meskan was behind his desk. And again, I was in position to do another carpet dance. Must have been some kind of a record, the second time with less than four weeks in the squadron. Not knowing what to expect from the looking glass atmosphere that I was again experiencing, I just listened!

Maj. Meskan unexpectedly said, "You're a good pilot, a basic pilot. You'll get to be a combat pilot, only through experience. I took you to that tree for one reason: I want you to be aware of just exactly where the tips of your blades are located. That will help you know whether or not you can fit in some of the zones in which you'll be asked to land. Now, have you apologized to the XO yet?"

254 | HAROLD G. WALKER

I responded to the CO that, as yet, I had not been able to meet with the XO. The CO continued, "He's probably in his quarters, go see him now!"

"Yes Sir!" I responded, turned heel and toe and got the hell out of his office.

Leaving the squadron office area and making my way toward the XO's hooch, I had time to think of the mess I was in and try to take from this lessons learned. The first lesson was to keep my mouth shut regarding any poor piloting on the part of senior officers. The second lesson was to avoid, at all costs, any interaction with the command structure of the squadron, any squadron. They were nothing but trouble.

The command hooch (a Quonset hut) was clearly marked with the words Heavy[107] Hooch written on the door. It was dark inside, and with the slight smell of mold, like a tomb, was similar to all of the Quonset huts. There was no sound. A dim light in the rear of the hooch provided just enough luminescence to make out the manner in which it was organized. There was a center isle with two bunks on each side in keeping with this being the inner sanctum of the CO, XO, OpsO, and AMO, the four flying heavies who held sway over the squadron.

"Major Whitfield!" I called out in a clear voice, intentionally neither meek nor aggressive. I thought it best to go in with my head up rather than my tail tucked between my legs. I would do as ordered by the CO, but not without explaining why I did what I did.

"Back here," came the voice, stark and direct.

"Lieutenant Walker here, sir."

"Come on back."

___

[107] The term "Heavy" was a slang term used to refer to the rank of the officers who reside there, being the top ranks in the unit. At that time, in 262, the highest position, CO, normally a LtCol's billet was held by a major. The XO was a major, and the department heads normally held by majors were staffed by captains and lieutenants.

Tentatively, I began to walk down the center corridor of the hooch toward the voice, the last poz on the port side. The symbolism was of a condemned man on his way, not to death, but something worse, a concentrated surefire Marine Corps ass chewing, like the time I stood before a circuit judge for the unforgivable offense of driving under the influence after a party. I steeled myself for the onslaught. The DUI had been reduced to careless and imprudent driving following an ass chewing by the judge, and paying a fine. However, I wasn't sure this particular infraction would be reduced. My stomach tightened and my mouth was dry.

The XO was seated at a small desk next to his bunk, over which hung that dim light, making his bald head gleam. He was not surprised at my presence. He knew why I was there, but let me speak. I carefully adhered to all military courtesies until he directed me to sit and talk at ease.

To my surprise and relief, he didn't appear angry or vindictive, just tired. To put this in perspective, that incident with me, an FNG First Lieutenant who had no clout, no support, and no place to go, was just one minor/insignificant event out of his year in Vietnam. I knew of his crash in May that resulted in the deaths of Marines and a copilot turning in his wings. I was aware that the 46 he crashed in didn't reveal any DEA, just exiting rounds from cooking off ammo. However, my thoughts were focused on why I was there—in front of him. Was it to "kiss the ring" and beg for forgiveness? Forgiveness for what...for having raised a safety concern? The XO had, in my humble opinion, damn near crashed, killing us all, because he was too high and too fast, that was it. And, rather than wave off, he choose to perform a quick-stop maneuver which entailed entering into a free fall, saved only through a large application of power, arresting the plunge. My sin? I was mad as hell just thinking about it!

Here I was, and the more I considered my predicament, the angrier I became with the XO, the CO, and myself. I wasn't upset with Stover or the others who may have run to the CO to tell on me. I had been forewarned of Stover's nature and had now become suspect of others. Now that I knew how the grapevine worked I would change my behavior. I would avoid the known assholes and say nothing about what happened in the air to anyone other than the closest of confidants, a classic example of "chilling effect." Damn it!

I swallowed my pride, hoping to salvage what was left of my flying in Vietnam. I literally tried to ignore, to myself, what I was about to say. Taking a breath, and overcoming my desire to simply say f**k you and leave, as carefully as was necessary to keep me on target, I apologized for speaking openly about the flight in the O'Club. He didn't ask to whom I spoke because he, no doubt, already knew it was Smokey Stover. He seemed to give considerable thought to what I was saying as I described my concern about the approach to that zone and mentioned that I had never heard of button red before that moment in the 46, but assured him I would never forget that frequency. To my surprise, he said little more. Granted, he had less than two weeks before the change of command, and he could have ground me up into little pieces and could still do it through my officer's fitness report. But, I couldn't detect the slightest resentment toward me and he courteously dismissed me, saying "Forget it."

I made my way out of the heavy hooch, feeling sick to my stomach for having succumbed to the CO and apologizing to the XO. I vowed that would be the last time I would humble myself before a ranking officer. I simply breathed a short sigh of relief and headed for the FNG hooch. The XO said to forget it, and that was what I intended to do. I knew this small, insignificant event could have adverse consequences for me, but it was never my intention to have a career in the Corps. I wasn't a Marine Corps career-ladder-climbing-kind-of-guy. I was there because of a deal cut with my OSO, Captain Larry Ogle of St. Louis postponing my entry into the war. He played fair with me and I would uphold my end of the deal, although the Marine Corps was beginning to take on a whole different look to me than when I was in college, on the outside looking in. But, I couldn't get over the image of Maj. Whitfield in his hooch. He seemed simply bone tired. His tenure of being XO in 262 would be ending within a few days, on 20 December and, it was my opinion that he was probably looking forward to it.

Note: On 6 December, First Lieutenant H. R. "Bob" Weber III who was the copilot with Lt. Whitworth on 4 December when I was copilot to Maj. Whitfield was again wounded. A Claymore mine exploded in close proximity to his helicopter, striking him in the elbow. He was medevaced off to Da Nang again, then to Yokosuka, Japan. That was number two. If he comes back, one more Purple Heart will send him home forever. Three Purple Hearts and you're out.

32: Jungle Environmental Survival Training School

On 7 December 1969, Pearl Harbor Day, First Lieutenant Eric Corsair McGrew arrived. His presence brought the hooch up to its maximum capacity of eight, the last pilot to be placed into the FNG hooch. Eric was another pilot with whom I had gone through OCS. We now had four FNGs: Allen, McGrew, Prigge and me in the hooch that had been together since arriving in Quantico, VA to attend the 48th OCS class. We were happy to have him. That evening we all gathered at the club to toast the newcomers. It was that day that Pete Hanner and I learned we would be leaving the following day to attend Jungle Environmental Survival Training (JEST) School in the Philippines.

That trip would be my second departure from Phu Bai since my arrival, not a bad job to date. JEST school, we thought, was Jungle *Escape* and Survival Training. It had me imagining myself being held in a bamboo cage. Upon receipt of my orders, however, I felt more at ease. The orders read, Jungle *Environmental* Survival Training. We were to be billeted at the U.S. Naval Air Station, Cubi Point, Republic of the Philippines (RP), comparable to a 4-star hotel.

Cubi, as it was called, was situated on the south side of Subic Bay, apart from and overlooking the Subic Bay Naval Base, RP— a sprawling deep water port, home to the U.S. Seventh Fleet and a deep water ship repair facility. It was also a notorious recreation port through which hundreds of thousands of soldiers, sailors, and Marines from all over the globe had passed during its long history. Separated from the naval base by a drainage canal, known locally as Shit River, it was the legendary liberty town of Olongapo City.

Pete Hanner and I were the only FNGs slated to attend the school at that time. Once I received my orders and spoke to a few guys who had attended JEST, I learned that it was more like a three-day bar hopping experience in the middle of the largest whorehouse in the world, with a few jungle classes tying it all together in a neat weekend package. There was no sitting in cages or being harassed by arrogant guards portraying themselves as NVA officers.

They said this was more of a nature study of the flora and fauna of the jungle, like a botany class. It taught what you might do to prolong your life in a jungle environment, if you were not captured. As a caveat, we knew there were few if any helicopter pilots or infantrymen kept as prisoners of war. Unlike the Fast Movers from Udorn or Task Force 77, the strike force of the U.S. 7th Fleet never flew into North Vietnam, where the captured pilots got their asses kicked and beat for years.

There was a less merciful end for those captured and kept in South Vietnam. It was rumored they were beaten, starved, and brutalized, then killed by drowning in submerged bamboo cages, like was recreated in the 1978 movie *The Deer Hunter* starring Christopher Walken and Robert De Nero, with starving rats feeding on them.

Not many were like the storied Marine Major Richard Risner, a powerfully built infantry officer, who after being captured by the VC near Chu Lai on 200868 successfully escaped on 220868. He physically overpowered and drowned one of his captors left alone to guard him.

Figure 59 Major Richard Risner

He spoke of his escape many times to civic groups wherever he was stationed. His captivity lasted less than three days.[108] They lost!

All things considered, though, I always viewed my old .38 cal. survival pistol like John Wayne taught me; save the last bullet for yourself. I was not about to be captured alive if I could prevent it.

---

[108] Major Risner was unable to satisfy some Marine brass that he was actually captured. The Naval Investigative Service investigated his story and never determined that he wasn't captured. I never doubted him.

Pete Hanner and I were due to leave the following day around noon from Da Nang. We didn't need much notice, and I was ready to leave after my run-in with the command element of 262. However, as I had noted upon my arrival into Vietnam, there were no scheduled shuttle flights to get us around to the other bases. Leaving Phu Bai to get to Da Nang where we would catch the plane to Cubi Point wasn't going to be as easy as going to Udorn. We were passenger listed on a C-130 leaving for Cubi Point, Philippines, from Da Nang Air Base, but first we had to get to Da Nang.

On the morning of 8 December, a heavy fog bank engulfed the Phu Bai airfield and all flights other than emergency missions were pushed back, including an Army flight scheduled to go to Da Nang that morning. I couldn't understand why the all-weather aircraft were affected by the fog, but the Army had their own rules, and it was an aircraft that we had to catch. As time ticked by, it was becoming increasingly necessary that we get out of Phu Bai in order to catch our flight leaving Da Nang for the Philippines.

Damn it, we were going to miss our chance to be JEST trained, and no telling if we would ever get another chance. Finally, we saw a Marine CH-53 heavy hauler from Da Nang break out of the low-hanging fog over the numbers of Runway 27 and begin taxiing into the Marine fuel pits on the north side of the runway. Now we had to make a decision: stay and wait on the weather, or try to catch a ride with the CH-53 if it was going to Da Nang. It was a pretty good bet they would be going back to Da Nang from here because there was nowhere else to land further north, unless they were going to Hanoi.

Not wanting to wait for an official vehicle to get us across the runway, we grabbed our gear and hauled ass. There was no interference from anyone. We were just two more guys crossing an active-duty runway with our gear; a normal day in Phu Bai.

We made our way to the 53's crew chief, who was supervising their hot refueling. We lucked out; they were on a routine instrument-training flight and were headed back to MMAF, and they would be happy to drop us off at Da Nang Air Base. I had never before been that close to the CH-53. We owed a debt of gratitude to Dimmer, the call sign of HMH-463. Crawling aboard the largest helicopter in the free world, I was in awe of its size. We stowed our gear and strapped into the cargo-net seats hung along each side of the cargo deck. The aircraft took the runway and began a take-off roll that was more like that of a C-130 than a helicopter. Picking up speed it leaped nose-high into the fog and rain that immediately engulfed us at about 200-300 feet. It was a wonder; cruising at airspeeds I hadn't seen since flying the T-28, it didn't feel like we were in a helicopter.

We broke out into a Smokey gray sky at 1000 feet, continuing to near 5,000 feet before leveling off. The geographical features of the lowlands were lost in the fog and clouds, yet the mountains in the west toward the A Shau Valley remained obvious. Finding a porthole window, I looked down on the area where I believed Highway 1 to be. Protruding from that layer of soup was the Hai Van Pass and the associated ridgeline that wove itself into the jungle-blanketed mountains of western Vietnam and Laos.

I had not previously seen the surface from this viewpoint. Flying at 500 feet over Highway 1 in a CH-46, you didn't get to see the whole, just a piece. The fog and clouds clearly backed up against the Hai Van pass, giving credence to the notion that the Hai Van was the dividing line between the ancient northern and southern provinces of Vietnam.

We were feeling at ease and thinking our way clear, but our faith in Dimmer didn't last. Pete and I found ourselves landing at First Med, the hospital near Freedom Hill! "Why the hell are we at First Med and not Da Nang Air Base?" I screamed to the crew chief over the engine noise. Pete looked at the crew chief as only he could—a bone-chilling stare.

"What is this chicken shit?" Pete hollered. Evidently, the Dimmer pilots had interpreted our need to get to Da Nang Air Force Base as simply needing to get to anywhere in Da Nang. They had landed at the First Med hospital pad because the pilots didn't want to try flying into Da Nang Air Force Base due to the hassle of flying into a jet corridor. This was strange to us as it was common for 46 pilots to fly into Da Nang AFB. We would certainly have done it for them. No amount of urging could make them change their minds, and the clock was ticking. I thought, what a bunch of assholes! A feud was born that day. *"Dimmer... Dimmer... Dimmer, won't you bite my ass?"* Departing, the 53 driver waved bye-bye to us like you would have done to a little kid, the beginning of a simmering need to get even. We both gave them the one-finger salute and never looked back.

Now we had to hustle. We had to find another way to get to the air base, and quick. After trying unsuccessfully to hitch a ride on a military conveyance, it was back to the streets for Pete and me. We saw a local bus operated by the armed forces—part of winning the hearts and minds of the Vietnamese people. It was stopping at Freedom Hill, just down the road from First Med. The little people watched in awe as we stumbled through the folding doors and up the steps into the bus, dragging our gear.

Every seat was taken. Pete and I, probably more than a foot taller than anyone else on the bus, were also the only two U.S. servicemen on the bus. We were decked out in our best; starched covers and bright silver bars reflecting our rank as first lieutenants, gold wings centered over the left-front pocket on our jungle utilities. The bus riders carried all kinds of goods, including a couple of chickens going to the cooker for lunch. We stuck out from the locals like sore thumbs and became the focus of their curiosity. But they seemed pleased. Rather than somber, vacant eyes, they wore great big smiles under their conical hats.

An unmistakable uneasiness swept over us. A home-grown VC could be anywhere, and two sets of gold wings and first lieutenant bars, taken from the carcasses of a couple of FNG officers would have made great war trophies for someone trying to work their way up in the ranks of the VC. We were sitting ducks, but so was everyone else with us. We scanned the crowd on the bus and Pete was doing his level best to keep things cool. He talked with the people. He had a gift of gab, like the comic character

Geraldine played by the comedian Flip Wilson. The Vietnamese on board began talking to him, neither understanding the other. It was the damndest thing. They pointed and laughed most delightfully. Some of the women were holding their hands over their mouths as they laughed, their eyes wide, reminiscent of school children. I grinned and thought...we're gonna get killed. I couldn't think of anything other than that anonymous 53 driver waving bye to us; what an asshole.

The one word that the Vietnamese on the bus understood as we rumbled down the street was "honcho." They pointed and asked Pete, "You honcho?" He laughed, then turned and pointed to me saying, "Me no honcho, he honcho."

"Damn it Pete, don't do that," I said. Then I returned the favor by upping it one. "Me no honcho, he honcho and SPY!" Pete laughed even louder. We began to see the humor of it all. These folks were just folks, not VC. They were just having a good laugh at what they instinctively knew were just a couple of FNGs out of their element. This back and forth babble went on until we came into view of the air base. When the bus stopped within a couple of hundred feet of the entry point we jumped off, leaving behind a dozen or so little people, two pigs that had eventually revealed themselves, and four or five more chickens I hadn't seen when we jumped aboard. Pete turned and waved goodbye to his new friends and I said, "Let's get the hell out of here. The flight is scheduled to be leaving right now."

"No hurry," said Pete. "We've got it made now."

We were cleared through the gate and made our way to the terminal, the same terminal that had hosted us when we came into Vietnam. The 130 was in the final stages of boarding. We just made it. Off to yet another adventure.

After getting on board I heard someone yell out, "Hey, Walker!" It was Wayne Stevens, a friend of mine from Southeast Missouri State (SEMO). Wayne was an outstanding half-back at SEMO, so fast they called him a "scat back." He was from Fredericktown, Missouri, a community northwest of Cape Girardeau, MO. He and I had taken classes together at SEMO. He was a Sigma

Phi Epsilon (SigEp) at SEMO, and I was in the Epsilon Iota Chapter of Pi Kappa Alpha (Pikes) at SEMO. My brother, Johnny, was a charter member in the chapter, and I was a legacy due to his membership. Now Wayne and I found ourselves in similar circumstances. We were both Marine Corps First Lieutenants, both pilots, yet still in opposite camps, similar to our fraternity affiliation. He was an F-4 Phantom pilot in VMFA-122, stationed at the Da Nang air base. Everyone who ever attended flight school wanted to be a Phantom Pilot and Wayne did it. I have always admired that fact.

The trip to Cubi in the C-130 was not comfortable. After what seemed like an eternity, I saw a few folks gathering around a small porthole window. The Philippine Islands were beginning to come into view. I had always thought the Philippines was one island, but what I saw from our high altitude were dozens of islands. They were beautiful—lush, green, surrounded by the deep-blue waters of the Pacific. Within a short period of time we were told to strap in. During the Vietnam War, the Philippines and Subic Bay in particular, was the service station and supermarket for the Seventh Fleet, providing upkeep and maintenance of ships and storage and distribution of food, fuel, and ammunition to sustain the war effort in Vietnam. From an average of 98 ship visits a month in 1964, the average shot up to 215 by 1967, and much more in 1969-70, with more than thirty ships in port on any given day; it was a busy place.

As the engines of the C-130 throttled back we began our descent. Shortly thereafter, a smooth approach and the slight screech of tires along with a reverse of thrust landed us at Cubi Point Naval Air Station. The view as we deplaned was magnificent. The dark-blue waters of Subic Bay and the Pacific came together into a lagoon-like bay, surrounded by lush green jungles framed by a deep blue sky with soft white clouds in random patterns from horizon to horizon.

We were met by a Navy chief who was assigned to get us through the next couple days of classes. The first thing was to billet us at the base officers' quarters (BOQ), which sat at the top of a steep drive, across from a small white chapel with a tall steeple. The last word from the chief who welcomed us was a warning. "Stay out of trouble with the local authorities in Olongapo. The Navy has good relations with the locals, but little authority outside the gated perimeter of the base."

Survival training was primarily taught by the Nigrito tribesmen of the Bataan Peninsula, a primitive people, historically mistreated by the Filipinos. They had an extensive knowledge of jungle plants, birds, animals, and insects—the original survivalists. The training was three days in length with two nights free to experience Olongapo City then back to Vietnam.

The Nigritos were similar in nature to the Vietnam Montanards. They knew how to live off the land and had been guerilla fighters against the Japanese in WWII. They made their own knives from the car springs of junked cars and encased them in wooden scabbards. The handle was made from some kind of wood they said could be used to treat wounds. They hunted with bows and arrows and used blowguns that hurled poisoned darts. All in all quite a bunch!

They showed us how to have a magnificent meal of bugs, leaves, some kind of wild berries and a long cool drink of water out of stalks of bamboo. I'd as soon have had a candy bar from my survival vest, for that is about as long as anyone I knew would be able to survive on their own in the jungles of Nam.

The escape portion of our training was not much. We were turned loose to hide in the jungle, after which everyone was promptly caught. We were then required to use a signal mirror to alert a rescue helicopter to our position. The helicopter crew knew exactly where we were, so no problem. They were supposed to bring us aboard the helicopter for purposes of authenticity, as if we were really being rescued. We took turns with a small signal mirror, the kind available in our survival vests, to signal the helicopter. The jungle, however, was so thick that we couldn't get the sun in order to use the mirror. We went to a stream, found a solitary sunbeam, stood on a small boulder in the center of the stream and took turns reflecting the sunbeam to the helicopter. We all did this and that was it...officially trained.

The actual survival part of this trip took place in Olongapo where, like Udorn, the dollar bill was king and every sailor and Marine on liberty had those bills stuffed into every pocket. During that period, Subic Bay always had the most sailors in port at any one time, from all over the globe. The only rule you had to remember was to make it to the gate before midnight or be locked out of the base. If discovered in town after the midnight hour, it was the brig for sure.

The Philippine Islands were full of retired service personnel (ex-patriots, or expats as they liked to be called) including Merchant Marines. It was a good deal if you had nothing to go home to. The expats were mainly retired seamen who were now working every supply ship in the world headed to Vietnam to support the war. They and their families received the best of care at the local naval hospital, and they also had access to the naval exchange while living in affordable luxury in this lush land, full of mainly friendly people.

However, the Philippines had its skeletons, one being the local communist group, the New People's Army, primarily just a ring of small-time criminals and thugs who used old political grievances to justify their lawlessness. They spawned little groups of assassins called Sparrow Teams, and a drunken serviceman, either just wandering or lured off the beaten path for some other erotic reason, could find himself alone in the wrong area and the target of one of those teams.

Their tactics were quite literally to run around the victim in Keystone Kop-style, shooting him several times, in a manner similar to sparrows attacking when they sense someone has wandered too close to their nest. (Real sparrows attack in numbers, diving at the intruder's head, pecking at him as he flees.) The response by the military was to encourage the buddy system, keeping at least two servicemen together throughout their stay outside the gates of Subic Bay.

Olongapo was an extreme replay of Udorn, Thailand. The main gate of the Navy base opened directly into the main street of Olongapo, a town primarily composed of gambling dens, saloons, and prostitutes. It was probably similar to the gold rush towns that flourished in the United States during the late 1800s, like Creed, Colorado, or Tombstone, Arizona. However, there was no end to the money coming into the liberty haven from the Godsend of the 7th Fleet. There were no problems unless someone got drunk and became unruly; then the private security personnel were brutally efficient in subduing the troublemaker.

The smells were the same as Udorn, Da Nang, Tijuana, Nogales, and a multitude of other lesser-known third world harbors: open sewers, booze, vomit, piss, and mystery meat sold by street vendors so thick with barbecue-like sauce the sinewy meat itself was camouflaged.

Marines and sailors gorged on the exotic food, too drunk to care that they'd be puking it up when standing in line to be tattooed from stem to stern. The image of helmeted Shore Patrol grabbing up rowdy drunks, thumping them with their batons and tossing them into the back of vomit laden military paddy wagons to take them back across shit river to Subic and Cubi Point is an image and smell I will never forget. The service personnel who found themselves in the Navy's brig were grateful, after sobering up, with the knowledge they were not in Olongapo's medieval jails. It was a hell of a show, and a mother's nightmare.

Again, mission accomplished. On Thursday, 11 December 1969, we received our certificates of satisfactory completion, signed by Lt. R.W. Ritz, U.S. Navy and made it back from Cubi alive, healthy and officially trained in Jungle Environmental Survival Techniques, which to me, meant stuffing your survival vest with Hershey bars.

Upon returning to Phu Bai, we found the much anticipated move to Marble Mountain was becoming more and more apparent, with more rumors of 46 squadrons being notified that they would soon be leaving country. HML-367, Scarface, was gone, tucked away in Marble Mountain as Operation Keystone continued with the rapid redeployment of Marines. Only our sister squadron, HMM-161 was still with us at Phu Bai, along with Third Force Recon as a rear guard.

33: Kit Carson

After surviving my interactions with the CO and XO, my time at Phu Bai was speeding along. Flying had become less rigorous due to the influx of more new guys, and the bad weather. "Heavy monsoon rains and low ceilings, however, continued to hamper flight operations."[109]

In mid-December, during a lull in our flying, Donnie McGlothlin and I took advantage of an exceptional opportunity. With other Marines who were available, we caught a ride in a six-by truck to Camp Eagle, a huge Army base nine miles west of Hue. Its main purpose was to protect Hue from another '68 Tet-like attack.

The purpose of the trip was to observe first-hand the methods employed by the infamous VC/NVA sappers. Historically, Roman sappers dug under mega-walls and brought down whole castles. The VC/NVA sappers had a near mystical reputation for being capable of wriggling through carefully placed obstacles—claymore mines and concertina wire strung with empty c-ration cans—without drawing the attention of posted sentries well within earshot. We had heard so much about those latter-day Ninjas that to have an opportunity to see a real Chu Hoi, a former VC sapper who had become what they call a Kit Carson Scout,[110] was just too intriguing for Donnie and me to pass up.

The ride to Camp Eagle, nine miles west of Phu Bai, was north along Highway 1 then west on red mud-caked roads full of vendors hawking bottled soft drinks and moving water buffalo from one rice paddy to another. The truck driver rolled along at a fast pace and again, blocking out the battle scars, the beauty of the countryside was breathtaking. I have never forgotten the natural beauty of Vietnam, nor its hidden dangers.

---

[109] The reference to "heavy monsoons" and "low ceilings" adversely affecting flight hours was routine in the monthly chronology of helicopter squadrons throughout the monsoon season.

[110] A "Kit Carson Scout" was a former enemy soldier, VC or NVA, who defected and was actively aiding American soldiers.

At the gate to Camp Eagle the Army sentries took a little more time with us. Being that we were Marines, we required more scrutiny by the posted guards, a mutual courtesy observed by both services. But after a few minutes of looking and checking, we were waved through.

The vehicle finally stopped in what appeared to be a training area fashioned in the manner of a firebase, with the approaches strung with the usual array of protective measures found around the perimeter of any fire base in Vietnam. These protective measures consisted of concertina wire, empty c-ration cans tied to the wire, and training devices mimicking the deadly anti-personnel claymore mines. What was missing, of course, were the sentries who light up the area with M-80 parachute flares. Those flares could hang in the air rocking back and forth under their own little parachutes and remain in the air for a period long enough that more flares could be launched assuring the area was, as bright as a full moon night, allowing deadly fire to be directed into the affected area. This was a tried-and-true method that made a forced breech a most deadly and suicidal affair. Stealth became the true weapon of the enemy, thus, the sapper.

At this advertised demonstration there were many Army Grunt units, a few Marine Grunt units, and us. An Army spokesperson announced the afternoon's event: a real live exhibition of a former (now a good guy?) VC sapper.

After the sapper was introduced, he revealed the small array of tools he used, mainly hooks made of wood used to separate the coils of concertina wire. He was very small in stature when compared to the normal size Vietnamese, much less than five feet tall and sinewy, weighing no more than 90 pounds. He dressed in only a loin cloth, revealing good muscular development. He could have been any Vietnamese vendor on the street. His demeanor was calm and seemingly un-coerced as he softly smiled at the crowd before whom he was about to demonstrate his prowess.

He portrayed what could only be described as a quiet dignity. The Army spokesperson described him as having been directly involved in many such operations while with the VC, prior to his decision to cross over to our side. I wondered if he would one day be coming through the wire to this base that he now knew so well.

The sapper took his place beyond the wire and upon being directed to begin, slowly went to his stomach and began a serpentine crawl through no-man's land. The pace was in slow motion; a glance in his direction within the dancing shadows of flares would not necessarily draw the attention of a sentry, especially in the early morning hours when the eye can become less trustworthy. Each and every movement was calculated to the extreme, reminiscent of the legendary Marine Corps sniper, Sgt. Carlos Hathcock's description of such movements as deliberate.

The sapper continued to successfully weave through the most restrictive barriers, generating no unnatural sounds that would attract attention. I found his movements to be hypnotic and terrifying. Slowly, he moved to each claymore, disarming them one by one.

My imagination raced to the unsuspecting sentry who may have been daydreaming about home or just resting with his eyes open, conditioned to react to the slightest noise, especially of anything metallic. The minutes passed as the sapper steadily inched his way toward the sentry, finally arriving at his intended target. At this point, we needed only to read the reports of the violence they had committed. I would see exactly what they could do before my tour in Vietnam ended.

The sapper, satisfied with his performance, displayed a humble smile. The Army spokesperson announced the successful conclusion of the performance and asked if there were any questions. There were some benign questions, but not from me. I had seen enough. That performance convinced me the sappers could do their grim work without interference. The next move for the sapper would have been to execute the plan.

The sentry would be killed with a silencing death blow. Satchel charges would be thrown into pre-identified locations and during the confusion and death brought by the sapper, a full out charge by the VC/NVA would come as a blitz screaming and throwing themselves at the firebase with their death almost a certainty and becoming an honored memory among their brethren also a certainty.

Once the exhibition was over, it was back to Phu Bai and one more night at the club. However, I have never forgotten that exhibition. At that time, I wondered how we could defeat an enemy so intent on our destruction. It would not be long before LZ Ross would be the target of sappers.

What did happen next was a very unexpected reaction to the continuing harassment of one of the old guys, First Lieutenant Chuck Fleisher. It was a normal morning at the ready-room. The weather was bad, as usual, and Fleischer made a huge mistake.

* * *

The atmosphere in HMM-262 from the former MAG 39 combat vets we called, "Old Guys," toward we FNGs greatly varied. The majority of those combat veterans welcomed us with a smile and a beer. Some, however, viewed us with thinly veiled contempt, a sneer or outright disdain. Especially prominent among them was First Lieutenant Chuck Fleischer who treated us like primary flight students, a behavior that had become excessive and annoying.

In mid-December, following the time when we FNGs were issued brand new Smith & Wesson .38 caliber revolvers and ammo. We enthusiastically made our way to the Mama San shop outside the gates of Phu Bai, alongside the Highway 1, the *Street Without Joy*.[111]. We each purchased western style holsters and cartridge belts, recommended by and prominently worn by the old guys.

[111] Bernard B. Fall's great book, Street Without Joy identified Highway 1 from Hue to the DMZ as The Street Without Joy, denoting a specific stretch of Highway 1. However, since 1968 TET occurred following the writing of the book, The Marines from Golf/2/5 under Capt. Chuck Meadows at Phu Bai were rushed up Highway 1 into the battle of Hue. Therefore, I have taken it on myself to extend the original Street without Joy, south, to Phu Bai.

However, comments by one of the old guys brought an unexpected yet deserved response.

Occasionally, but not often, there were All Pilots Meetings (APMs) as opposed to All Officer's Meetings (AOMs) bringing everyone into the ready room. The gloomy days of low dark rumbling clouds and constant monsoon rains ushered in hours and hours of ready room boredom for us all until a partial scud layer allowed us to air taxi to and from Marble Mountain.

On one of those mornings when we were grounded at Phu Bai due to hundred foot ceilings and fog, A.C. Allen, a new resident of our FNG hooch was in the meeting. His wearing of a new holster with a full cartridge-belt of new .38 rounds caught the attention of Lt. Fleischer, a known hard-ass toward us FNGs.

However, that morning, Lt. Fleischer made a mistake. He took an opportunity to make a sneering observation in that room full of pilots. He said to Lt. Allen, "Well, look at that. Isn't that cute? You got a brand new gun and a lot of bright and shiny bullets on your new holster." And, he chuckled as he sipped his coffee and eyeballed the area looking for an admiring glance from his brethren, the old guys.

What Lt. Fleischer didn't know, was anything about First Lieutenant Allen. A.C. was from a small river town in Kentucky and a tough as nails son of a Baptist preacher and "B" Company Honor Man in the 48th OCS Class at Quantico, VA. His natural wit and intelligence along with self-effacing humor made him a welcome favorite on any occasion. He was a self-described "skinny kid from a scruffy section of a small river town full of bullies." He described occasions when he and his brothers experienced bloodied noses and hide scuffing from fights on the school playground. Those battles with bullies taught him many lessons. Bullies, he'd say, "were talented at discerning who they could shove around. Bullies would size up a circumstance and select a target to assure success." To A.C., Fleischer was just another bully.

Fleischer was also unaware of a certain philosophy developed by A.C. during those childhood skirmishes. Nor did he know what off- the-rails violent behavior could come following a simple smart-ass remark, once he had established himself as an asshole. Chuck was about to be the recipient of what A.C. referred to as the, "instant escalation rule."

Being close to AC as he (Fleischer) glanced around the room to see who was grinning at his childish remark, a right hand shot out and grabbed him by the collar. Fleischer's eyes widened and his mouth gaped open as he spontaneously grabbed the hand with both of his hands. He couldn't pull the hands from his collar as AC (who was left handed) simultaneously pulled Fleischer close and with his right hand, pulled that brand new .38 S&W from his brand new holster and placed it near Fleischer's smug face and whispered... "How would you like it if I put two of these brand new f**king bullets up your nose, you son-of-a-bitch."

The room grew quiet. Even the old beat up coffee peculator seemed to stop bubbling. The quiet continued as A.C. slowly loosened his grip, lowered his pistol and then with his right hand, straightened the collar of Fleischer's flight suit and quietly backed away. In the rear of the room, Mike Delong asked, "Anyone for a game of Ping-pong?" The event was never again mentioned and Fleischer was never again unkind to us FNGs or for that matter, any FNG. But, Lt. Fleischer would, in time, fully redeem himself.

34: Change of Command

On 20 December 1969, HMM-262 had a Change of Command (COC) from the stewardship of Major Donald J. Maj. Meskan to that of Lieutenant Colonel Richard A. Bancroft. It was a time of great celebration. My thoughts, however, were more personal as I briefly allowed myself to focus on why fate had played such a trick on me. Why couldn't I have avoided both Majors Meskan and Whitfield until this moment? After some thought, a very little thought, I simply accepted my experience as traditional Walker luck. I had asked myself the same question when I received my second mandatory (had to go) draft notice that steered me to the Marine Corps.

* * *

The day was also significant for another reason. During the early hours of that day, Phu Bai, a large Marine Corps and U.S. Army XXIV Corps base surrounded with massive amounts of firepower and ringed with layers and layers of defensive measures was pretty much believed to be impenetrable. However, on that day, 20 December, a rare and bizarre attempted breach of its defensive perimeter occurred.

It was the last thing anyone expected. However, two wannabe sappers, in the early morning hours of that day, attempted to infiltrate Phu Bai by tying themselves to the underbellies of water buffalos. One sapper was killed; the other was captured, questioned and turned over to the Vietnamese National Police field force that specialized in the neutralization of suspected members of the National Liberation Front of South Vietnam. There was no word as to the fate of the water buffalo.

Having witnessed the Chieu Hoi sapper demonstration at Camp Eagle, strapping oneself to a water buffalo in hopes of getting inside the wire seemed amateurish, far-fetched and just plain stupid. I had never heard of this type of encroachment by the VC/NVA anywhere else. They were not stupid and much too good at their business to be tying themselves to water buffalo.

And just how did they plan on getting the water buffalo to side-step the Claymores that awaited them?

What I took away from that reported incident was a fascination with the mindset of the VC/NVA. Although they didn't have a chance, they attempted to penetrate the defenses of Phu Bai in a very bizarre manner. This brought to mind that the Vietnamese people, the offspring of Mongols and Islanders, had been in a state of concentrated occupation or war for a 1000 years, and we should never underestimate them.

* * *

As a new guy I had no assigned responsibilities in the Change of Command, and I much preferred to be on the flight schedule during the ceremony. The old guys, for the most part, were overjoyed at the prospects of Majors Meskan and Maj. Whitfield being relieved by someone...anyone! Some were outspoken regarding their displeasure with the current leadership, but most were more guarded lest the COC be cancelled for some reason. However, Maj. Meskan's perceived arrogance and lack of leadership skills, as addressed by the old guys, was the first thing they brought out in any conversations I had with them regarding their disdain for him. Some said that his belief in his uncommon flying skills allowed him to get into difficult situations that others might avoid, and he had come out of situations smelling like a rose that others might not have come out of at all.

One point of dissatisfaction with the leadership of the squadron at that time was that when Maj. Meskan, former OIC of S-1 and Maj. Whitfield, former Safety Officer of HMM-262 respectively became the CO and XO of the squadron, they allegedly mandated that only one of them (Meskan or Whitfield) would be scheduled to fly to the hospital ships *Repose* or *Sanctuary*. That trip was considered by the squadron pilots to have been choice duty and an opportunity to get out of the combat arena and simply see the American nurses (round eyes) aboard the ships, even if they never left the cockpit of the 46, it was deemed an innocent delight from which all the squadron pilots were summarily restricted.

Meskan's flying skills and lack of fear were never questioned by anyone. He was the dark and brooding master of the ship; not unlike Major Alex Lee, the overlord of Third Force Recon. I believe I was allowed a brief window into Meskan's piloting skills and level of self-confidence when he flew the last portion of our trip back to Phu Bai, when I pruned the tree for my test.[112]

He was beyond relaxed, as I carefully pushed the forward edge of that blurred arc into a tree, reflexively pulling back at the first sign of debris flying into the air from the limb under assault. Furthermore, his obsession with setting an altitude record in the 46 was evidence of his belief that he could extricate himself from any trouble in the air, especially any trouble I might have gotten us into.

Although Meskan had been generally described as a medal monger, out to collect as many medals as possible before his tour was up, many first lieutenant CH-46 pilots who flew in those same battles from 1965 to October of 1969 had earned similar amounts of recognition. Theirs was a war of attrition, like the whole of the Vietnam War since Operation Hastings when Tim King, a journalist for the Salem-News wrote: "Marines flying the CH-46 helicopter in combat scenarios are among the boldest and most precise pilots and aviation crews in existence."

I never realized the depth of the resentment until decades later after attending several reunions. Meskan, to my knowledge, never attended a 262 reunion. When I asked, "Does anyone know the whereabouts of Don Meskan?" I got back rumors that he became the XO of H&MS-16 and retired from the Corps with the rank of major, an oddity given his reputation of combat prowess and personal decorations that included a couple

[112] First Lieutenant Larry Fenton, who walked out of the DMZ with Capt. White and a recon team in June 1969, told of flying with Major Meskan in MAG-39 when they were within inches of tree limbs while flying down a river covered in trees. It may be that Maj. Meskan was indeed concerned with keeping blades out of trees when he had me trim a tree with my blades.

of DFCs, a Silver Star or two, tons of air medals and having commanded a combat helicopter squadron at the rank of major.

It was as if he disappeared off the Marine Corps map. In a way I felt that my test by Meskan, just 16 days before the change of command was peculiar and unjustified. But, in another way, it was a gift. I got to experience his flying skills and demeanor on full display. I think I might have learned to like him if I had had an opportunity to fly with him in combat. And, I never got my blades in the trees again.

Figure 60 Lt. J.D. Jeffryes "Mountain Man"

On or about 16 December, 4 additional FNGs arrived. They were First Lieutenants John "Juan" Arnold, John "Ski" Kosinski, Lowell "Ollie" Olsen and 1 second lieutenant, the only second lieutenant in MAG-16, Joe "Silky" Gulvas[113]. With their arrival, my luck seemed to have changed for the better upon learning that I had been scheduled to fly a Third Force Recon mission with First Lieutenant "Mountain Man" J. D. Jeffryes on December 20, the day of the Change of Command.

That mission with Jeffryes was my second opportunity to participate in a Third Force Recon insert, which was a rarity for us Marines. It was well known that Maj. Alex Lee, CO of Third Force Recon, who reported directly to LtGen. Nickerson, CG of IIIMAF, preferred to work with the Army's 101st Airborne Division, particularly the 2d Squadron of the 17th Cavalry. What wasn't common knowledge was that Maj. Lee was LtGen. Nickerson's son-in-law, giving Lee access to the ear of the most powerful Marine in Vietnam. The reason given by Lee, in his book, for

---

[113] Second Lieutenant Joe Gulvas was soon a first lieutenant. He had gone through the Army training program like so many did. The difference was that he got into combat so quickly. It took me a full year longer than Joe to complete Naval Flight School.

using the Army was the resistance he received from the 1st MAW, versus the ready-and-willing aviation assets of the 101st Airborne Division. Dialogue between Lee and the 1st MAW was contentious.[114] Lee dealt with disagreements he had with the 1st MAW by going directly to Gen Abram's staff in Saigon as present- ers of the desires of LtGen Nickerson. Maj. Meskan was known to have accompanied Lee to meetings with the 101st Airborne Divi- sion where they both were held in high esteem. Learning of all the fraternization with the Army by Third Force was disconcert- ing. Weren't we, the Marines, the best pilots?

That day, 20 December, became even more memorable to me when I learned we were going into the A Shau Valley, the Valley of Death, with all of its startling beauty and mystery. I had heard stories about the A Shau primarily from flight instructors during advanced training at Ellyson Field in Pensacola FL and HMMT-302. The name itself brought forth chill bumps and descriptive terms such as dark and foreboding, often used in narratives that described the valley. Flying west with the Third Force Recon team on our aircraft, escorted by Scarface, HML-367's new Co- bras, and OV-10s with the Hostage call sign watching over us, was a thrill I would never forget, a true Marine Corps team.

As we entered the valley, it was like the first time I looked into the Grand Canyon. The most stunning sights were of long silvery streams cascading down the sides of peaks from such heights the water, sparkling like diamonds, transformed itself into a churning mist at mid-plunge. Deep, dark, heavy jungle flowed gently up the slopes of the mountains that formed the valley below that was a sea of elephant grass with those razor

[114] The incoming XO, Maj. Wiley Sellers, had some direct contentious talks with Lee about Lee's bad-mouthing Marine helicopter support. Lee's book *Force Recon Command*, pages 144-145, reveals that Major Lee and Major Meskan, CO, HMM-262 were "boisterously welcomed" by Maj. Gen. John Wright, Commanding Officer of the 101st Airborne Division, on New Year's Day, 1970, where Gen. Wright "...made it clear that we were considered to be important to the 101st Airborne Division" and, he "was quick to point out that he knew about [Third Force Recon] being...harshly judged, in Da Nang for fly- ing more with the Army than with the Marines." Lee's infatuation with the Army led to future problems for his command.

edges, the height of which was level with the cockpit of the 46, some 10 to 14 feet high.

Figure 61 Elephant Grass in the A Shau Valley. Notice height and thickness.

An old French resort sat atop one of the peaks, all grown over except for the remains of a tennis court where the French vacationed to cool off. An oft repeated tale, by Marines, was that it was an R&R center for Mr. Charles. The mummified remains of what was once a cable car system leading up the side of the mountain from the valley's floor was absorbed by the jungle. The barely recognizable form, discernible from a distance due to the symmetrical flow of the jungle over the cable, was a vestige of French colonialism like the resemblance of the hull of a sunken ship melting away, covered in rust, crustaceans and sand.

The French colonial influence in Vietnam was inescapable in both the language, peppered with French phrases, and the architecture. That mountain-top resort had provided an elite class of Frenchmen a cool respite from the syrupy heat, humidity and mosquitoes found in the lowlands.

Snapping out of my tourist mode, I glanced at Jefferys, the mountain man who was locked onto the controls. I quickly located our position and became engrossed in following the map with my finger as we traveled across the geological contour lines, some so close together they appeared to be a solid line, indicating a drop of several hundred feet, followed by a spacious distance between the lines revealing a vast level field. Our mission was to insert the recon team into that field. Our intent was to deposit them near one of the hundreds of craters created by bombs of all sizes dropped from a variety of warplanes over the years.

I could almost visualize ancient warriors fighting to the death, just as our Marines and our Army comrades were doing that day. The radio was squawking and squelching as Scarface set up in a wagon wheel, covering us and looking for bad guys. Marine speak went on between the gunships and Jeffryes. I completed the landing checklist and quickly stated in between their breaths, "Landing checklist complete." Jeffryes dropped the collective and rolled the 46 to starboard into that patented nose-down death-spiral approach.

Rolling out on final into an area near a bomb crater, Jeffryes pulled the nose higher than usual, our unprotected belly exposed, using aerodynamic braking to remain short of the crater. The elephant grass enveloped us as our main mounts settled onto terra firma. The heavy razor grass flailed against the hurricane force winds of the blades that were at full flight RPM as the nose-wheel gently settled onto the ground. I dropped the ramp upon the crew chief's call and glanced into the cargo bay through the narrow passage.

The Marines were prepared to exit the helicopter as rapidly as possible. They moved in unison into the thick grass and became one with that green world. The reality of the moment buoyed me. The radio belched out bursts of chatter from the gunships, looking for Charlie. There were no outward signs of Charlie, but he was there...watching and waiting, hunkered down. To my naïve observation of, "Wow, so this is it, the Valley of Death?" Jeffryes replied, "Yep, Charlie owns this place, and we're just visitors." How right he was. We were just another foreign foe following in the footsteps of France.

Third Force Reconnaissance was in the business of relaying information as to what was being moved into Vietnam from Laos. The reports of that team reinforced what was known; there were heavy movements of enemy troops and large trucks carrying supplies, all headed east from the Ho Chi Minh trail. The term *infestation* was liberally used to describe the growing number of our enemy.

Jeffryes smoothly raised the collective. It seemed such a disparity; Jeffryes, a mountain of a man, handling the controls as delicately as a brain surgeon's scalpel.[115] The engines began to scream that comforting sound of power as the nose raised high above the sea of grass. The old warhorse literally leapt into the air, clawing for altitude, as if it inherently knew that anything less would result in catastrophe. The vertical speed indicator (VSI) was pegged. In moments, we were at an altitude placing us out of small arms range. Following a brief response from the team to Scarface, consisting of a double squelch, all was well. The radios fell silent. The insert was complete.

With a quick change of frequencies we were out clean and on our way home, back to the COC. My part in the war was over for the day. It felt strange to think that we had deposited recon warriors into the heart of the A Shau only minutes before. What a strange, beautiful and dangerous place, this Vietnam.

---

[115] In the book, "Steinbeck on Vietnam: Dispatches from the War", Steinbeck went to Vietnam to do a series of reports. Steinbeck spent time with a CH-46 Squadron and made the following observation. "...these pilots. They make me sick with envy. They ride their vehicles the way a man controls a fine well-trained quarter horse. They weave along stream beds, rise like swallows to clear trees, they turn and twist and dip like swifts in the evening. I watch their hands and feet on the controls, the delicacy of the coordination reminds me of the sure and seeming slow hands of (Pablo) Casals on the cello. They are truly musician's hands and they play their controls like music and they dance them like ballerinas and they make me jealous because I want so much to do it. Remember your child night dream of perfect flight free and wonderful? It's like that, and sadly I know I never can..."

Figure 62 First Lieutenant Mike Harr was the last of the FNG arrivals in 1969.

Upon our arrival back at 262, I learned that another FNG had arrived just in time for the COC: it was First Lieutenant Mike Harr, an easygoing Marine from Iowa. Mike's presence strengthened the number of FNGs in the squadron.

* * *

I never enjoyed the pomp and circumstance of ceremonies, having bypassed The Basic School in which you are drilled on the ceremonial aspects of being a Marine officer, including the proper use of the Mameluke officer's sword, other than having it as a memento of our service. We Aviation Officer Candidates turned Second Lieutenants in a few harrowing weeks at Quantico learned how to march in a straight line, but were never entrusted with swords. Colonel Conroy, the Great Santini,[116] and commanding officer of the Marine Aviation Detachment at Pensacola (The M.A.D. house) attempted to rectify our lack of swordsmanship with an impromptu sword drill class on a hot, sultry Friday afternoon. We gathered in an alley next to the MAD house, near the base Exchange when practice began. Following a horrible display of awkwardness with the Mameluke, Conroy dismissed us following a colorful rendition of what he saw as a direct threat to our future as aviators and thus, the security of the country, should we put someone's eye out whose fate may

---

[116] The Great Santini was a 1979 movie based on the 1976 novel by the same name by Pat Conroy. The film starred Robert Duvall. Pat Conroy was the son of Col. Donald Conroy, the CO of the Marine Aviation Detachment at Pensacola Naval Air Station, Pensacola, FL. He was the CO when the majority of us going to Vietnam were going through flight training at Pensacola.

have been to save the world. We were then ordered directly to Happy Hour at the Mustin Beach Officer's Club—pure Santini.

* * *

As for our 262 COC, I was told that at the precise moment LtCol Bancroft gripped the colors representing 262, and Meskan released his grip on same, an audible sigh of relief could be heard throughout the old guys' officer ranks. LtCol. Bancroft and Maj. Meskan both made equally forgettable comments, and it was done. As for Majors Meskan and Whitfield, I never saw them again.[117] They seemed to disappear into thin air with no fanfare and no notice, but they left behind a mess of mediocre fitness reports that could adversely affect those wanting to have a career in the Corps.

Figure 63 LtCol R.A. Bancroft

LtCol Bancroft, the former Commanding Officer of H&MS-16 and a former A-4 pilot with no serious helicopter piloting experience other than a brief field-grade transition, was now our new commanding officer. At some point in the past, the Marine Corps had taken a list of jet pilots, and, without regard to experience or any other objective criteria, went down the list choosing every other name for forced transfer to service in the helicopter community.

[117] I never saw Major Meskan or Maj. Whitfield again. However, Maj. Whitfield's name showed up on some 262 flight schedules when we were in Marble Mountain.

Figure 64 Major Wiley J. Sellers

HMM-262 had a new boss and a new XO, Major Wiley J. Sellers, a second tour CH-46 pilot who was originally a Douglas F4D Skyray pilot, kinda like flying a ballistic missile. Then Major, now LtCol (Ret), Sellers advised there had been a forced transition of jet pilots into helicopters years ago, when there was a severe shortage of helicopter pilots. He became a seasoned CH-46 combat veteran and primo maintenance officer who, as a first tour helicopter pilot with HMM-164, participated in Operation Hastings. During that horrific battle for Hill 362 in July 1966 north of the Rock Pile near the DMZ, five CH-46s crashed or shot down while inserting troops into LZ Crow in the Ngan River Valley. That valley, which holds the broken remains of five CH-46A helicopters, would forever after be known in the annals of Marine Corps Aviation as Helicopter Valley. Seller's helicopter credentials were solid.

* * *

At the end of Majors Meskan and Maj. Whitfield's reign, we were directed, or, at least we new guys had been directed, to sign blank, undated fitness report forms with no opportunity to review or respond to any portions of the written evaluation. That furtive evaluation was sent to Headquarters, Marine Corps, Washington D.C. and placed in our permanent personnel files.[118]

---

[118] The practice of having officers sign blank fitness reports without any right to review or respond was commonplace at that time except from the most benevolent commanding officers and not until years following Vietnam was the policy changed to allow review and responce. But, having started my career essentially as a draftee, I wasn't much interested in the evaluations.

With the experience of signing blank fitness reports, the words of Major Meskan soon after we arrived at 262 were ominous. He stated at an All Officers Meeting (AOM) that there were none of us that he "particularly desired" to have due to our inexperience. He further stated that many of us would become "good" Marine officers should we continue our careers and cautioned us not to judge the Marine Corps by what we observed in our tour in Vietnam.

* * *

I couldn't believe we were going to have a CO, LtCol. Bancroft, who was not a real helicopter pilot. The Marine Corps wouldn't do that, would they? Col. Bancroft and Maj. Sellers, however, would prove their loyalty to us much sooner than anyone could have expected, and in turn they would receive our full support and loyalty.

Let the party begin!

Traditionally a day of celebration, the COC provided the squadron an opportunity to launch into a fiesta. Upon recovery of the day's flights, all were expected to join in the squadron party which began in the hangar following the ceremony and moved on to the O'Club. The occasion had the effect of ushering out the old and celebrating the new.

The FNGs were becoming stronger in number and more confident, losing the flight student feeling and coming into our own as fully qualified H2p copilots. Toleration of being treated by some as perpetual flight students was being tested as we became less obliged to take a backseat when it came to flying. Bancroft's arrival marked the emergence of this new era that would include the movement of the squadron to Marble Mountain.

However, now was not the time to reflect, but to party! Col. Bancroft, a powerfully built man with heavy jowls and a bulldog appearance that belied his gentle nature, was immediately liked by all. The sense we had upon meeting him was that he liked us. He seemed genuinely happy to be with this group of men and to be in Phu Bai. He was a refreshing change in persona and style from the brooding Meskan.

With the completion of my mission after action paperwork, I wasted no time in joining the squadron at the O'Club. I was feeling salty after having flown into the A Shau.

An Australian band was performing on that special night. It was always a treat to see blonde female singers in the club who seemed perfectly at ease in that bawdy environment. The booze was flowing and there was a holiday atmosphere.

John Arnold and Lowell "Oly" Olson, two FNGs with whom I had gone through the training command, were already in the club and forming the FNG party nucleus. Hanner, as usual, was busy with maintenance test flights, but would make his way to the club, not missing much of the happenings. A.C. Allen and McGlothlin arrived at the club along with Gary Rainey. Soon, Ron McAmis, Roy Prigge and Gene Mitchell arrived. Bill Davis, Fred McCorkle, Mike Delong, arrived. Soon everyone was there, along with guests: honored guests, Col. Mann from HMM-161, still at Phu Bai, and Third Force Recon CO Maj. Lee. His XO, Capt. Hisler, and First Lieutenants Buck "Igor" Coffman and Robert "Beak" Hinsley[119] were also in the house, along with some Army commanders who were friends of both Maj. Meskan and Maj. Maj. Whitfield. The only thing that brings out more dignitaries than a COC is the funeral dirge of a fallen Marine.

LtCol. Bancroft, as it turned out, was no slouch when it came to booze. He drank a peculiar green colored liquid, straight. It was a cocktail called a sidecar, made with crème de menthe, cognac and lemon juice. Ugh! Odd. I thought, for a tough, brawling Marine colonel to drink such a fancy drink was an oddity. John Wayne would never have done that. The majority of the squadron drank beer from keg and can. Some drank whiskey straight, or scotch and water, but not a drink called a sidecar. The Colonel's drink soon became his nickname when he wasn't in hearing

---

[119] First Lieutenant Hinsley, following his tour of duty with 3d Force, transitioned to the air wing in an A-4 Sky Hawk.

range—Sidecar 6.[120] Wine was also on the tables—the familiar dark green Mateuse bottles.

No one knew the flight schedule for the following day. The possibility of being on the flight schedule had no visible ill effect on the intake of booze.

Figure 65 First Lieutenant John W. Arnold

The party lasted until late into the evening. By early afternoon John "Juan" Arnold, although already assigned to the S-1 office, further distinguished himself by running around on the roof of the O'Club. Why John was on the roof was a subject for discussion. Some said he wanted to be closer to God. John said he may have been trying to retrieve something.

Lowell "Ollie" Olson, his close friend, was more understanding. Ollie said, "He's on the roof, because he wants to be on the roof." That settled it. Although Arnold had only been in-country for three days and had been assigned to S-1, he demonstrated that he met all the necessary qualifications to be placed into a very special job yet to be announced by the CO.

The hardcore FNGs remained at the club as long as it was open. Bancroft, during this revelry, was found in the head by A.C. Allen. "There he was," said Allen. "Our new CO, drunk as a monkey, standing there with his head leaning against the bulkhead, crank in hand, pissing on the deck between two urinals," [A la *Das Boot*.[121]] A.C. teased Bancroft by saying, "Sir, if you can't aim

[120] The number 6 was attached to the commanding officer's call sign. Cattlecall 6 was the commanding officer's call sign of HMM-161. Chatterbox 6 was the call sign of LtCol Bancroft, CO of HMM-262. Ancient Scout 6 was the call sign of Maj. Alex Lee, the CO of Third Force Recon, etc. The number 5, represented the XO.
[121] "Das Boot" is a German movie produced in 1981 and considered by some to be among the best war movie made, albeit from the German perspec-

well enough to hit one of two urinals how are you going to hit an LZ?" Future events would shed light on Bancroft's ability to get the 46D into a zone.

The club was packed with pilots, both Marine and Army, Third Force Recon officers, and a contingent of Army helicopter pilots who flew Maj Lee's Third Force in and out of the A Shau. As always, there's one person in every group of five or more who can't hold his booze and becomes very obnoxious. One of the Army pilots fit that profile. Col Bancroft was seated front row center with Maj. Sellers and other ranking officers and visiting warriors, conducting himself in an admirable manner, like that of a Viking warlord, considering all the drunk first lieutenants and warrant officers in the club.

However, as Ron McAmis, Gary Rainey and I were standing near the rear of the room, a drunken warrant officer began to elbow his way through the club. This was overlooked for a while as one of his friends tried to quiet him down. No one wanted any trouble, but this guy was beginning to piss off everyone, even his buddy.

As things progressed, he finally broke away from his friend, and it was my bad luck that he was coming my way. Well, I also had plenty to drink by that time and was waiting for this idiot to do something stupid. He did!

His path placed him between Gary and me with Ron McAmis to my left, and as a drunk would do, he pushed by Gary then elbowed me. I pushed back. His arrogance and sense of entitlement was more than I could stand. He mumbled something obscene about jarheads while at the same time taking a drunken swing at me. His blow glanced off the left side of my head. It didn't hurt; his punch was feeble, but it did push me back.

---

tive. A scene in the movie caused me to immediately recall A.C. Allen's description of LtCol Bancroft in the scene described above. The captain of the German U-Boat was passed out in the men's restroom when an officer demanded to know where the commanding officer of the rowdy submarine crew was so that he could make a report of their bad behavior. The enlisted man pointed to a body lying face down in the restroom passed out in a pool of urine. "There Sir," responded the submariner. "<u>That</u> is our CO."

I took full advantage of the weak punch and spontaneously turned and caught him flush on the jaw with a pretty good punch, knocking a cigarette out of his mouth that shot by Gary's face. He staggered backwards. This brought the other warrant officers to his side, which then brought the Marines to my side, and all of a sudden it was time to dance. He was acting as if he wanted to fight, and I was hoping he would. It was the nasty side of my nature. I had always been able to control this urge except on a few provoked occasions.

Outside the club, in the lighted area under the watch tower, we pushed and shoved each other like a couple of schoolyard kids. Col. Bancroft and his guests, who had front row seats at the show, weren't disturbed, or so I thought. The party was beginning to have the feel of a Viking celebration what with the band, the Australian singers, an almost brawl, and the warlord surrounded by his faithful senior officers while filling himself with that green liquid. Pandemonium was on display, and we were home.

After getting outside I knew it was going to be a dog fight. He was my size and very drunk, which would give me the edge. But to my surprise, the guy seemed to sober up once we were outside in the cool air. Three or four warrant officers gathered, and a similar number of Marines, all of whom appeared more ready to fight than even me or him.

The Corps was tough: Excluding the old guys, we had some great athletes, boxers, grapplers and brawlers in the FNGs. Hell, Pete Hanner, tough as nails went through four years in the Navy, could flatten you with a stare, and Eric McGrew had boxed throughout high school and college. A.C. grew up fighting in a tough, southern river town. Donnie would rather throw fisticuffs than talk. McAmis was a former Golden Gloves boxer and Gary was just plain tough. And, they would have been with me no matter what if necessary. But so was the Army Warrant Officers Association (WOA) with my adversary, and they were a few years younger than us. It would have been an all-out, down in the mud brawl, a real dog fight, had it happened. The political fallout would have been thunderous had cooler heads not prevailed. But prevail they did.

No one shook hands, no one lost face literarily or physically, and the rift was over as quickly as it had begun. It was never again mentioned. I never knew the name of the offending warrant officer, nor he mine. We both walked away and, again, I was unable to keep a low profile and the night was very young.

35: The Great Raid

The partying that began in early afternoon of that day began to fade near 2100 hrs. The band was packing up and our new commanding officer staggered out of the club with help from the new executive officer as Country Joe and the Fish blared from the TEAC 4010. Captains Stover and White walked with the new leadership and Majors Meskan and Whitfield just disappeared. The Lieutenant's were unleashed!!

The posted closing hour for the club was 2200. A small contingent of first lieutenants was still working on a case of Mateuse. Corks broke in half as clumsy fingers applied too much pressure, causing them to have to push the remaining cork into the bottle.

Figure 66 Interior of O'Club following the COC reception. L to R, Larry Ridgeway, Bob Lloyd, John "Wags" Wagner. Rear, Art Gillidette and Dean Davis. Far rear, Pete Sawczyn.

They laughed, chugged wine, and talked about their exploits in Provisional MAG-39, in support of the 3d Marine Division. Yet, unlike helicopter pilots of which I was familiar, those 46 drivers to my astonishment used their hands like fighter pilots to illustrate maneuvers into difficult zones on ridgelines and buttonhooks into insecure zones to pick up the dead and wounded. They spoke of facing the terror of quad-fifties and a mid-air collision between a 46 and an Army Huey in the fog of war. They also spoke of funny things that had happened during their year; and in soft tones they remembered those no longer with them.

The Marines from our hooch were still present, along with other FNGs, when someone came up with the idea of going over to the Army side of Phu Bai. The flight schedule for the following day, 21 December, had not yet been completed and probably wouldn't be posted, as usual, until sometime in the early morning hours. Therefore, there was always the chance you wouldn't be scheduled. So if you didn't know you were on the schedule, the mind-set was to party on. We were on the board to move to Marble, and we were flying most all of our missions in the Da Nang area. There was a certain amount of "What the f**k?" going on about everything. It was apparent to me that the squadron, now under new leadership, was undergoing a change, a new mentality, that of short-timers.

My day was over; however, someone suggested that it was a perfect time to head over to the Army side because the Army clubs remained open until 0100. That idea struck a note with the group consisting of myself, John Arnold, Gary Rainey, John Kosinski, Bill Davis, Gene Mitchell, Lowell Olson and three or four additional Marines whose names have been lost to time. A.C. Allen, Donnie McGlothlin, Eric McGrew, Ollie Olson, Pete Hanner, Roy Prigge, and Ron McAmis did not come with us, and I have no recall as to why not.

Before long, those who were going walked into the drizzle of rain and crawled over the back tailgate of a covered 6x6 driven by the duty driver for that night, a corporal who wasn't sure this trip fit the description of an emergency or anything close to necessary. However, with a generous donation of the military's answer to real money, MPC, he was convinced the trip was exactly what was meant by exigent circumstance.

The night was cool by Vietnam standards, and it was the middle of the monsoon season, red super-mud blanketed everything as a continuous light drizzle alternated with blinding downpours that taunted us each day. On our way to the home of the Screamin' Eagles 101st Airborne's XXIV Corps located on the Army side of Highway 1, the truck groaned and moaned in low gear as it moved through knee deep mud like an Arctic icebreaker.

I personally knew nothing about the Army side; apparently they had many clubs available to us. I was also unaware of the Army's living conditions, figuring the Air Force to be the ones who pampered themselves. But it appeared the Army also lived well, especially the Screamin' Eagles, and they didn't bar Marines—yet.

We eventually made our way through the Phu Bai gate onto Highway 1 then made the short trip to the Army's main gate. Following a cursory look, the sentry waved us through. We were beginning to sober up as we entered the gate. The 3.2% beer was akin to drinking Kool-Aid. The club we were looking for was the Spud Officer's Club, home of the Army's Mohawks.[122]

Our driver was asked to be back at the club no later than 2200. He agreed, as he deposited the MPC into his pocket and lit up a Camel. "I got a radio," he said. "If I'm needed back at the base, they'll call. So I'll just hang around here waiting for you sirs unless I'm called. Then, just call me again, and I'll get right back over here."

We entered the club and found a few Army Mohawk pilots who were at the bar in the same shape we were. They greeted us with wrinkled brows and stone faces wondering what we were doing there.

[122] The Army's 131st Aviation Co. flew the OV1 Grumman Mohawk, a twin turbo prop that carried two crew members, a pilot and an observe and was armed with a 30MM cannon. Its mission was observation and artillery spotting. They primarily flew over the Ho Chi Minh trail and its missions were classified.

"Has there been some kind of meeting with you fellas?" one asked.

"Nope," responded one of us. "We just wanted to see how the other half lives."

"Not too goddamned good," was the response. "But," he said, "we do have the luxury of a steam bath and massage parlor."

"No shit!" one of our group spouted off. "Where?"

That was it. Last call was announced. We gulped down our drinks and thanked the Army pilots for the information.

It was time to sober up, and what better way to do that than sit in a steam bath and then get a massage? Two of our group, First Lieutenant's Bill Davis, Gene Mitchell, John Arnold and Ollie Olson separated from us and went their own way to another Army club that was also open until the 0100 hour. We lost track of them, but figured they'd come to the steam bath.

The steam bath was similar to the one I'd discovered in Okinawa. I couldn't believe that this was in the Army's own compound. What a deal! It was apparent that someone in the Army was offsetting the cost of the war here.

The place was a rough-hewn steam bath operation populated by massage parlor girls who, for the most part, appeared to be Cambodian, although it was difficult to know for sure. I wondered aloud as to how much clout you had to have to get this on a U.S. Army base.

I couldn't imagine the local Vietnamese taking part in this, although they may have. There was no overt prostitution going on, but behind closed doors there was most certainly plenty of time for monkey business. The Army apparently allowed Marines, albeit reluctantly, the use of the facility. I suppose that since the Army's XXIV Corps was under the command of III MAF in Da Nang, they felt obliged to be somewhat conciliatory toward us. Hell, I learned that the Army even had an outdoor swimming pool. What a gig, just like the Air Force!

For the Army and Marine Grunts who lived in the bush, a swim in a real swimming pool, in water that wasn't infested by blood-sucking, disease-ridden leeches, was a distant dream. Although there was some leisure time through what was called In-country R&R for both Marines and soldiers at China Beach in Da Nang or the Freedom Hill complex, a steam bath followed by a massage would have done wonders for their morale.

Upon entering the Army's sanctuary, the worst possible thing happened; an Army guy wrapped in a towel had tried to ignore our group, but couldn't remain quiet to our presence and made some disparaging remarks about Marines. The remarks may have been justifiable, but under the circumstances it showed poor judgment. As if to subdue our enthusiasm, someone shouted, "He's a colonel." How were we supposed to know his true rank? He was standing there in his towel, madder than hell, his face redder than red, and cussing a blue streak over seeing Marines there.

We had been, up to that point, rather docile. We hadn't even been able to check in. And it was getting late, maybe too late. The alleged colonel neither commanded nor received our respect. We were beyond caring what his rank or station in life might have been. And he knew we didn't care, which didn't do anything to soothe his rage.

I don't recall the remark, or who owned it, but a disparaging comment was directed in the general direction of the "colonel," who took further exception to our presence and, I believe, our very existence. The manager asked that we calm down, and we in turn asked that the towel man calm down. Then things escalated. The manager resorted to ordering us to leave. We saw this as a hostile act toward the Corps by the Army and its representative, the manager. Then it all degenerated into a full-scale attack on the facility with the Marines scrambling throughout the area tossing cold water on unsuspecting Army personnel after kicking open the doors to their massage retreats. There was panic. Towels flew into the air as "massage girls" took flight, screaming, laughing, and running in every direction.

There was the smell of steam and sweat-soaked wood, and cheap perfume with Army personnel in complete disarray: partially clothed and jumping up and down on one leg while trying to get their pants on. Their attempt to mount a counterattack was neither organized nor fast enough.

A clear and consistent rant uttered through their clinched teeth. "You goddamned Marines!" or: "You f**king jarheads!" A smattering of comments about Marines being little more than animals were thrown into their rants for added measure. The manager, with the phone in his hand, made a loud and clear declaration that moved us into full retreat. "The MPs are coming, you sons of bitches!"

It was time to make our getaway!

Our loyal corporal had the motor running earphones on, listening to a cassette tape. Someone in our merry band had obviously had the foresight to arrange a signal, because as we came running out of the massage parlor he began flicking the lights on and off so we knew which way to run. Our retreat was somewhat harried as we ran into the dark followed by a few brave Army souls cussing and throwing rocks. One had a handgun that was silhouetted by the lights of the buildings in the immediate vicinity.

The corporal was like the driver of a bank heist, cool and calm; his job was to get us away as fast as possible. With tires spinning and mud and gravel being slung from the big knobby tires, the truck bounced along the muddy roadway on the way to the gate. We lay in the back in a pile, laughing.

Did we all get aboard? Was anyone missing? Remember, no Marine will be left behind. As the truck coughed, spit, and lunged forward on the way to the Army gate, we felt we had escaped. No one had been hurt, no one gave their name or rank, and it had been great fun. The good-natured rivalry between Marines and Army personnel had been reestablished. We thought of it all as tradition. There was no harm, no foul!

Only two more obstacles remained to make good our escape: getting through the main gate guards onto Highway 1, and through the gate into Phu Bai. To our surprise, the Army sentries waived us through the gate and onto Highway 1 with little notice. Apparently, the Army "colonel" was satisfied that we were gone and did not notify the sentries to block our escape. So far, so good!

A short distance on Highway 1, past the Combined Military Police (CMP) post, was the turnoff east into the Marine side of the base. We followed the dirt road lined with concertina wire to the heavily guarded gate, the Marine guards did a cursory check of our ID cards, and while amused at our poor condition, they allowed us into the camp. After making our way back to our hooch, we realized we just might still be missing some Marines.

We counted noses and found that four FNGs, First Lieutenants Bill Davis, Gene Mitchell, John Arnold and Ollie Olson were not with us, nor were they in their hooches. Oh Shit! What a mess! It was the day of the COC, and we had lost two Marine officers. It was now the early morning hours of 21 December 1969 and missing anyone in Vietnam could be a problem! The flight schedule had come out, and I was scheduled to fly with Jeffryes again. The brief was 0745 for a Code 1R8 mission (visual reconnaissance). It didn't look like there would be much sleep, if any, for me or anyone else.

36: The Getaway

One of our group did some detective work and learned that Steve Bravard had recently left the O'Club with Bill Davis and Gene Mitchell to go to the Army side. Also, John Arnold and Ollie Olson had come back with Mitchell and Davis in the Jeep. At that time, we knew nothing about Arnold and Olson having been with Mitchell and Davis. They went to their hooch and were out of what was to come. I believed they were all still on the Army side, at another open bar or running for their lives from the colonel in the massage parlor. This was confusing, very confusing.

"Hal, if they were here, how did they get there?" Gary opined. "And, more importantly, why would they go back to the Army side?"

"Where did they get a Jeep?" I thought out loud.

"OK, something is wrong, and we have a new CO who hasn't even sobered up from the COC ceremony."

"Yep," said Pete, who had been listening to this debacle with an amused look on his face. "sounds like this is the time for some adult leadership!"

"Well, Pete, what do you think?"

"I think someone is in a world of shit."

"Okay, Roy, what do you think?"

"Oh, nooo! Don't get me involved with this." responded Roy, laughing as he looked over from his bunk at the think-tank that had evolved.

"OK, what do we know?" I said.

"Not much, apparently," responded A.C.

"Those guys at the club said that Bill and Gene had a Jeep they said they borrowed from an Army major and that the three had left the club on their way back to the Army Club."

"Sounds like bullshit to me," responded Donnie. "Let's just go to the MP shack out there on Highway 1 and see if there's been an accident or anything."

"Okay," responded Gary. "Let's get the truck back and get out of here."

The decision was made. Upon re-securing the use of the duty truck, Gary Rainey, Don McGlothlin and I, among others, headed for the Combined Military Police Station on Highway 1. The night had turned cold, with low hanging clouds and mist. We were now half-asleep, dog tired, and determined as we once again made our way through the Marine sentries.

Upon arriving at the CMP, where both Marine and Army police personnel milled about, we made our way into the office area, hoping to learn whether or not Bill, Gene, and now Steve were in custody. It was our intent to be casual, even in this atmosphere.

A new round of harassment and interdiction (H&I) fire had begun. The 105mm howitzers were pumping high explosives off to the west into no-man's-land as we walked into the office area. Our intent was to find someone, hopefully a Marine, from whom we could trust and elicit information leading us to the whereabouts of our friends.

Our worst fear was that the three had been caught and locked up following the massage parlor raid. If so, we wanted to spring them before the command learned of the event. Hopefully, someone at the CMP station would be understanding and "cut us a huss."[123] However, our appearance became immediately suspect. The drizzle had turned to rain, and we were the only Marine first lieutenants wandering through their compound.

Our casual inquiries resulted in our being directed to the CMP Duty Officer. The circumstances in which we found ourselves made it necessary to address him lest we incur more suspicion.

We found the D.O., a weary, red-eyed first sergeant MP, seated at a large desk set up on a landing, not unlike those found in any large municipal police station in any city in the states. He eyed us suspiciously as we advanced to his desk. I got straight to the point of stating our primary purpose by saying, "Sergeant, we're here to see if you've picked up any Marines tonight?"

---

[123] A "huss" is a Marine term for giving someone a break, a favor.

The question itself sounded suspicious, yet I couldn't figure out any other way to say it. Even as I asked, I cringed, thinking this doesn't sound right. How do you say we've lost two Marine officers, and they were last seen after we were thrown out of the Army's massage parlor, without being suspicious? (At that same moment, Bill, Gene, and Steve were seated in the Army Club that was trying to close.)

The D.O. settled back into his chair, took a hard long drink of bust head coffee and with both eyes locked on us asked, "Who the f**k are you sirs looking for?" The directness of his no-non-sense response struck me dumb. I didn't want to give their names—I wouldn't.

While I was thinking about it, Donnie and Gary began backing up. He continued, "What did they look like, and where and when did you last see them?" Finally, after receiving some ahhhhs and uhhhhs, the D.O. began turning color. As we tried to be conversant while not saying a word, the D.O. continued asking appropriate questions—who, what, when, where, how and why kinds of questions—appropriate questions that we couldn't answer without also identifying ourselves.

I responded almost cheerfully, "Well, never mind. They're probably back inside the base and asleep by now."

Gary chimed in with his rendition. "Listen, if you haven't seen any of these guys, it's okay." Like me, he said, "They're probably back at the base somewhere."

Having smelled a trap, Donnie had already left the office area and was back in the truck. The tone of the D.O. had changed to that serious tone you hear when an otherwise personable state trooper becomes real official-sounding "Please, sir, step out of the car" after examining your driver's license and registration.

Oh shit!

The tone had also become similar to, "Where were you the night of the murder?" We said, "Thanks, but we have to be going." I was certain that had we not been officers, we would have been escorted to the lockup for more questions. It was definitely time to get going.

Fortunately, though he had left his chair behind the desk to stand and speak to us, the D.O. did not try to stop or block our retreat, nor did he directly ask us to identify ourselves. He knew who we were. Our units could be none other than the Marine helicopter squadrons sitting on the north side of the Phu Bai runway. Those we were seeking were officers, or it would have been a senior staff NCO, a gunny, with equal rank to the D.O., who would have come. No rank less than the D.O's would have had a chance to get a Marine out of that place. Feeling tired and depressed, we made our way back through the gate into the Marine side and to the hooch. We had done all we could. Now, we could only wait.

During the time period immediately following our disastrous meeting with the CMP, Bill, Gene and Steve were approaching the Army gate that would allow them back onto Highway 1. Information about them, Marine officers having taken what was officially identified as a general's Jeep, not a major's Jeep was already at the gate. A small security shack sat near the heavily guarded gate where the sergeant of the guard was watching over the happenings at the gate.

As the Jeep approached, rather than doing a cursory check of the three officers and waving them through, a guard stepped in front of the Jeep with his hand stretched out, signaling a halt, stopping them cold. The guard stepped into the shack, retrieved a clip board as other guards watched the Jeep. Returning to the Jeep, the guard with the clip board wiped away thick layers of monsoon mud on the hood to reveal the Army serial number, prominently displayed in white paint. The MP checked and rechecked the vehicle number with the information on his clipboard, spoke briefly with another guard, then turning to Steve, who was sitting in the front passenger seat, "Please step out of the Jeep, Sir!"

Bill Davis, as calm as could be, was sitting behind the wheel as if he had nothing to fear. Steve, in the front passenger seat, was just glad to be going back to his hooch, unaware he was riding in what the Army had determined was a stolen Jeep and Gene, sitting in the back seat, was nodding off.

In response to this unexpected turn of events, Steve hesitated to leave the Jeep, saying in the most sober manner he could muster, "I beg your pardon?" The MP's polite-demeanor abruptly changed. "Sir, this is a stolen vehicle, and all of you are under arrest."

Now, the problem for the MP was one of adhering to proper procedure. Bill was behind the wheel and Gene was in the back seat. The MP ordered the passenger, Steve, to get out of the Jeep and when Steve hesitated and questioned the order, the MP announced that they were all under arrest without first having assured that flight was impossible. Could the MP have imagined what was about to happen?

Steve was stunned with what he heard as he relented and began to slowly climb out. Bill, as if he was just coming awake, reached out with his right hand, grabbed Steve's shoulder and pulled him back into the Jeep while simultaneously flooring the accelerator. The Jeep lurched forward in the morning mist, tires spinning and mud flying all over the guard post and any MPs who happened to be standing behind it as it careened onto Highway 1, lights out, heading north towards Hue.

Pandemonium ensued and curses rang out. Three drunken Marine officers had just escaped by running through the Army's sentries in a general's stolen Jeep, ignoring orders to halt after they were placed under arrest.

The three had heard the distinctive bark of an M16 and lowered themselves below the seat backs, but no bullet holes were found in the Jeep. Maybe the guards had fired high in hopes they would stop, but they didn't! Bill was essentially driving blind. He and Gene were laughing their asses off, but what of Steve? Well, he was holding on for dear life.

Steve shouted, not knowing how the Jeep had been acquisitioned, "What the hell is going on?" even though his senses were telling him exactly what was happening. Having been almost

304 | HAROLD G. WALKER

killed in a crash, left for dead by the NVA and barely escaping death from close air support, he was now being fired upon by Army MPs because of a prank similar to West Point Cadets stealing the Navy's mascot goat before the big game. Whew! His tour to this point had been anything but a cakewalk, and his innocent involvement in this current situation was indicative of his luck so far—all of which was bad!

The three desperadoes lumbered north toward Phuong, a small village immediately north of Phu Bai along Highway 1, known to us as a Chieu Hoi[124] village where many pardoned NVA and VC, now supposedly loyal to the south were settled. During the evening hours, it was not uncommon to receive small arms fire from this area while in the landing pattern of Phu Bai. The three desperadoes got their heads together and hatched a plan.

There were no apparent chase vehicles from the Army, although the event was sure to have alerted all MPs, both Marine and Army, in the area. The plan was to abandon the Jeep, split up, and get back to Phu Bai, but how? Recall that the preceding night two sappers from this area had tried to enter Phu Bai while tied to water buffalo. This was a dangerous area.

It was decided that the Jeep should be hidden from view alongside Highway 1. They ran it into the roadside ditch as planned, but the Jeep was still readily visible from the highway— not planned. It was early in the morning, but too late to fix this problem. They couldn't pull the Jeep out of the ditch and start over. The plan now was just to split up and get out of the area, back south down Highway 1 to Phu Bai—back to the safety of the Marine base.

With no weapons and, in a unsecure area where only armored vehicles would normally dare to tread, they began their walk. Steve separated from Bill and Gene, walking down Highway 1. His decision was to be direct; just walk back to the base,

---

[124] Chieu Hoi is Vietnamese for "open arms" a program whereby enemy soldiers could surrender without penalty.

identify himself and hopefully enter the base without difficulty. He didn't see Bill and Gene until much later.

Steve covered the distance from Phuong to the Marine gate with no difficulty. As he approached the main gate, he again steeled himself and resolved to come clean, come what may. He was feeling the adverse effects of being hung over, exhausted, and covered in mud. The hour was approaching 0200, Sunday, 21 December 1969.

Upon approaching the gate, he was halted by Marine guards and directed to identify himself. He handed over his military identification card, which was logged in by the guards. He thought to himself that it wouldn't take a brain surgeon to figure out he might have had something to do with the incident, having come into the base, on foot, in his condition. Yet the original concern was with three Marine officers in a stolen Army Jeep last seen heading north on Highway 1, not one lone officer on foot. Regardless of the situation, Steve made it in.

Steve's most personal thoughts, he said, were of his family. Had he been killed by the MPs or the VC/NVA, or worse, captured, how would the telegram read? "Dear Mr. and Mrs. Bravard, We are sorry to inform you that your son was shot by Army sentries while attempting to evade authorities in a stolen Jeep." What could possibly have been worse?

When it was learned that Steve had shown up, everyone was relieved; everyone could now turn in, without worry. There was still time for a few hours of sleep before launch time. But when we learned that Steve didn't know the whereabouts of Bill and Gene, the anxiety returned to us all.

At approximately 0300 both Bill and Gene walked into our hooch, muddy, tired, hung over, and delighted at their narrow escape. Their arrival was applauded. We all were elated that they were back. The feeling upon their arrival was incredible relief that the night had come to an end without anyone dead, captured, or in jail.

Bill and Gene had decided it would be unwise to follow Steve through the gate. One disheveled Marine officer might be okay, but three would raise too much suspicion and risk to them all. They decided they had no choice but to sneak through the security by crawling through the wire! Yes, they crawled through the wire! Like an NVA/VC sapper! It was difficult to believe, but there was no record of them having come through the gate and both were covered from head to toe in mud. They had pulled it off. They had come through the wire, through the Army's security posts undetected...or so it seemed. So, my thought was that we weren't that well protected!

All three then went together to report the situation to LtCol Bancroft. However, Col. Bancroft was still suffering the effects of the Change of Command. Major Sellers, the new XO, met with them. The first words to Maj. Sellers from Steve were, "Sir, we're in deep shit."

"Well, let's hear it," was Major Sellers' response. After hearing what had happened and what they had done, Maj Sellers responded, "Yes, you are in deep shit."

Seller's ordered the three immediately to their quarters for thirty days, and there could be no booze in their quarters. They could fly scheduled missions and attend church services only. What a beginning it was—the Black Sheep Squadron, all over again.

The night passed with the usual random booming of H&I fire. I slept for a couple of minutes, showered in what felt like ice water as the community showers' water heater was broke again[125] and flew a six-and-a-half-hour resupply with the mountain man,

[125] It sounds implausible, but, the community showers in that tropical land had only two temperatures, cold and super cold. There was a hot water heater of sorts, but it hardly ever worked. Lieutenant Art Gillidette was the only person in the officer's area that knew how to maintain the hot water heater and how to fix it. His flight schedule literally affected the showering habits of some pilots. There were occasions when, walking by the showers, you'd hear someone yell out "Whoa, shit! Where in the hell is Art?"followed by a line of unprintable curses. I never said anything about this to any Grunts, us complaining about the cold water, when those poor bastards would have given anything to have had any kind of a shower. I knew I was damn lucky to be in the Wing.

Jeffryes, all the while wondering what was happening back at Phu Bai.

The Army, it seems, was seriously upset and humiliated that their general's Jeep had been stolen/taken/used by Marines, not to mention they had been unable to catch the culprits who were in their grasp and who escaped under their noses. The Army's Criminal Investigative Division (CID) knew the rank of the officers and had sentries who spoke to the culprits before their harrowing escape. The melee at the Steam and Massage also pointed directly at the Marines, specifically helicopter pilots as we had made no attempt to conceal our identity. The pool of suspects quickly centered on 262.

37: The Aftermath

On the morning of 21 December, LtCol Bancroft woke to two headaches, a hangover and a briefing by Maj. Sellers of the goings on with the Army. Although Lieutenants Steve Bravard, Bill Davis and Gene Mitchell were restricted to quarters, Steve was called to the CO's office. It was there, that LtCol Bancroft made clear the full impact of what could happen.

Steve, during the writing of this book, recalled the following conversation:

"Do you realize what can happen as a result of your behavior?" asked Bancroft with the seriousness the moment deserved. "C.I.D.[126] wants to charge those responsible for the theft of the general's Jeep with grand larceny. All of you can be held in-country on legal hold as long as necessary to investigate and conduct a general court martial. And, if found guilty, the consequences could mean doing time in Leavenworth. Is that clear?"

The situation could have been as hard hitting to Bancroft's career as it could have been to Steve, Bill, and Gene's. To give up the identity of the 3 Marines to the Army would have been a crap shoot for Bancroft. If he went along with the general's wishes it had the potential to put Bancroft at odds with the pilots and cause the squadron, 98% of which were first lieutenants, to implode.

At that point in time, Redeployment and Vietnamization was in full stride, with many midcareer Marines (majors and lieutenant colonels), who wanted to have red ink (combat time) in their log books and maybe a DFC or Silver Star, were ready and willing to jump into any available billet that might get them there. Bancroft could be replaced at any moment with the stroke of a pen for not going along with the general. The tension in the squadron was palpable.

---

[126] CID is the U.S. Army's Criminal Investigative Division responsible for investigating felony crimes and serious violations of military law.

Bancroft confirmed Maj. Seller's decision to keep the 3 in hack,[127] allowing them to fly scheduled missions under the terms dictated by Maj. Sellers in the early morning hours of 21 December.

Later that week, in response to a U.S. Army Criminal Investigative Division (CID) request,

LtCol. Bancroft permitted a lineup of available pilots before flight operations were to begin. The young MP who had attempted to place the 3 lieutenants under arrest before they burst through the gate like Bonnie and Clyde onto highway 1, was brought to the squadron ready room by an Army CID Major. A primitive lineup of available pilots, like nothing that had ever occurred except in shaded recollections of Pappy Boyington's famed WWII Black Sheep Squadron, was staged in the ready room. In that lineup of available Marine pilots, was Grottoite Don McGlothlin.

Years later, Donnie recalled the following:

"The lineup was, by all accounts, a carefully planned and choreographed event. Maj. Sellers was present, as was LtCol. Bancroft. Sellers selected Marines, all of whom were chosen for their similar height and weight and were dressed in jungle utes, no flight suits. Donnie said that those chosen had no mustaches and all had the traditional high and tight haircuts, an oddity in the squadron. It appeared to be a lineup of clones. The MP who walked down the line of lieutenants carefully looked at each man, finally turned to the Army CID major and said, "Sir, I can't tell them apart ... I just can't recognize the person I saw." PERFECT!

The Army major was livid. He yelled out, "I can't believe this shit!"

He complained to Bancroft, Sellers and anyone within shouting range that the lineup was a setup, an obvious attempt by the

---

[127] In hack: is unofficial punishment, when an officer is confined to his stateroom, hooch, etc.

Marines to protect those responsible for the theft of the general's Jeep. This drew a sharp rebuke from the bull himself, Col. Bancroft, who took the comment as it was intended—disrespectful.. Bancroft reminded the Army major that it was he, the major, who had asked for the lineup and that he, LtCol. Bancroft, had complied with his wishes. If the major was not satisfied with this arrangement, then he should address his concerns through proper channels, because, 'we (the Marines) have a war to fight.' That was the end of the lineups. Everyone had now met LtCol Bancroft, the bull of the woods, and any further disruptions due to the event had come to an end. The lineup became the joke of jokes on the Army. Maj. Sellers was the main operative, making sure the lineup revealed nothing and placing marine look-alikes within the staged lineup.

A few days later, following the lineup, Lt. Bravard was once again alone with Col. Bancroft in his office when Bancroft was on the phone with who Steve believed was MajGen. Thrash, Commanding General, 1st MAW at Da Nang. It was apparent to Steve that the Army Major had done what Bancroft told him to do, address his concerns through the proper channels. Steve recalled portions of Bancroft's side of the conversation.

Bancroft, Steve advised, vehemently denied to the person on the other end of the phone that he was hindering military justice by not turning over the three Marines to the Army. Furthermore, he responded that he was not hindering justice, but that he might 'possibly be guilty of slowing it down a little.'

Bancroft, according to Steve, was apparently being ordered to give up the three Marines to the Army. Steve overheard Bancroft clearly state, "Sir, I cannot turn my Marines over to the Army," and that was that. The general apparently didn't insist any further that the Marines be turned over to the Army following Bancroft's firmly stated position.

Bancroft and Sellers had, with this decision, solidified their positions as standing up for the Marines, and our squadron. The fact that Col. Bancroft was a former A-4 pilot was forgotten ... almost. He had proven his mettle to the squadron. The rumor of his decision made its way through the squadron, giving everyone a feeling of relief and pride in having Col. Bancroft as our commanding officer. Needless to say, the night of 20-21 December 1969 was the last time I visited the Army side of the base.

When Steve Bravard departed Vietnam in April 1970, the following citation was read during a spoof award ceremony:

Marine Corps/Army Public Relations Medal with Oak Leaf Cluster to 1stLt Steven Douglas Bravard, United States Marine Corps Reserve, for service as set forth in the following citation:

For heroic achievement in an inebriated condition while serving as Marine Corps Army liaison with Marine Rotary Wing Tactical Pursuit Squadron 262, Marine Aircraft Group 16, First Marine Aircraft Wing in connection with combat operations against the United States Army in the Republic of Vietnam on the evening of December 20, 1969. First Lt. Bravard was the team leader for the traumatic three, a highly trained group of reformed hubcap thieves assigned a top secret mission which would avenge the outrageous affront by the staff of the 85th Evacuation Officers Club for having, a week earlier, thrown LtCol "Blades" Bancroft out of the club just prior to his becoming the commanding officer of 262.

Lt. Bravard's two junior officers (Bill Davis and Gene Mitchell) had returned from a harassment and interdiction patrol in treacherous 24th Corps area where they had seized an enemy general's personal vehicle. Lt. Bravard's ingenious military mind immediately recognized the possibilities of using the vehicle to reconnoiter the enemy's area of operations undetected. Disregarding all personal safety, Lt. Bravard led his team back across the enemy's heavily guarded line after collecting a great deal of information. Lt. Bravard instructed his driver to exit at the nearest gate. The guard had been briefed on the stolen vehicle, however; he immediately accosted Lt. Bravard, requesting to see his credentials. Realizing the fact that his guise had been detected, Lt Bravard cleverly replied, 'ABA ... ABA ... ABA' which the driver correctly construed to mean, "Let's get the f**k out of Dodge."

As the vehicle came under intense enemy fire from its six o'clock position, Lt. Bravard wisely assumed the prone position on the vehicle's deck as he directed the driver in his evasive maneuvers. Once out of range of enemy ordnance, Lt. Bravard directed his team members to abandon the vehicle along the side of the road as it could be of no further tactical use. He then instructed his men to split up and inspect the perimeter as he walked in the main gate. Realizing that the guard would not be aware of the authorization of his top secret patrol, Lt. Bravard cleverly gave them his correct name, thinking that nobody would believe he would be stupid enough to tell the truth. Lt. Bravard's bravery in the face of imminent danger, and his ability to think clearly in the most difficult situations, are in keeping with the highest traditions of the Marine Corps and the United States Naval Service.

For the President,

I. M. Trashed [a play on the name of General Thrash, CG, First Marine Air Wing]

All in all, the HMM-262 change of command in Phu Bai on that December day in 1969 was quite a party, never yet duplicated, until documented.

38: El Mossy Grotto

Nearing mid-December, a total of 21 new pilots, all of whom had gone through the training command together, had arrived in 262. The old leadership was gone and the new leadership gave the squadron the sense that a new era had arrived. The old guys were rapidly approaching the end of their year of service. Many had already left country and we new guys were becoming more and more comfortable in our surroundings. It was during this period of time that the eight personalities making up our FNG hooch began to reveal themselves.

The hooch was becoming the unofficial gathering spot for the new guys. There was most always a cold beer, a game of Acey Ducey, cards, or just plain camaraderie available at any hour of the day or night. Therefore, we decided to discard the FNG identifying letters that had been anonymously written on our hooch door upon our arrival. It was time for a new beginning.

The idea was to come up with a new image. The renaming of our hooch would be the manifestation of that idea. The name had to reflect the character of the abode: humidity, mold, age and attitude. Writings on the walls from previous Marine occupants might have been seen in caves where ancient civilizations mocked their own mortality. "Lose not thy turns lest the earth rise up and smite thee." "All that I feel when I kill is recoil." "The difference between the Boy Scouts and the Marine Corps? The Boy Scouts have adult leadership." and, "This is a holy war, God hates the gooks too."

The debate dragged on. What to call our hooch? Finally, someone came up with The Cave, which had some appeal. However, it wasn't a cave. But, maybe something like a cave, a GROTTO. Okay, but what about some character....add some adjectives...humidity and mold, maybe MOSSY... Mossy Grotto? It was missing a touch of flair and needed some refinement. Okay. Let's go with an EL...El Mossy Grotto. Yeah, that gives it some class...Spanish flair, like El Matador. The unanimous decision became, "The El Mossy Grotto." There were drinks all around and a ceremonial erasing of the FNG initials with back and forth swipes from a black paint spray can and a rendering of the new name, like the christening of a battle ship. However, in short order, it became just "The Grotto."

Figure 67 The author in front of the newly named El Mossy Grotto, visible on door.

During this period, another Phu Bai tradition was being passed along to us—a beer-drinking ballad: a traditional depiction by song of thinly veiled contempt directed toward the leadership of past squadrons. Here it is:

The Phu Bai Song

> Phu Bai, ol' Phu Bai's one hell of a place.
> The organization's a f**king disgrace.
> With captains and majors, and light colonels, too,
> Their thumbs up their a***holes with nothing to do,
> They stand by the runway, they scream and they shout,
> About many things they know nothing about.
> For all of their value, they may as well be

Shoveling shit in the South China Sea.
Ring a ding a ding ding, blow it out you're a**.
Better days are coming bye and bye... Bullshit!"
You'll wonder where the yellow went
When the H-bomb hits the Orient.
Nuke 'em, Nuke 'em, Nuke 'em!
Ho Chi Minh's dead!

The inaugural ceremony of El Mossy Grotto demanded an alphabetical listing of the eight original plank-holders.

Figure 68 First Lieutenant A.C. Allen

Allen, A.C.:Say it in either direction and it's always the same, Allen C. Allen. A native of Henderson, Kentucky, and a product of the same 48th OCS class from which Eric, Roy and I had come, with one large difference. A.C. was the B Company honor man, an impressive achievement given the high quality of candidates in that superb group of men I am honored to have known. Married to Terri, also of Henderson, Kentucky, they had no children.

A.C. as he was known by all was easily the most complex of all the Grottoites, a natural leader whose left hook was as quick and as dangerous as his wit. He was a for real son-of-a-preacher-man. A.C.'s appearance was remarkably reminiscent of Paul Newman. His character was captured by a combination of Newman's HUD, and Burt Lancaster's mythical Elmer Gantry. I could easily visualize A.C. pastoring the largest Baptist church in Tennessee, or running the most successful nightclub, or more likely, doing both simultaneously.

Figure 69 First Lieutenant N.F. "Pete" Hanner

Hanner, N. F. "Pete": Pete, from Eureka, Illinois, had completed a four-year tour of duty in the Navy, then completed a four-year B.S. degree at Illinois State University, Bloomington, Illinois, while simultaneously participating in the Corps' summer platoon leadership class (PLC) program. He received his commission as a second lieutenant upon receipt of his baccalaureate degree from Illinois State, and went directly to Pensacola for flight training. At 28 years old, he was the oldest and most mature of the group.

He was married to Sharon, whose picture was placed in a prominent location on his shelf. He was a no-nonsense fellow with a clear understanding of the dynamics of a military unit which few of us understood. He was affable and a military man through and through; occasionally he served as an interpreter for me regarding Marine Corps tradition and policy. It was clear to me that he tolerated us and was not entirely comfortable in The Grotto. His eye was on a long career in the Corps. My eye was on getting home. I expected Pete would become a general officer in the Corps.

Figure 70 First Lieutenant Ron McAmis

McAmis, Ron: He was a Kansan—Liberal Kansas—right off the prairie, Dust Bowl country, known for its pancake races in conjunction with its sister city in England. He also joined the Platoon Leadership Course (PLC) program in 1965, like Pete Hanner did. He did two summers in Quantico, graduated from college in 1968 and went straight to Pensacola for flight school. He was a bright cheery fellow who was happy to be in Phu Bai and had been a Golden Gloves boxer. He made friends quickly and soon became one of the favorites in the squadron. He was engaged to Jennifer, a Pensacola, FL. girl whom he met while in flight school. He was in the S-1 shop (Admin) and frequently stood the post of Operations Duty Officer (ODO). He was fun to be around and had strong piloting skills. His conversation was intelligent and brisk as his wide grin. I expected big things from him in his not-yet-chosen career field.

Figure 71 First Lieutenant Don McGlothlin

McGlothlin, Don: Donnie was a family man, he was married to his college sweetheart, Jan Whitney and had two boys, Pete and Doug, upon whom he doted, often speaking of them in glowing terms. He was, by his own definition, a Marine brat, a legacy, whose father, Pete McGlothlin, was a renowned Marine Colonel who piloted the Corsair in both WW-II and Korea and flew with legendary Marine Aviator, Joe Foss, a Medal of Honor recipient at

Guadalcanal. He had two brothers; one, his twin brother, had enlisted in the Air Force, and his younger brother was a future Marine officer. Like all children who grew up in the Marine Corps, they lived all over the place.

Donnie was gregarious and fun to be around. He was tough, full of life, and a close friend of AC Allen's. He had a quick wit that could cut like a knife and was known to enjoy a cold beer, a round of fisticuffs, or even better, both. In my opinion, Donnie would have made a great general. His nickname, Mini-General, solidly captured his military bearing and straightforward character. I always knew that Donnie's life would lead him away from the Corps. In quieter moments of reflection he had said he wasn't going to be a lifer, because, he had "already done that."

Figure 72 First Lieutenant Eric C. McGrew

McGrew, Eric Corsair: A Louisiana man who was married to his college sweetheart, Willy vanLuipen from the Netherlands. They had a year old daughter, Audrey. Eric escorted his wife and child back to the Netherlands to remain there with her family until he returned from Vietnam. He was a Marine legacy, whose middle name was a tribute to the F4U-4 Corsair aircraft his father Marine Capt. Henry McGrew, flew. Based upon Capt. McGrew's personal experience while in a power dive from an altitude of 50,000 feet that ripped both wings of his Corsair, it is believed that he most probably was the first man on the planet to have experienced breaking the sound barrier and lived, prior to Chuck Yeager's record-setting flight. "Calm and focused throughout the catastrophic event," he had survived by parachuting out of the aircraft under the most extreme circumstances and lived to fly again, receiving the Distinguished Flying Cross for his exploits.

Eric, his son, "Didn't fall far from the tree." Eric was also a product of the 48th OCS. He was also a no-nonsense practical fellow who was a world class storyteller, a journeyman carpenter, builder of sandbag bunkers, and digger of foxholes. Upon arriving in the Grotto, Eric set to work improving the old sandbag bunker next to it and making routine repairs to the place. On one occasion he had cut about a half-inch off the old battered outside door of the Grotto, allowing the door to close easier. Trouble was, according to Donnie McGlothlin, after the repair was completed by Eric, "the rats could walk in under the door standing on their hind legs." Maybe a little exaggeration.

Eric had the lean look and chiseled features of a bare-knuckled prize fighter from the 1800s, and had boxed as an amateur in both high school and college. His character and professionalism were as solid as any who wore the uniform. He became known to the Grottoites as "Bones" due to his chiseled features. I would characterize Eric as possessing the unique traits of those pioneers who tamed the old west. And, like all the Grottoites, I believed he was destined for good things.

Figure 73 First Lieutenant Roy Prigge

Prigge, Roy: A devout Lutheran from Minnesota, married to Faith, with no children. He was also a graduate of the 48th OCS and a very likable fellow, but not totally comfortable in the Grotto. He, like Pete, tolerated us, taking part in the fun but not to excess, which was what we did best in the Grotto. I expected Roy to return home to Minnesota, where he and Faith would have a large family. I could clearly see Roy sitting on his porch, smoking his pipe (an oddity in the Marine Corps) and overseeing the farm with his wife cooking up a feast. Roy's faith was apparent in his tranquil manner through his daily life. His given Grotto nickname, "Ton-of-Fun," was not what he was. He was a rock solid Marine, a great pilot, and someone you could trust and count on.

Rainey, Gary: He was a Wyoming cowboy, by way of Lake Charles, Louisiana. Like Pete, Gary was also a product of the Platoon Leadership Class (PLC) and was commissioned a second lieutenant upon graduation from college. Gary was a lifer; unmarried and a near-confirmed bachelor we weathered the same flight program, moving from one syllabus to another in the same flights. My wife Kathy and I were close friends with Gary. He watched with Kathy and me as Neil Armstrong made his "one small step for man" and accompanied us in a two-car caravan as we returned from California to our respective homes to prepare to leave for Vietnam.

Figure 74 First Lieutenant Gary Rainey

Gary's brother served in the Corps in Vietnam at the same time Gary was there. Gary very much reminded me of Jack Webb's character in the classic Marine Corps drill instructor film, *DI*. Gary also had my vote to become a high-ranking Marine officer. A.C. Allen bestowed upon Gary the nickname "Rain Tree," with no good reason other than it somewhat rhymed with Rainey. Gary worked in the squadron's S-3 department, Operations, and he was like a brother to me. His devotion to the Marine Corps was clear and unambiguous.

Figure 75 First Lieutenant Harold G. Walker

Walker, Harold G.: I entered into the 48th Marine Officer Candidate School as an Aviation Officer Candidate in November 1967 along with A.C., Eric and Roy following a couple of draft notices, the last of which I could not avoid.

The deal with Capt. Larry Ogle and the Corps was: pass the written tests, pass the flight physical, graduate from SEMO State College, attend officer's candidate school, receive a commission as a second lieutenant, enter flight school (marry Kathleen on 29 June, 1968, fresh out of college with a B.S. Degree in Elementary Education), complete flight school. Then, do a tour of 12-13 months in Vietnam. If everything went according to plan, and I was still alive, I'd be getting off active duty in December, 1972, or thereabouts. Now, however, I was in Vietnam.

I was happy to be in HMM-262, in Phu Bai, with a group of men any one of whom I would have and did entrust my life. My goal in life at that time was simple, live through Vietnam and get back to Kathy. Had I not been drafted, I'd probably have been teaching a biology class in a local high school in the Missouri Bootheel. Instead, I had become a Marine officer and squadron helicopter pilot in Vietnam, not a bad trade.

I was along for the ride and the thrill of it all. Looking back, I realize I was in the company of heroes, living a fantasy with a front row seat to the first and probably last great helicopter war. I vowed never to forget a moment of it, both the laughter and the horror.

* * *

There was some movement of pilots in and out of The Grotto, including one person who moved in unannounced. The hooch

322 | HAROLD G. WALKER

was at maximum capacity with eight pilots; A.C. Allen, Pete Hanner, Ron McAmis, Donnie McGlothlin, Eric McGrew, Gary Rainey, Roy Prigge, and me. Yet, another pilot checked into the squadron and without speaking to us, pushed aside the existing racks, displaced personnel gear and scrunched us up to the extent we could hardly move between bunks. Upon our return to the Grotto that evening, as everyone in the hooch was flying on that particular day, we found the mess that was made. We took the intruders gear and sat it all outside, removing him from The Grotto. Upon his return he angrily informed us that he was a senior first lieutenant, and that we had no choice other than to defer to him. He never returned and may have requested a change of squadrons. In time, with the big move to Marble Mountain coming up, there would be more changes bringing new Grottoites into the fold as some left the friendly confines just when it was becoming more interesting.

39: Dreaming of a White Christmas

Only four days till Santa was scheduled to arrive. The monsoons were still with us twenty-four inches in twenty four hours, some kind of record, somewhere, but not in Vietnam and the schedule never slowed, but the flying surely did. The low ceilings, fog, and rain kept us out of the air and the Grunts in the paddies wet and sick. My penalty flight with Meskan being over, I felt much lighter. I survived. Yet, the rumors of when we were leaving never stilled, the latest rumor being a repeat of a much earlier rumor. We were soon leaving Phu Bai, but not for Marble Mountain Air facility; we were going to Hawaii, the ancestral home of 262...yes...no...maybe?

Kathy and the other married Grotto guys' wives sent Christmas packages with all kinds of goodies. I received a Ouija board I had requested in order to see our future, along with cookies, and a package of Tootsie Roll Pops for Gary. Kathy never failed to provide Gary with Tootsie Roll Pops. Also enclosed were cassette tapes; one of the Mommas and Poppas album, *If You Can Believe,* in which their block buster song "Monday, Monday" was first introduced, and another cassette of the Beatles, "Hey Jude,' along with a family tape of everyone yelling Merry Christmas. Unfortunately, I had no opportunity to deal with gift giving and responded to the goodies by letters home with the promise that I'd have to make up for Christmas '69, come 1970.

Makeshift Christmas trees began springing up in the hooches, some no more than limp twigs from some bushes on base with those stringy aluminum icicles and empty c-ration cans hanging on them. First Lt. Ed Mowry[128], one of the old guys by our standard, a PMAG-39 combat vet who arrived in Vietnam in July of '69, received a small aluminum Xmas Tree with some real ornaments from his mother. A beautiful tree.

---

[128] Author of "So Close to Dying," a memoir of his journey of remembrance from childhood to Vietnam, when it was in full swing. Registered Copyright2013 by Edward F. Mowry. One of the good guys from Provisional MAG-39.

Lieutenants Mowry, John Parnham, and John Whitworth teamed up to organize a 262 Christmas celebration, pooling their memories to come up with lyrics to "Hark the Herald Angels Sing," "Silent Night," and other standards for some Christmas choral activity. The party was to be held in one of the many vacant Quonset huts rather than in the O'Club so the party would be exclusively made up of 262 folks. Everyone was supposed to dress in civilian attire, wear dress slacks, white shirts with a button down collar and tie, etc.

I briefly stopped by the party, wearing my flight suit and snapped a picture of the gathering. I however simply didn't want to get into civilian attire. I really didn't want to be reminded of past Christmases.

Figure 76 Christmas Party" Far left is Fred McCorkle. Far right is Pete Hanner.

I wanted to celebrate Christmas Eve in my own way, in a flight suit, in Phu Bai, in Vietnam. So, me and some of my other nonconformist friends that included John Kosinski, did Christmas Eve at the O'club where John Arnold and Lowell "Ollie" Olson (Civilian Affairs Officer) were busy running the bar and Joe Smith, our friend from HMM-161, passed around rumors about when 161 was leaving Phu Bai. Soon he said, sometime in early January.

Meanwhile, our three heroes, Steve, Bill and Gene, were still in hack. However, they had a visitor. Major Sellers stopped in early in the evening to see how the three were behaving and proceeded to see that they were abiding by the restriction policy. However, being that it was Christmas Eve, he off-handedly asked them, "Why aren't you Marines at the party?"

Their response was, "Why, Sir, we're still in hack."

"No, you're not. You've done your time. Hell boys, it's Christmas."

With that proclamation, Maj. Sellers, our new pipe smoking XO, a former jet jock and second tour 46 driver set everything right. "Merry Christmas!" he said, just like Santa Claus.

A group of our 262 crew chiefs, gunners, and mechanics surprised everyone with Christmas songs. They were Christmas caroling. There in Phu Bai, it was really strange, seeing those men who flew into and out of hell every day, looking like they were at a church picnic. It looked like one of those junior high school parties where everyone just stood around, but hard cider was the fare. But, the boys were out of hack and that was a good thing.

Meanwhile, in our world, the U.S. Army was still smarting from the great raid and their inability to identify the three mysterious lieutenants who breached their security and embarrassed their general. LtCol Bancroft had grown taller in stature due to his support of the three raiders and his willingness to accept the fact that he needed more stick time[129] in the 46.

---

[129] "Stick time" meant the time a person was actually flying the craft, the stick being the cyclic and collective. More stick time meant more experience in the 46. A tendency inherent in the piloting world was "transference," the belief that a pilot of the same or greater rank had similar piloting experience in a particular model of aircraft. Many majors and colonels who were flying helicopters may have had less time in a particular model of aircraft than a person of lesser rank, i.e. first lieutenants. This was a common phenomenon in Vietnam at the time of my tour, when we were on our way out of Vietnam. The tendency was for mid-level career pilots, majors and lieutenant colonels to rush in to Vietnam to get as much combat time as possible and any kind of medal that might come with it. The Air medal upwards through the Navy Cross in their record books could boost their career opportunities in what was an incredibly competitive environment. There wasn't much time remaining for Marines in Vietnam.

The flow of FNGs was still coming as the old guys continued to go home. The NVA/VC were still causing trouble but nothing like previous Christmas holidays in Vietnam. They too were hunkering down into whatever cave or trench they were living in while getting blasted to hell on the Ho Chi Minh trail.

Back in the States, the first drawing of the draft lottery took place that month; those 19-year-olds whose birthdays were September 14, and whose last names began with "J" would be the first called. In later life, those whose number placed them out of harm's way crowed about their achievement and were saluted for not going or fleeing to Canada—whilst I bit my lip.

The Christmas meal plan was posted in the club with a Christmas prayer by James A. Skelton, the staff Chaplain for Phu Bai. The prayer contained the following prayerful request: "May the Star of Bethlehem which guided the Wise Men from the East also guide each of us safely home from Vietnam, through the remaining days of life to our eternal home in heaven. Amen."

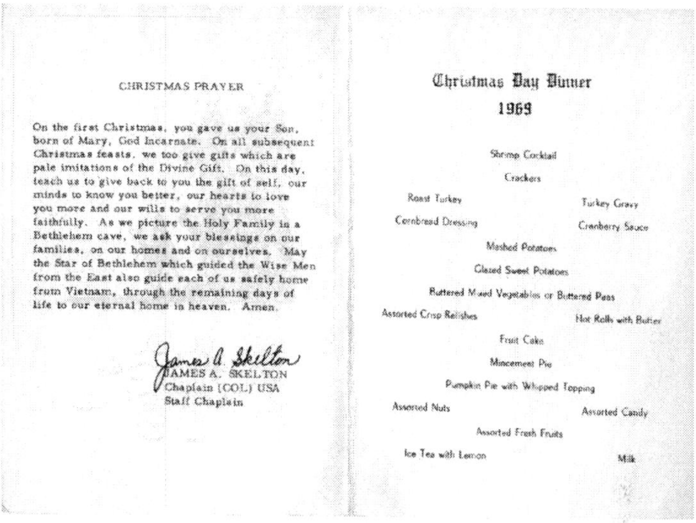

CHRISTMAS PRAYER

On the first Christmas, you gave us your Son, born of Mary, God Incarnate. On all subsequent Christmas feasts, we too give gifts which are pale imitations of the Divine Gift. On this day, teach us to give back to you the gift of self, our minds to know you better, our hearts to love you more and our wills to serve you more faithfully. As we picture the Holy Family in a Bethlehem cave, we ask your blessings on our families, on our homes and on ourselves. May the Star of Bethlehem which guided the Wise Men from the East also guide each of us safely home from Vietnam, through the remaining days of life to our eternal home in heaven. Amen.

James A. Skelton
JAMES A. SKELTON
Chaplain (COL) USA
Staff Chaplain

Christmas Day Dinner
1969

Shrimp Cocktail
Crackers
Roast Turkey
Turkey Gravy
Cornbread Dressing
Cranberry Sauce
Mashed Potatoes
Glazed Sweet Potatoes
Buttered Mixed Vegetables or Buttered Peas
Assorted Crisp Relishes
Hot Rolls with Butter
Fruit Cake
Mincemeat Pie
Pumpkin Pie with Whipped Topping
Assorted Nuts
Assorted Candy
Assorted Fresh Fruits
Ice Tea with Lemon
Milk

Figure 77 1969 Phu Bai Christmas dinner menu

As the squadron party died down, they all wandered over to the club. It was a good time. We toasted our friends who were no longer with us, sang the Phu Bai song, and wondered quietly to ourselves what the next day might bring, and if we'd ever see another Christmas Eve. A classic Christmas movie, *Rio Bravo*, starring John Wayne and Dean Martin, along with cold Black Label Milwaukee beer and those odd looking bottles of Mateuse, carried us through Christmas Eve of '69.

BOB HOPE AT CAMP EAGLE—CHRISTMAS DAY 1969

Wags made me aware of a truck leaving Phu Bai at 0900 the following morning on Christmas Day headed for Camp Eagle to see Bob Hope. The next morning, the six-by filled up with

Marines from 161 and 262. Wags, A. C. Allen, John Arnold, John Kosinski, Lowell Olsen, me and many others piled into a six-by.

Figure 78 Lowell "Ollie" Olsen on the way to see Bob Hope at Camp Eagle

Figure 79 John "Wags" Wagner clowning around with M16 on the way to Camp Eagle

I was lucky not to be on the flight schedule. The missions assigned to the squadron never let up and now there were always new guys who needed familiarization flights. This gave me an opportunity to take advantage of that trip to Camp Eagle, headquarters of the 101st Airborne Division, located west of Hue and Highway 1, where Bob Hope was scheduled to appear on Christmas Day with Miss America and a troop of dancers. We boarded the six-by military truck at 0500 and began our journey to "spend the day with Bob."

The ride to Camp Eagle was exciting as I had seen very little of the countryside from anything other than a helicopter. The going was bumpy as we drove north along Highway 1 and veered west toward Camp Eagle. The red clay was striking. Maybe Christmas brought out the red color more than usual as a salute to Santa. It was also on this trip that I saw the picturesque scene of a small boy riding on a huge water buffalo.

Figure 80 Small boy on the back of a water buffalo – LZ 401

The beast had no halter or any type of harness or controlling apparatus. The boy, so comfortable on the back of the beast in close proximity to the heavy military traffic was disconcerting. I didn't realize water buffalo were so domesticated. I thought water buffalos were like mules that were used on our farm when I was a child, mules whose names I still recall, Tom and Jerry, like the old cartoons seen at the Saturday matinees all over the United States. I know that if our Tom and Jerry had been faced with the kind of traffic I saw on Highway 1, and they weren't harnessed, they'd have run like hell, and no father would have allowed his child to ride on the back of the farm mules. But this was Vietnam, not the Bootheel of Missouri. I learned that the Water Buffalo was highly domesticated and as much a pet and family member as anyone else in the Vietnamese family unit. I began to have an admiration for those Vietnamese farm folks, just trying to get to his farm around all of those big tanks and APCs and us. What a sight it was.

Furthermore, small displays alongside the road of sodas: coca cola, orange and lemon drinks and candy bars were endless. How they got those drinks and candy bars I had no idea, but there were Army GIs buying drinks and dipping cups into a box of ice. That ice was always suspect to me, and as I earlier stated, I stayed away from ice that wasn't from the O'Club.

As we approached Camp Eagle, there was a loud explosion off to the southwest from us. A big white cloud blossomed into the skyline. Thinking the worst, we did as usual, nothing. Wags raised his M-16 in jest, and I took his picture. I mentioned that we were ready to defend ourselves, right after the Bob Hope show. That drew a laugh. But apparently the blast was a controlled explosion at an Army ammo dump, or, it was Mr. Charles wanting to disrupt our day. Either way, not much happened.

A little further on, we were stopped in a line of trucks and Jeeps making their way through the Army's main gate. A long line of military policemen was conducting cursive inspections and gave our truck a longer look than non-Marine vehicles, a mutual courtesy since the raid on XXIV Corps a few days earlier. Eventually, we were waved through, taking our place in a long procession of vehicles to a crude amphitheater set into the side of a hill they called the Eagle Entertainment Bowl named for the 101st Airborne Screaming Eagles. Jumping out of the truck, we looked every bit the tourist, everything from exotic 35mm cameras and long range lenses to small Kodaks hanging from each of us.

Making our way to the makeshift amphitheater near a helicopter landing zone, I was struck by the size of the area. I had never been to an outdoor concert nor much more than a movie theater. This was a big area which that day reportedly held

16,000 plus soldiers and Marines. A large makeshift stage, surrounded by massive amounts of lighting sat on large scaffolds with big mounted cameras directly in front and to the sides at about a 45-degree angle.

Hoping to be seated up front and near the stage, we once again ran into the biggest MPs I ever saw. They were directing everyone to seating behind the scaffolds, leaving the up-front seating vacant. We scrambled to bleachers set up in the very rear of the amphitheater, occupying a viewing area that allowed us to see the center of the stage. The performers would be far away, but the sound equipment was of such size and power that the performance could probably be heard as far away as the DMZ, maybe all the way to Hanoi. I hoped the POWs in the Hanoi Hilton would hear us and know that we'd be coming for them. At least at that time, at that place, I hoped we'd be coming. As the hour of the performance drew near, the excitement increased.

The entertainers accompanying Mr. Hope were: Les Brown and his Band of Renown, Miss World, Eva Rueber-Staier of Austria, Connie Stevens, Suzanne Charny, Laugh-In's Teresa Graves, the Gold Diggers, a dance group seen on the Dean Martin Show, and Neil Armstrong, who only a few months before had walked on the moon. Just before the show began it became apparent who would occupy the choice seats stage center. It was going to be the real combat soldiers, the Grunts! They were ushered in by the MPs, and from their appearance I believe they must have come directly from the bush. Can you imagine, one moment watching Charlie, the next moment watching this star-spangled show. It was surreal but so was this place called Vietnam.

Hope joked about the proximity of the base to North Vietnam, saying that when he put milk on his cereal, the snap, crackle and pops caused everyone to lay prone on the floor. This joke was a common refrain from Hope, adjusted according to the location of the show. His jokes didn't have to be too sophisticated to get a laugh from us. He also solidly validated where we were when he said, 'You guys are certainly the 'tip of the spear.' [130] However, it made me think, was it our spear or theirs? We were occupying and backing down to Da Nang and going home, not going forward. What were we really doing?

Figure 81 The 1969 Bob Hope Christmas show, Camp Eagle, Vietnam from our remote seats.

The show was one-and-a-half hours and over too soon. I was thankful for the time and soon we were back in the six-by, headed to Phu Bai. When first seeing *Apocalypse Now*, the 1979 movie produced and directed by Francis Ford Coppola, I concluded that our celebration was tame when compared to the one depicted in the movie. Yet the shows yet to come at the MMAF O'Club may well have come very close to the movie version.

I had been in-country for 46 days. My experiences thus far were not wild- eyed enemy charges and intense battles, but more learning the dos and don'ts of both squadron politics and combat flight survival (i.e., "Lose not thy turns lest the earth rise up and smite thee," the truest of all epithets) and all the while acutely

---

[130] The "tip of the spear" was the first to go in, the part that starts the process to bring down prey.

aware of the Angel of Death lying in wait, lurking. Yet I was still wide-eyed and thrilled to be where I was. I wanted to get on with the experience. My next step was to accumulate the requisite 500 total flight hours to be eligible for a HAC check ride. I needed 111.6 more hours following my last fight in 1969, a long way to go for that sought-after HAC qualification.

BLOODY INCIDENT IN THE READY ROOM:

First Lieutenant Ron McAmis had his first Squadron Duty Officer (SDO) watch on 26 December. The following account is directly from Ron's recollection with the name of the individual in this incident having been masked:

* * *

On 26 December I was assigned SDO for the first time. When I took the watch at 1600 hrs. SgtMaj. Duke came to the ready room with an enlisted Marine. Duke told me the Marine was to remain in the ready room until the next day when he would be transferred to Marble [Mountain Air Facility] because he had received threats that he was going to be killed. Being a good first lieutenant, I said "Aye, Aye SgtMaj." and carried on.

The Marine was a strange bird, very quiet. He went off in one of the admin spaces by himself. Around 2000 hrs. I was working in the awards office when he came in and asked if he could stay in the same room and accompany me when I checked the aircraft. I of course answered "Affirmative." He then did something peculiar. He sat on the floor in the corner. I tried to carry on a conversation with him but he wouldn't talk. I remember offering him some chewing gum but he declined.

Two enlisted Marines on the duty crew were in the ready room playing ping-pong. At approximately 2230 hrs. the Duty Phone "bat phone" in the ready room rang. I left the awards office to answer it. When I returned a minute or two later I walked to the door (the scene is etched in my mind like a snapshot) he was sitting on a chair with a claw hammer gripped in both hands, and he is swinging it up from the floor impacting the top of his head as hard as he could with the claw end. Thunk!! Thunk!! The sound was like a ripe watermelon being thumped very hard. Chunks of hair and blood were splattering all over the room.

Only a fraction of a second had passed, but it seemed like minutes while I pondered over what action to take. My first thought was to rush over, grab the hammer and stop him! Then, I thought….what if he uses the hammer on me? So I took the only option open. I… very calmly…screamed 'GET A CORPS MAN!!!' The two enlisted men in the next room ran over and one of them seeing the scene, instead of using the phone, dashed out of the building, running to sickbay.

I yelled at the Marine to lay the hammer down. To my surprise, he did so. Then, he stood up. Only after he laid down the hammer did I move from the doorway to where he was standing. He was bleeding like a stuck pig. Facing him I grabbed him by the shoulders. He looked at me and said 'What did you do it to me for?' I thought, oh shit! Nobody else saw this, and he is going to blame me.

"The Marine was literally covered with blood and now, my arms were covered with his blood from my elbows down. I managed to get him out to the ready room, and the other enlisted man and I got him to lie down on the floor. He bled a pool of blood two feet across while he was lying there. When we tried to put a pressure bandage on his wound he got agitated. He got up saying; 'Keep away from me.' He dashed out of the ready room and down to the hanger where the night crew was working. I'm chasing after him with my side arm slapping against my leg.

The Marine ran into the hanger screaming at the top of his lungs 'Help me, help me….They're trying to kill me.' The Marine had the appearance that 'they' have almost succeeded with thick, clotted blood covering his head, face and upper body and still bleeding profusely. Following the Marine into the hanger was me, an out of breath new 1st Lt. hardly any of the men knew, with blood all over my hands and arms. The entire night crew stopped what they were doing, watching the scene wide-eyed.

I explained to the nearest man that the Marine was crazy and to keep him there until I returned. I sprinted back to the ready room and called security and told them to 'send four very big MPs because this guy is crazy.' I called the O'club to get hold of Col. Bancroft. I was severely out of breath and gasping as I explained what had happened. Col. Bancroft kept telling me 'Calm down lieutenant, Calm down.' My reply was 'Yes sir, I am. I'm just out of breath.'

Having reported the events to Col. Bancroft, I ran back to the hangar where I left the Marine. The MPs and an ambulance were just arriving. I told the MPs to remain out of sight until I determined what was happening with the Marine. As I entered the hanger, the night crew had backed the Marine into a corner. When he saw me, he began screaming again and made a break for it. The men grabbed him. The corpsmen came and the Marine was strapped down on a stretcher. He continued to fight and scream against the straps as they placed him in the ambulance.

Afterwards, I washed up and cleaned up the blood in the ready room. I had the two men that were in the ready room write statements, and I wrote mine. I collected the hammer, which had big chunks of skin and hair on it. By now it was midnight, and I sat down thinking it couldn't get any worse, when in walks one of the guards. 'Sir we have a man out here who took a whole bottle of aspirin and tried to wash it down with Plexiglas cleaner.'

My thought was, Jesus Christ...its gonna be a long year!

* * *

And, for all of us FNGs, it was just beginning!

40: The 70s, A New Decade

(Total flight hours: 388.4)

55,000 Marines were in Vietnam on 1 January 1970, a reduction of some 24,000 Marines from the same time in 1969. Redeployment was taking its toll, and the overall effect on the helicopter community was that dependence on helicopters increased. The missions never diminished, unit names and locations were just rearranged to cover ground responsibilities. TAORs, once the responsibility of Marines, were simply disappearing as Redeployment and Vietnamization exponentially increased the areas for which the ARVNs were assuming responsibility. The HMM 262's Command Chronology[131] for January 1970 revealed the pilot strength to be at 50.

El Mossy Grotto (The Grotto) was at its max capacity as more new guys were checking in and the tour was ending for the PMAG-39 veterans. The can-do attitude prevalent in the Marine psyche caused HMM-262 and HMM-161, the last two Marine squadrons north of the Hai Van Pass, to overcome the formidable obstacle of being based in Phu Bai while working in the Da Nang area, a good 30 minute flight from Marble Mountain, depending on the weather. Both squadrons were advised that they would be moving to Marble Mountain when it was finally deemed that remaining in Phu Bai was inefficient and undesirable. HMM-161 would be moving down to Marble Mountain in early February. HMM-262 would be moving between 15 February and 1 March 1970. But, really, who knew what would happen?

On New Years Day 1970, a full schedule was published. Three Grottoites were scheduled to fly that day. Ron McAmis was scheduled to fly maintenance test flights with 1stLt. Frey. Pete Hanner was scheduled to fly with Dean Davis on a ROK Marine Command and Control mission. I was scheduled to fly with Bill Babs Babcock on a 1st Battalion Reconnaissance mission. Three

[131] http://vva.vietnam.ttu.edu/repositories.

other new guys were also scheduled that day: First Lieutenant Gene Mitchell was scheduled to fly with Hugo Beck; Second Lieutenant Joe "Silky" Gulvas, the only second lieutenant Marine helicopter pilot in Vietnam at that time, was scheduled to fly maintenance test flights with First Lieutenant Mix; First Lieutenant W. "Bird" King was scheduled to fly maintenance test with First Lieutenant Jeffryes; and, First Lieutenant Fred McCorkle, was scheduled to fly ROK resupply with John Parnham.

Camp Reasoner, LZ 401, where the First Recon naissance Battalion was located was named for First Lieutenant Frank Reasoner, a recon Marine posthumously awarded the Medal of Honor. LtCol W. C. Grace was their commanding officer. Their LZ was a large Marston matting that could easily accept two CH-46s, and could, if necessary, accept two CH-46s and one Cobra or Huey at the bottom of the hill upon which the recon base sat. A makeshift control tower stood beside the matting and a steep stairway approximately 40-50 feet high was the way up to the base camp where we received our briefings.

Figure 82 The makeshift control tower at the Recon Pad.

They owned us that day, and I looked forward to seeing where we would be flying during the year to come. It was a good day for me to get plenty of stick time. Babs was good about that.

He didn't hog the stick. The flight consisted of a few inserts and extracts of Recon teams from the Que Son Mountains, and from the area of Antenna Valley, between LZ Ross and An Hoa, plus one distinct mission that reaffirmed our traditions.

That mission was to input a Recon team into a crash site where a fixed wing aircraft had slammed into a medium-height mountain along the Hai Van Pass ridge, north of Da Nang. Babs allowed me to take the helo into the area designated by the Recon briefing. The brief for the insert was there couldn't be a landing. It would be another type of insert, by what they called fast rope.[132] This would be a hover with the aft pylon rotor blades near the trees. A normal wind of about 10-15 knots was expected.

The winds however were a little more than I expected. Maneuvering the 46 into position was difficult. We were being blown around to the point that I couldn't steady the aircraft. My grip on the cyclic was too tight, and I was over correcting. The harder I tried the worse it became. Seeing my anxiety building, Babs said, "Let me take it for a while and see if I can steady it down."

Babs' demeanor was one of teaching, but I was embarrassed. His words calmed me down as he steadied the craft and gave the crew chief the word, "Tell em to go."

"Yes sir," was the response from Cpl. Flores, an experienced and savvy crew chief. After what seemed like a long time, but in reality were only moments, all seven members of the team were gone. I realized that I needed much more stick time in these precarious circumstances where the aft pylon blades are only a few feet from the trees, and the cockpit is hanging out in space with nothing in view to judge your stability.

[132] Fast-rope or fast-roping is a technique used in special operations and assaults or in areas where a landing is not available to a helicopter, as in heavily wooded areas or on the slopes of mountains. A specialized thick rope is used and the person fast-roping utilizes hands, knees, and foot pressure on the rope to control the descent. See fast rope techniques http://www.imef.marines.mil/News/News-Article-Display/Article/759525/helicopter-rope-suspension-technique-masters-teach-marines-fundamentals-of-fast/.

The coordination between Cpl. Flores and Babs reflected a unique chemistry between the pilot and crew chief, brain to brain. It was that thing for which I have no name. It was that cerebral connection between the pilot and crew chief that comes with time. I had seen this with Dean Davis and now with Babcock. I wondered if I would ever achieve that skill level.

The team had fast roped into an area no more than a few feet wide, between trees some 40 to 60 feet high. Once the team was clear, and we had a thumbs-up from them, Babs graciously turned the flying back over to me. Back at the Recon LZ, the fast-rope was removed from the aircraft, and I expressed my concerns to Babs regarding my apparent inability to hold that 46 still in those winds. Babs said it simply. "It's a big sail and any wind can blow it. Handling it in a cross wind or hovering, on the side of a mountain, while a recon team dangles under it is a learned skill, like riding a bicycle...it'll come with time" he assured me. "Your brain is like a gyroscope; it will automatically handle the winds through your hands."

The mountains presented all kinds of problems for a helicopter. There is the burble, the turbulence that occurs when flying into a high zone where omnidirectional wind gusts varying in speed and intensity in the last 100 feet or so of what began as a smooth approach, can ruin your day. But, if you are carrying enough power to push through the turbulence and yet safely land in or deliver an external load of supplies, you'll live another day. I had a lot to learn. A fraction of a second off on power has caused many helicopters and external loads to be lost down the side of the mountain.

Once we were free of the mountain, we headed back to LZ 401 where we parked near the western edge of the pad. Babs rolled the power back to idle RPM as the fast rope attachment was being removed from the helicopter. A recon lieutenant who had made his way up the ramp and up to the cockpit area through the main cabin to the small passageway, placed his right hand on the back of Bab's armored seat, leaned in toward Babs, yelling something. Babs, through the intercom told me, "Hal, take the controls, I'll see what he wants."

I nodded and took control of the cyclic and collective as Babs removed his helmet. The lieutenant began speaking to Babs as I held the cyclic and collective stable. I could hear their voices, but could not understand them. The lieutenant ended his talk to Babs by handing him a note. Babs nodded his head in agreement with the lieutenant, who shook hands with Babs, then, turning briefly towards me, gave me a thumbs up. Babs placed his helmet back on his head, tightened the chin strap, pulled the mic close to his lips, placed his hands on the cyclic and collective and keyed his mike.

"I have the aircraft," he said, in accordance with procedure.

"You've got the aircraft. What's up?" I asked.

"We got one more thing to do."

"What?"

"We get to take a hot New Years Day meal to a recon team down around the tennis courts."

"Damn, that's great. Where's that?"

"The high bluffs just west of Arizona territory near Thuong Duc and An Hoa."

"No shit?"

"Yep," said Babcock.

"Flores?"

"Yes Sir."

"Are you good with this?"

"Hell yes...those guys deserve a good meal. Especially on New Year's Day! "

"We got enough fuel?" I asked.

"Yeah" said Babs. "We'll top-off[133] at Marble on the way back to Phu Bai,"

"Ok, let's do it.'

"Yes sir," said Corporal Flores. "Let's do it...but there's one problem."

---

[133] "Topping-off" slang for filling the fuel tanks.

"Yeah...what's that?"

"There's no food back here."

"They're bringing the food now." responded Babs.

While we sat waiting for the food, I thought of the day thus far. Beginning that morning in Phu Bai, then bouncing around the Da Nang area fast-roping those guys into that jungle zone and picking up and depositing a couple of recon teams. There was not one shot fired throughout the day. Maybe that was foretelling how the coming year would be?

A small vehicle called a mule showed up. It was the food. We were soon on our way, calling DASC for clearance. We were cleared to Hill 55 direct from Cau Do Bridge. The afternoon was on us and the flight was unremarkable. I felt good about this special trip to the men in the bush, yet I didn't understand why it was safe for them to receive the hot meal there in the bush.

Upon making radio contact with the recon team, we spiraled down, flared, and were in the zone. The team was jubilant. Babs said to them, "We got some New Years Day hot food and cake for you guys from your brothers back at camp"

"Yes, sir," came the response. "We've been waiting."

After Flores delivered the food, a recon team member came up to my side of the helicopter (port side) and pushed a folded piece of paper through the small window opening. I took the paper. It was a hand written note.

"Happy New Year! Thanks A Lot BRAVO BASTARDS 1st PLT. 1st RECON".

It was a real nice thing they did, after showing it around to everyone. I folded the note and placed it in my personal papers and orders packet that I kept throughout my tour of duty, transferring it into my Marine Corps papers upon retirement, where it remains to this day. The mission was complete and the day was ebbing. We got back to Phu Bai at 1525 hrs. for a total of 5.2 hours of flight.

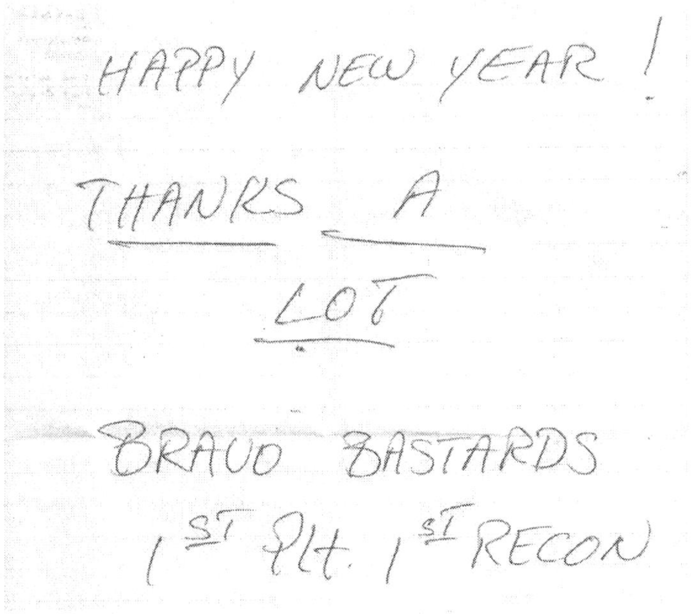

Figure 83 Happy New Year note from BRAVO BASTARDS 1st PLT. 1st RECON.

41: A Visit to Hue

In this new decade a unique opportunity soon presented itself to me...a trip to Hue. Third Force Reconnaissance Marines had a Jeep for the day; I was lucky enough to have a day off from flying and Wags gave me permission to go on a sight-seeing trip with them. The Recon Marines who asked me to go with them were on one of the flights into the A Shau when I was flying as copilot with Jeffryes. I couldn't think of a safer group to be with, so off I went on a real adventure.

The trip took us north on Highway 1 through Phuóng (pronounced Fu-Long), near where the three lieutenants dumped the generals's Jeep. Highway 1 was full of military traffic moving at a snail's pace going both ways as we entered from the south. XXIV Corps. battle tanks, armored personnel carriers, and big six-bys full of cargo or troops were on the move.

Figure 84 Military traffic into Hue.

The Recon Marines knew the area, and I felt very comfortable with them as driver, guide and body guard. As we approached the outskirts of Hue, I could see no immediate signs of battle damage, but very soon, signs of that battle began to appear. This trip into Hue was surreal...The ancient imperial capital of Vietnam, the citadel, the epicenter of the battle of Hue, the longest and bloodiest battle of the Tet Offensive which began on 31 January 1968 when at 0800, the NLF (National Liberation Front) flag was flying over the ancient city. For the next 25 days until the end of the mop-up that ended on 02 March 1968, the U.S. Marines and elements of the First Cavalry Division (U.S. Army) and South Vietnamese Marines (ARVNs) fought a brutal house-to-house battle to retake the city of Hue.[134]

I noticed the architecture of Hue was primarily French, like New Orleans, reflecting the influence of the French colonization of Vietnam in the mid-1800s that led to the Indo-China War, when Ho Chi Minh kicked the French out of Vietnam. We were next in line, but they couldn't have done it had we been allowed to hold ground and move forward rather than sit and take it—fight the war as it should have been fought.

As we moved through the streets in our Jeep, making turns into narrow thoroughfares, a large church was coming into view. It was a Catholic church, with a huge statue of Jesus standing in front of it.

I didn't expect to see a Christian church in this area which was, I thought, 100% Buddist. I couldn't believe the South or North Vietnamese would tolerate Christianity. But I was very wrong. I was told by the Recon Marines, the church was famous following the battle. The story was that the church was full of parishioners and probably some Buddhists too, seeking refuge from the NVA, who were busy slaughtering people (thousands of civilians were found in shallow mass graves as the communists settled old scores and eliminated "enemies of the people," identified as teachers and doctors and such).[135]

[134] Wirtz,231.
[135] Wirtz,228.

Figure 85 Hue Catholic Church.

A priest in this church allegedly dared defy the NVA during that battle. What a show of guts! It was said that an NVA officer, intent on killing everyone in the church, held a pistol to the head of the priest in what appeared to be another summary execution. The officer, red-faced and angry, spitting out vitriol and hate, miraculously decided against killing the priest. Instead, he holstered his weapon and stomped out of the church in a fit of angry words and gestures. The incident was considered a miracle, but not the only miracle credited to the church.

The church had an extremely tall cathedral window. A cross, made of steel, occupied the center of the window, an impressive sight when viewed from either outside or inside the church.

An NVA mortar launched toward the church during the battle crashed through the window, hitting the cross and bouncing off. It landed outside the church where it harmlessly exploded. That event was also deemed by the church to be direct evidence of God protecting his flock. In the last two years since the battle, the church, I was told, had become a place of healing with a daily overflow crowd of people seeking the healing grace of God.

That area, during the battle of Hue, was indeed a hot spot where many Marines fought to the last man. It was a place of respect and held a special place in a Marine's heart. To see this place where such a historic battle had been fought was humbling. The walls of the buildings all bore the markings of war. None were completely free from defacement by bullets from both sides. Homes remained in ruins and the narrow side streets were piled high with battle debris. Being in the jeep, I flashed

Figure 86 Close up of picture of HUE Catholic Church cross window

back to WWII news reel films of GIs in Europe moving through ancient narrow streets just like we were doing. The facts were that it was amazing to me how our Marines, used to jungle warfare at that time, transitioned to total urban house to house and hand to hand fighting against an enemy just as fanatical and disciplined as the Nazis. It was never so apparent to me that the Marine Grunt was the best weapon in our inventory.

Another odd structure caught my eye. In the middle of all this destruction was a Shell Oil gas station that looked like a station you might see in any small town in America. It was intact with what appeared like new concrete paving, and it was open for business. One of the Recon Marines, pointing toward the station said, "that's what we're really fighting for," as he gestured toward the station.

Figure 87 Hue Shell Oil gas station

"What?" asked one of the Recon Marines.

"That oil company, you dumb shit."

That gas station[136], I later learned, played a very important part in the battle for Hue. Captain Charles L. Meadows, Golf 2/5 (Golf Company, 2d Battalion, 5th Marines), a recipient of the Silver Star for his actions in the Battle of Hue, found a wall map for the city of Hue in that station. That map was the only map available to him to maneuver his company of Marines in Hue. His unit Golf 2/5 was a highly decorated, having earned seven Navy Crosses.

We then made our way toward the Citadel, within which is the Imperial City, the ancient capital of Vietnam. There were two bridges within a few feet of each other across the perfume River (Song Huong) to the southwest corner of the Citadel. One bridge

---

[136] The brand name of the gas station I saw in HUE was Shell. It has been identified as an ESSO station. However, Capt Meadows, CO of Golf/2/5, in 2005, identified the shell station pictured above as the one in which he took cover and from which he recovered a street map of Hue.

was for civilian traffic. The second bridge, built for heavy military traffic: battle tanks, armored personnel carriers and such all built by combat engineers.

The battle of Hue will be studied by military academies all over the world. Marine Grunts, U.S. 1st Cavalry Division, and dedicated ARVN Marines fought block to block, man-to-man and hand to hand more reminiscent of the epic urban battles of WW II rather than the island campaigns of the Marines in WWII. The Citadel with its centuries old heavy thick walls was a perfect defensive position for the enemy and when we approached the southwest corner of the citadel one of the Recon Marines accentuated the site by saying, "Right f**king here was where it happened," like he was talking about Normandy, Iwo Jima, Tarawa or Okinawa. The battle rated those comparisons. It now was sacred ground, where the Marines "sold their lives dearly."[137]

I was in awe, like standing at the bloody angle of our nations Gettysburg battlefield where north and south met in a hand-to-hand battle. The similar feelings I experience at both historic sites shook me. The rubble, still evident, strung alongside the scarred remnants of the wall, proof that a great battle had taken place there, the Battle of Hue.

* * *

Upon preparing to leave the Citadel, our driver said, "Since we are this far, we should visit the oldest Buddhist Temple in all of Vietnam." It was "just a couple of miles" west along a less traveled river road called the Kim Long Road. The temple was the Thien Mu Pagoda (Heavenly Lady), a Buddhist Temple with a seven story tower whose construction had begun in 1601. It was situated on high ground, on the north bank of the Perfume River.

---

[137] The phrase "sold their lives dearly" is taken from the words Col. William Barrett Travis spoke to two-hundred Americans gathered at the Alamo. He said, they would fight until they could fight no more. They would, "sell their lives dearly."

In June 1963, the year I graduated from High School, Thich Quang Duc, a 73-year-old monk from the Thien Mu Temple, traveled to Saigon and on 11 June 1963 he set himself on fire in an intersection in Saigon protesting the Diem regime. I did see this on the Huntley-Brinkley Report, NBCs flagship evening news program when I was 17. My mother never failed to watch that program and gleaned all the news of the day from them; I was about to graduate from High school at that time; the impression it made on me was that people who set themselves on fire were crazy.

Figure 88 The burning monk on the 14 June 1963 cover of Time Magazine was captured by Malcolm Browne, Associated Press Photographer. Most other periodicals in that era featured the stunning picture.

The question in my mind when in high school (1965), upon seeing the picture of the burning monk, was whether or not that burning man in Vietnam was the enemy? Where again is Vietnam? To many of my friend and me, the grisly picture revealed the true nature of the enemy — the Viet Cong. It appeared that the enemy was determined to fight to the end, like I saw on Victory at Sea footage on Sunday afternoons. It was the United States Marines who used flame throwers to burn out Japanese soldiers on those islands. Was that what happened to the monk? Also, the picture reinforced our loosely drawn opinions that they, the enemy, had to be destroyed at any cost to once again save the world — just like WWII.

* * *

This portion of my outing was the most exciting part of the trip. I began feeling uncomfortable as we drove farther and farther out of the city going west along the north bank of the Perfume River on a small dirt road. I took some comfort in the fact that the Recon guys appeared very comfortable and at ease, so why shouldn't I? As we traveled farther and farther, I was becoming acutely aware that it was getting late in the afternoon, and the sun was sinking fast behind the mountains on the western horizon. Even in the presence of Recon, I didn't want to be out of Phu Bai after dark.

At about the same time that I was becoming a little anxious, we neared our objective. A group of Vietnamese was milling about in the road wearing what appeared to be black pajamas which was not reassuring, but the Recon men seemed not to be at all concerned. "Militia?" I nervously asked. "Who are those guys?"

The Recon Marines then began to appear more alert; no talking, no laughing, as they eased their weapons into a position where they could be easily brought into action if necessary. We were too close to them to stop, turn around or show any hesitancy. We could only slow down, so as not to be provocative, and keep moving. As we neared the group, there was a moment of anticipation. The Jeep slowed and the group stared intently at us, then slowly parted, allowing us through. The Recon guys relaxed their grip on their weapons as they noticed that the group was not armed with M-16s or AK-47s, but older firearms, maybe old French carbines, which gave me some degree of comfort. The banana clip of the AK-47 would have very much identified them as "bad guys." As it turned out, they were no threat to us. They must have been Popular Forces (PFs), local militia. If they had been a threat, we would have all been dead, or worse, captured.

Eventually we arrived at the temple. My nervousness subsided to some degree, but the day was getting away from us and again, I didn't want to be back there in the dark of night.

I still felt it odd that for the first time I did have some degree of concern for my safety. We were armed only with side arms and a couple of M-16s, and my sense was that there would not have been a very long fight if it had been Mr. Charles' band of VC/NVA. The reason for my discomfort was now becoming clear. In the cockpit of the 46 I was, and would be, comfortable in some of the most uncertain circumstances; there, I was in my element. When both of my feet were on the ground, I was in a world that was not so comfortable. Just as some of the most hardened Grunts shut their eyes and their guts tightened when in the canvas seats of the 46. However, when the ramp came down and they moved into the jungle, they were in familiar surroundings and if not totally comfortable they were confident.

The scene, as a whole, appeared to be a set from an old Tarzan movie. As we progressed up the ancient steps into the temple plaza area, a seven layer tower was the most obvious centerpiece of this ancient place. It was very quiet, solemn, cathedral-like. A nimble wisp of saffron, resembling the light stroke of an impressionist's brush drew our combined attention to a deeply vined corner of the courtyard. An apparition feigning a presence escaped as we cautiously moved up the ancient stones, smoothed by a thousand footsteps, leading to what appeared to be the sanctuary.

Approximately eight golden Buddhas, each near three feet high, situated on individual pedestals covered in glass, guarded the pagoda (interior of the temple). The gardens affected a feeling of enchantment seldom experienced. This was indeed a special place, and I felt that our mere presence was having an unsettling effect.

* * *

Figure 89 One of the Golden Buddhas inside a large glass bell.

There were other places later in life where I experienced that same feeling: The Grand Canyon was one. My first in-person glimpse of the Grand Canyon was breathtaking. When Kathy and I were traveling from Santa Ana, CA to Missouri during my preparation to go to Vietnam, we took a ride in a Bell 13 type helicopter referred to by most as a whirly bird. The pilot was a former Army helo pilot, and we spoke about the eccentricity of flying helicopters. He asked if I would like to fly it. I rapidly declined, and we all three squeezed into the bubble. He began by remaining on the top of the trees running headlong toward the canyon. Being as low as we were, I couldn't possibly anticipate what I was about to see. Bang...passing from the forested area over the south rim into the magnitude of the canyon was stunning. It burst upon me as if I had entered a dreamscape.

The second place I experienced that feeling was on 6 March 1987 when visiting the Alamo. I went to the plaza before dawn. My intent, to see what the defenders could see as dawn broke across the plaza and Col. Travis rushed to the north wall. What all three of these experiences shared: the Buddhist Temple, The Grand Canyon and the Alamo was a natural quiet, a solitude, a grandeur that came together in one rare moment of inspiration. It all blew me away.

I wondered if the Buddhas were covered in real gold or simply painted with a gold colored paint? The Recon men said they believed it was real gold and reaffirmed that this temple was the oldest temple in Vietnam and that no one dared damage it, neither the VC/NVA ARVN nor the American forces. The place was enveloped in sea green jungle and mystery. When I asked the rhetorical questions as to where the Buddhist Monk had disappeared, and why we had not been approached, the recon men didn't respond. It was time to go. The feeling I had was that the Buddhist Monks had tired of our meddling and were ready to send us on our way. Yet, for a very few moments, in that garden, I was allowed a special treat—to see and feel the true Vietnamese culture. That moment was the deepest I would ever get into the culture of Vietnam. And I would never forget it.

Figure 90 The three of us, two Recon Marines and me in the middle of no-where at one of the most revered locations in all of Vietnam. It was history, mystery, danger and intrigue all in one, a grand adventure.

Yet, I was more than ready to return to the security and comfort of Phu Bai. We left the temple and headed back. I had plenty of time to think of all I had seen that day. Upon arriving at Phu

Bai, I thanked my hosts and was happy to be back within the protective inner ring of the base. Another day in the Nam had passed. I passed the time that evening writing Kathy and telling her of my special experience that day. It was a special thing that happened because as a helicopter pilot you rarely got a chance to be on the ground unless you were under fire and lying in an old bomb crater (which I never had the bad luck to do), or a FAC (Forward Air Controller.) I had a beer afterward and retold the Grottoites of my experience. Gary said he would like to make the trip, but I don't think he did. It was a unique happenstance that was interwoven into my memory, with the other unique experiences happening on a near daily basis. I made a few notes in a small memo book about the trip, then sleep took over.

42: Night Vision School

I don't know why or who arranged it, but following the change of command, Col. Bancroft became more lenient than Maj. Meskan when it came to pilots getting out of country. This may have been happening under Maj. Meskan, but I think not. In this regard, Gary Rainey and I received orders to take a trip out of Phu Bai. We would take an Air Force C-130 leaving Phu Bai for Udorn, Thailand, one of five outposts near the northeast border of Thailand from which Operation Rolling Thunder[138] was launched.

We were told this was a night vision school, but not until we arrived did it become evident that night vision school actually meant running wild in Udorn, Thailand, for two nights and three days. My first thought was, where is Udorn, Thailand? Logically, it was in Thailand. However, my familiarity with Thailand began and ended with a faded wall map in high school and maybe, the 1957 movie, *Bridge over the River Kwai* that starred William Holden and Alec Guinness. The fact that the movie was supposed to have been in Burma, not Thailand, didn't matter. I figured it all looked the same. For certain, the nations to the west of Vietnam were all notorious and overrun with brutal jungle gangs, loosely categorized as communist guerillas. Thailand had their Communist insurgency or Liberation Army, and Laos had the Pathet Lao. As far as I was concerned, it was all associated with the North Vietnamese Army and Ho chi Minh. Furthermore, I was vaguely aware that Rolling Thunder air attacks, the coolest name ever for an attack operation, were launched into North Vietnam and the Ho Chi Minh Trail from Thailand, but from where in Thailand, I didn't know.

* * *

It seemed to me that all of Southeast Asia, not just Vietnam, was

---

[138] Rolling Thunder was a sustained aerial bombardment of North Vietnam by the Air Force, Navy and Republic of South Vietnam Air Force from 2 March 1965 to 2 November 1968. The vast majority of missions were launched by the Air Force from bases in Thailand, included in which was Udorn, Thailand.

made up of communist revolutionaries trying to kick over the first domino to begin the takeover of the world. Therefore, it was important that we be ever-vigilant, guarding against the fall of that first domino. Perhaps, however, the first domino had fallen. Didn't France get kicked out of Indochina by Ho Chi Minh? If so, what was a country boy like me and the thousands of others like me, grabbed up in the draft or otherwise going to be able to do against those people? Didn't anyone read Bernard Fall's *Street Without Joy*? Hmm ... To think back on it, I didn't read it either. My thoughts were not of history in that era of my life. What I always believed about going to Vietnam was once you were there you did whatever you had to do to survive, regardless of history. We attendees were not the decision makers. We were just following orders.

I immediately recalled a friend of mine from Kennett, Missouri, Jimmy Dale Moody. During the summer of 1966 I had worked at the Riggs Wholesale Supply Company with Ronnie Morgan, from Holcomb. I was also friends with Tom Crunk Jr., Mike French, Ken Stewart, Richard Whitehorn and other Kennett folks. It was during that era that I met Moody. He was a tough guy, who didn't show any interest in going to college. He became a friend, not a close friend, but, an acquaintance who was fun to be around. I was present one night when he got beat up pretty bad by a Kennett High School football stand-out. It was about a girl, what else? She apparently had dumped Jimmy for the football player.

The fight appeared to have been prearranged. It was going to take place out on a country road north of Kennett, called the billboard road. Hell, there must have been a hundred kids there. I remained back from the crowd, watching. Jimmy was no match for the star athlete, he got beat up real bad, but never turned his back. Jimmy was never the same after that. I went back to college in the fall and forgot about the whole thing. Years later, in 1982, when in Washington, D.C., I saw his name on the Vietnam Wall.

It seems that Jimmy licked his wounds and joined the Marine Corps, the kind of guy that made up the Corps, tough, wild and smart. He like so many others was putting Kennett behind him. The Marine Corps had the feel of the French Foreign Legion, because they took tough guys who had a past and told them they could begin anew. I couldn't see Jimmy in any other service. I could see him as a Grunt, the best of the best. The information on the wall filled in a couple of blanks. The date of his death was 24 March 1967. He was 20 years old. I spoke to him in my mind, *what happened to you Jimmy, where were you?*

I learned that he was in the thick of it near the DMZ, with Headquarters and Headquarters Company of the 3d Battalion, Third Marine Division. The Marines were in a hell of a fight with many hardcore NVA units coming across the DMZ into South Vietnam. I looked further. Not to my surprise, I found that he was posthumously awarded the Silver Star.

He was a mortar man. His job was to keep the mortar shells available to the gunner. He had to break open ammo boxes and run back and forth to the mortar tube to the team firing the mortar. He keep them supplied in what became a duel to the death between the Marines and the NVA, head-to-head, man-to-man. A few Marines against an NVA Division, and, they never turned their back.

His job was to keep his mortar team supplied with ammo during the intense enemy attack that day. Enemy mortars landed all around them, clearing the way for the enemy infantry. Jimmy's mortar team was practically wiped out. They were dead or dying. Now, it was up to Jimmy alone. He was badly wounded. Knowing there was no one else to man the mortar, to halt the enemy advance, Jimmy crawled to the mortar tube. He was able to return fire by himself which he did, in agony from his wounds. I can only imagine the horror of it all. Again, it must be said, he never turned his back. He was a real hero, someone to be remembered, not any make-believe bullshit. Not everyone who wore the uniform was a hero. Jimmy was!

* * *

There was never any doubt in my mind that we would win our

fight with North Vietnam, like our WWI and WWII heroes had done in Europe and Pacific island fighting before us. John Wayne had done it in his movie *Green Berets*, hadn't he? But, John Wayne himself was known to have said, he was, 'just Marion Morrison, from Winterset, Iowa, playing John Wayne." He was never in the military, and he was quick to say to friends that he was an actor playing a part, and they shouldn't lose sight of who the real heroes were. The truth is, no one cared that he was just playing a part. His screen presence was our template. He was how we wanted to be. Yet there were major differences between both world wars and Korea and Vietnam. The difference was how it was categorized. The word *war* was the difference. Korea was a *police action* and Vietnam was a *conflict*. I suppose, if Korea or Vietnam had been recognized as a war by Congress, we would have been allowed to fight like it was a war. Korea was declared a draw and Vietnam was an illusion brought about by overly used nonsensical phrases such as Peace with Honor, Vietnamization and Redeployment.

The Marine Corps however has a legacy more dear than such categorizations; it was the image of John Wayne as Sgt. John Stryker in the *Sands of Iwo Jima,* and the real life Chesty Puller, the most decorated Marine in history. Chesty himself was present at the 2 February, 1968 commissioning ceremony of the 46th OCS class in which his son, Louis Puller Jr. was commissioned a second lieutenant as was Jimmy Stewart, the famous actor and bomber pilot present as his step-son, Ron McLean, was also commissioned a second lieutenant. A.C. Allen, Eric McGrew, Roy Prigge and I were also commissioned as second Lieutenants in that same ceremony.

Marion "John Wayne" Morrison in his movie roles defined the soul of the Corps as did the legacy of Col. Puller whose war record and famous quotes summed up his simple philosophy. In Korea, just before Christmas 1950, when Chesty was in command of the 7th Marine Regiment[139], 1st Marine Division and surrounded by 22 Chinese Divisions in the Chosin Reservoir he motivated his Marines with the following comment: "We've been looking for the enemy for some time. We've finally found him. We're surrounded. That simplifies our problem of getting to these people and killing them." Pure Chesty. The subsequent Marine breakout from the Chosin Reservoir through Koto-ri is regarded as a classic in the annals of modern American military warfare and assured Chesty's elevation to the rank of Brigadier General and his iconic role as the Marine's Marine.

* * *

Our flight from Phu Bai to Udorn was shorter than I expected. Disembarking in the middle of a lush jungle I noticed a gray T-28 Trojan, a propeller-driven aircraft with a Radial 1820 cubic inch engine that generated 1475 shaft horse power, coming in on final; it was the sound that drew my attention and made goose bumps rise up on my arms. Most pilots, like myself, who ever flew the T-28 will never forget the sound of that engine; it's unmistakable, the Harley Davidson of the sky. The last time I flew solo in the T-28 was in Pensacola, Florida, at Saufley Field during my carrier qualification. It was held on the World War II aircraft carrier USS Essex during its decommissioning cruise. The side number on my T-28 was 707 in big bold numbers. I never tired of saying that I carrier qualified on the Essex with a 707. At that time, the 707 was the largest commercial airliner manufactured by Boeing, so it was a joke among the flight students.

With the canopy of the T-28 open, the pilot taxied close enough to our C-130 that I couldn't help but notice he was wearing a Hawaiian-like short-sleeved shirt. Hell, I couldn't believe it. The pilot had on military-style sunglasses with the dark visor on his helmet in the up position. The prop wash billowed his shirt as he maneuvered his craft into a chocked row of T-28s. He glanced toward our group deplaning from the C-130. The T-28

---

[139] The same 7th Marines headquartered at LZ Baldy.

bellowed with the deep nostalgic roar of that R-1820 rotary engine, not unlike the sound of a big Harley just lumbering by, reminding me of the magnificence of that craft. It was painted flat gray and carried a gun pod and bomb racks under both wings. I later learned that Air America's T-28s carried 500-pound bombs, rockets, and a .50-cal. pod and had been flying missions since the early 1960s. I loved the T-28 and thought that was where the real action was taking place. From that moment on, when possible, I mimicked this style: visor up and sunglasses on.

* * *

Figure 91 Air America T-28D, at Udorn, Thailand, 1969

I later learned that the T-28D was piloted by Laotians trained by the USAF at Udorn Thailand. The Royal Army of Laos, under the leadership of General Vang Pao, led a CIA-backed secret army that included Air America, fighting against a communist takeover of Laos. In 1975, when the United States pulled out of South Vietnam, Vang, without further CIA backing, immigrated to the United States. He died on 6 January, 2011 in Fresno, CA[140] His funeral cortege was escorted by two T-28s.

* * *

I wish I had a picture of that moment. It made a real impression on me, probably like the impression James Dean made on people. I would never know who that pilot was, but he represented the image of what I wanted to project—confidence and coolness in a real war plane. I would do my best in the CH-46. You fly "what brung you" and the 46 Phrog "brung me" to Vietnam.

Udorn was an outpost of the Royal Thai Air Force where the United States Air Force maintained a frontline facility under the

---

[140] "Vang Pao Gets Hero's Farewell, But not at Arlington," VIETNAM, Volume No. 1 June 2011,8.

command of the United States Pacific Air Forces. It was from Udorn that courageous airmen flew the F-105 Thunderchief, called the Thud, at Mach 2 (twice the speed of sound) into North Vietnam. Their roar became Rolling Thunder. Udorn was also the Asian Headquarters of Air America—an American passenger and cargo outfit covertly owned and operated by the Central Intelligence Agency (CIA). It supplied and supported covert operations in Southeast Asia during the Vietnam War.

We were greeted by a local Thai in a minivan from Ben's Jewelry. This seemed strange; why were we not being greeted by a military host telling us about the school and when we would start and stop and how to stay out of the local jail. Oh well, go with the flow. We were ushered to a beautiful hotel. The name said it all, The American Hotel. There were other hotels in Udorn, the Princess Hotel and the Charoen Hotel, rumored to be owned by Air America. The day was beautiful and the airbase-dependent city was crawling with uniforms of all kinds, but U.S. Air Force and Thai Air Force uniforms were prominent.

All I had ever heard of Thailand was that it was beautiful. The monks with their shaved heads, draped in their colorful orange robes accentuated the kaleidoscope of people and color from what seemed to be all parts of Asia. The temples appeared to be gold plated and sprinkled with jewels, luxurious and beautiful when compared to the local palace of the King of Thailand, whom I was told never ever came to Udorn, so he could always feign ignorance. Their local legal commodity held a world monopoly on black star sapphires; a beautiful stone found only in Thailand, they say. The huge illegal product from the area of the golden triangle that encompassed major portions of Asia, Burma, Thailand and Laos was heroin. During the 1960s and '70s, the DEA fought a secret war in that area.

Once we had been taken to The American Hotel, we checked in with about a dozen other service personnel and were free until the next day when our guide advised he would pick us up and take us "shopping." Meanwhile, have a good time, and oh yes, spend lots of money. I had some U.S. currency and some MPC, both of which were valued currency to the local money changer. Gary and I changed our money into Thai money called *baht* (pronounced "bot"). It was a ridiculous exchange rate, and we were rolling in baht.

Our first order of business was to have a custom-made shirt and trousers made for us as we had left all of our civilian clothes in Phu Bai. I ordered a double breasted gangster suit, the kind that wives throw away the first time they see it. The hotel had a host of services, including the Release Me massage service which looked and operated more like an old west bordello.

After being measured for our suits, Gary and I, and many of the other military types, made our way to the hotel swimming pool. The pool was fancier than anything I had ever seen, and they had all types of Asian beer available and would be happy to just put it on your room bill, something like 50 cents a beer. One beer in particular was necessary to drink if you were in Thailand; it was called Singha beer, 6% alcohol, with a Bengal Tiger's head on the label. One percent stronger than what we had in-country. I thought the tiger on the label looked like our squadron logo. The beer was served in what looked like quart-size bottles, chilled to almost freezing. We were used to Black Label, Old Milwaukee and an occasional delight, Budweiser beer, back in Phu Bai. After a quick dip in the pool, Gary and I began ordering Singha which we drank with much gusto. However, weren't prepared to drink Singha. After a couple of bottles of that brew, the buzz began and before long I could feel myself becoming numb and slipping off to sleep, which I could not let happen, for the night was just beginning. Before much longer, upon trying to get off the chaise lounge at the pool's edge, I couldn't feel my legs. Wow! Gary laughed and ordered two more, but the oncoming night forced me up and at it.

Udorn was overrun with bicycle-driven buggies or rickshaws, very colorful and seen throughout the Pacific Rim countries. It was an inexpensive and convenient way to get around town, but it seemed to me that it was just a little too close to the local color for my comfort, or, I was not drunk enough to risk it.

We hailed a cab instead and told the driver to take us to the center of the nightlife in Udorn. Off we went into that unholy night, the kind that when you woke up in the morning you hoped your wallet and keys were not missing.

The honky-tonks were innumerable, with the best labels of booze being plentiful and cheap. It looked just like Guam and smelled like the streets of Da Nang and every Mexican border town I ever ventured into. The smell of mystery meat barbecued by roadside vendors and open sewers tainted the night air. The streets were overrun with prostitutes and peddlers hawking their wares. Sirens and red flashing lights blared as MPs grappled with drunken servicemen as background music from Hendrix's anthem, "Purple Haze" and the "Doors' "Light my Fire" wafted through the streets. An eerie glow and the high pitched hum of generators powered a garish buzzing and popping jungle of neon signs. Colorful rickshaws raced through the narrow, winding streets, as smashed Americans laughed and taunted them with dollar bills to go faster and faster in a race to nowhere.

It was a whirling mixture of sensuous color and mind-numbing sound. The experience could be eerily likened to Captain Willard's (Martin Sheen in the film *Apocalypse Now*). Like Captain Willard, when you were in Udorn, you had already passed the fictional Do Long Bridge and, "had left the boat." Willard's thoughts were poignant, "Never get out of the boat, unless you are going all the way." Civilization was nowhere to be seen here and in most every way it was a horror brought forth by atrocity.

All in all, this place was just another cow town with dirt streets, brothels, saloons, and cheap night clubs. It was beyond the red line where every doorway into every den of depravity brought a new vision of pulsating hard rock accompanied by rhythmic twisting dancers, pushing drinks and selling themselves to mine the true mother lode—cash from the U.S. military.

In that place, it was apparent the United States military, especially the Air Force and Air America ruled. There was an Americanized bar in Udorn that catered to Air America pilots. A quick turn into that bar placed you back in the States. However, if you weren't one of them, it was best to move on to a less hostile bar. That rule was ignored, on one occasion, when a besotted visitor from Vietnam attempted to dance with the wife of an Air America pilot. Needless to say, that led to his misfortune. It was a tough place, filled with tough people fighting a war far darker than Nam.

Military and Thai police intermingled amongst the twenty-four-hour revelers, not unlike Dodge City, Kansas, during the height of the cattle drives, or Tombstone at the zenith of the silver boom. Gary and I ended the day that began in Phu Bai with each of us in a rickshaw, hoping the bicycle cabby knew where the hotel was located.

The next morning found us safe, sound, famished, and sobering up in the hotel. A breakfast of fresh cut pineapple with scrambled eggs was adequate. Ah yes, and a bit of the hair of the dog was in order before getting a haircut and having my eardrums cleaned, a procedure I had not requested. As the haircut came to an end, I felt a sharp instrument deep into my ear. The barber continued as though he did this to everyone. I was afraid to protest and held my head very still hoping he didn't puncture my eardrum. He didn't. But, I practically ran from the shop.

Gary and I took possession of our new suits; my double-breasted, yellowish-beige pinstripe suit was boxed up and ready to go. I purchased a necklace and earrings set of Black Star sapphires for Kathy. They were beautiful, but I don't believe she ever wore them, nor did I ever wear the suit. Its appearance was sufficient evidence of my step into the whirlwind that was Udorn.

The King of Thailand had a residence in Udorn should he ever want to visit the place. It was a small, but very luxurious looking palace. It should have been expensive looking, for many millions of dollars flowed into the King's coffers from the United States for allowing us to build these bases in such close proximity to the border of Laos for what was a short run to North Vietnam. The Buddhist Monks wore various colored robes and were prominent in the vicinity, although, I thought at first they were the Hare Krishnas I had seen beating drums and chanting in San Francisco. I guess I was wrong on that count. But, it was time to go. Our brief visit over with, we boarded our C-130 and headed back to Phu Bai with a haul of goodies, little to no money and wonderful memories of a land I would never have known nor forget had it not been for the "Nam".

The trip was what the military calls *basket leave* which is when the command authorizes a specified period of leave time with the necessary paperwork, only to discard the paperwork into the trash basket upon the individual's uneventful return to base. In this instance, there was no paperwork, just a list of who was going. It was a perk of being in Vietnam—no, it was a perk of being in Phu Bai and close to the 101st Airborne, for it was the Army that had set up the shuttle in the first place.

43: "Blades"

(Total Flight Hours: 423.7)

A Third Force Reconnaissance "secret" mission scheduled on 3 January to go into the A Shau Valley—now under control of the Army's XXIV Corps—was the one mission that caused the former 262 operations officer, Captain Stover, to tremble just thinking of it. Everyone was wondering how this A Shau Recon mission would go with the new squadron leadership in place as both the CO and XO had very different aviation experiences in Vietnam.

The concerns of Maj. Lee, Commanding Officer of Third Force, who preferred the 2d Squadron of the 17th Air Cavalry to using Marine Corps Squadrons, were apparently resolved, at least for this coming mission. But bad weather, always a wild card, would be the variable that would again stop this mission—probably forever—since we were on our way to Marble Mountain in little more than a month.

Operations put together a good team. The section of helicopters would be crewed by two seasoned combat veterans, First Lieutenants, Bill "Fuels" Nelson and John "Wags" Wagner III, combat veterans who were familiar with the A Shau Valley, and who had begun their Vietnam tour with PMAG-39 under the auspices of the Third Marine Division (now gone) under Operation Keystone.

Lt. Nelson was the designated flight leader and HAC. Maj. Wiley Sellers, the new XO was scheduled to fly as Nelson's copilot until NATOPS could designate him a HAC. Cpl. Jerry Jay "J.J." Hall, an experienced combat crew chief, was placed with Nelson and Sellers. The gunners were Corporals Todd and Hayes, both experts on the .50 cal. Their helicopter would carry no Recon Marines. Their job was to provide support and extract (if necessary) for the aircraft designated to insert the Recon team

LtCol. Bancroft, our new CO with a minimum of helicopter experience, was a designated HAC and placed in the second aircraft, making Wags his copilot. Although Col. Bancroft was designated a HAC, he was not as yet designated a section leader. He was on his second tour. His first Vietnam tour had been as an A-4 Skyhawk jet pilot. He started his second tour of duty as CO of Headquarters and Maintenance Squadron 16 at Marble Mountain, a position that required minimal flying time in the CH-46D, mostly for flight pay purposes. Now here he was, a newbie and the CO of a CH-46 combat squadron flying what to him was a new aircraft in an intense combat scenario.

Figure 92 PFC Donnie K. Sexton

The crew chief was Private First Class (PFC) Donnie K. Sexton an absolutely fearless individual and recipient of the DFC, as well as a holder of a double handful of Air Medals including single mission air medals and various other awards. He had become a living legend for having wheeled and dealed his way into remaining in Vietnam through two previous back-to-back tours, called cross-decking. This was Sexton's third back to back tour in Vietnam.[141] The .50 cal. gunners were Corporals Danny L. Radish and Lance Corporal P. E Coley.

The gun cover would be supplied by HML-367, Scarface, in their new Cobras with the serpent's powerful jaws and fangs poised in full striking posture painted in bright colors on the

---

[141] PFC Sexton's lack of rank was due to his unique inability to go on liberty without ending up before the Commanding Officer for "Office Hours," administrative or a summary court martial. He was honored by us all, and he was the only crew chief they would have placed on the helicopter with the CO. His eventual ticket out of Vietnam came after he was taken into custody by a Marine MP for being drunk and rowdy. Lt. Donnie McGlothlin, the squadron duty officer was approached by the MP who offered to drop any charges against Sexton if he, the MP, could just "take Sexton out behind the wood shed," and have it out with him. Donnie agreed after consulting with Sexton. And, that happened. Sexton proceeded to break the MP's jaw in three places. Following a court martial, Sexton was sent back to the States as a Pvt. Still. if he has an opportunity to read this book, Sexton, please contact me.

nose of the aircraft for all to see and fear. The goal of the mission was to find an elusive super-cache of NVA weapons hidden away in that bloody valley where Operation Dewey Canyon (The Green Hell) took place early in January through March 1969. The Cobra Pilots were also veterans of Quang Tri and very familiar with the A Shau.

Years later Wagner talked about the flight. His opening comment was, "Bancroft overshot the zone and damn near killed the whole crew."

Wagner said that Bancroft came in "too hot and too high to stop at the zone. He overshot the LZ and ended up in a copse [grove] of bamboo trees near six inches in diameter. We couldn't set down for fear of impaling the aircraft on heavy bamboo stalks. The blades were taking an awful beating from hitting those big stalks, and worst of all, Bancroft, over the objections of me and Sexton, ordered the Recon team to jump out of the aircraft, which they did. God help them!"

Radish, one of the gunners, later said, "The helicopter was taking a real beating, twisting back and forth as the Recon men jumped from some 10-12 feet above ground." Radish said that expecting a crash, he sat down on the nylon seats the Recon team had just vacated, in order to buckle himself in. However, "for some reason I couldn't find the metal buckles on the end of the nylon straps." So, he said, "I tied myself onto the seat with the nylon straps then, the colonel took off and climbed to around twelve hundred feet in an attempt to join up with Nelson and Sellers in the lead 46."

Wags said, "When we got high, the real damage to our helicopter became apparent. The blades began to delaminate and Sexton came up to the cockpit, standing in the doorway of the tunnel behind the cockpit, bracing himself on the center console, expecting us to crash. I saw an 8-foot piece of blade fly off into the distance, and the helicopter began to shake uncontrollably."

Radish said he never ever experienced anything like it. He could hear pieces of the blades coming apart and whistling through the air over the sound of the engines and wind noise.

Bancroft, fearing the helicopter was going to come apart in the air, tried to enter an autorotation by reducing the power. However, he didn't control the RPM which zoomed to 107%, a very dangerous situation.

Wags expected the delaminating blades to deteriorate more rapidly, at the dangerously high rotor RPM, that would result in catastrophic failure and certain death at any moment. Seeing that Col. Bancroft was locked onto the controls, holding the collective down without monitoring the RPM, Wags took hold of the controls and tried to overcome the CO's grip, but, he couldn't. Seeing what was happening, Sexton added his hand to the collective. Now, two men, Wags and Sexton were trying to overcome Bancroft's weight and strength. It wasn't happening.

Radish recalled, "I heard Col. Bancroft screaming over the intercom system to our chase helicopter (Lt. Nelson and Maj. Sellers), 'We're gonna crash! We're gonna crash!' The whole crew heard him through the ICS, and it seemed that they would for sure go down. It was at that point when I heard the damndest thing, over the intercom, Sexton in one of the strangest things that happened was heard quietly saying, or singing into the ICS, 'What goes up, must come down.' Maj. Sellers and Lt. Nelson both could hear the commotion as Wags and the CO both were inadvertently squeezing the UHF while pulling and pushing against each other on the collective. Wags' efforts to pull up on the collective were ineffective against the powerful Bancroft. Major Sellers, however, recognized the extreme danger that was unfolding, and he knew that anything could happen at any moment. So, he squeezed the UHF trigger and yelled at Bancroft, 'Give the aircraft to Wags. Give the aircraft to Wags.' Bancroft, upon hearing Seller's voice, relaxed his grip on the collective and cyclic allowing Wags to take control.

Wags immediately raised the collective, thus reducing the rotor RPM back to 98-100% and set up a controlled landing that was half autorotation and half power, making a smooth landing onto one of the abandoned airstrips in the A Shau, thereby saving the aircraft and crew from certain disaster. Lt. Nelson and Maj. Sellers immediately landed their helo on the airstrip near Col. Bancroft's helicopter to pick them up, but their crew chief Hall said the crew on the downed helicopter was not hurrying, even though the NVA normally just waited for someone experiencing circumstances such as what was happening to kill them all. "Whether you saw them or not," said Hall, "in the A Shau Valley the NVA were always nearby."

Radish said that after the helicopter touched down on the air strip and the engines were shut down, he was having difficulty untying the knot he had tied around himself for a safety belt. Wagner had quickly unstrapped from his seat and was coming back through the cabin, stopping long enough to remove the firing pins from Radish's machine gun. Then, while running out the back of the helicopter with his helmet on, he hit his head on the upper portion of the helicopter above the rear ramp and was knocked flat on his back on the ramp. Radish said they all thought Wags had been hit by enemy fire the way he was slammed against the deck. LCpl. Coley had already removed the firing pin from his .50 cal. and was headed out along with Col. Bancroft. Radish said that he finally got the knot untied and began carrying items from his downed helicopter to Lt. Nelson's aircraft.

Hall said it seemed to be a long time before the pilots and crew began to move toward his helicopter. He learned that Cpl. Radish had been trying to get a large coffee maker from the downed helicopter, but to their dismay, it was secured to the bulkhead, and they couldn't get it loose. Hall said that he and Radish still laugh about the fact that they were in a disabled aircraft on the floor of the A Shau, one of the most dangerous places in Vietnam, maybe the whole world, delaying their getaway while trying to rescue a coffee maker.

The battered CH-46 was recovered after the blades were cut off. A CH-53 picked it up and took it back to Phu Bai where new blades were fitted onto the aircraft. Hours later it was back in service, and the coffee maker had made its way back to Phu Bai.

Years later, Wags, the best copilot in Vietnam, who saved the aircraft and the lives of those aboard, said this about the mission, "The Recon Marines never found the cache of weapons. The mission was a bust."

The A Shau had won that day, as it often did, and from that moment forward, LtCol Bancroft was known as "Blades" Bancroft. The talk that night in the Grotto was of the mission, which seemed funny at the time, what with all six blades destroyed in one landing that had not entailed any direct enemy action.

You had to give Col. Bancroft credit. He was not much of a helicopter pilot, yet he led from the front and never faded from his role as our beloved Commanding Officer, and never ran from his nickname, "Blades". His colorful commentary about the incident was told in the ready room. It was delightful.

Figure 93 LtCol Bancroft telling how he was able to destroy all six blades on a CH-46 without any interference from the enemy.

In keeping with Phase III of the Operation Keystone drawdown of Marine forces, HMH-361, one of only two CH-53 Squadrons located at MMAF, deployed back to the states on 03 January 1970. With the departure of HMH-361, HMH-463 would be the only heavy lifter remaining in-country. I had two friends who would soon come to Vietnam with 463, Douglas Raupp and Robert "Bob" Carlstrand.

44: A Bad Day

Marble Mountain Air Facility (MMAF) was on the Tiensha Peninsula, about 5 miles southeast of downtown Da Nang, separated from Da Nang by the Han River where Gary, Roy and I had checked into MAG-16 on 11 November 1969. It seemed to be the safest place on earth, belying its reputation as "Rocket City" from the earlier days of the war. Yet, on 4 January 1970, the VC/NVA managed to lob a few rockets onto the base. They harmed no one, but it was a reminder that even though Marine units were leaving Vietnam on a weekly, sometimes daily basis, under Operation Keystone, we were still in Vietnam. With this as a backdrop, the next move on the chess board by the VC/NVA was a blow struck at the 7th Marines, LZ Ross.

Figure 94 Soviet 122 millimeter night rocket attack into DaNang. Photographer unknown.

CARNAGE AT LZ ROSS:

On 6 January 1970 at 0130 during a heavy monsoon down-pour a local VC sapper battalion, identified as the 409th VC Battalion attacked LZ Ross.[142] Ross was a firebase that had been occupied by both the Marine Corps and Army on separate occasions and had been the target of vicious attacks over the years.

There were 560 Marines on Fire Support Base Ross at the time of the attack: Headquarters and Service Company and Companies A and B of the 1st Battalion, 7th Marines, Battery K, 4th Battalion, 13th Marines, elements of Battery G, 3d Battalion, 11th Marines, the 2d Platoon, 1st 8-inch Howitzer Battery, and a small detachments of support troops.[143]

The base was battered with more than two hundred 82mm mortar rounds, followed by a massive ground attack, with bugles and whistles blaring. Thirteen Marines were killed, 40 seriously wounded, and 23 were slightly wounded. Thirty-eight enemy soldiers were killed, five of whom made it inside the wire without being detected and tossed satchel charges and grenades into command bunkers. The Marines met them head-on, rolling out of their racks, grabbing their weapons, and fighting the enemy hand to hand. The assault was a throw-back to the earlier days of the war—the battles on the borders, from Con Thien to the A Shau Valley, and all the numerous unnamed ridges on which Marines and Army infantrymen had fought and died.

The ground assault was done by "sappers" who got inside the wire and hurled satchel charges into bunkers and machine gunning every direction. During the fighting inside the wire, some two hundred 82mm mortar rounds were flung into Ross,

---

[142] Cosmos, Graham A. and LtCol Terrence P. Murray, USMC, *U.S. Marines In Vietnam, Vietnamization And Redeployment, 1970-1971.* History and Museums Division Headquarters, U.S. Marine Corps Washington, D.C. U. S. Marine Corps, Washington, D.C., 1986, 48-50.

[143] A CO, 1st Bn, 7th Marines, 1st MarDiv Republic of Vietnam 1970****A Note from the Virtual Wall.

374 HAROLD G. WALKER

killing both Sappers and Marines[144] and providing insight into the suicidal warfare being conducted by the NVA. The battle raged on until 0330 hrs.

Not scheduled to fly that day, I was busy talking with Wags and Sgt. Patton on how the packing was going for the squadron's move to Marble. Following our discussions as I was walking over to the ready room, I was called over to the Ops desk.

"Got an add-on[145] today."

"What?" I asked.

"An add on"

"What's that?" I asked.

"A mission added onto the already written schedule, for an unexpected mission, usually an emergency situation. Seems all hell broke loose at LZ Ross last night. So you and Parnham are up."

First Lieutenant John Parnham and I were directed to go to Da Nang, pick up some newsmen, and take them to LZ Ross. That would be the only time I got to fly with what I would call a legend. John Parnham earned 3 DFCs and a handful of single mission air medals and was almost killed in a fighting hole with the Third Force Recon Marines in April 1969, along with Steve Bravard. John and Steve were on their way to becoming legends to us new guys.

Parnham and I flew single bird[146] down to Marble Mountain, picked up a group of news people with cameras and notebooks, and upon getting clearance from DASC[147] flew down the coast to

---

[144] Although suggested by the movies that this was a tactic, it only occurred when the archers failed to let their arrows fly into the rear of the enemy's attack columns, thereby avoiding their own forces. Braveheart was an example of what did not happen.

[145] An "add-on" was a mission that just popped up. It wasn't scheduled by our Operations team, it was at the request of a higher authority, cycled through the commanding officer. The crews were those who were available. Many were never logged in our log books. This was one of those. Contact with Parnham for this book revealed that he had no distinct recall of the flight.

[146] Single bird is jargon for one helicopter.

[147] Direct Air Support Center (DASC) controls and coordinates helicopters operating in support of Marine & Army forces on the ground in Vietnam. Helicopter missions were controlled by DASC. When initiating a mission, DASC

the Hoi An. We turned in toward the twin bridges, back south over Highway 1, then west on route 535 toward LZ Baldy, the home of the 7th Marines. We requested clearance from their

Figure 95 A 1970 bird's eye view of LZ Ross in 1970 following attack.

tower to go through Baldy's traffic control area on our way to LZ Ross further west on 535 into the badlands.

"LZ Ross, Chatterbox zero-niner"

"LZ Ross, go ahead Chatterbox"

"Ross, we got a group news people with us. You got room for us?"

"Sorry, we're in the middle of medevac activity."

"Well, this is a special mission from Wing. Check it out?"

"Roger, will do."

A few moments later... "Chatterbox zero-niner, you're cleared."

"Roger that Ross, niner out."

We were all familiar with LZ Ross; it had that bad look about it. It always smelled like trouble, and I didn't like to stay put in that zone for long. But there we were. John put us into the perimeter of the small firebase, situating our 46 near a medevac helo.

Upon shutting down the engines, we were told by the Marines in the compound that we could remain only for about 20

was who we contacted. When the mission was completed we notified DASC. DASC would also, when necessary, ask for volunteers to take an additional mission.

minutes. It was a difficult scene to take in: the rugged landscape, the smell of battle, smoldering bunkers, cordite hanging in the air, and the smell of fresh death. Seeing a new battle field was a rarity since 3d MarDiv left country. We 46 pilots were all involved in medevacs to those lonely squads in the middle of nowhere, when they were ambushed.

Death and carnage was always present. But a large scale full frontal assault by a VC sapper battalion was not something seen every day. Bodies of both the VC and our Marines were being recovered. The VC, I was told, normally do not leave bodies in the field. But they did there, in and around Ross, in the fields of fire. The Marines who fought off the assault, in hand to hand combat, were exhausted.

What I saw in the faces of those warriors was a toughness that can only come from having lived through a massed charge of sappers; it can't be disguised. Some of the Marines were standing with their M16s held muzzle down along their side with one hand, a cigarette in the other, their faces smeared with clinging sweat and smudges, their hair, not long, but not high and tight either as they spoke with news people and each other. Others sat in stark weariness, their heads held high. Damn I was proud of them.

I overheard them in a small group speaking to a reporter, commenting on the fight. "It happened real fast, and they were all over us," one said. Another said, "I prayed that my M16 wouldn't jam." I stood outside their group, silent, listening then walked slowly away. It was their story to tell and the job of the news people to relay their story of a night in hell to the folks back home.

I used what little time was left before we had to leave, to continue my walk around the area. It was well under control and 367 Cobras and 167 Hueys were roaming low in the area south of Ross where the assault had originated, along with a large force of Marines and ARVN in the bush trying to make contact and exact some revenge. The aura was a calm tenseness, with intermittent bursts of heavy machine gun fire echoing off the surrounding hills.

I overheard another Marine describing the battle. He said, "It was pitch black dark, with mortars falling all around and the rain was hard, and they unleashed hell upon us." I couldn't expect to hear a more accurate description of the battle.

The sappers had made their way through a field of concertina, tangle foot,[148] razor wire and claymore mines. It was considered to have been an impossible feat. I wondered again if the sapper Donnie and I had witnessed at Camp Eagle was one of the attackers. Some of the Marines on watch died without knowing what happened; they were caught from behind and had their throats slit. The warning to the camp came in the manner of explosives tossed into the radio bunker and command bunker. Bedlam ensued as the mortars began to fall like rain and the howling attack followed.

Many sappers were still lying where they fell. The bodies of the Marines had been collected and placed in body bags that laid in a row. There were Marines watching over their fallen brothers, staying with the body bags. As the loading began, the bloatflies searched for their feast. Small fires inside barrels created a smoky atmosphere adding a surreal appearance to the battleground; the smells of rice-paddy muck mixed together with the after-odor of cordite and burnt rubber seemed odd, but appropriate in that grim and desperate scene.

The reporters were doing their thing, interviewing and videotaping whatever the Marines allowed. I felt so damned useless. I could see the blonde hair of one of the lads killed as the body bag was being zipped closed, and I wondered who he was and where he was from and what his family was doing at this precise moment, a world away. I wondered if his mother knew. Sometimes, I was told, a mother has a sixth sense, a kind of extraordinary empathy with the dying child that allows her to somehow

[148] Tangle foot is single-strand barbed wire strung in a meshwork pattern at about ankle height. A barrier designed to make it difficult to cross the obstructed area by foot. Usually placed around defensive positions.

know when death captures her child. A deep sadness came over me, not something I had as yet experienced in Vietnam, but something I swore not to forget.

Seeing the aftermath of that stand by the Marines I felt I had not earned the right to be there. The term Marine Grunt became more to me than a nickname. They were exceptional human beings. The 14 who were killed were all young: PFCs, Cpls, and Sgts. My mind flashed again to my cousin, Sgt. Owen Ray Walker a squad leader in the American Division who in January 1967 was terribly wounded by a booby trap and PFC Jim Moody a friend of mine from home, a mortar man in the 3d MarDiv, killed in March of 67, near the DMZ, a posthumous winner of the Silver Star.

As a CH-46 pilot, all I could do was fly them into battle and be there to take them out as medevacs, or take their bodies out as a permanent routine. That's the best we could do as was exemplified by the Ugly Angels, the first H-34 squadron in Vietnam, HMM-362. Yet, at that moment, in that place, it seemed to be so little. The Grunt's ultimate goal was to kill the enemy. We 46 pilots' and aircrews' ultimate goal was to get the most dangerous weapon in the world, Marine Grunts, safely to their battle, to supply them and medevac them and to leave no one behind. My thoughts reaffirmed my personal commitment to each and every one of them. Rest in peace my brothers.

I didn't recognize any of the news people, but it was clear that this was going to be on the news back home. With the imminent pullout of Marines, this battle, I thought, signaled a huge problem. This battle at LZ Ross made me think that the enemy wasn't going to let us simply pack up and go home. Everyone knew we were pulling out, so why this assault? It was my belief that LZ Ross was an indicator of what might be a very large offensive in the making. We soon left the scene and headed home. It was another awakening for me.

FIRST AIR MEDAL

On that same day, 6 January 1970, upon returning from LZ Ross, I received an official letter from the Marine Corps in my packet of mail. The letter was dated 18 December 1969. I was receiving my first Strike/Flight Air Medal that represented 20 sorties, or mission credits.

The letter read as follows: "The Commanding General, 1st Marine Aircraft Wing, Fleet Marine Force, Pacific takes pleasure in presenting you the Air Medal (1st Strike Flight Award) in recognition of your meritorious service while performing combat missions assisting Republic of Vietnam Forces in countering guerilla operations in the Republic of Vietnam."

The words made you feel like you were doing something special. But having just walked through the fresh battlefield of LZ Ross, I had no such feeling except humility.

Figure 96 Don McGlothlin and A.C. Allen with Miss Noa at the Grotto

Yet, this was a beginning for me. I really felt that I had now accomplished my original goal—that was to be a combat helicopter pilot. Having been in the unit for almost two months and having received my first air medal, I began to feel as though I was making some headway. But the fresh memory of Ross placed a pall over any sense of celebration I might have had.

* * *

The Grotto was becoming more and more like home, even though we knew we would soon be moving to Marble Mountain.

Missy Noa, our hooch maid, was like a house mother, taking real good care of us: washing clothes, polishing boots, cleaning, and even getting Donnie and AC to eat some of her rice with Nuoc Mam, a traditional Vietnamese sauce, made of fermented fish, the smell of which was nauseating to the uninitiated. However, a worrisome occurrence of some letters from home having gone missing from hooches was troubling.

* * *

Note: On 11 January 1970 Major Robert M. Fitzgerald, our new Aviation Maintenance Officer (AMO) checked into the squadron.

Figure 97 Major Robert M. Fitzgerald

45: VIP

Mid-January 1970: The road was coming to an end in Phu Bai. The 3d MarDiv was long gone, and our missions were under the auspices of MAG-16, 1st MarDiv. The areas we would serve were primarily within Quang Nam (Da Nang) and Quang Tin (Chu Lai, LZ Baldy and FSB Ross) Provinces. We also flew a few Third Force Reconnaissance inserts, extracts into the A Shau Valley as Maj Lee, CO of 3d Force Reconnaissance, stubbornly held onto his command with support from the Army's XXIV Corps as his advocate. LtGen. Nickerson, III MAF CG (commanding general) who was Lee's main supporter, was poised to be relieved by LtGen. McKutchen in March 1970. There would be no more 3rd Force without Nickerson. A loss.

I generally considered the above areas to be everything south of the Hai Van Pass to Chu Lai and west to the border of Laos. The familiar names for pilots were: Hills 37, 55, 65, An Hoa, the Coal Mines, Thuong Duc, LZ Baldy, FSB Ross; ROK Marine Corps', Camp of the Blue Dragon and a series of manmade landmarks. Those included Liberty Bridge, Twin Bridges and the French Fort. There were also geological formations: the Que Son Mountains, Charley Ridge, Arizona Territory within which was an area called Dodge City (never mind that Dodge City was in Kansas, it was its reputation that was similar), Thuong Duc, the Tennis Courts, Happy Valley, Antennae Valley, Alligator Lakes, Go Noi Island and many lesser known areas.

There were all kinds of missions as I have already addressed. However, the VIP mission was something special. It meant flying chase on a Huey slick with no armament, normally flown by First Lieutenant Joe Hutton of HML-167, carrying LtGen. Nickerson throughout the Da Nang TAOR to meet and greet the troops.

On that occasion, I was flying copilot to Bill "Fuels" Nelson, who took the picture of me at the General's quarters, LZ 400. We were there in our 46 to rescue the general if the Huey went down, so we were prepared to be SAR (search and rescue) or a medevac, whichever was needed.

Figure 98 Landing at LZ 400

Figure 99 First Lieutenant Bill Nelson with helicopter in back-ground.

Figure 100 Author standing under non-deciduous pam tree at General's quarters, LZ 400..

Figure 101 Dining room in III MAF general's quarters.

On another of my VIP flights into and out of LZ 400 as copilot to First Lieutenant Bill Nelson, we escorted Major General Edwin B. Wheeler, Commanding General, 1ˢᵗ Marine Division, code-named Cactus Pete. I suppose he must have been from the southwest United States, maybe Arizona, where the Saguaro cacti grow to gigantic proportions. During our meandering trip through the Da Nang area following the general's Huey, the subject of being shot at was the topic of conversation between me and Nelson and our crew chief over the ICS. We had no sooner begun talking about it when the crew chief said, "There's tracers at our seven o'clock."[149]

"What?" responded Nelson.

"No shit sir, there are tracers arcing up at us."

"Are they at our 7 or the general's 7?

"Our 7."

Nelson responded, "What color are the tracers?"

[149] All calls about something outside the helicopter were called by the clock position of the location of the thing causing the disturbance. twelve o'clock was dead ahead. Six o'clock was directly behind the helicopter. With the visibility from the cockpit limited by armored seats, etc. the pilots were restricted to a near 10 and 2 o'clock range of vision. The crew chief and gunners were as always, our radar.

"Well, can't really tell, but I think they're red."

"Red huh? You sure they're not green?"

"Yep, they were red alright."

"We take any hits?"

"No sir, not that I can tell," said the crew chief. "There wasn't more than a coupla tracers."

"The tracer rounds are every fifth round," said Nelson, "so, we had a burst sent our way. Hell, that could have been anyone taking a shot at us, probably from an AK, or a PF cadre with an M-16...happens all the time."

"What's that about the color?" I responded.

"Flying over near the border with Laos," said Nelson, "you'd see green tracers coming at you. That meant the ammo was not our ammo. Red tracers coming at us means the ammo is probably stolen from us or was ARVN ammo."

"I've hardly seen red tracers, much less green tracers," I said. "Sounds like Disneyland when the park was closing."

"I'll let Joe (Hutton the Huey VIP pilot flying the general) know," said Nelson, "just write it down with the coordinates and what kind of fire it was, .30 Cal, .50 cal. B-40s, rocks, or arrows, and how many rounds we fired back at 'em, and you will put all of that in the AA report. Hutton'll do the same at 167. Our Operations folks will get the report, call it in to MAG-16, and someone in the bunker will place a pin on a huge map on the wall, and when there's no more room for pins, then, they'll clear the map and start over. That happens all day long...as common as flies.

"Each sighting of someone shooting at us is considered a strike and each strike equals two mission credits, Twenty mission credits is an air medal documenting our heroic stand for the peaceful residents of South Vietnam."

"We get an air medal just for that?"

"No, just one strike credit., sounds like you need a math degree to figure this stuff out."

"Ain't that something!" said the crew chief, with a chuckle. "Welcome to the Nam."

Flying along at a much lower altitude, depending on the VIP's rank, we remained behind them at near 2000 feet where possible. It was generally presumed the tracer rounds were probably from a Vietnamese farmer who was out for a stroll and performed his commitment to some VC cell to throw a round or two at a passing helicopter or his whole family would be killed that night or some night soon. "And if our patrols find him with that AK-47, he's done for too. So, damned if you do and damned if you don't," said Nelson with a straight face. "It's just how things are here."

I said, "kinda like that medevac (on 28 November) when we both got a few holes in the helicopters?"

"Yep," responded Nelson.

* * *

The next flight on our VIP mission would take me to the Da Nang Air Base on behalf of the General, to pick up something from air freight. I had flown a few missions since being in-country, but none that took me into the big air base. I had become acquainted with the manner and method of flying our low level routes around the big base and what frequencies to use; what to expect from the tower operators and how to stay out of the way of fast movers departing from and landing at Da Nang Air Force Base, but, as yet, I had never before landed on the base. So, I was anxious to see what the procedures were to do so.

Da Nang Air Base was state of the art. The big commercial jobs landed and took off throughout the day on their double runways (35 right and left) interspersed with VMFA-542 F-4B Phantoms loaded down with bombs and rumbling like a thousand Harleys.

On this flight, I had an opportunity to observe the entry and exit routes for helicopters. Staying low and hopping over the defensive perimeter under control of the tower operators was the ticket. We landed at the very large terminal/freight area, located on the east side of the runway. Upon contacting the tower operators, Nelson was directed to land on the taxiway nearest to the shipping area. We were to pick up some boxes of freight.

As we landed, I was able to visually record the area for future flights. The base was obviously Air Force, but there was a strong Marine presence, and it had the feel of being stateside. Also, I was told that the squadrons there had swimming pools, like were at the 101st at Phu Bai. They were also rumored to have a great O'Club, just like stateside, although I never had an opportunity to visit the Air Force base on a day off.

Scanning the area from the cockpit of the 46, I noticed at the southern-most portion of the freight area, a very large aircraft. Freight was stacked about on pallets, and a large loader, similar in appearance to forklifts found in all warehouses, but much larger, was carefully making its way up the ramp into the belly of the plane. The man driving the big loader was cautious, very cautious, moving slower than I was used to seeing freight loaded and unloaded into big planes. The freight being loaded had the appearance of long aluminum boxes, gleaming in the sun. From where I was observing there could have been as many as six of those strange boxes on a pallet. There were several more pallets of the same, stacked and strapped and protected by armed security personnel.

The sight captivated me. What was it? My curiosity unquenched, I asked Nelson, "What the hell is that they're loading?" He glanced up in the direction I was looking and without hesitation and, in a somber matter-of-fact-manner, he replied, "coffins," then turned his head away. He said no more, and I asked no more. Nuff said. A pall came over me. This was the ugly truth of it all, wasn't it? This is where it all ends; the fun, the drama, the excitement. Any one of us could have been in one of those boxes that day. What I experienced was a rare moment of silence and reflection, and a reaffirmation of reality, of where we were.

* * *

In general, I was beginning to get a little bit comfortable with flying into and out of Camp Reasoner, LZ 401, First Battalion Reconnaissance Headquarters, and doing inserts and extracts into and out of the Thuong Duc Corridor, the Que Sons and Charley Ridge. We were also still doing a few Third Force Recon inserts and extracts into the A Shau, when I supposed Maj. Lee couldn't get an Army chopper in which to ride. Third Force was documenting significant sightings of an ever-increasing flood of North Vietnamese crossing into Vietnam from Laos along the Ho Chi Minh Trail. The word infestation was being used a lot in reference to the numbers of NVA making their way into our area. I always felt that if we could get a giant comb and pull it through that triple canopy jungle out there, the teeth of the comb would be filled with NVA.

Third Force Recon, who carried the death head playing cards they left on the bodies of VC/NVA, had changed the rules of the game. They were an elite mix of snoop and poopers[150] and ambush squads who were themselves becoming the hunted with North Vietnamese bounties on their heads. We were hearing things about Third Force that didn't surprise me...that they were in heavy combat each time they jumped into the elephant grass of the A Shau. One team reported 26 kills with 10 probable kills of NVA infiltrators; one Marine was killed and fourteen wounded. I had heard they also collected ears. I never saw a severed ear, making me believe there was only talk of such things. But, If anyone knew whether there were severed ears or not, Pete would know. Pete was friends with First Lieutenant Hensley, a 3d Force staff officer. When I asked Pete, he said there were no severed ears being worn by Third Force. But, I thought, those Recon Marines are different. They are true warriors that scared

---

[150] Third Force Reconnaissance Company (snoop and poopers) was a "long-range reconnaissance asset that worked in the most dangerous areas of Northern I Corps. They gathered intelligence and verified questionable intelligence that was submitted directly to the Commanding General, III MAF.

the pants off of the NVA,[151] and they might just have a few appendages hidden away.

* * *

Everyone in the Grotto was busy during our getting ready to move, but not as busy as Eric. He was still working with Gene Mitchell and Roy Prigge, building those big green boxes that would be filled with everything that makes a squadron tick. My thoughts during this period began to turn to where we would live at Marble Mountain. I was unfamiliar with officer housing and who lived where. In that endeavor, Eric was our man of the hour.

Where did we want to live? This brought forth a full-fledged Grotto meeting. Would we be in a SEA Hut or Quonset Hut? There were a lot of differences. The Quonsets had air conditioning, but were meant for company and field grade officers, Capts./Majs./LtCols. So there probably would not be a Quonset for us. Yet we had confidence in Eric getting us into the right spot. We all wanted an ocean view, and to be close to the Officer's Club and the community toilets and showers.

Donnie wanted to be able to walk right out on the beach and body surf. I just wanted to be in the seawater. The salt was medicinal. It helped with the ever present jock rash caused by the heat and humidity.

Eric was the most practical of the bunch. He wanted something safe, and if it wasn't safe enough he'd put his carpentry skills to work. A.C. was content to pop the top of a Budweiser and let the thing work its way out, having full trust in Eric's decision.

Gary was certain that access to the club was the most crucial point, and I agreed with them both, but leaned toward Gary's

---

[151] Quang X. Pham, was a Vietnamese-American and a Marine aviator, whose father, Pham Van Hoa, was a LtCol in the ARVN Air Force, flying the A-1 Skyraider. In Pham's memoir, "A sense of Honor," he tells of his mother's comments to him regarding how the VC felt about the U.S. Marines fighting in Vietnam. "The VC were scared of the Marines." she said. "They [the Marines] were vicious." She added, "During the war, we never saw Marines in Saigon. They did all their fighting up north."

point. Ready access to the Officer's Mess (chow hall) and Club was the most important. Gary made a point that if we were real close to the Club, we could find our way back to the Grotto after "a few beers" without getting lost.

On 26 January, Maj. James M. Perryman Jr. checked into HMM-262 as the new Executive Officer, at which time Maj. Sellers, the acting Executive Officer, slid over to Operations, S-3. This was indicative of a strengthening of the squadron, bringing it into line with the rank structure of other squadrons in MAG-16.

The last couple weeks in January 1970 were devoted to packing up the squadron for the move which was now scheduled for, of all days, Valentine's Day. A highly touted one-day stand-down to move an entire squadron to MMAF would better 161's move by one day. Everything was a contest between 161 and 262. Like that 1000 hour deal between 161 and 262 at Quang Tri that got Wags in trouble.

46: Moving South

(Total Flight Hours: 441.6)

HMM-161, our sister squadron at Phu Bai and before that at Quang Tri, was the squadron with whom we felt the most camaraderie. Our squadrons had been through the thick and thin of that war together. With the departure of HMM-161 on 1-2 February, HMM-262 would be the last Marine helicopter squadron based north of the Hai Van Pass.

The convoy carrying HMM-161 squadron equipment was guarded by low flying gunships and heavily armed gun trucks as it made its way down Highway 1, up and over the Hai Van Pass, around Da Nang Bay, and through the streets of Da Nang proper to the Marble Mountain Air Facility by the sea.

Figure 102 "Rough Rider" Motor Transport Battalion

I took the above picture of the 7th Motor Transport Battalion's "Rough Rider" convoy, loaded with HMM-161 gear leaving Phu Bai. Two weeks later, on 14 February, HMM-262's convoy would make the same trip.

* * *

The Vietnamization (de-Americanization) of the war was ongoing and more and more often we would be assigned missions to support ARVN units. The efforts would be to protect Da Nang from mortar and rocket attacks. The Thuong Duc Corridor was the super highway from the Ho Chi Minh Trail through the Annamite Mountains to the coastal flats and lowlands south of Da Nang.

During that period of time in the early 1970s, the Vietnamization of the war was being implemented in coordination with the redeployment of the Marine Corps out of the country. Operation Keystone was the master plan. Following the Battle of Hue in January '68, the First Marine Division, at the direction of III MAF, was tasked to build a concentric physical barrier some 600 meters wide called the "Rocket Belt," 12,000 meters (7.45 miles) from the center of Da Nang in all directions. The dimension of the Belt was determined by the known range of North Vietnam's 122mm and 140mm Russian-made rockets. The Belt was patterned after the failed McNamara Line, intended to alert South Vietnam to attempted incursions by the North through the DMZ. The effort, constructed by Marine engineers, depended upon state-of-the-art listening devices, devices found to be susceptible to winds, rain, water buffalo, NVA incursions and false alarms. It failed miserably.

Therefore, in the finest tradition of Washington-think, they tried it again, encircling Da Nang. But who would have suspected the costly effort would once again fail when local farmers began crossing through the area to get to their rice paddies and the coastal lowland winds set off false alarm after false alarm. The benefit of the Belt, if it had worked, would have been to free up 5,000 Marines for offensive actions elsewhere. That didn't happen.

In January 1970, only a small portion of the belt was completed. Additional efforts to construct the barrier existed only on paper. The entire focus of the Marine Corps at that point in time was to protect Da Nang[152] and the Marine Corps as we redeployed through the airbase and deep water port. Alas, with technology not working as proposed, as per usual, the Belt had to be protected the old fashioned way, with boots, bombs and helicopters.

THE MISSION:

First Lieutenant Martin "Marty" Benson, in HMM-161, was one of us FNGs. He had endured the same naval flight training program with us at Pensacola and had gone through advanced helicopter training at New River, North Carolina, along with Donnie McGlothlin and A.C. Allen. The three of them had arrived in Phu Bai back in December. Originally slated to come to 262, Marty gave up his slot and went to HMM-161, so that the good friends, McGlothlin and Allen, could report into the same squadron. Marty, A.C. and McAmis played handball, and we all were as one unit, there in Phu Bai.

On 5 February '70, three days after 161 planted their flag at Marble Mountain, a section of CH-46s led by Captain Brian Duniec and his copilot, First Lieutenant Marty Benson, with their chase 46 piloted by First Lieutenant Barry Fitzhugh Lee, launched out of Marble Mountain. Their mission that day was to insert forty CIDGs from the Mobile Strike Force Command (Mike Force), twenty in each helicopter, into the Tennis Courts.[153]

Duniec and Lee would take turns leading their lone flight of two CH-46Ds (a section), not an uncommon occurrence decided between aircraft commanders. They would be inserting the Montagnards into an area known as the tennis courts, a rela-

---

[152] Cosmas, Graham A., Murray, Terrence P., U.S. Marines in Vietnam, Vietnamization and Redeployment, 1970-1971 (History and Museums Division Headquarters, U.S. Marine Corps Washington, D.C.), 31

[153] The "tennis courts" was a flat geologic area along the top of a high ridge that bordered the western edge of the Arizona Territory, north/northwest of An Hoa, overlooking Arizona Territory within the An Hoa basin.

tively flat area on top of a high bluff that was the western boundary of Arizona Territory, to conduct a bomb damage assessment (BDA). The mission was commonplace for Marine Recon, typically conducted by 1st Battalion Reconnaissance out of LZ 401 west of Da Nang. However, during that era of Vietnamization, the mission went to the CIDGs.

The bombing was probably an arc light by U.S. Air Force B-52s. Over the years, countless such missions dropping 500, 750, or 1000 pound bombs from the stratosphere pulverized the earth and disintegrated anything made of flesh and blood. There have been reports of finding NVA and VC body parts hanging in trees for miles surrounding the target. Once the CIDGs were on board the helicopters, and the Comprise gunships were in the air, they headed south ...into a nightmare.

Upon arriving in the vicinity of the insert area, Duniec's section cruised to a higher altitude, waiting for the Comprise gunships to do their jobs prepping the zone with 40mm. Once the prepping was accomplished, and there was no indication of enemy troops, the Huey's job was to cover the 46s during their landings. Both Duniec and Lee were designated section leads, so like most of us, they took turns leading the section. Lee had led the section during the morning's missions. Duniec set up for the first landing and began his approach into what was a one helicopter LZ. Without another word, Duniec began the approach.

"The approach was normal," said Duniec. "There was no obvious enemy activity." As he neared the desired point of landing, beginning the early stages of the flare, with airspeed and altitude slowed to touchdown speed just prior to the main mounts touching down, Duniec described a torrent of AK-47 fire "coming from directly in front of us causing the cockpit to burst into shards of bullet fragments and glass. I wasted no time," he said. "I pulled all the power available to get out of there realizing that Marty had been hit several times."

"The No. 2 (right) engine was knocked out immediately, along with the SAS (stability augmentation system) and the No. 1 hydraulic system, with the No. 2 hydraulic system failing. The

THE GROTTO – BOOK ONE | 395

aircraft was, quite frankly, barely flying and blood was splashed all over the cockpit from the hits Marty took. The .50 cal. gunners had spontaneously opened up, sweeping their fields of fire with .50-cal rounds and filling the air with the acrid smell of cordite. But, we had already taken the hits into the cockpit, and I didn't see any gunships anywhere."[154]

Duniec exhibited exceptional flying skills, keeping the 46 in the air. Although he had received a shower of shrapnel into his right upper arm and face, he maintained control of the aircraft. Intuitively, he knew he had not been hit by any of the .30-cal rounds.

"We cleared the trees," he said, speaking slowly, recalling each moment. "But, with the loss of one engine, I couldn't climb." Utilizing what power was available to him, he kept the old Phrog in the air. He recognized his only opportunity to get away from the danger was to dive off the high ridge of the tennis courts, head-first into the Arizona Territory, picking up airspeed in the descent.

Barry, his chase pilot said, "I saw that Brian was in big trouble. I saw blue/gray puffs of smoke from the tree line, in front of and behind him, and I saw the belching of smoke from his .50 cal. gunners. But I had no radio contact with him."

The gunships were working out on the tree lines where Duniec had been ambushed as Lee concentrated on Duniec, his wingman. Lee called Comprise and passed them the coordinates of the zone, telling them to call in all the artillery they could get into that zone and to follow him to wherever Brian ended up.

Duniec said, "I had to use the airspeed I got from diving off that ridge, trading airspeed for altitude. Marty was unconscious and bleeding heavily. I didn't know how he was doing." He, however, managed to maintain flight at tree level over the landscape

---

[154] This situation Brian found himself in, taking fire directly into the cockpit, highlights what we 46 drivers feared most, no way to protect ourselves from the dedicated enemy who know that to kill the helicopter, all they have to do is kill the pilots.

of ancient rice paddies for a short time, before realizing he was steadily losing altitude.

Lee, flying above Duniec, could see the rotor RPM deteriorating. The normal blur of blades was slowly becoming individualized. With no communication, Lee dove downward, pushing his 46 to where Duniec was limping along still airborne and noted that Duniec appeared to be having some trouble controlling the aircraft. So, Lee flew at a safe distance along the starboard side of Duniec's helicopter, so that he could be seen by Duniec's crew chief who was visible in the upper portion of the crew door that was open. Lee wanted Duniec to know that he wasn't alone, that he, Lee, was right there with him.

Duniec realized he couldn't go much further before losing the surviving engine and made the decision to land the helicopter in what he called "a soft crash landing" into a thousand year-old rice paddy. Duniec's aeronautical skills were tested under the most trying of circumstances: his copilot, Benson, shot up; the helicopter shot up (25 bullet holes were later counted in his helicopter, most of which entered into the cockpit); and himself, slightly wounded. Duniec's skills saved the lives of his crew, the helicopter and the twenty ARVN soldiers who were aboard.

Once he set down in the paddy, the gunships arrived. Their job was to keep any curious VC/NVA troops at bay. The ARVNs in the rear of Duniec's 46 scrambled out of the helicopter and formed a defensive perimeter, expecting an attack at any moment. The Arizona Territory was notorious and known to be saturated with enemy troops.

Duniec ran, carrying Marty, to Lee's 46. Lee, upon receiving word from the crew chief that Duniec, Marty, and the crew from Duniec's 46 were on board, whisked them away at full throttle to the NSA hospital complex next to Marble Mountain at full throttle, reaching speeds of near 160 kts.

Marine A-4s from Chu Lai, OV-10s from VMO 2 plus artillery comprised of 155-mm Howitzers and 175 mm self-propelled guns at An Hoa and Hill 65 pulverized the vicinity of the LZ. All other air activity in the area was immediately stopped. The CH-53s operating in the general vicinity of the zone where Duniec and Benson were ambushed were forced to leave the area because it had become too risky for them.

Upon arrival at NSA, who were expecting them, Duniec, covered in Benson's blood and Lee, leaving his idling 46 in the hands of his copilot, followed alongside Marty's stretcher as he was being rushed directly into the operating room.

The best trauma surgeons in the world immediately began working on Marty, who had taken three point-blank hits from an AK-47. Fifty pints of blood were required during the procedure and his right kidney, heavily damaged by the bullets, had to be removed. Only when Marty was safely off the operating table and in bed did Duniec and Lee feel they could return to base at Marble Mountain.

Later that evening there was a USO show at the Marble Mountain O'Club. The place was full of pilots, probably at least a

Figure 103 Photos courtesy of Brian Duniec.
"These pictures are of the repairs being made on the
CH-46 flown that day, 12 Feb 1970.

couple of hundred, maybe 300. Duniec had been a standout tackle in Big 10 football and was the starting right tackle on the 1964 University of Illinois (Illini) Rose Bowl team and a standout on the Marine Corps football team and the Navy's Goshawks, when Lt. Roger Staubach, destined to be in the NFL Hall of Fame, was quarterback. Among Duniec's Illini teammates were Dick Butkus and Jim Grabowski, both of whom were destined to become NFL greats. But Brian wasn't telling stories about football that night. His thoughts were of that day—of what happened, what didn't happen and what might have happened had he been sitting in that zone with the ramp down, the most vulnerable of positions, before the rattle of the AK-47s began. Brian said, "We would have been shot to pieces had we been on the ground with the ramp down. We'd never have gotten out of there."

Brian's wounds were superficial to him. He had bled more in the first quarter of football games than he did that day and like everyone else he was a hard drinker. His thoughts were on Marty's precarious grip on life. The news about what happened to Marty had spread through the squadrons like those incidents always did. Duniec and Lee were peppered with questions from concerned pilots. "What happened?" "Is Marty going to be okay?"

Upon hearing some CH-53 pilots bragging about some hot zone they had flown into that day, within proximity, to where Brian and Marty were ambushed, he took immediate offense at their giddiness and seeming lack of respect for what had happened to Marty. He got mad and before he knew it, he had decked two or three of the 53 pilots before he could be hustled out of the O'Club by friends, not an unusual occurrence in the club at Marble Mountain, or any other club in Vietnam[155]. The tension in

---

[155] Again, it must be stated that the CH-53 pilots were under unusual restrictions by the Marine Corps due to the cost and limited number of those behemoths and for them to be near a zone taking fire was an oddity. Those pilots also wanted to be in action, in the zone, and soon that is where they would be. On that occasion, they apparently did get close to that point.

those places was always at a fever pitch and the slightest thing could start a brawl.

Captain Harrison Brand, another pilot from HMM-161 and close friend of both Marty and Brian, went to the hospital early the following morning. Harrison said that Marty was lying in his hospital bed, not saying anything, just staring into nothingness, waiting to be transferred by a 46 to the USS Repose hospital ship.

According to Harrison, he said to Benson in hopes of raising his spirits, "You're looking good, Marine," he said, with as much cheerfulness he could muster. In response, Marty replied, "Really...really...you're not just saying that are you?" Harrison said it tore his heart out to see Marty like he was, knowing there was only slim hope that he would recover on the hospital ship. Others who were there said that Marty managed a weak smile and a thumbs-up as the hospital staff carried him aboard the 46. Having learned of this, we HMM-262 pilots in Phu Bai who knew Marty felt a little better about his chances.

"They said he was smiling, giving a thumbs up...he'll be okay...won't he?"

On 26 February, 21 days following the ambush, Marty Benson died when taken off dialysis. "Peritonitis, we were told," said Brian in a solemn tone 48 years later, as he sat in the well-appointed family room of his fashionable home, overlooking the bucolic Fox River. For Brian, it was as if the incident were yesterday.

Marty's death was a blunt reminder to all of us 46 drivers of just how thin a line there was between life and death each time we went up. All Marine CH-46 pilots drank a toast to our fallen comrade, something we would do on many occasions that year...in the Nam.

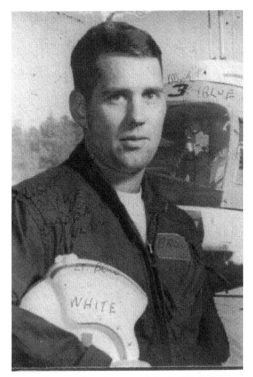

Figure 104 First Lieutenant Martin "Marty" Benson when in the training command.

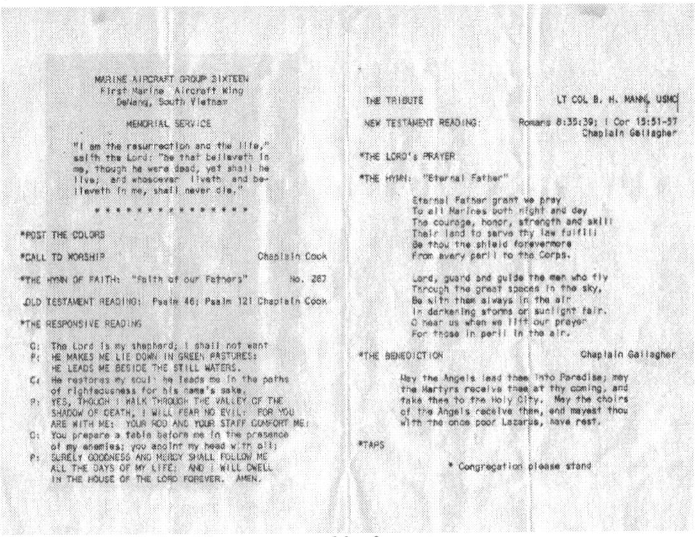

MARINE AIRCRAFT GROUP SIXTEEN
First Marine Aircraft Wing
DeNang, South Vietnam

MEMORIAL SERVICE

"I am the resurrection and the life," saith the Lord: "he that believeth in me, though he were dead, yet shall he live; and whosoever liveth and believeth in me, shall never die."

* * * * * * * * * * * * * * * * *

*POST THE COLORS

*CALL TO WORSHIP — Chaplain Cook

*THE HYMN OF FAITH: "Faith of our Fathers" — No. 287

OLD TESTAMENT READING: Psalm 46; Psalm 121 Chaplain Cook

*THE RESPONSIVE READING

C: The Lord is my shepherd; I shall not want
P: HE MAKES ME LIE DOWN IN GREEN PASTURES:
HE LEADS ME BESIDE THE STILL WATERS.
C: He restores my soul: he leads me in the paths
of righteousness for his name's sake.
P: YES, THOUGH I WALK THROUGH THE VALLEY OF THE
SHADOW OF DEATH, I WILL FEAR NO EVIL: FOR YOU
ARE WITH ME: YOUR ROD AND YOUR STAFF COMFORT ME;
C: You prepare a table before me in the presence
of my enemies; you anoint my head with oil;
P: SURELY GOODNESS AND MERCY SHALL FOLLOW ME
ALL THE DAYS OF MY LIFE: AND I WILL DWELL
IN THE HOUSE OF THE LORD FOREVER. AMEN.

THE TRIBUTE — LT COL B. H. MANN, USMC

NEW TESTAMENT READING: Romans 8:35:39; I Cor 15:51-57
Chaplain Gallagher

*THE LORD's PRAYER

*THE HYMN: "Eternal Father"

Eternal Father grant we pray
To all Marines both night and day
The courage, honor, strength and skill
Their land to serve thy law fulfill
Be thou the shield forevermore
From every peril to the Corps.

Lord, guard and guide the men who fly
Through the great spaces in the sky,
Be with them always in the air
In darkening storms or sunlight fair.
O hear us when we lift our prayer
For those in peril in the air.

*THE BENEDICTION — Chaplain Gallagher

May the Angels lead thee into Paradise; may the Martyrs receive thee at thy coming, and take thee to the Holy City. May the choirs of the Angels receive thee, and mayest thou with the once poor Lazarus, have rest.

*TAPS

* Congregation please stand

Figure 105 Memorial Service pamphlet for Lt. Benson

Figure 106 Memorial Service pamphlet for Lt. Benson

47: Goodbye Phu Bai

The continuing redeployment of aviation assets: On 10 February 1970, MAG-11, Da Nang Air Base: VMFA-542 (F-4s) and VMA 223 (A-4s) redeployed back to MCAS El Toro, Orange County, CA. and MAG-12 and VMA-211 (A-4s) re-deployed from Chu Lai to Iwakuni, Japan.

MAG-16 helicopter activity continued unabated:[156]

The movement from Phu Bai was happening. It was no longer conjecture. Phu Bai began to feel vacant as we were the last squadron on the base. The "Redeployment" was taking its toll. How long would it be before we left Vietnam entirely like F-4s and A-4s identified above ? No one knew. The story of Phu Bai began in March 1965, when Major General Lewis W. Walt was the Commanding General, III MAF in I Corps. He was in charge of all American military operations in I Corps including the U.S. Army, and thus exercised the same authority as an Army Field Force Commander. Phu Bai was the first area the Ninth Marine Brigade moved to, following their landings on 8 March 1965 at Red Beach, on the west side of Da Nang Bay.

In June 1965 the 9th Marines moved out of Da Nang to Phu Bai. The Army's 509th Radio Research Group was already there and welcomed the Marines presence. Normally, the Marines would be there first, but not in Vietnam. The U.S. Army had been there in various forms beginning in the 1950s on the heels of the Korean Police Action. Special Forces Green Berets followed in 1961, giving them a foot-hold long before the Marines were brought into the fray.

The Marines immediately began building with sandbags and assumed the job of defending Phu Bai, which was not much more than a spot on the map. The Marine combat base at Phu Bai was originally named Camp Hochmuth.[157] The ARVNs, of course,

[156] http://www.vietnam.ttu.edu//reports/images.php?
[157] Camp Hochmuth was the little known name of the Marine camp in Phu Bai. It was named in honor of Bruno Hochmuth, Commanding General of the Third Marine Division, who was killed in a helicopter explosion north of

were there and by all accounts not worth much. Discipline was handed out by the ARVN officers to their undisciplined soldiers via summary execution; it was a rough place to call home.

With the imminent departure of HMM-262, the U.S. Army would once again be the only American service holding ground there. The Grottoites were busy with the move and flying missions. In our last few weeks at Phu Bai, Missy Noa, our hooch maid, was replaced by another Vietnamese woman, another Missy. We got nothing but rumor about why Missy Noa wasn't returning. Lieutenant Olson, our Civilian Affairs Officer, heard a rumor that Noa had been caught trying to smuggle letters to Marines from their families back home out of the gate. She was allegedly caught through routine searches of Vietnamese employees, but who knows?

The hooch maids were hired based upon "stringent background checks" by the Republic of Vietnam National Police in coordination with Marine authorities. The fear was that she was responding to threats by the local VC leadership to bring them something. The VC operatives in the villages of Vietnam were known to extort military information from Vietnamese employees through threats and intimidation. She may have had no choice. She may have been told that her family would all be killed if she refused to work with the VC. Or, she might simply have been a hardcore VC operative with most of her family hiding in the mountains.

We couldn't believe she was grabbing the letters for any reason other than for VC intelligence operatives. We were all cautioned through our S-2 Intelligence section to secure any letters from home to ensure our families were not subjected to or used in any propaganda by the North Vietnamese. Missy Noa certainly couldn't decipher the letters—no more than we could read Vietnamese writing—and none of us in the Grotto had been missing any letters. I assumed we all kept a few personal letters and

Hue in June or July 1968. The base was used by Marines until early 1969. https://www.revolvy.com/topic/Bruno%20Hochmuth (09/04/2017).

destroyed the remainder. I kept one or two from Kathy, but for the most part I put them into a burn barrel. I never knew what or whose letters were being taken by Missy Noa. It could have been from anyone as the hooch maids seemed to be a close knit group. Whatever was going on, she was taken by the Vietnam National Police. We never heard any more about her.

The O'Club remained the gathering place. John Arnold remained the manager, and his friend Lowell "Ole" Olsen was almost an assistant manager.

Figure 107 The author at the O'Club bar with Lt. John Arnold tending bar. Note the mud on author's boots.

John Arnold was behind the bar, and I had finished my flying for the day and was on the stool. John used to say, back when the club had been raucous, "Every day was like Saturday and each Saturday was like New Years Eve." Now, it was as if it was our very own man-cave. Once we leave for Marble Mountain this luxury will definitely be missed[158].

---

[158] Years later, the NVA made a direct hit on the club with a rocket or mortar, destroying the best Marine bar north of the Hai Van pass—a pity to this day.

On 11 February, things were percolating along. It was two days before the big move, although many things had already been moved. HMM-161 required two days of stand-down from flying missions to move. In the spirit of competitiveness, we were going to do it with only one day of stand-down. In those last few days before our official date to move to Marble, I was involved in packing up and making sure things were not lost. Eric, always the organizer, was the one we counted on to get our personal gear to the new hooch in Marble. Yet, missions were still being flown at a break-neck pace. We had been flying missions down south in the Da Nang Area since I arrived in early November. So, we were familiar with the area where we would be living. The death of Cpl. Thomas Rogers on 17 November 1969 in an emergency medevac with Lieutenant Don Esmond was the squadron's first combat death since becoming a MAG-16 component and since that day, there had been no serious combat losses[159]. But that was about to change.

Don McGlothlin had been scheduled to fly a night medevac at Da Nang on 11 February with Mike Ragin, a veteran of combat in Provisional MAG 39, and the eventual recipient of two Distinguished Flying Crosses.

Donnie was due back in Phu Bai the morning of 12 February 1970, following a night medevac at Marble Mountain. But he didn't return as expected which was normally around 0800. It was a normal day for missions. There were several helos out that day, all in the Da Nang area. Around the noon hour, I grabbed some chow and returned to the Grotto, our hooch. I was glad to see that Donnie was back and sitting in the common area. He was reading or writing a letter or something. He didn't look happy. He looked worn out, tired, and his mind seemed to be elsewhere. Maybe it was what he was reading, or he was thinking about his sons and what they might have been doing that day.

---

[159] Cpl. Rogers was KIA on that flight and the gunners and aircraft commander were wounded. They were picked up by Lt. Babcock and rushed to medical facilities in Da Nang.

406 | Harold G. Walker

"What's up Donnie?" I asked in passing. But he didn't immediately respond. "You okay?" I asked.

"Oh... yeah," he haltingly responded, in a measured tone. Turning away, he stared for a few moments at something that wasn't there, then said, "Hal, you ever see anyone just blow up?"

"Do What?" I asked. We had been in Vietnam long enough to have seen a lot of things. But, seeing someone blow up wasn't one of them.

"You know, someone walking along and BOOM they just f**kin' blow up!"

"No. Not recently," I said, adding a bit of skepticism, thinking he was just kidding around.

"Well," he said, "I did... this morning."

I saw the look on his face and that he wasn't kidding around. I sat down in one of the worn-out, hand me down chairs in the common area and said, "What happened out there?" Donnie explained that their night medevac had gone okay, a typical night with a few emergency extracts for Marines who were almost dead...but, they all made it to the hospital alive, therefore, no problems. But there was a sick Marine they couldn't go after in the night because it wasn't deemed an emergency. As I said, to be medevaced at night, you had to be at death's door. Donnie began, "This morning, when the next shift of medevac crews arrived, Ragin asked the arriving crew if it was okay with them, he'd like to pick up that sick Marine we couldn't get to during the night and get him to the hospital on our way back to Phu Bai. They were okay with that and a call was made to Luminous Base to get permission to keep the corpsman on board for one more pick-up."

Donnie continued, "We flew to the coordinates where the Marine was to be picked up (a position out in the bush). I had a good view from the copilot's seat. I could see the Marines carrying him in a poncho liner. There were 4 Marines, one on each corner of the liner. He looked real sick. The Marines were struggling with the poncho, coming toward us through the brush. It really was an emergency, and it made me sick that we couldn't have come for him in the night. I watched as they approached us and all of a sudden, BOOM! A tremendous blast occurred. A dust cloud so thick you couldn't see and the concussion from the blast rocked our helicopter. "Hell," he said, "I thought we were going to be turned over by the blast."

"Ragin [the Hac and a veteran combat pilot from P MAG-39 who knew what it was like to be mortared in the zone] just pulled power, a reflex action, and sprang from the zone, thinking we were being mortared. We cleared the zone while the ramp was still down. It's a wonder our crew wasn't slung out the back. But, they held on. I immediately raised the ramp as we circled. We heard a banging against the side of the helicopter and the helo was shaking badly. We thought at first we must have received structural damage, maybe an RPG or B-40 rocket had hit us. Our chase 46 looked us over and advised that the noise was caused by the flopping around of open access panel doors on the port side of our helo, including a large access door that when opened was a platform to stand on for inspections of the aft tail rotor, etc. on my side of the helicopter.

"Once we were satisfied that we were not being mortared, Ragin brought the helo around and landed back in the same spot...which was at that point believed safe from booby traps because that blast would have set off any other booby trap in the zone. It was then, as the dust cleared, that I saw the death and destruction caused by the blast. Marines who had rushed up to help were all over the place. Our corpsman and crew chief, Cpl. T. Dolan, jumped out to help carry in the dead and wounded and reset the popped panels.

"We now had two Marines dead and more wounded. One of the Marines was trying to pick up the original med-evacuee still wrapped in the tattered and torn poncho liner....I watched as he fumbled with the bloody torso of the Marine we had come to help, trying to find a way to pick-up what remained of him. Finally, he resorted to picking up the dead Marine's upper torso by the hair of the dead Marine's head. Damndest and hardest thing I've ever saw."

Donnie stopped in mid-sentence. He had said all he wanted to say. I asked if there was anything I could get for him. He declined, saying "Thanks, but I gotta get some sleep."

On my way back to the paraloft, I saw a group of mechanics gathered around a 46 parked in a revetment near the hangar with water hoses leading to it. Curious, I wandered over to see it. It was the 46 Donnie and Ragin had flown. I saw Cpl. Dolan busy cleaning his helicopter. He was using a water hose to wash the blood and gore off of the cargo deck. The water ran blood red down the ramp, not an uncommon sight at the conclusion of a medevac. However, other somber Marines were carefully picking and scraping the port (left) side of the helicopter (Donnie's side), the side that took the brunt of the blast. The material being scraped from the skin of the helo was body parts—specks and pieces of brains, sinew and blood. The flesh looked like browned hamburger meat beginning to draw flies, a sickening sight. Those small pieces were living, breathing Marines that morning. But now...it was hard to think about.

I continued to the paraloft, picked up some mail and made my way to the ready room. There was a Recon mission being run by First Lieutenant Dean Davis with his chase bird commanded by First Lieutenant Ridgeway that hadn't shown up yet, and a Baldy Medevac being run by first lieutenant Chuck Fleischer that reportedly had run into trouble.

Second tragic mission that day:

That same morning, First Lieutenant Dean Davis was the designated flight leader for a section of 46s scheduled for a 0700 takeoff. He was assigned aircraft No. ET-08. He briefed his copilot, First Lieutenant Sullivan, and the chase bird HAC, 1stLt Larry Ridgeway and his copilot, Bob Weber. They would be assigned aircraft No. ET-12.

Thirty two CIDGs, sixteen on each aircraft, were headed for that same area, where Hell always seemed to be breaking loose. It was the off ramp to Da Nang from the time-worn corridor called the Ho Chi Minh Trail. NVA troops by the thousands and tons of supplies were in a never ending slog from North Vietnam to the Da Nang area 24 hours a day, seemingly undeterred by constant bombing. They eventually ended up at one time or another in the Que Sons, Tennis Courts or Charlie Ridge where double and triple canopied jungle flowed down the slopes of the high ground into the lowlands right up to and thru Da Nang's Rocket Belt .

Lieutenant Marty Benson, gravely wounded the previous week on the Tennis Courts while attempting to insert CIDGs, was barely clinging to life on the *Repose* hospital ship. Mike Ragin and Donnie McGlothlin were almost blown away that very morning by a booby trap. I began to recognize what we could expect as the winter months turned to spring. The Marine brass and all the military intelligence agencies expected the enemy to build up for a big push into Da Nang, like the 1968 Tet offensive on Hue. The absolute sense of security Marble Mountain exuded would be dispelled as the Marine pullout continues to its inevitable conclusion.

I found some time and jotted down a few lines to send to Kathy, mainly benign information. I never mentioned anything that would distress her. I just missed her. I began to wonder about R&R in the letter, suggesting Hawaii. I was writing that I didn't want to go on R&R until I was more than halfway through my tour when I heard someone say, "A helicopter is missing."

"Who...where?" I spoke aloud, more from reflex, than reasoned thought. I folded the letter, stuffed it into the large leg pocket of my cammys.

"It was either Davis or Ridgeway," came a response.

Being in Phu Bai was great; we weren't bothered by stateside garrison policies or brass who wanted us to cut our hair shorter or shine our flight boots. But the disadvantage was not getting timely and relevant information about our flights from down south.

Questions abounded. Which one was it? The word was that the crew chiefs were Cpl. Seaworth on Davis' helo and Cpl. Perrett on Ridgeway's helo. The .50 cal. gunners were LCpl. Massey and Cpl. Parker on Davis' helicopter, and Cpl. Bunting was one of the .50 cal. gunners on Ridgeway's helicopter. Maintenance Marines were on edge. The air was tense and the maintenance cassette tape player that was always on, was off.

I departed the paraloft and headed to the Grotto. On the way, I stopped briefly at the maintenance desk– nothing new. I spoke with A.C. and Eric about the missing bird. They also knew nothing. I said "Let's go to the O'Club." It was near 2000 hrs.

Walking into the club we found John Arnold, who was behind the bar with a clipboard of documents, talking to one of the Vietnamese bar girls. We learned that Dean Davis' helicopter, ET-08, had just returned. The good news was that no one from our squadron was killed. But ET-12 would not be returning, nor would Perrett, Bunting, or Ridgeway's copilot, First Lieutenant H.R. Weber, who had recently returned to flight duty after having been wounded by a Claymore mine in an LZ. They were all subsequently medevaced out to the USS *Repose* hospital ship, by a U.S. Army Dustoff helicopter.

The flight had begun with both Davis and Ridgeway's helicopters filled with 16 CIDGs each supported by two Comprise gunships. The LZ was on one of the mountainous ridges northwest of Thuong Duc in that never-never-land.

An Aussie, whose heavy accent would become very familiar to us during the coming year, was in the LZ directing traffic coming into the zone. There was just enough room to land one CH-46 at a time with strong and variable gusting winds complicating the task. First in was Davis, the flight leader.

According to Cpl. Perrett, Ridgeway's crew chief, who had an open view of Davis' approach from his plane captain seat, "He [Davis] seemed fast into and out of the zone. I believe he must have overshot the zone and waved off, or it was one of the fastest deplanings I had ever seen. So I'm not sure if he unloaded his Vietnamese or not. But, in any case, it was our turn."

Cpl. Perrett, years later, told the tale: "The zone was actually a knoll on top of a plateau that was an almost-mountain. The best approach was reportedly from west to east into the prevailing winds at the time. I could see the grass whipping around as he

[Lieutenant Davis] started to flare. He seemed to come to a hover out of the flare, but had already overshot the zone and was hovering over the eastern edge of the slope, a long steep drop off the hill, kinda like a cliff but with some slope to it. Davis couldn't seem to get a steady hover. Something, maybe unreported winds from the west was causing the problem as there was no smoke in the zone with which to made a good determination on wind direction and speed. Davis appeared to hover over the edge of the LZ, over the slope for a few seconds...then waved off. His second approach was successful and his team deplaned.

Next in was Cpl. Perrett in Ridgeway's 46. Perrett recalled that he felt they were approaching the zone too fast and too high. "I remember keying the mic and saying to Lt Ridgeway, 'Sir...we're coming in too high'.....but he didn't respond."

"Ridgeway at the bottom of the approach flared. Yet, it didn't feel like we were slowing down enough. We were fast, but it may have been caused by gusting winds coming up and over the LZ that pushed us forward–an unexpected tailwind—like what happened to Davis. " The result was that at near 25 feet above the LZ, when the forward airspeed should be at zero, they were being pushed forward by a tailwind, overshooting the zone. Perrett, at his post, hanging out of the top half of the crew door, watched as the LZ passed beneath them.

Ridgeway increased the flare angle while pulling in power, successfully slowing their forward momentum but not stopping it. The helo settled into a wobbling hover over the approximately 45 degree downward slope of the mountainous zone. A drop-off of several hundred feet lay below the 46.

"I told him [Lt. Ridgeway] 'Sir...wave off...go around!'"

"He responded, 'Shut the f**k up and just...talk me in.' I pushed the troops out of the way and stuck my head out of a portside port-hole window and saw that 5-10 feet of the aft blade path was only about 10-15 feet above solid granite, red clay and elephant grass.

"Up...up..." advised Perrett. "We have to come up!" was Cpl. Perrett's urgent response to what he saw.

Perrett said he was guiding Lieutenant Ridgeway through a string of directions, "Back...left...left...back...up, up, up." a clear example of intimate communication between the crew chief and pilot in such circumstances. "Talk me in," or "Talk to me," was the key phrase uttered by the pilot. "In the attempt to recover the landing, the left main mount touched upon a boulder covered with red clay as the right main mount was hanging out over the drop-off. It was a one-wheel balancing act on a wobbly insecure platform."

Having momentarily found a point where the ramp could breach the void to land, Perrett called out to Ridgeway, "hold it there ... hold it there!" The ramp rested upon the slope when it was halfway lowered, and I began kicking the CIDGs off."

"I had to kneel down to see we were within only a few feet away from the blades striking the surface of the LZ as the helicopter wobbled back and forth in the wind."

As the precarious nature of the situation deteriorated, Perrett was able to get a few of the CIDGs off into the LZ before the helicopter dropped five to ten feet off of the one wheel resting spot. The blades had begun thrashing into the elephant grass, filling the air with debris, at which time Perrett called for Ridgeway to, "Take it up, take it up, forward, forward, take it up."

"Get em off, Goddamn it...get em off," responded Ridgeway.

The helicopter once again gained a footing lower than the last footing with the same left main mount, placing the blades to within five feet of the hill. Perrett once again began pushing the CIDGs off the right side of the ramp into the zone. He then saw CIDGs in the elephant grass. They had dropped their weapons and were crawling around beneath the helicopter. Upon seeing what was happening, Perrett once again called for Ridgeway to, "Wave off, Goddamn it...wave off."

There was no reply from Ridgeway, as Perrett struggled with the winds and the situation they were experiencing.

At about that same moment, Perrett noticed motion over his right shoulder and turned to see what was happening. He saw a CIDG crawling back into the helicopter through the starboard port-hole window. He then knew why there were so many of them still on the helicopter. They had dropped their weapons outside and were coming back into the helicopter over the starboard port stub wing and entering the helicopter through the large window, none of which had Plexiglass in them. Perrett said he reached back and smacked them with his intercom cord, while simultaneously pushing three more CIDGs toward the ramp.

A strong gust of wind again rocked the helicopter at that precise moment and the port main mount once again dropped from the precarious perch upon which it had been sitting. There were three very distinct metallic thuds as each of the three blades impacted the granite crown of the zone and disintegrated.

The impact slammed Perrett to the floor. The torque from the forward blades no longer offset the aft blades. The helicopter, being seated against the slope of the zone, began to twist, going inverted. The starboard engine flew from its mounts, flying to pieces as it fell onto two or three Vietnamese within arm's reach of Perrett. "They couldn't have survived" he said. The front of the helicopter pitched down, at which time the tail section rose some forty feet into the air from the slope, breaking the helicopter in-half near station 410. The gas tanks in the stub wings burst open spewing fuel all over the people in the cabin and on the slope. Fire was the horror he expected.

LCpl. Bob Bunting, the port gunner, spoke of it years later. "There was an awful noise and the helicopter just began to disintegrate. We tumbled forward, breaking in half in mid-air, flipping end over end. The front half in which I was located along with the pilot, copilot and other gunner, whose name I don't recall, kept tumbling down the steep side of the mountain coming to a stop very far down. The rear half, with Cpl. Perrett and the Vietnamese, was scattered all over the place. The large back portion with the engines was nearer the top of the mountain than were we, in the front portion. I had been thrown back and forth between my machine gun and the radio closet like a rag doll. My helmet, my M-16 and my sidearm, a .45 semi-auto were gone. I must have lost consciousness quickly, but when everything stopped moving, I slowly came to. Blood was in my eyes and I could hardly see.

"The CIDGs had been standing or sitting in their passenger seats, not secured with seat belts because they were getting ready to leave the helicopter when we crashed. They and LCpl. Perrett were at the mercy of gravity and were thrown all over the place. I had no idea at that time what might have happened to Bill [Perrett]. I supposed anyone left alive was just plain lucky. I was lucky.

"I awoke and found myself entangled in the wreckage, partially inside the small passageway between the cargo deck and cockpit. Surprised that I was still breathing and fearing fire, I worked my way clear of the wreckage and crawled to a pretty deep bomb crater a short distance from where I found myself. I could hear what I thought was a spray of AK-47 fire, with bullets buzzing around me, rounds slamming into trees and leaves cut to pieces and showering down. I don't recall if I was the first to get to that crater or not, but the copilot [Weber] was there with me. His left arm and shoulder were in bad shape, torn and bloodied. At first I thought his arm may have been torn off. I figured there was a lot of folks that didn't make it.

"Since I had lost my firearms in the crash, I was looking for a weapon. I saw one of the CIDGs wandering toward us. He appeared to be in shock and wasn't using his M-16 that was hanging loose on him. So, I managed to take his M-16 and the bandolier that was strung around his shoulder and crawled back to the crater. The CIDG never really acted like he knew anything and simply wandered off into the bush. We were in that crater for a long time—for hours, it seemed.

"Lieutenant Weber and I acted together to defend our position. Although I was almost blinded by my head wound, I could still operate the M-16. Lt. Weber couldn't hold an M-16 because of his injuries, but he could see much better than I could, so he would direct me as to which way to shoot. I believe we were just shooting at muzzle flashes, or the sound of the AK-47s. What a pair we were. I never saw an enemy soldier. But they were there...shooting at us."

Perrett recalled, "I hung onto the ramp along with a couple of the Vietnamese CIDGs, who were dead, crushed when the starboard engine fell on them. I thought maybe I was dead too. But I was knocked unconscious. My helmet was split open from being slammed headfirst into the fuselage. When I halfway regained consciousness, barely awake, I thought I was dead. But, my head wound was gushing blood, so I thought I must be alive. It was like a scene from hell. As I regained full consciousness, I began clawing my way back up the mountainside to the LZ and looking back down I saw the gunners, the copilot and Lt. Ridgeway too, crawling up that drop-off to the LZ. The enemy continued firing at us as we took what cover we could, which was not much."

The Australian, who was wearing tiger stripe camouflage, was busy calling in Dustoff, the Army medevac chopper. More fighting was going on around us and there was a wounded NVA soldier taken prisoner. He was in the zone with us. The enemy finally melted away when both the Huey and Cobra gunships began sweeping the surrounding area with heavy machine gun fire and rockets. There were also two or three OV-10s firing rockets into the area as a section of F-4s screamed low through the valley. They didn't drop any bombs, but I guess they were just letting the V/C know they were there. Soon, everyone ended up at the USS *Repose* hospital ship, Lt. Weber, Cpl. Perrett, and LCpl. Bunting and the POW. The POW, according to Bunting, "took a beating from a couple of Kit Carson scouts who were being treated on the *Repose*, and when I last saw him, he was in pretty bad shape."

After arriving on the ship, Perrett and Bunting didn't see each other for about two weeks. When they finally returned to the squadron, Perrett resumed his crew chief duties and Bunting resumed his duties as an aviation mechanic and soon-to-be crew chief. Lt. Ridgeway was extremely lucky. He got away "with just a scratch" and went to work in the MAG-16 communications bunker. H.R. "Bob" Weber, the copilot wasn't so lucky. He never returned to HMM-262. His last known address was the U.S. Naval Hospital, Seattle Washington.

The HMM-262 Chronology entry for February, 1970 addressed the above event in the following manner:

February 1970:

While flying a reconnaissance mission in support of the 1st Reconnaissance Battalion a section of Chatterbox helicopters was called upon to insert 16 CIDGs to exploit recent enemy contact discovered by Recon. The difficult mountainous zone, located some 9 miles southwest of Thuong Duc, required a one wheel hover to disembark the team. Gusty winds caused the aircraft to move off position, the aircraft settled in a level attitude, resulting in the aft blades contacting the slope of the hill. The aircraft became uncontrollable, rolled inverted and tumbled some three hundred meters down the slope, resulting in Alfa damage to the aircraft. Miraculously, there were no fatalities and only minor injuries to the five man crew"

HMM-262 CHRONOLOGY

Third tragic mission that day:

On that same day, 021270, Corporal Danny Radish earned his Silver Star as he began his extraordinary and distinguished tour of duty as a CH-46D Crew Chief.

First Lieutenant Chuck Fleischer, Chatterbox 16 and his chase pilot, First Lieutenant Pete Sawzyn, Chatterbox 19, took position at the LZ Baldy medevac pad, the home of the 7th Marines. That day, 021270 would become infamous to HMM-262.

The helos crews were as follows:

	Lead 46	Chase 46
Pilots	Lt. Chuck Fleischer	Lt. Pete Sawzyn
Copilots	Lt. Joe Gulvas	Lt. Pete Hanner
Crew Chiefs	Cpl. Dan Radish	Cpl. P. Flores

Gunners	LCpl D.L. Pierce	G.J. Soucie
Gunners	L.A. Sartain	Sgt. Stuart
Corpsman	E.R. Reed	
Corpsman	D.T. Sink	

About 5 miles southeast of LZ Ross, Lieutenant Fleischer was ambushed by 20-40 NVA regulars in what was called a beautifully set up and very well executed ambush by elements of the same NVA unit that assaulted LZ Ross on 6 January.

Corporal Radish was the crew chief aboard the lead aircraft in a flight of two transport helicopters assigned the medevac mission of picking up twelve wounded Marines while the zone was still under a heavy volume of fire from North Vietnamese Army soldiers occupying well-concealed emplacements. Nevertheless, Cpl Radish in an exposed position at the open door [crew door] of the helicopter provided direct instructions to Fleischer which enabled Fleischer to place their 46 between the Marines and the hostile soldiers. The .50 cal gunner was sweeping the area keeping the enemy's head down.

Cpl. Radish left the aircraft and rushed across the fire-swept terrain to where the wounded men lay and assisted the Corpsman who was rendering first aid and helped carry a stretcher to the helicopter. Although accurate sniper fire wounded one of the casualties, Radish continued traversing the hazardous area with rounds impacting around him. He made trip after trip until all were safely aboard. There is nothing more to be said. Danny Radish, who performed in the manner that brought others the Navy Cross, was awarded the Silver Star. He was as humble as a man could be. He, like all real heroes, never mentioned it. Like all our magnificent crew chiefs, he just kept on doing a great job, under the most demanding circumstances. Also, Lt. Fleischer, although still a complicated man and our old nemesis, revealed the mettle of which he was made. He would do much more in the near future.

* * *

On Saturday, 13 February 1970, the next day, missions were flown as usual. We had our personal gear ready to be flown to MMAF on the 14th and the men were gathering for a last hoorah at the club.

Some of the pilots and personnel were already at Marble Mountain, making ready for the influx of Flying Tigers. Again, at our club in Phu Bai, the TEAC 4010 was blasting out hard rock and the liquor flowed freely. As the night dragged on, things went from bad to worse. The shout, "Don't leave it to the Army," began to ring out. Soon the original pile of discarded plywood furniture was torched and the beginnings of a bonfire flared up. More and more furniture was heaped on till the flames were reaching some ten to twenty feet in the air and could have been seen for miles.

Figure 108 The great bonfire and last night at Phu Bai.

Dean Davis walked from his hooch with a very large one-piece homemade desk and shelf arrangement from his poz. His form, silhouetted against the flames with the awkward structure held high above his head, reminded me of the Titan, Atlas, who held the weight of the world on his shoulders. Dean walked slowly to the fire and heaved the mammoth conglomerate piece high into the air and onto the fire. It was also wild and inevitable that someone, wound tight, would choose to throw some old ammo into the fire. Art Gillidette, the fixer upper of the hot water heater in the showers was dutifully burning a large amount of letters from home, in accordance with the policy not to keep personal mail where it could get into the hands of the enemy.

Art had started a fire in a bucket outside his hooch and was throwing letters into the fire after perusing them, not paying any attention to the Tom Foolery going on about him, First Lieutenant Mike Ragin snuck up on him and had jokingly said, "Let me see some of those letters?" to which, Art refused, telling Mike to kindly "Go to hell." Or something of that magnitude.

Mike left the area, returning with some .38 cal ammo and dropped them into the fire, then, took off, laughing. Art, not having noticed Mike dropping those rounds into the flame, just sat there, head down, still re-reading and sorting the letters.

Bang, bang....the rounds cooked off, throwing soot and debris in Art's face. He let out a howl and saw that it was Mike who had done the deed. With his face covered in dark soot, Art, grabbed a pistol and chased Mike through the hooch area as we all ran for cover. Art never caught up with Mike, but, there were no more fireworks displayed, as the fire burned higher and higher.

Returning to the club, we finished off the night with shots of something Arnold served up as the "last supper." Then, upon leaving the club, it was time to say goodbye to the Army guards in the tower, one last time. The guards, quite used to our rude, abusive behavior, did what they always did when they tired of us. It was an unmistakable message delivered by the sound of a heavy bolt slamming shut on an M60 machine gun. We shouted "Good night" back and "good luck" to our comrades whose faces we'd never seen. To my surprise, they yelled back, "Good luck, you f**kin' jarheads," and with a series of "f**k yous" back and forth, we bid each other adieu and goodbye, a begrudging salute to each other. That kind of goodbye could only have happened in Phu Bai on that night, like the Christmas Truce of 1914 when the Germans and the allied French and British soldiers, bitter enemies, agreed to a truce for a brief period of time as they celebrated Christmas. True or not, it was a good story.

But in this instance, we had to say that both Phu Bai and our U.S. Army brethren were indeed all right!

The last moments of Phu Bai as a Marine base:

The last one out, turn off the lights, the party's over, as the hooch maids hauled away the plunder before the Army could take command. HMM-262, The Flying Tigers, the last Marine helicopter squadron to leave Northern I Corps was going south.

Figure 109 Hooch maids carrying off the last vestiges of the Marine Corps presence.

Epilogue

I arrived in Vietnam on 101169 (November 10, 1969) to learn that we would soon be leaving. President Nixon had declared there would be "Peace with Honor" through Operation Keystone the code name for Redeployment and Vietnamization aka withdrawal. My earliest concern, at the time, was whether or not I would have an opportunity to become a Vietnam Combat Helicopter Pilot. The fear of that not happening vanished as the need for the CH-46D medium lift helicopter never faded, but increased. The arrival of more FNG pilots who were beginning their tour of duty never lessened as we took hold and learned how to fly from those bloodied PMAG-39 veterans. The men before us had flown into the maelstrom in support of the legendary 3d Marine Division at Con Thien and taking Route 9 west from Quang Tri and Dong Ha to Camp Carroll, the Rockpile, Khe Sanh, and the battle of the hills and Mutter's ridge down to the A Shau Valley to Hue and Dewey Canyon, and nameless ridges throughout the region where Marines were locked into mortal combat with an intransigent and ruthless enemy. That war in the north was now Marine Corps. history. The men who flew in that unforgiving raw environment, had set the standard for us in blood and courage and were now the legacy for all CH-46 squadrons.

At Phu Bai, we had learned from those warriors, flying through monsoon rains and low and no ceilings to Marble Mountain Air Facility, only to be told to stand down due to unflyable weather conditions. The Marine Corps was indeed leaving, but the need for the CH-46 grew. On 14 February 1970 we would move to Marble Mountain Air Facility, MAG-16, Da Nang, to begin again. We former FNGs would slowly become HACs as unfamiliar FNG faces took their place in the left seat. We would become even more familiar with Charlie Ridge, Arizona Territory, Baldy, An Hoa, Gonoi Island, Barrier Island, Elephant, Happy and Antennae Valley and that bloodiest of all areas, the Thuong Duc Corridor. What once was bold division size charges along the

DMZ and Laotian border turned to ambush tactics: 51-cal machine guns, B-40 rockets, RPGs, AK-47s and insidious land mines and booby traps fashioned from random unspent artillery shells. It was an era when each insert and extract of reconnaissance teams had the potential of becoming a battle in itself and large sweeps of ancient rice paddies kept the beast at bay.

The thing that didn't change was the extraordinary efforts to maintain the tradition that no Marine be left behind. When a CH-46 was sitting in an LZ waiting for wounded Marines to be brought to the helo, the flight crews took the enemy fire and responded in kind rather than leave anyone behind. Ooh-Rah!

A friend of the Grotto, a combat vet from PMAG-39 was First Lieutenant Marty Lyman. He arrived in-country on 5 September 1969 and had recently left Phu Bai on R&R to Australia and wasn't around for the celebratory departure of 262. However, we would see much more of him when he returned to MMAF.

Figure 110 First Lieutenant Marty Lyman

The Grotto, Book Two will follow to the end as we meet new challenges both external and internal, as the Marine presence in Vietnam winds down.

Acknowledgements

First and foremost, I wish to express my gratitude to my wife, Kathleen, for her unwavering support, encouragement and patience, without which this project would not have begun. The following individuals are those who have worked difficult hours editing the story, and the many Marines who lived in that year with me and whose memories have helped add context to the many stories. Many were beta readers who added insightful recollection. But, all believed in the true story of that unique group of men who flew the CH-46, the work horse of the Corps, in Vietnam.

Special thanks go to my editors: Laura Slivinski, line editor; Heather Ruffalo, Proof Reader; Laura Walker Volmer, finishing micro-editor; Kevin Moriarity: formatter, editor, IT guru and co-host of Waterline Writers, Batavia, IL. a place for published and non-published writers of the written word to display their wares; William Pack, historian, magician, author and book cover designer extraordinaire; Keith French, former Marine Corps Captain and an EA-6B Prowler pilot, noted commercial photographer and photo lab genius, Elgin, Illinois, who brought those old 35mm slides and Kodak Polaroid camera pictures to life.

Special thanks go to: Beth Crumley, noted Marine Corps historian and current U.S. Coast Guard Assistant Historian and former reference historian with the USMC History Division, MCB Quantico, VA. author of several military articles including the following: *The Marine Corps, Three Centuries of Glory; Walking with Giants-The Tigers of HMM-262* and *The Green Hell - Operation Dewey Canyon.*

And

John and Linda Kosinski: John, former first lieutenant, HMM-262, 1969-1970 now Major, USMC (Ret) has the distinction of having been in 3 direct enemy action shoot-downs in which there was death to crew and passengers and alpha damage to two of the helicopters. One of the incidents was caused by an enemy booby trap in which the aircraft commander was killed. John has been a great help in identifying micro events and elements directly attributed to his experiences in 262 and those shootdowns that will appear in Book Two and to Linda, an accomplished teacher who also provided invaluable assistance throughout the writing and editing of book 1.

Editors, Reviewers and Beta readers who took the time to read and/or offer suggestions and observations were:

A.C. Allen, then, first lieutenant and Grottoite, HMM-262, Vietnam, 1969-70, now, a United States Navy Captain, retired. Allen found his calling in the USN Chaplain Corps where he rose to the level of Chief of Chaplains (CHC) and head of the U.S. Chaplain Corps in the command of Lieutenant General Marty Berndt USMC.

John Arnold, then, first lieutenant, HMM-262, Vietnam 1969-70, whose collateral duty was to be the Phu Bai officer's club manager and later, as will be related in Book Two, he was a forward air controller (FAC) with the First Battalion, First Marines on Hill 10 (AT865681), the best of both worlds. John was known for driving a Jaguar XKE convertible in flight school. He is not a Texas oil executive (Ret), living in a grand hacienda near San Antonio, Texas.

Dr. Steve Bravard, then, first lieutenant, HMM-262, Vietnam 1969-70, now, a practicing ophthalmologist whose passions lie with his wife Dawn, a family of beautiful Border Collies, Harley Davidson and HMM-262 "The Old Tigers" reunion activities.

Bill Bunting, then, a lance corporal, HMM-262, Vietnam 1969-70, recipient of the Purple Heart and an outstanding .50-cal. gunner and crew chief, whose experience on 12 February 1970 when ET-12 crashed, he recalled in vivid detail. Mike Butler, then first lieutenant, HMM-161, 1969-70 and HMM-262, 1970-71, Vietnam, now, Colonel, USMC (Ret) and a much respected and lauded CH-46 helicopter pilot whose flight logs contain more than 2000 combat helicopter missions and whose combat experience is second to none. Butler following his end of tour with HMM-161, returned to Vietnam within a short period of time. His "tongue in cheek" response to the question, "Why?" was "I couldn't find anyone to date in Jacksonville." But it was much deeper than that. Mike was the genuine deal, a superior pilot whose energy and expertise was second to none. Flying combat was his passion, that's why he returned to Vietnam. The same can be said for a myriad of Marines and soldiers who found stateside a boring place to be.

Lou and Lola Deleonardis are our friends and neighbors who are great readers and from whom suggestions and encouragement were so very welcome.

Terry Driskill, then, first lieutenant, HMM-262, Vietnam 1969-70 (deceased on 19 July, 2017, his ashes will be interred in Arlington National Cemetery) entered Vietnam on 23 September 1969 and played out the year in a quiet dignified manner. He was somewhat of a reluctant celebrity, having been a former band member, along with Boz Scaggs in the Steve Miller Band and whose image appears on Miller's second album, *Sailor,* a psychedelic blues rock sound, released by Capital Records. He and his closest childhood friend, Bill Davis, also a first lieutenant in HMM-262, were inseparable. Terry, like everyone else, flew every type of mission, with two horrific missions that changed his life, to be identified in the next submission of *The Grotto Book Two.* Over the past several years, through email correspondence, Terry, an expat whose life following Vietnam was primarily in Southeast Asia and Europe revealed what had happened during those horrific missions and his life experiences following the Marine Corps that will be revealed in *The Grotto Book Two.*

Brian Duniec, former captain, HMM-161, Vietnam, 1969-70, a for real tough guy and former Illini football standout as right tackle in the 1964 Illini Rose Bowl rout over the Washington Huskies along with teammates Dick Butkus, Jim Grabowski, Lynn Stewart and Archie Sutton, then, to Marine Corps football at the Marine Base in Quantico and on to flight training and the Navy Goshawks football when Roger Staubach was quarterback, then to Vietnam. Now, a commercial real estate sales executive, taking life easy with his wife Patti, in a lovely home on the banks of the Fox River west of Chicago, IL.

Larry Fenton, then a first lieutenant, HMM-262, 1968-69, in Vietnam, now, LtCol. USMC (Ret) who along with Captain Dave White and the Recon team "Fighting Mad" walked away from their shot down CH-46D. It was a four day trek through thick jungle during which time they were under fire from NVA forces probing and snipping at them continuously. He was shot in the knee during that escape as they carried a dead comrade with them in the fulfillment of the Marine pledge to leave no one behind, a feat worthy of the big screen.

Jerry "J.J." Hall, then Sergeant, HMM-262, 1969-70 the consummate crew chief whose recall and experiences filled in many gaps. J.J. always smiled and worked day and night as did all the crew chiefs and maintenance Marines. It was always a pleasure to have J.J. on board.

N.F. "Pete" Hanner, then first lieutenant and Grottoite, HMM-262, Vietnam 1969-70, a consummate maintenance test pilot, day and night who transitioned to the A-4 Skyhawk following his tour in Vietnam, now, a LtCol USMC (Ret), then, with nothing else to do, he became a FedEx® pilot, then a maintenance test pilot for FedEx®. Now retired and a doting grandfather to his grandchildren, he is known to hunt on his farm in Arkansas whenever possible. Pete was a solid Marine and seemed to always be flying test, recovery and combat.

Joseph "Jake" Jacobs, former 18-19 year old HMM-262 crew chief during the first battle of Khe Sanh *The Hill Fights* December 66-67, now, 45 years with Deseret Industries and current Vice President of the International Division and, in his spare time since 1996, the guiding helm for reunions of the Old Tigers of HMM-262. His actions during that period of time helped develop the legacy of HMM-262.

Gerald "Jerry" Johnson, then first lieutenant, HMM-262, Vietnam 1970-71, A CH-46 driver turned Phantom pilot, now a LtCol USMC (Ret). Following retirement from the Marine Corps, he flew a variety of helicopters and fixed wing aircraft including Cessna 210s, Beach 58s and Lear jets, with Evergreen International, for 3 years out of Galveston, TX, before becoming a contract pilot and eventually an employee of NASA at the Johnson Space Center, Houston, TX. While with NASA, he flew F-18s and T-38s and Hueys from which he retired in 2005. A person who at one time was told he was "too aggressive to fly helicopters" was also an artist, an author and philosopher.

Pat Kenny, former first lieutenant, HMM-364, Vietnam, 1970-71 the Purple Foxes and fellow alum from Southeast Missouri State University, Cape Girardeau, Mo., particularly noted for his participation in the "Cam Sa" raid on August 4, 1970, now, retired from Cargill Grain Management following 29 years in the Agri-business. He became a riverboat captain on the Columbia River that flows through the Hanford Reach Wildlife Area of Washington State, "for the fun of it" and is a doting grandfather who brings his grandson with him to Pop-A-Smoke reunions, to meet his fellow warriors from The Nam and to listen to their tales.

Martin "Marty" Lyman, then a first lieutenant and later, a Grottoite , HMM-262, Vietnam 1969-70, now, a Colonel, USMC (Ret) and an olympic alpine downhill racing aficionado living in the good life near lots of snow in Utah. His piloting ability and easy going and cheerful mannerism made him a favorite in the squadron and a good friend to all.

Dr. Ron McAmis, then, a first lieutenant and grottoite, HMM-262, Vietnam 1969-70, now, a Commander, U.S.N. (Ret) and practicing Oral Surgeon in the Kansas City area and boxing aficionado. Ron, a golden gloves boxing aficionado had the best experiences while standing watch as the Squadron duty Officer (SDO). His quick wit and sense of humor were welcomed traits that made him an instant favorite in the squadron.

Fred McCorkle, then, first lieutenant, HMM-262, Vietnam 1969-70, now lieutenant general retired and former Deputy Commandant for Aviation, who spanned helicopter history from the CH-46 to the V-22 Osprey and who built a legend for himself in Vietnam. Fred's stories became legendary, giving credence to the saying, "when the legend becomes fact, print the legend." His tales about his attack cat "Grady" and really, performing "90 degree angle of bank and zero-air-speed," thrills for those who flew with him was his mainstay. However, his love of flying and his thoughtfulness for fellow Marines is his true character.

Don McGlothlin, then, a first lieutenant and Grottoite born and raised in the Marine Corps by a WWII Corsair Pilot, his father, whom he held dear, as did we, the friends of Donnie. He was a dedicated Marine who had the blood of an Irishman pulsing through his veins. He enjoyed a beer or a round of "fisticuffs" equally well. Donnie was a pioneer in Hughes Aircraft who worked in the desert surrounding Yuma, AZ., helping to produce the AH-64 Boeing Apache attack helicopter. Later, as an Apache Production Executive (Ret), he dedicated his life to the world of attack helicopters. He is now retired and living the good life with his wife Elin in his Arizona hacienda.

Eric McGrew, then, first lieutenant and grottoite, HMM-262, Vietnam 1969-70, now, a legendary Delta Airlines Pilot (Ret) recognized, in-person, by then Vice President of the United States, George H. W. Bush, for having talked an armed highjacker out of his weapon. Eric is now at ease on his farm in Georgia with his very understanding wife, Mrs. Willy.

P.T. Nemitz, then first lieutenant, HMM-362, 1968-69, H-34 pilot in the legendary Ugly Angels, 1968-69 Vietnam and former commanding officer of HML-776, MACG-48, Fourth MAW (Reserve Squadron) Glenview, IL., now, Colonel, USMC (Ret) and retired corporate helicopter and business jet pilot who has flown all over the world in various capacities.

John Parnham, then, first lieutenant, HMM-262, Vietnam 1969-70, now, a lauded honorable senior judge from Escambia County (Pensacola) Florida's Division "W," Ret. John was one of the most respected pilots that sprang from Provisional MAG-39 in Quang Tri to HMM-262. His understated humor and southern-gentleman persona served him well.

Grit Patton, former Sergeant, Paraloft/Flight Equipment, HMM-262, Vietnam 1969-70, now a gentleman farmer in North Carolina, was the heart of the paraloft. His leadership and sense of duty kept me out of trouble, almost. His recollections of times and events are laudable. He is a good friend and regularly attends both the HMM-262 squadron reunions and the yearly Pop-A-Smoke reunions.

Bill J. Perrett, then corporal, HMM-262, Vietnam 1969-70 was the crew chief of ET 12 that crashed on 12 February, 1970. He is now a Major, USAR (Ret). His enthusiasm for aviation has been the guiding light in his life. He is the Executive Director of the Blackhawk Flight Foundation, Inc. Mandeville, LA. in alliance with the National Flight Academy, Experimental Aircraft Association, & Mississippi Department of Education. His riveting recall of the disastrous loss of ET-12 along with Bill Bunting's recall provided a riveting moment to moment account of the catastrophic loss of ET-12.

Danny Radish, then, corporal, HMM-262, Vietnam 1969-70 crew chief, now, a master gunnery sergeant USMC (Ret) and inspiration for the Danny L. Radish award annually presented by the Marine Corps Aviation Association to the Marine enlisted air crewman of the year for superior performance under extreme conditions, like enemy fire and booby-traps.

Gary D. Rainey, then, first lieutenant and Grottoite, HMM-262, Vietnam 1969-70, is now, LtCol. USMC (Ret). He is a Wyoming cowboy by way of lake Charles, LA. His Marine Corps career placed him in hot spots all over the globe. He participated in the April, 1975 evacuation of Saigon and later stood up HMM-266 as its first commanding officer. He relocated to Denmark where he was assigned the responsibility of being the USMC Staff Officer at Headquarters, Allied Forces, Baltic Approaches of the NATO Military Command. Later, he became a flight instructor in our beloved T-28s in Pensacola, FL. before retiring. He now resides in his home state of Wyoming and is the doting grandfather of two beautiful little girls and a constant companion throughout the writing of this Book.

Dale A. Riley, then Sergeant, HMM-262, Vietnam 1968-69 crew chief, downed with First Lieutenant Steve Bravard and the

Fighting Mad reconnaissance team on April 24, 1969. Riley provided extraordinary details of the event as he searched through the crash site to locate the pilot and copilot of the craft.

Wiley J. Sellers, then Major, HMM-262, XO, AMO and OPSO, Vietnam, 1969-70, a veteran of Operation Hastings during his first tour in Vietnam, now, LtCol. USMC (Ret) and living on the gulf coast, he provided substantial meaningful context to the HMM-262 experience as related to the leadership and squadron highlights. His input regarding helicopter operations and individuals serving in high positions was very informative.

Dave White, then, captain and AMO of HMM-262, 1968-69 a former artillery officer in his first tour of Vietnam, turned CH-46 pilot for his second tour, whose recall of the squadron, the people and his trek with 1st Lt. Fenton, aided in the description of the time and events associated with HMM-262 and its leadership, when the squadron was under both the standard of Provisional MAG-39 at Quang Tri and MAG-16 at Phu Bai. A quiet man with deep thoughts suits him well.

Richard "Dick" Wiggins, then, a 21 year old Marine Corps Sergeant in the combat engineers, now, retired from Caterpillar Corporation, described his participation in the construction of Con Thien and the attempted construction of the McNamara line through the DMZ. It was the same type of line they tried to construct around Da Nang that upon failure became the "rocket belt." His story of being wounded by a Chicom grenade during the fight, that was a brawl, was reminiscent of the Chinese human wave attacks in the Korean conflict, providing insight and context for those on the ground, we called Grunts.

With the best of intentions, I have tried to acknowledge those who have accepted my late night phone calls that began with, "Do you remember when...."? And, for those who I have not mentioned, I owe you a round of cheer at our next reunion.

On May 8, 1967 at 0300, 2 battalions of NVA Sappers from the 4th and 6th Battalions of the 812 NVA Regiment assaulted Con Thien with satchel charges, hand grenades and flame throwers. Their intent was to stop the construction of both Con Thien and the McNamara line. The engineers were backed up by two companies of Marines from the 1st Battalion, 4th Marines, and several tanks from Company A, 3rd Tank Battalion, 3rd Marine Division. The assault was brutal. Every Marine is first and foremost a rifleman and this assault was a lesson well learned by the NVA. The enemy sustained nearly 200 dead and 8 captured. Mortar and rocket fire accounted for 80% of the Marines killed that night. The Marines suffered 44 killed and 110 wounded one of which was Sergeant Wiggins with shrapnel from a Chicom hand grenade hurled toward the Marines at point blank range. Afterwards, the Marines licked their wounds. Sgt. Wiggins was patched up and received his Purple Heart. They then continued the constructing and strengthening Con Thien, known thereafter as with M14 mines known as the "toe poppers", M16 mines called "Bouncing Bettys", and M18 Claymores, with embossed instructions, "Front Toward Enemy." They widened route 9 west through Quang Tri, Dong Ha, Camp Carroll to Khe Sanh and other similar outposts at which the 3rd MarDiv fought the most vicious battles of the war and Marine Air, both fixed and rotary wing, honed their skills for the battles that were to come. The battle was planned and carried out by NVA General Vo Nguyen Giap. He learned from this battle, that attacking a Marine unit with overwhelming numbers did not assure him victory.

Larry Zok, then Sergeant, HMM-262. an expert .50 cal gunner and crew chief who flew with us through thick and thin, now, a Pop-A-Smoke reunion coordinator for all Marine Corps combat helicopter and rotary wing aircraft squadrons.

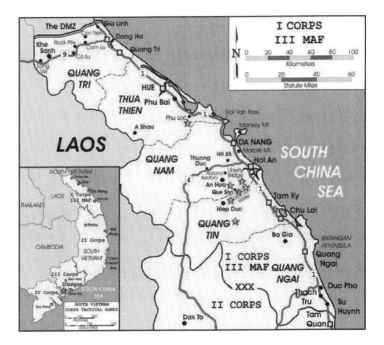

Bibliography

Barden, Thomas E. *Steinbeck in Vietnam: Dispatches from the War.* Charlottesville: Univ Of Virginia Press, 2013.

Bingham, Clara. *Witness to the Revolution: Radicals, Resisters, Vets, Hippies, and the Year America Lost Its Mind and Found Its Soul.* New York: Random House, 2017.

Caputo, Philip. *A Rumor of War.* New York: Ballantine Books, 1978.

Cosmas, Graham A., Terrence P. Murray, William R. Melton, and Jack Shulimson. *U.S. Marines in Vietnam: Vietnamization and Redeployment, 1970-1971.* Washington, D.C.: History and Museums Division, Headquarters, U.S. Marine Corps, 1986.

Crew, Randolph E. *A Killing Shadow.* A Novel. Greenville, SC: Aztec Pub., 1996.

Crumley, Beth. "Green Hell"– Operation Dewey Canyon." Marine Corps Association. January 12, 2018. Accessed July 25, 2011. https://www.mca-marines.org/mcaf-blog/2011/08/22/green-hell-operation-dewey-canyon.

Crumley, Beth. "Walking With Giants – The Tigers of HMM-262." Marine Corps Association. January 12, 2018. Accessed July 25, 2011. https://www.mca-marines.org/2011/07/25/walking-giants-tigers-hmm-262.

DeBenedetti, Charles, and Chares Chatfield. *An American Ordeal: The Antiwar Movement of the Vietnam Era.* Syracuse, NY: Syracuse University Press, 1990.

Fall, Bernard B. Street *Without Joy: The French Debacle in Indochina*. S.1. Stackpole Books, 1964.

Garfinkle, Adam. *Telltale Hearts: The Origins and Impact of the Vietnam Antiwar Movement*. New York: St. Martin's Press, 1995.

Halstead, Fred. *Out Now!: A Participant's Account of the Movement in the U.S. Against the Vietnam War*. New York: Pathfinder, 1992.

Hildreth, Ray, and Charles W Sasser. *Hill 488*. New York: Pocket Books, 2003.

Kellum, Michael Dan, *Book II, American Heroes: Grunts, Pilots & "Docs", Leathernecks Find 'em, Fix 'em, Kill 'em, Vietnam Combat Stories, '69-70,* (Longview, Texas: Navarro-Hill Publishing Group 2011).

Lake, Bruce R. *1500 Feet over Vietnam*: A Marine Helicopter Pilot's Diary. Haverhill, NH: Almine Library, 1990.

Moore, Harold G., and Joseph L. Galloway. *We Were Soldiers Once—and Young: La Drang, the Battle That Changed the War in Vietnam*. New York: Ballantine Books, 2004.

Murphy, Edward F. *The Hill Fights: The First Battle of Khe Sanh*. New York: Ballantine Books, 2004.

Nicosia, Gerald. *Home to War: A History of the Vietnam Veterans' Movement*. New York: Carroll & Graf, 2004.

Pham, Quang X. *A Sense of Duty: My Father, My American Journey*. New York: Ballantine Books, 2008.

Puller Jr., Lewis B. Fortunate *Son: The Autobiography of Lewis B. Puller, Jr.*, New York: Grove Weidenfeld, 1991.

Sheehan, Neil. *"Page 717." A Bright and Shining Lie: John Paul Vann and America in Vietnam.* New York: Modern Library, 2009.

Smith, C. R. *U.S. Marines in Vietnam: High Mobility and Standdown. 1969.* Washington, D.C.: History and Museums Division, Headquarters, U.S. Marine Corps, Washington, D.C., 1988.

Sturkey, Marion F. *Bonnie-Sue: A Marine Corps Helicopter Squadron in Vietnam.* Plum Branch, SC: Heritage Press International, 1999.

Telfer, G. L. *U.S. Marines in Vietnam- Fighting the North Vietnamese 1967.* Marine Corps Vietnam Series 4. Washington, D.C. 1984.

Webb, James. *Fields of Fire.* Annapolis, MD: Naval Institute Press, 2000.

Wirtz, James J. *The Tet Offensive: Intelligence Failure in War.* Ithaca NY: Cornell Univ. Press, 1994.

List of Pictures

Chatterbox Numbers

Known Chatterbox numbers
11 November 69 – 6 November 70

2nd Lieutenant

Gulvas, J.	***

1st Lieutenant

Allan, A.C.	18
Arnold, J.	01/09
Beck, H.	20
Bresnahan	02
Butler, M	24
Connell, J.C.	19
Cronin, J.	31
Davis, D.	13
Davis, W.	36/24/13
DeLong, M.	15
Driskill, T.	21
Esmond, D.	07
Faulk, R.E.	26
Fears, B.	15
Finley, E.	18
Fleischer, C.	16
Forbes, R.	35
Gillidette, D.	01
Glynn, M.	15/33
Graham, W. ****	22
Guerrero, G.	31
Hanner, N.F.	16
Harr, M.	13
Hart, J.	35
Holls, W.	12
Hudson, W.	27
Jaquish, M.	29

Jeffryes, J.D.	10
Johnson, G.	17
King, W.C.	24
Kosinski, J.	20
Lloyd, R.	30
Lyman, M.	25
McAmis, R.	22
McCorkle, F.	32
McGlothlin, D.	34
McGrew, E.	14/21
Mitchell, E.	12
Mowery, E.	26
Olsen, L.	NA
Page, J.	02
Parnham, J.	09
Prigge, R.	11
Proctor, D.	19
Ragin, M.	14
Rainey, G.	23
Randall, J.	39
Ridgeway, L.	10/18/19
Reid, W.T.	08
Sawzyn, P.	19
Simpson, A.	37
Sublette, W.	20/44
Sullivan, J.	22
Wagner, J.	***
Walker, H.	28
Whitworth, J.	11
Wood, M.	17
Wright, T.	***

Captain

Appel, R.	07/10
White, D.	07
Johnson, K.	09

Major

Collins, B.	04
Fennell, H.	07
Fitzgerald, R.	07
Lawson, H.	03
Lockwood, R.	05
Meskan, D.	06
Perryman, J.	05
Sellers, W.	05/03
Watson, J.	03/08
Whitfield, H.	05/30*#

Lieutenant Colonel

Bancroft, R.	06
Pate, G.S.	06

*** Chatterbox number not found
**** Promoted to Captain while in Vietnam
*# Whitfield's chatterbox number in February 1970 following his tenure as XO of 262.

Additional Reading

So Close to Dying, a memoir, by Edward F. Mowry - Copyright 2013 by Edward F. Mowry.

Bonnie-Sue A Marine Corps Helicopter Squadron in Vietnam, a memoir by Marion Sturkey - Copyright 2010 by Marion F. Sturkey.

Index

Travis, William Barrett, 348
Vanek, "Panic", 15
Vang, Pao, 360
Verbanik, "Buzz", 99, 111, 154
Vo, Nguyen Giap, 430
Volmer, Laura Walker, 423
Wagner, John "Wags," III, **108**, 109–11, **110**, 152, **292**, **328**, 329–31, **332**, 366–71
Walker, Harold, 26
Walker, Harold G., **20**, **22**, **23**, **195**, **198**, 292, **314**, **321**, **353**, **382–84**, **404**
Walker, Johnny, **22**, 263
Walker, Kathleen B., 4, 6, 14, 15, 16, 17, 18–19, **20**, 21, 22, **23**, 27, 31, **32**, **35**, 130, **131**, 138, 174, **195**, 197, 320, 321, 323, 352, 364, 409, 423
Walker, Owen Ray, 76, 378
Walt, Lewis, **203**

Webb, James, 36
Weber, H. R. "Bob", 204–6, 207–13, 216–22, 223, 257, 408–16
Wheeler, Edwin B., 384–86
White, David L., 98, 123–28, 141, 145, 154, 236, 292, 430
Whitehorn, Richard, 356
Whitfield, Howard M., 98, 110, 115, 138, 144–46, 203–6, 207–13, 216–22, 223–28, 232–35, 236–37, 239–40, 253–57, 276–77, 284, 292
Whitworth, John R., 204–6, 216–22, 223–28, 324
Wiggins, Richard "Dick", 430–31
Williams, Jack "Gorilla Monsoon", 199
Wood, Marion, 94
Gen. Wright, 278
Wyatt, Austin, 1
Zok, Larry, 431

Made in the USA
Lexington, KY
02 September 2018